Kamichama Karin Chu 2

KOGE-DONBO

Translated and adapted by Alethea Nibley and Athena Nibley
Lettered by Foltz Design

Ballantine Books ★ New York

A Del Rey Manga/Kodansha Trade Paperback Original

Kamichama Karin Chu volume 2 copyright © 2007 by Koge-Donbo
English translation copyright © 2008 by Koge-Donbo

Published in the United States by Del Rey Books, an imprint of The Random House Publishing Group, a division of Random House, Inc., New York.

DEL REY is a registered trademark and the Del Rey colophon is a trademark of Random House, Inc.

Publication rights arranged through Kodansha Ltd.

First published in Japan in 2007 by Kodansha Ltd., Tokyo

ISBN 978-0-345-50593-4

Printed in the United States of America

www.delreymanga.com

2 3 4 5 6 7 8 9

Translators/adaptors: Alethea Nibley and Athena Nibley
Lettering: Foltz Design

CONTENTS

A Word from the Author

It's *Kamichama Karin Chu* volume 2! This time they all go to the beach and have a school festival; it's just as lively as ever! And furthermore, *that* character from the first series makes a *Chu* debut, and the wackiness just keeps on increasing, so please let your heart pound along with Karin-chan!

HONORIFICS EXPLAINED

Throughout the Del Rey Manga books, you will find Japanese honorifics left intact in the translations. For those not familiar with how the Japanese use honorifics and, more important, how they differ from American honorifics, we present this brief overview.

Politeness has always been a critical facet of Japanese culture. Ever since the feudal era, when Japan was a highly stratified society, use of honorifics—which can be defined as polite speech that indicates relationship or status—has played an essential role in the Japanese language. When addressing someone in Japanese, an honorific usually takes the form of a suffix attached to one's name (example: "Asuna-san"), is used as a title at the end of one's name, or appears in place of the name itself (example: "Negi-sensei," or simply "Sensei!").

Honorifics can be expressions of respect or endearment. In the context of manga and anime, honorifics give insight into the nature of the relationship between characters. Many English translations leave out these important honorifics and therefore distort the feel of the original Japanese. Because Japanese honorifics contain nuances that English honorifics lack, it is our policy at Del Rey not to translate them. Here, instead, is a guide to some of the honorifics you may encounter in Del Rey Manga.

-san: This is the most common honorific and is equivalent to Mr., Miss, Ms., or Mrs. It is the all-purpose honorific and can be used in any situation where politeness is required.

-sama: This is one level higher than "-san" and is used to confer great respect.

-dono: This comes from the word "tono," which means "lord." It is an even higher level than "-sama" and confers utmost respect.

-kun: This suffix is used at the end of boys' names to express familiarity or endearment. It is also sometimes used by men among friends, or when addressing someone younger or of a lower station.

-chan: This is used to express endearment, mostly toward girls. It is also used for little boys, pets, and even among lovers. It gives a sense of childish cuteness.

Bozu: This is an informal way to refer to a boy, similar to the English terms "kid" and "squirt."

Sempai/
Senpai: This title suggests that the addressee is one's senior in a group or organization. It is most often used in a school setting, where underclassmen refer to their upperclassmen as "sempai." It can also be used in the workplace, such as when a newer employee addresses an employee who has seniority in the company.

Kohai: This is the opposite of "sempai" and is used toward underclassmen in school or newcomers in the workplace. It connotes that the addressee is of a lower station.

Sensei: Literally meaning "one who has come before," this title is used for teachers, doctors, or masters of any profession or art.

-[blank]: This is usually forgotten in these lists, but it is perhaps the most significant difference between Japanese and English. The lack of honorific means that the speaker has permission to address the person in a very intimate way. Usually, only family, spouses, or very close friends have this kind of permission. Known as *yobisute*, it can be gratifying when someone who has earned the intimacy starts to call one by one's name without an honorific. But when that intimacy hasn't been earned, it can be very insulting.

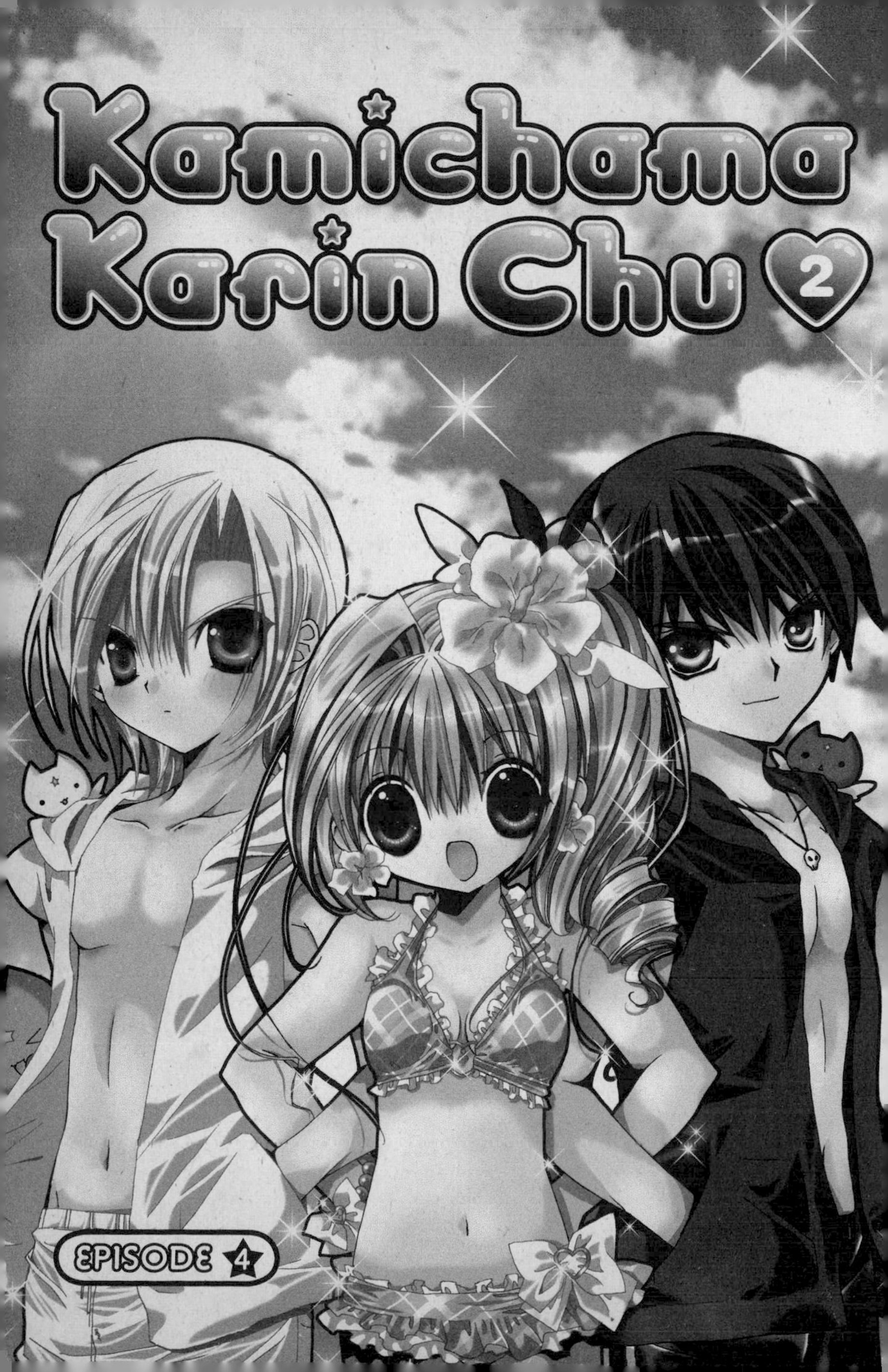
Kamichama Karin Chu 2
EPISODE 4

KAMICHAMA CHU WORLD GUIDE

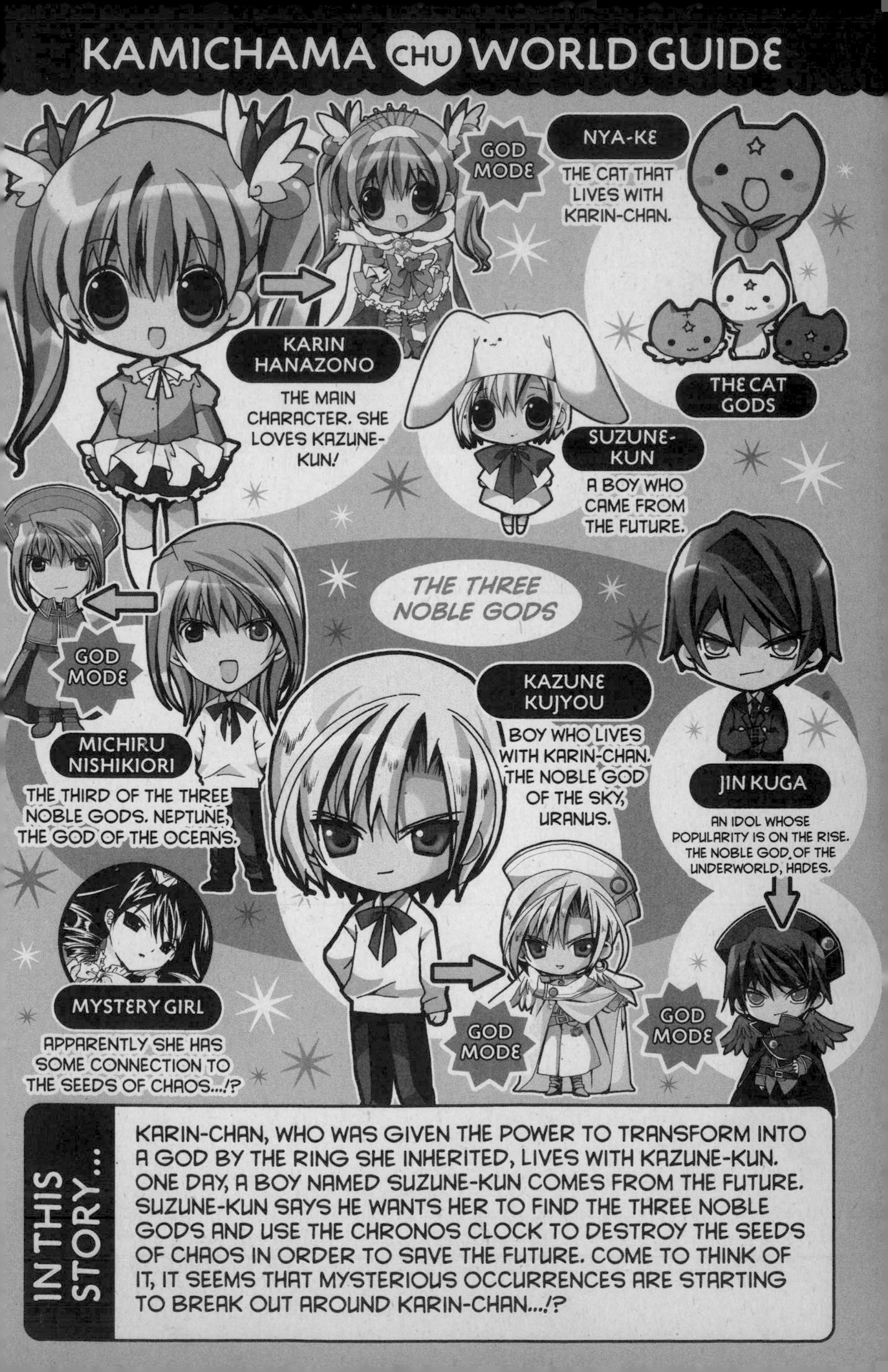
GOD MODE
NYA-KE
THE CAT THAT LIVES WITH KARIN-CHAN.
KARIN HANAZONO
THE MAIN CHARACTER. SHE LOVES KAZUNE-KUN!
THE CAT GODS
SUZUNE-KUN
A BOY WHO CAME FROM THE FUTURE.
THE THREE NOBLE GODS
GOD MODE
KAZUNE KUJYOU
BOY WHO LIVES WITH KARIN-CHAN. THE NOBLE GOD OF THE SKY, URANUS.
MICHIRU NISHIKIORI
THE THIRD OF THE THREE NOBLE GODS. NEPTUNE, THE GOD OF THE OCEANS.
JIN KUGA
AN IDOL WHOSE POPULARITY IS ON THE RISE. THE NOBLE GOD OF THE UNDERWORLD, HADES.
MYSTERY GIRL
APPARENTLY SHE HAS SOME CONNECTION TO THE SEEDS OF CHAOS...!?
GOD MODE
GOD MODE

IN THIS STORY...

KARIN-CHAN, WHO WAS GIVEN THE POWER TO TRANSFORM INTO A GOD BY THE RING SHE INHERITED, LIVES WITH KAZUNE-KUN. ONE DAY, A BOY NAMED SUZUNE-KUN COMES FROM THE FUTURE. SUZUNE-KUN SAYS HE WANTS HER TO FIND THE THREE NOBLE GODS AND USE THE CHRONOS CLOCK TO DESTROY THE SEEDS OF CHAOS IN ORDER TO SAVE THE FUTURE. COME TO THINK OF IT, IT SEEMS THAT MYSTERIOUS OCCURRENCES ARE STARTING TO BREAK OUT AROUND KARIN-CHAN...!?

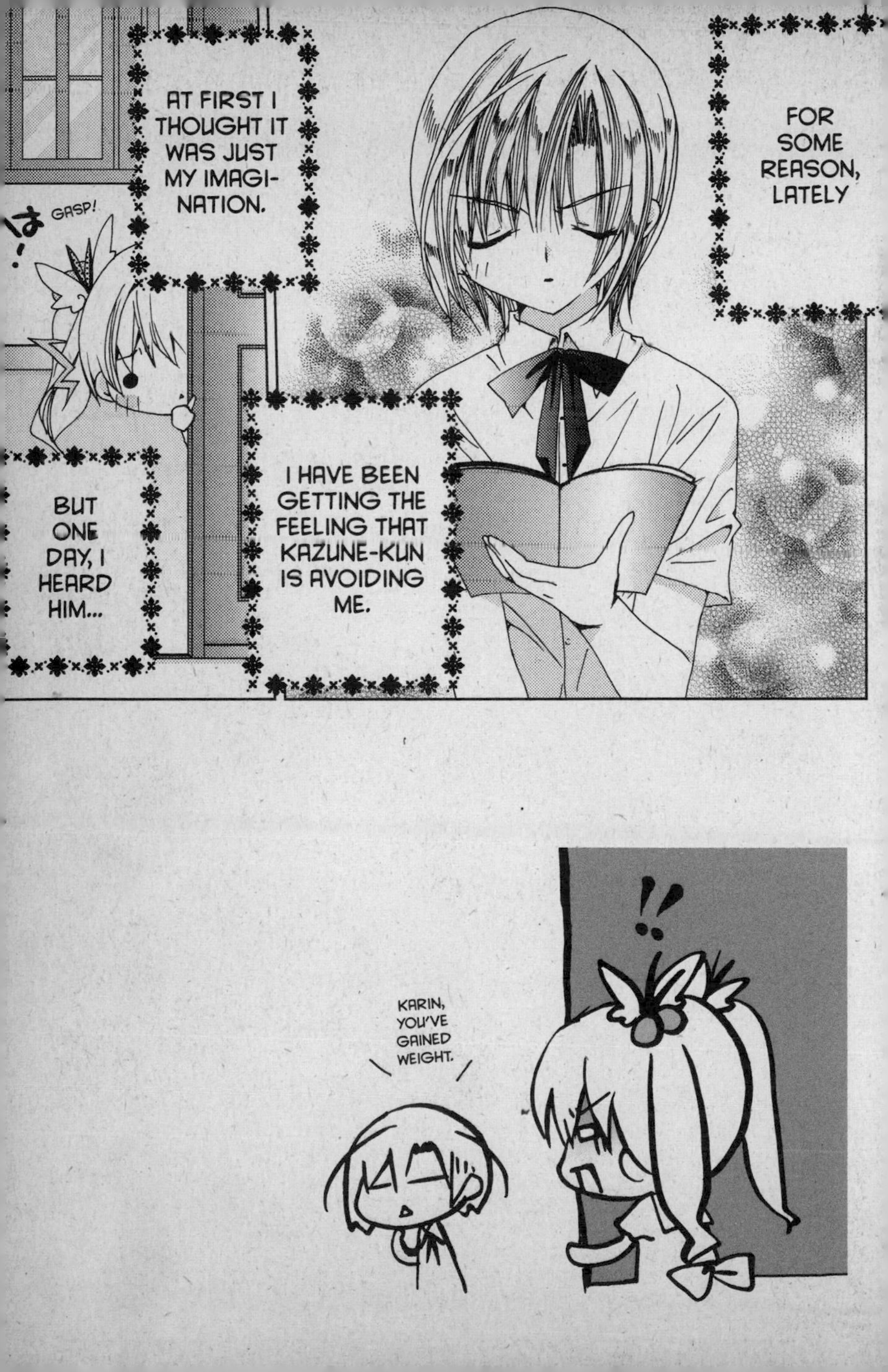
FOR SOME REASON, LATELY
I HAVE BEEN GETTING THE FEELING THAT KAZUNE-KUN IS AVOIDING ME.
AT FIRST I THOUGHT IT WAS JUST MY IMAGINATION.
は!
GASP!
BUT ONE DAY, I HEARD HIM...
!!
KARIN, YOU'VE GAINED WEIGHT.

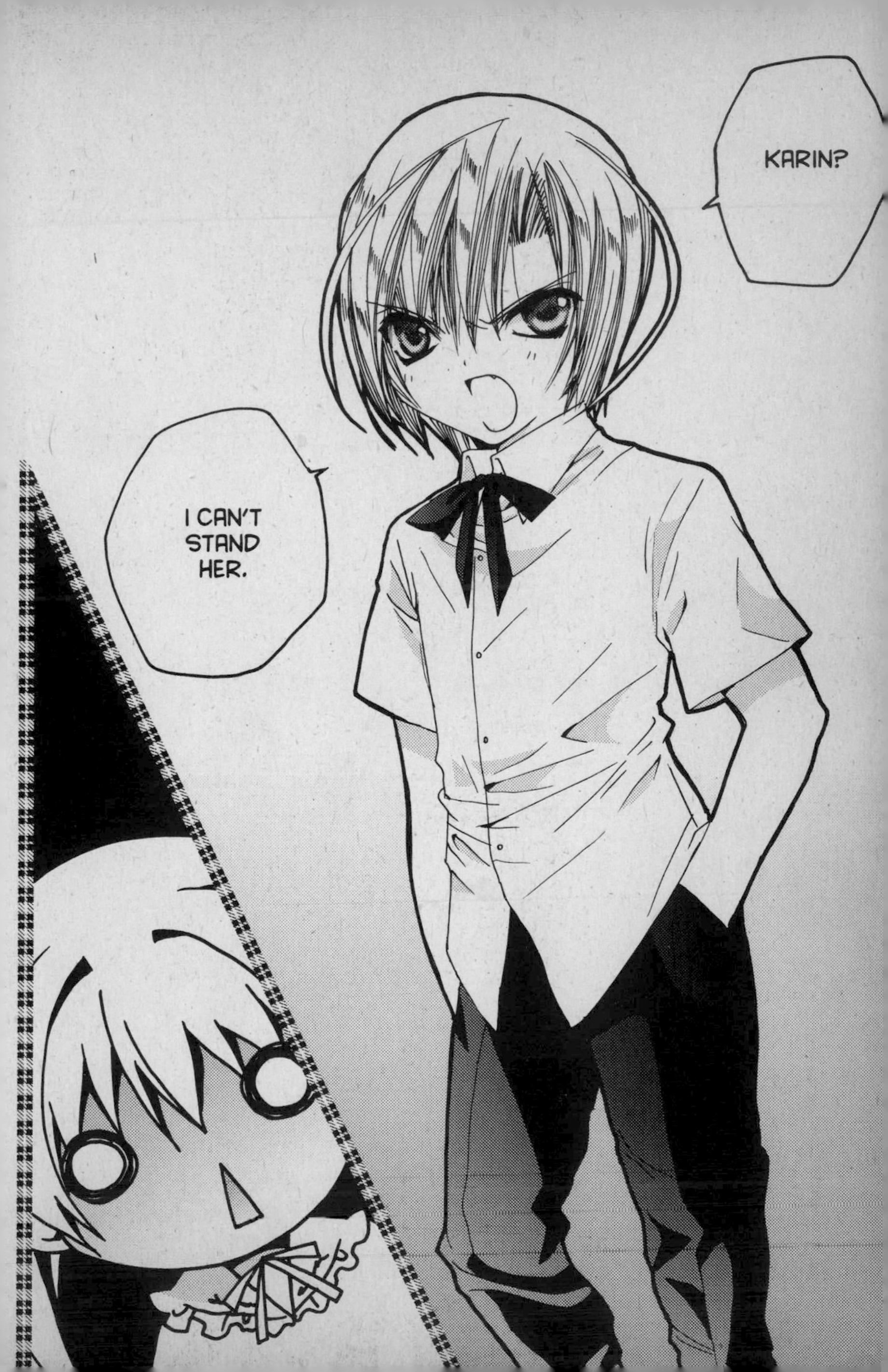
KARIN?
I CAN'T STAND HER.

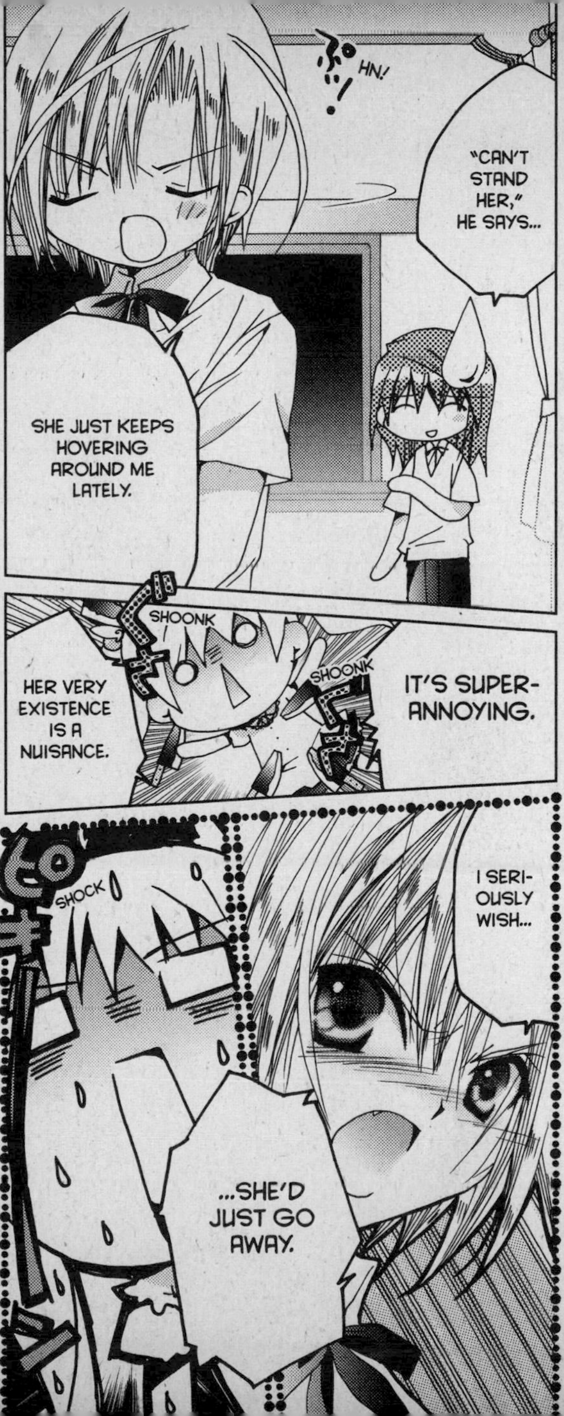
HN!
"CAN'T STAND HER," HE SAYS...
SHE JUST KEEPS HOVERING AROUND ME LATELY.
IT'S SUPER-ANNOYING.
SHOONK
SHOONK
HER VERY EXISTENCE IS A NUISANCE.
I SERI-OUSLY WISH...
...SHE'D JUST GO AWAY.
SHOCK

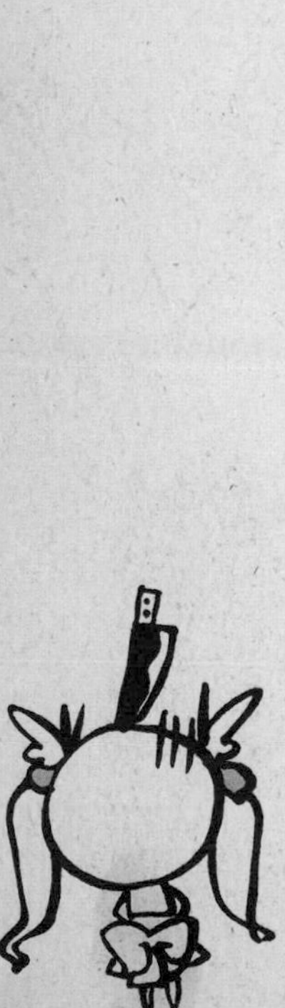

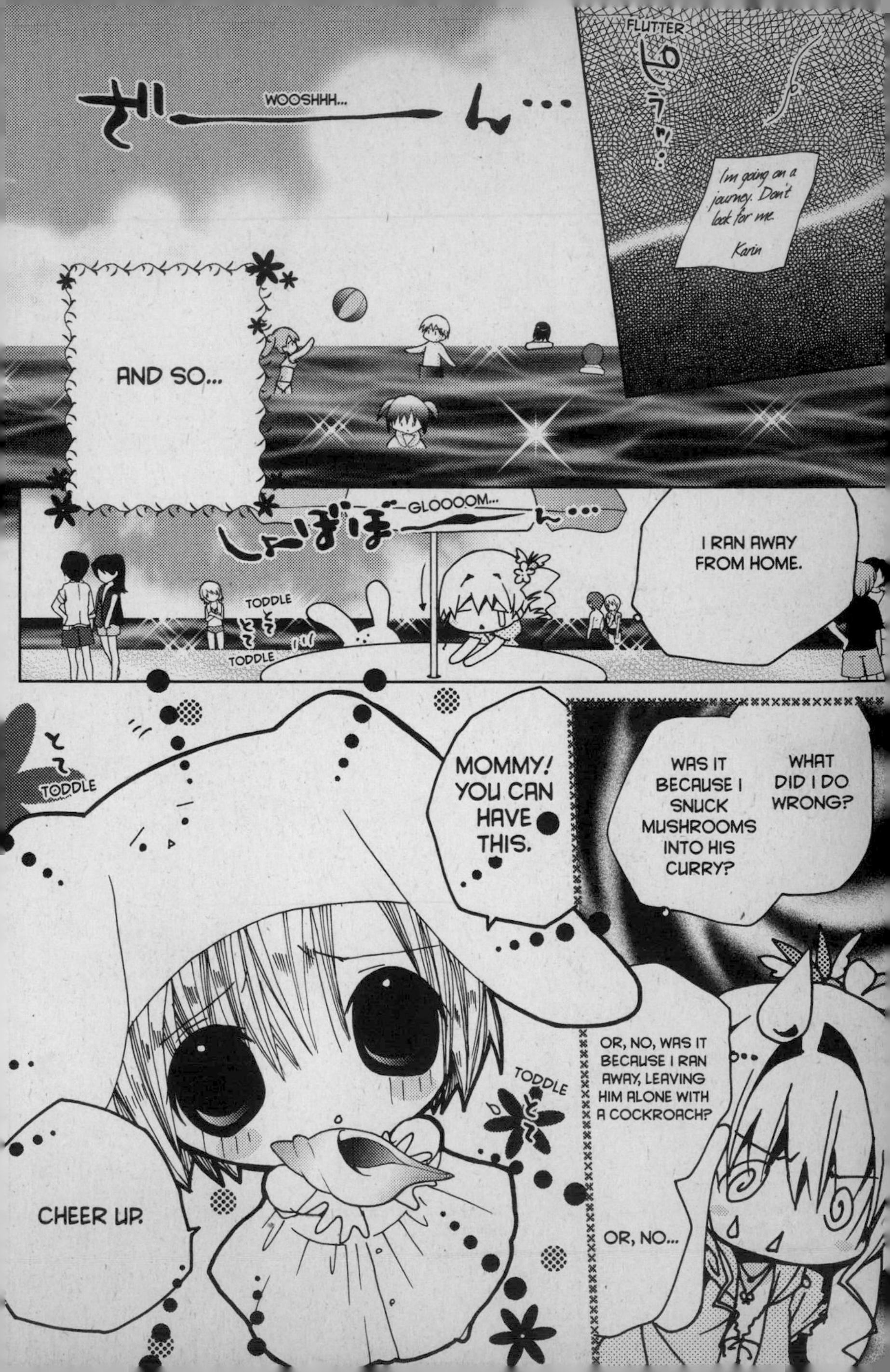
FLUTTER
I'm going on a journey. Don't look for me.
Karin
WOOSHHH...
AND SO...
GLOOOOM...
I RAN AWAY FROM HOME.
TODDLE
TODDLE
WHAT DID I DO WRONG?
WAS IT BECAUSE I SNUCK MUSHROOMS INTO HIS CURRY?
OR, NO, WAS IT BECAUSE I RAN AWAY, LEAVING HIM ALONE WITH A COCKROACH?
OR, NO...
TODDLE
MOMMY! YOU CAN HAVE THIS.
TODDLE
CHEER UP.

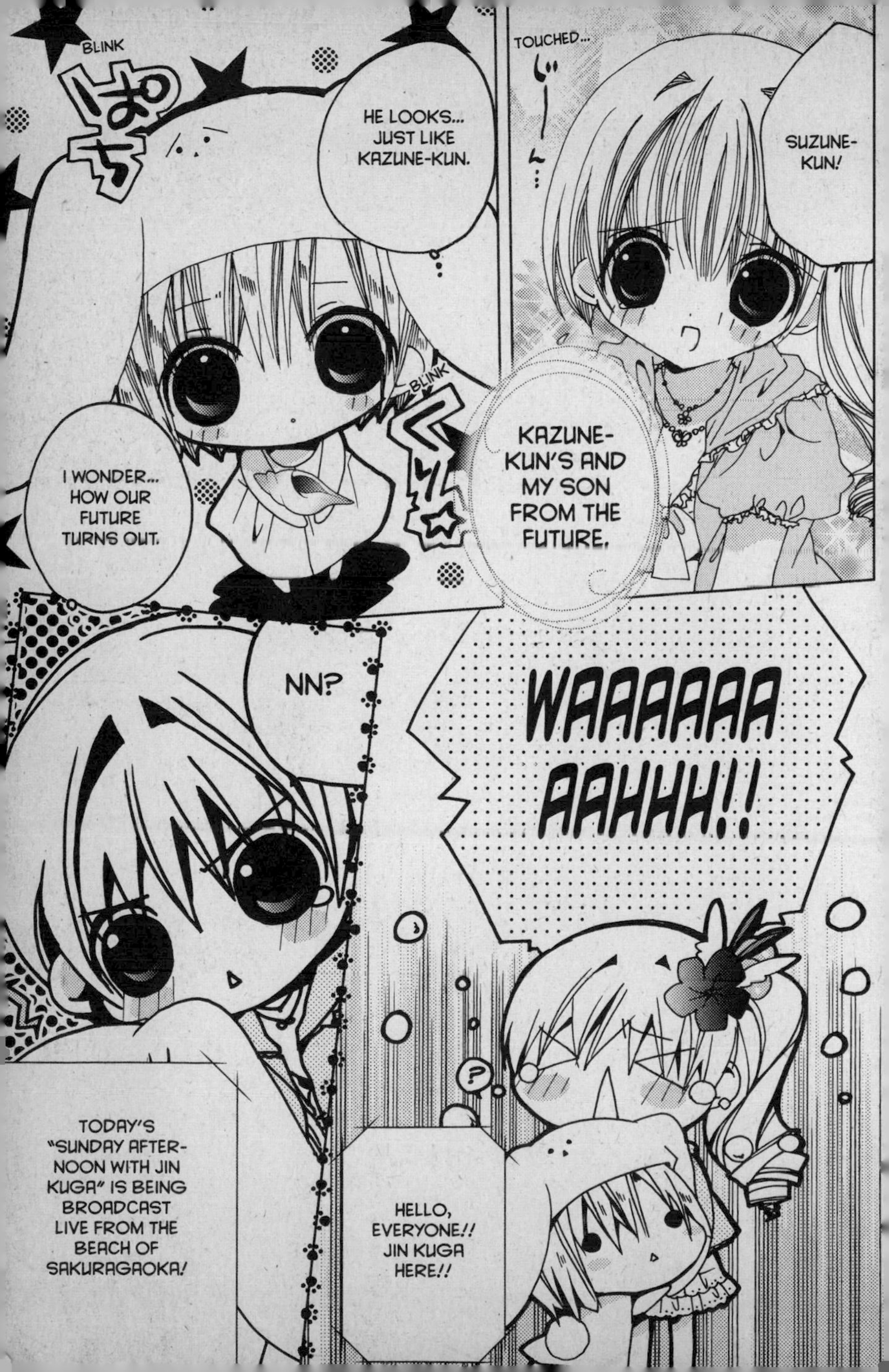
TOUCHED...
じーん…
SUZUNE-KUN!
KAZUNE-KUN'S AND MY SON FROM THE FUTURE.
BLINK
ぱち
HE LOOKS... JUST LIKE KAZUNE-KUN.
BLINK
くりっ
I WONDER... HOW OUR FUTURE TURNS OUT.
WAAAAAAA AAHHH!!
NN?
?
HELLO, EVERYONE!! JIN KUGA HERE!!
TODAY'S "SUNDAY AFTER-NOON WITH JIN KUGA" IS BEING BROADCAST LIVE FROM THE BEACH OF SAKURAGAOKA!

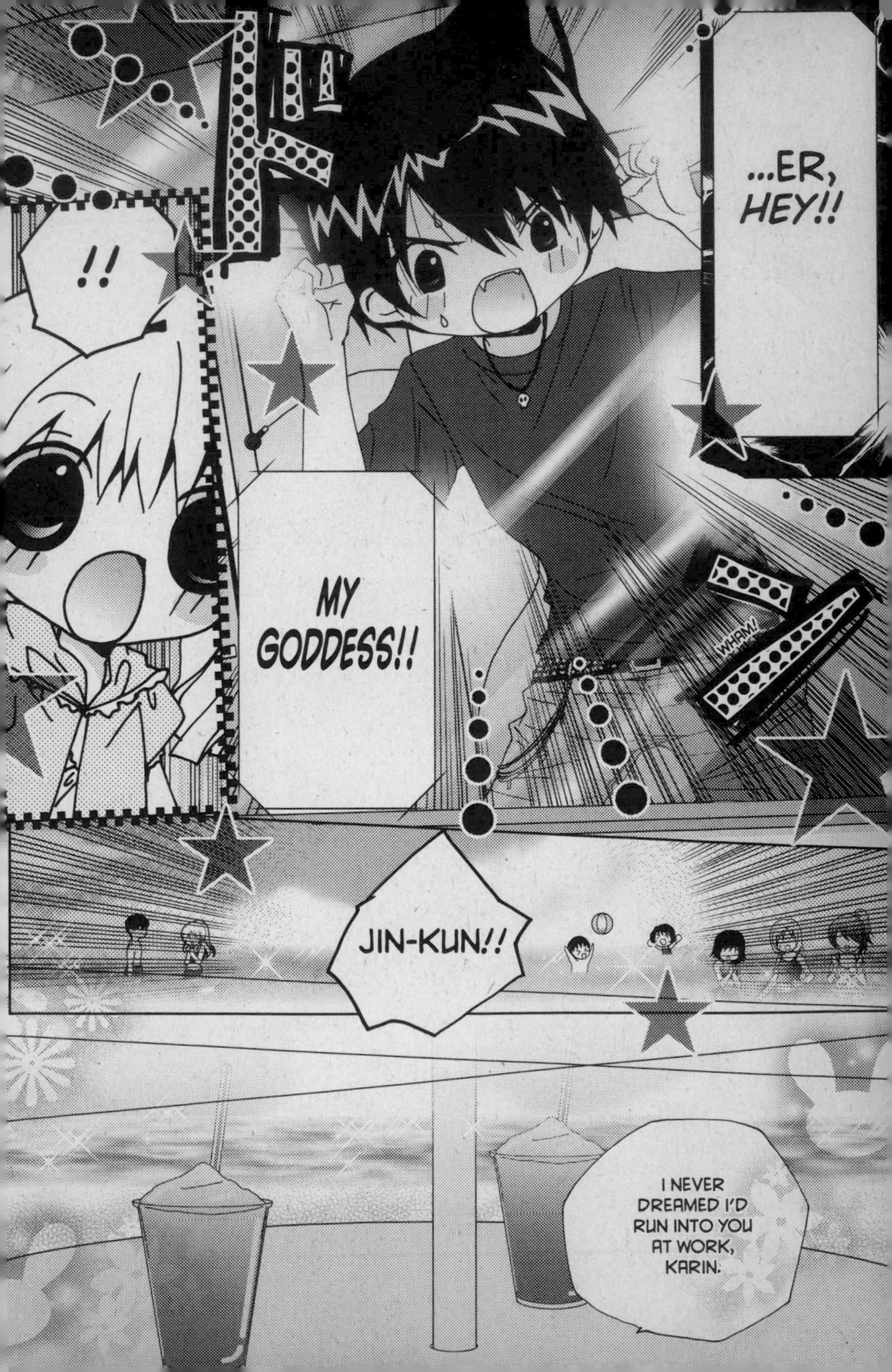
...ER, HEY!!
WHAM!
MY GODDESS!!
!!
JIN-KUN!!
I NEVER DREAMED I'D RUN INTO YOU AT WORK, KARIN.

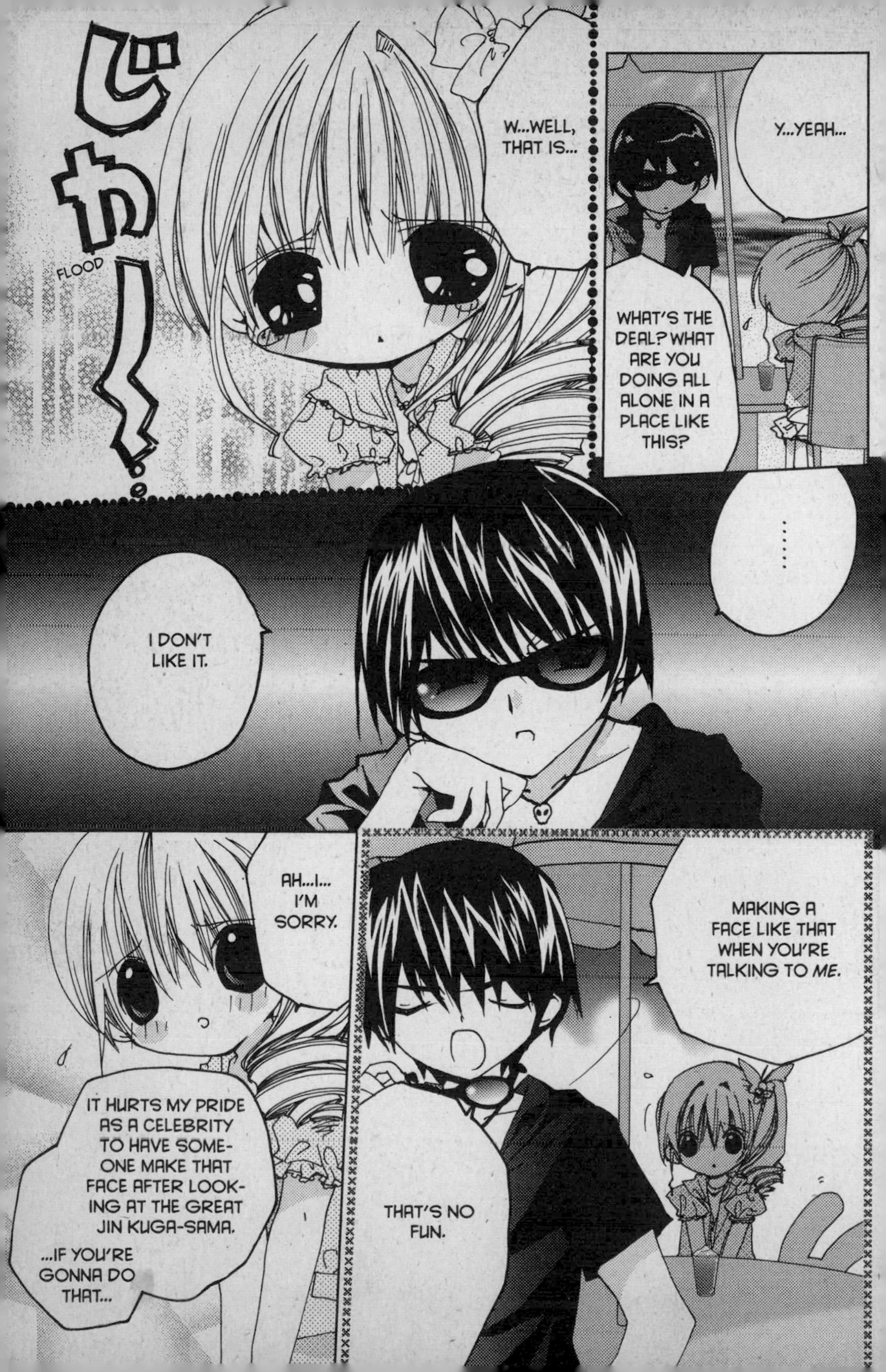
Y...YEAH...
WHAT'S THE DEAL? WHAT ARE YOU DOING ALL ALONE IN A PLACE LIKE THIS?
W...WELL, THAT IS...
じわ～。
FLOOD
......
I DON'T LIKE IT.
MAKING A FACE LIKE THAT WHEN YOU'RE TALKING TO *ME*.
THAT'S NO FUN.
AH...I... I'M SORRY.
IT HURTS MY PRIDE AS A CELEBRITY TO HAVE SOME-ONE MAKE THAT FACE AFTER LOOK-ING AT THE GREAT JIN KUGA-SAMA.
...IF YOU'RE GONNA DO THAT...

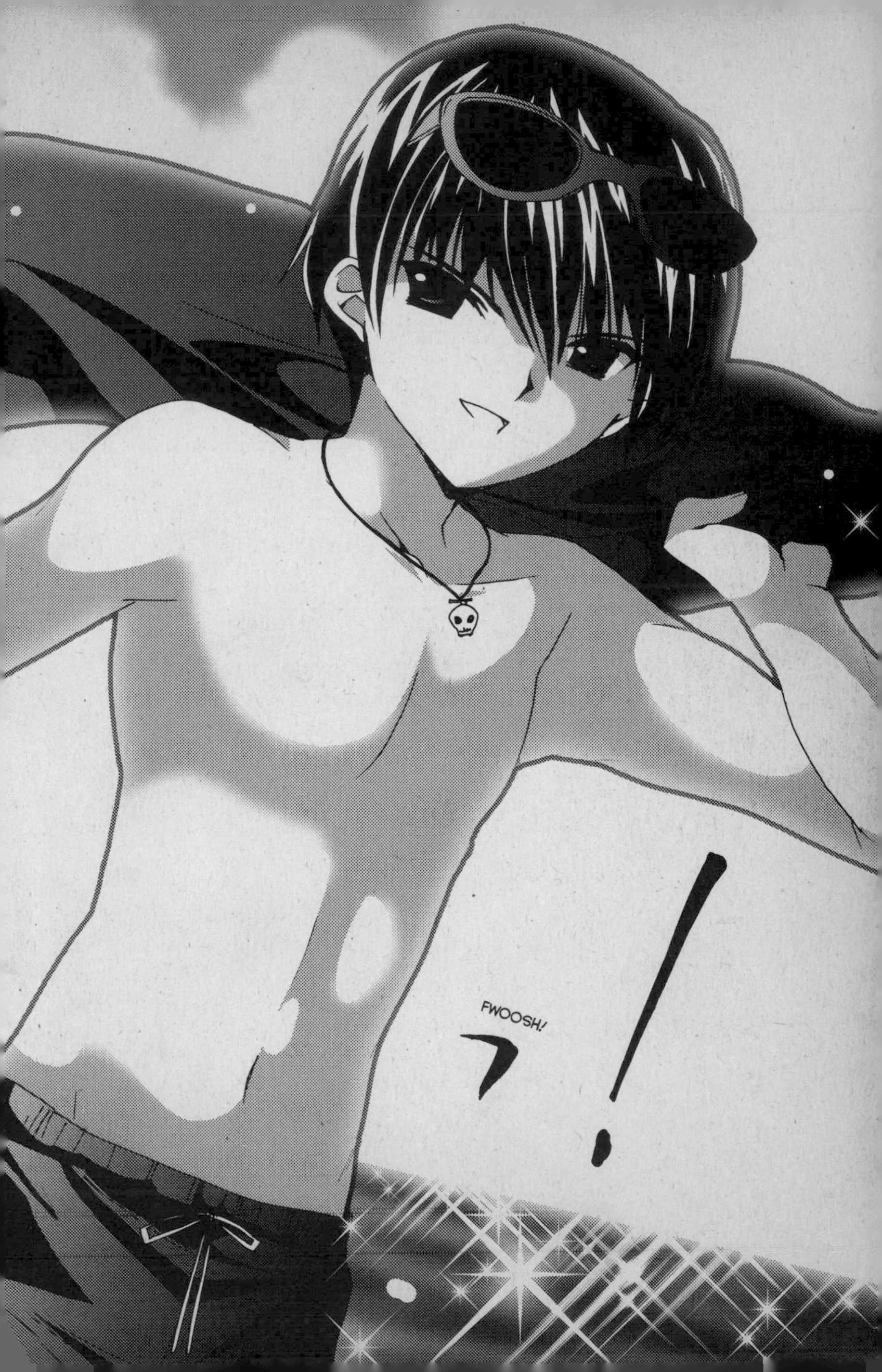
FWOOSH!

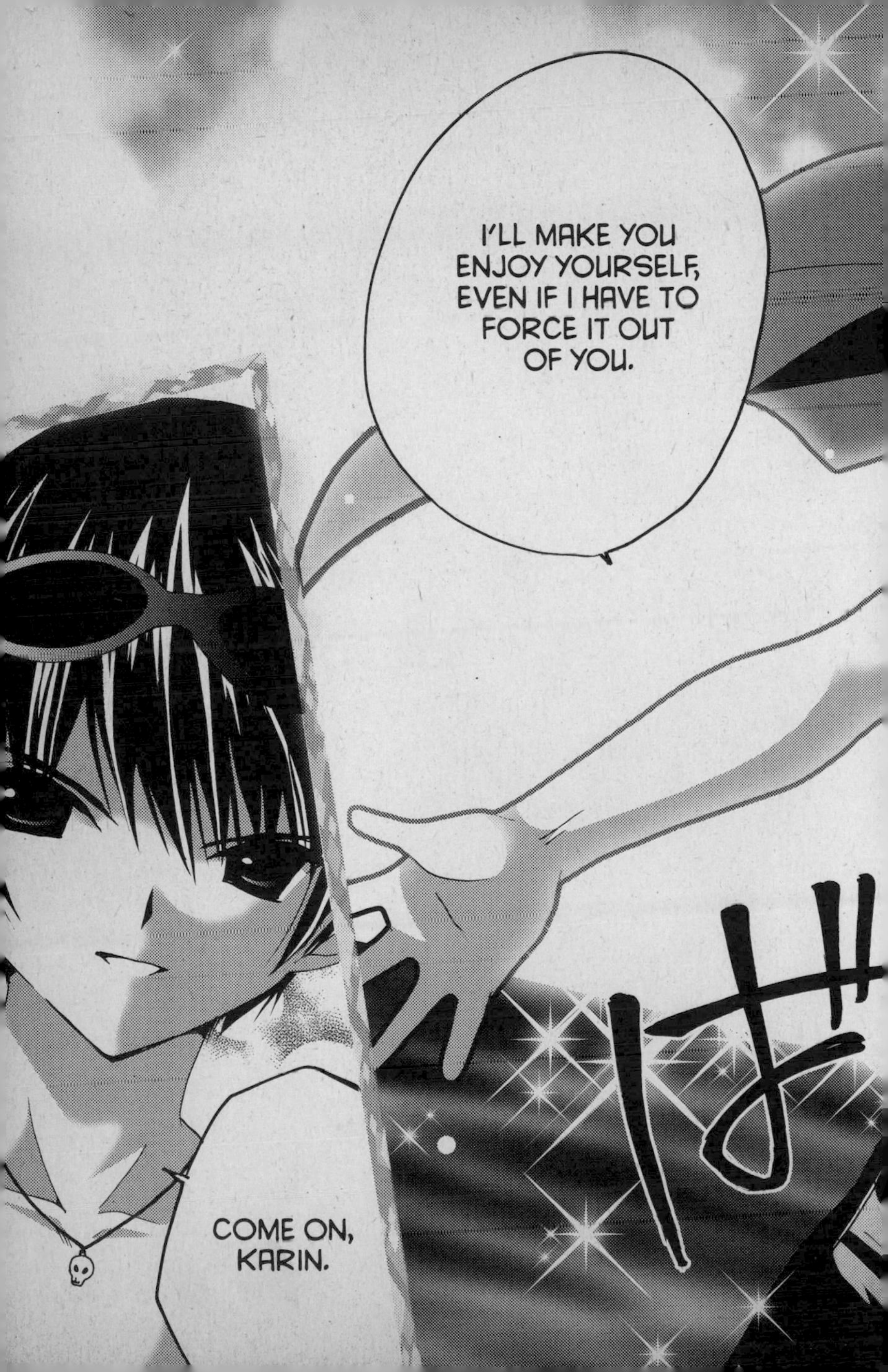
I'LL MAKE YOU ENJOY YOURSELF, EVEN IF I HAVE TO FORCE IT OUT OF YOU.
COME ON, KARIN.

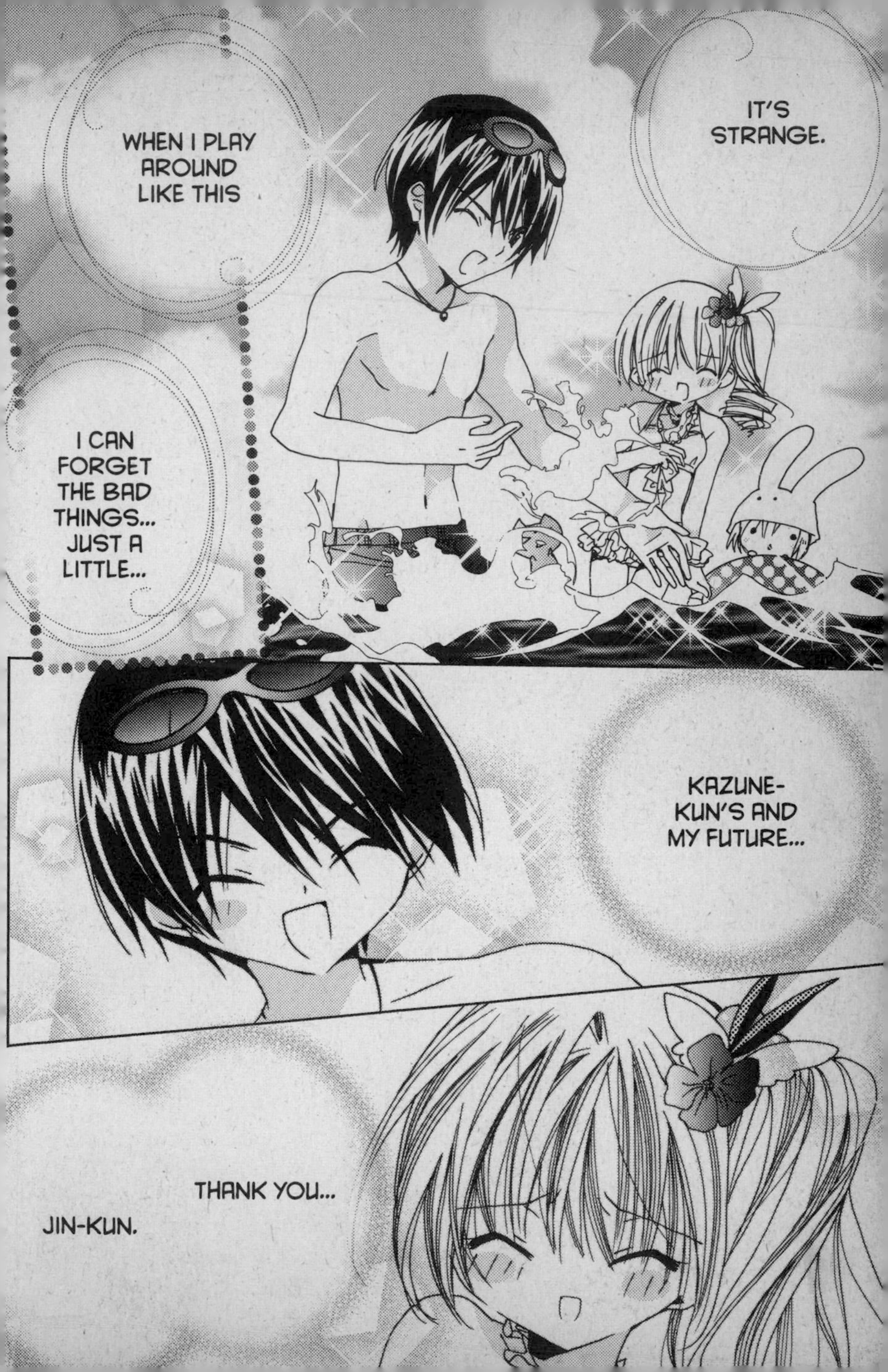
IT'S STRANGE.
WHEN I PLAY AROUND LIKE THIS
I CAN FORGET THE BAD THINGS... JUST A LITTLE...
KAZUNE-KUN'S AND MY FUTURE...
THANK YOU...
JIN-KUN.

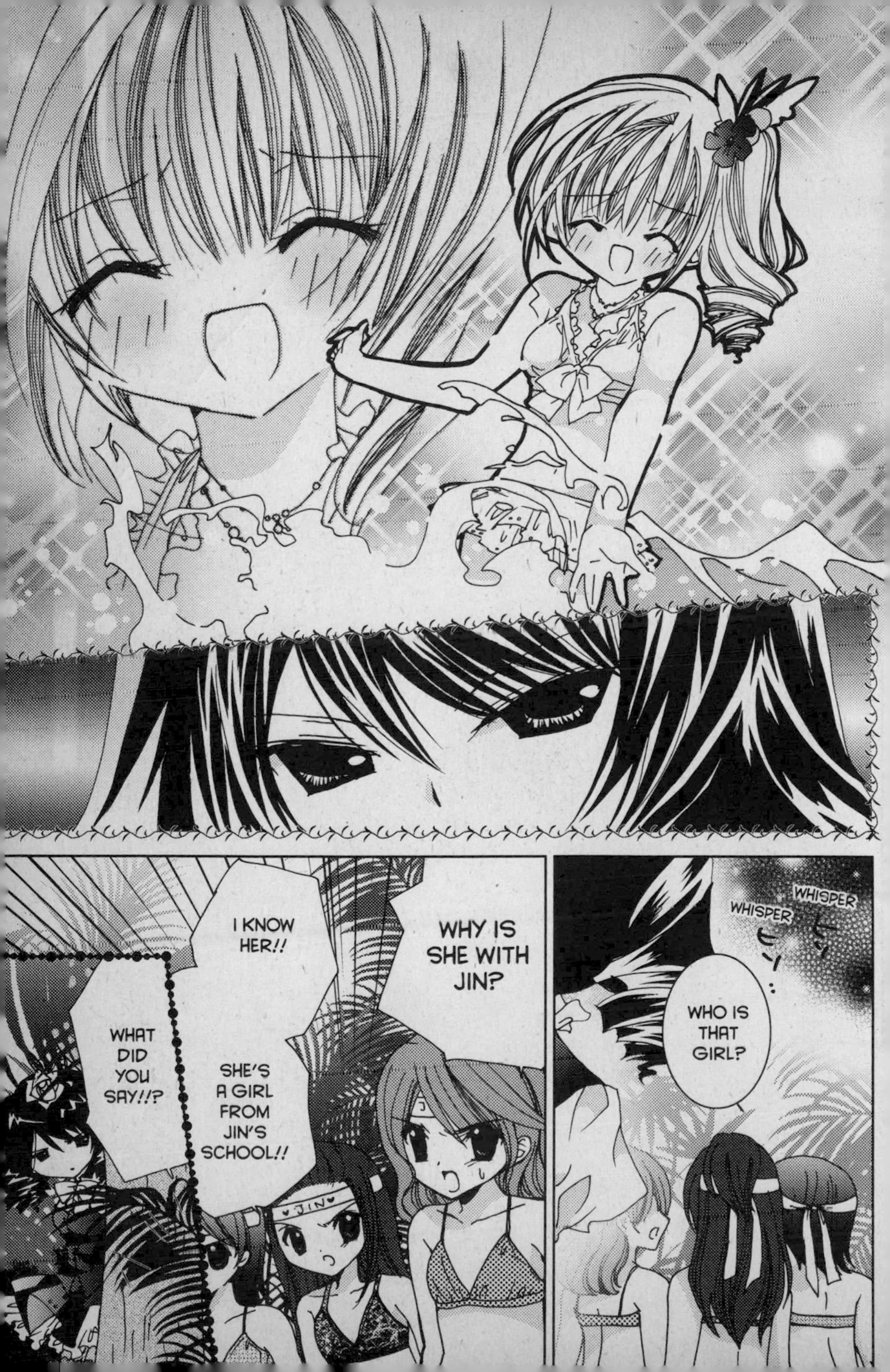
WHISPER
WHISPER
WHO IS THAT GIRL?
WHY IS SHE WITH JIN?
I KNOW HER!!
SHE'S A GIRL FROM JIN'S SCHOOL!!
WHAT DID YOU SAY!!?

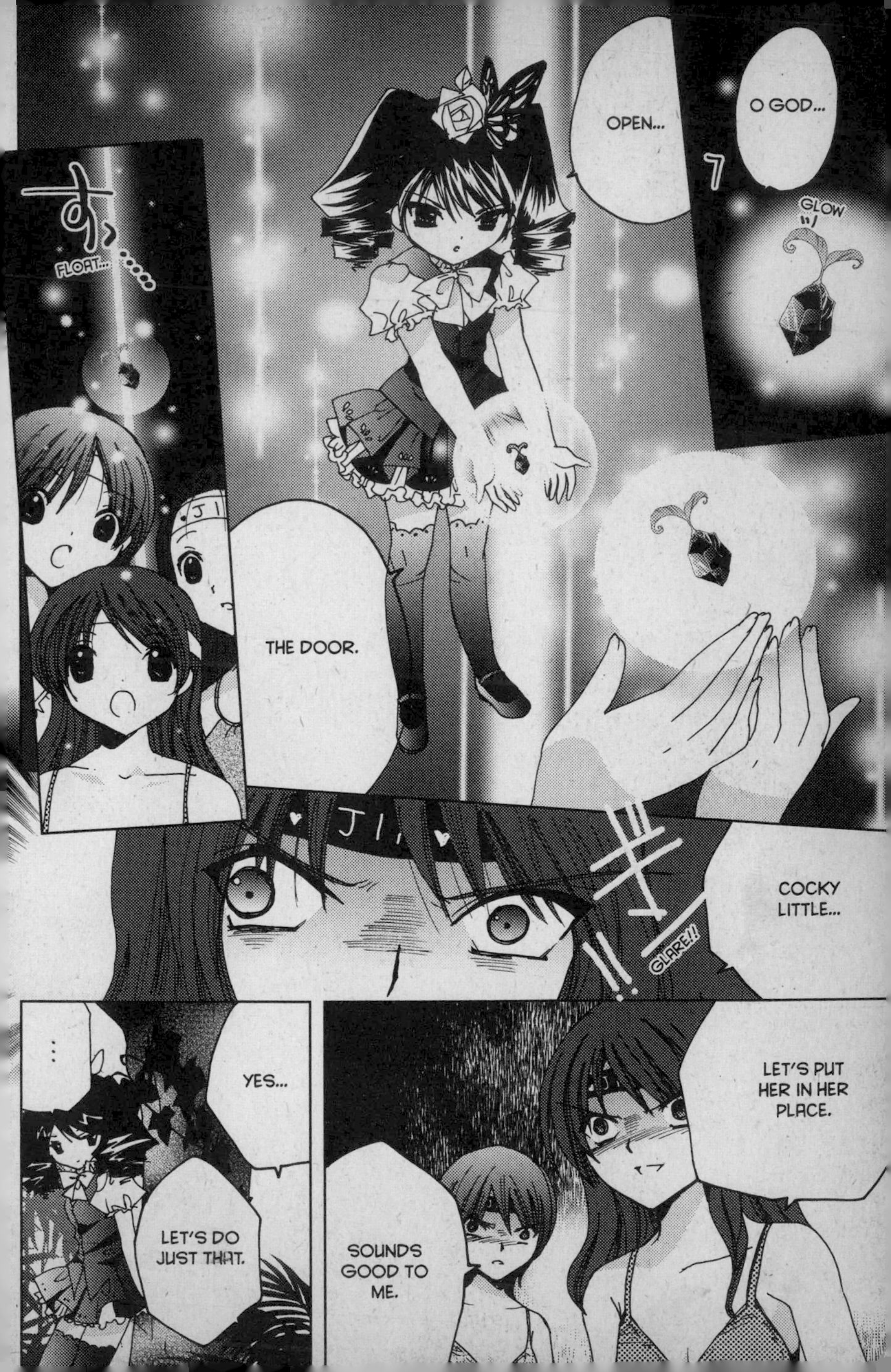
O GOD...
GLOW
OPEN...
THE DOOR.
す
FLOAT...
COCKY LITTLE...
GLARE!!
LET'S PUT HER IN HER PLACE.
SOUNDS GOOD TO ME.
YES...
LET'S DO JUST THAT.

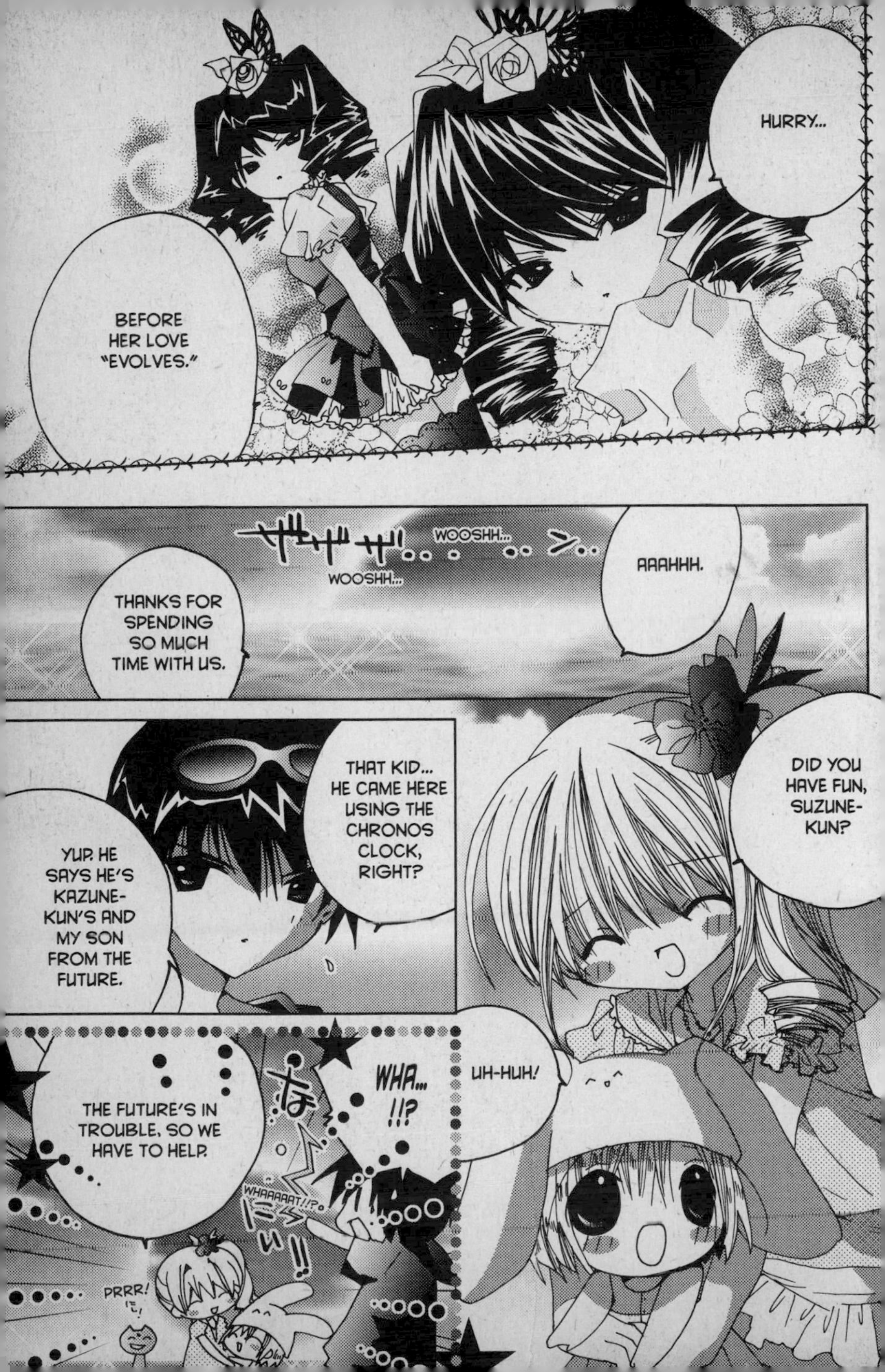
HURRY...
BEFORE HER LOVE "EVOLVES."
AAAHHH.
WOOSHH...
WOOSHH...
THANKS FOR SPENDING SO MUCH TIME WITH US.
DID YOU HAVE FUN, SUZUNE-KUN?
UH-HUH!
THAT KID... HE CAME HERE USING THE CHRONOS CLOCK, RIGHT?
YUP. HE SAYS HE'S KAZUNE-KUN'S AND MY SON FROM THE FUTURE.
WHA... !!?
WHAAAAAT!!?
THE FUTURE'S IN TROUBLE, SO WE HAVE TO HELP.
PRRR!

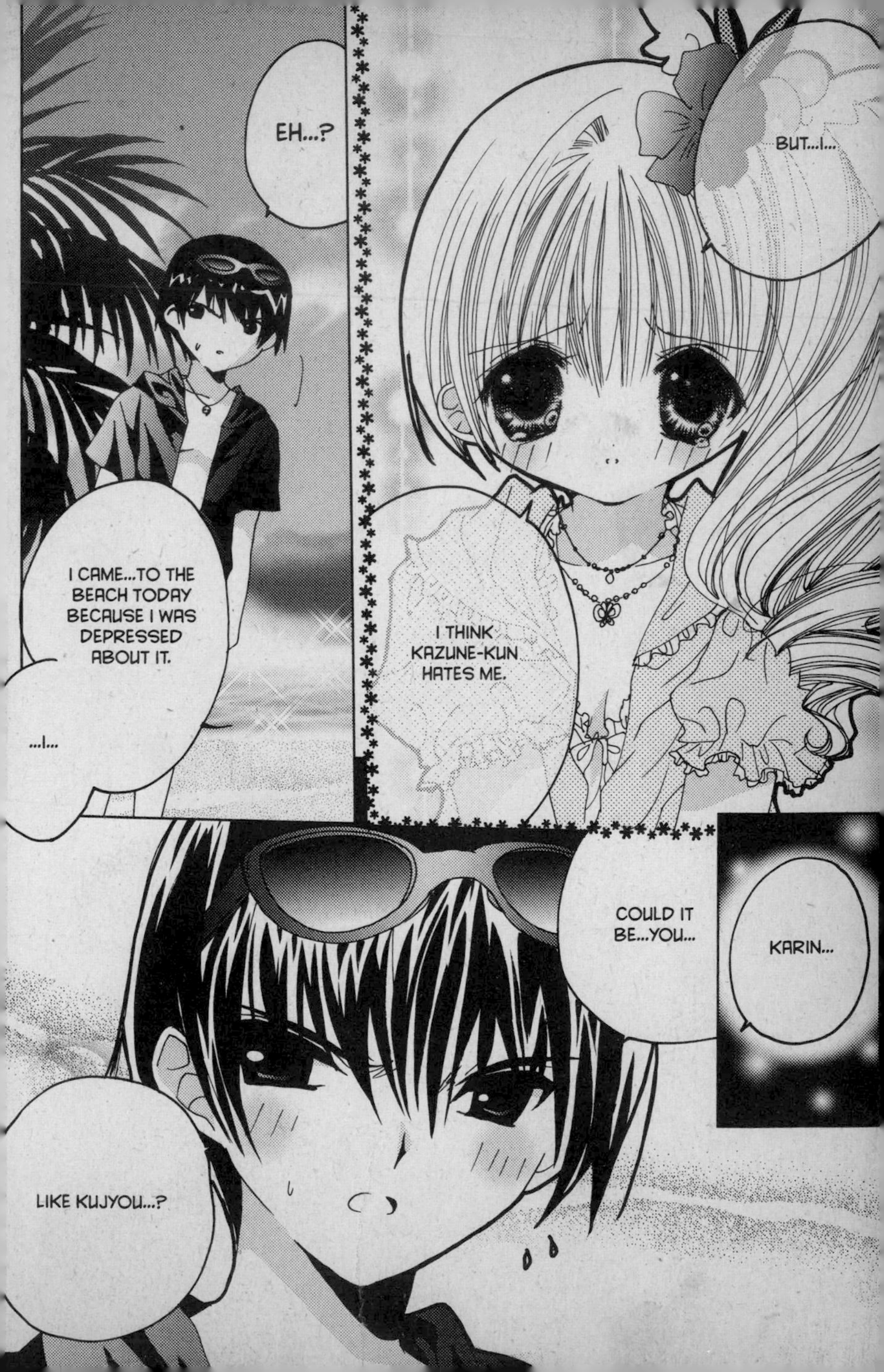
BUT...I...
I THINK KAZUNE-KUN HATES ME.
EH...?
I CAME...TO THE BEACH TODAY BECAUSE I WAS DEPRESSED ABOUT IT.
...I...
KARIN...
COULD IT BE...YOU...
LIKE KUJYOU...?

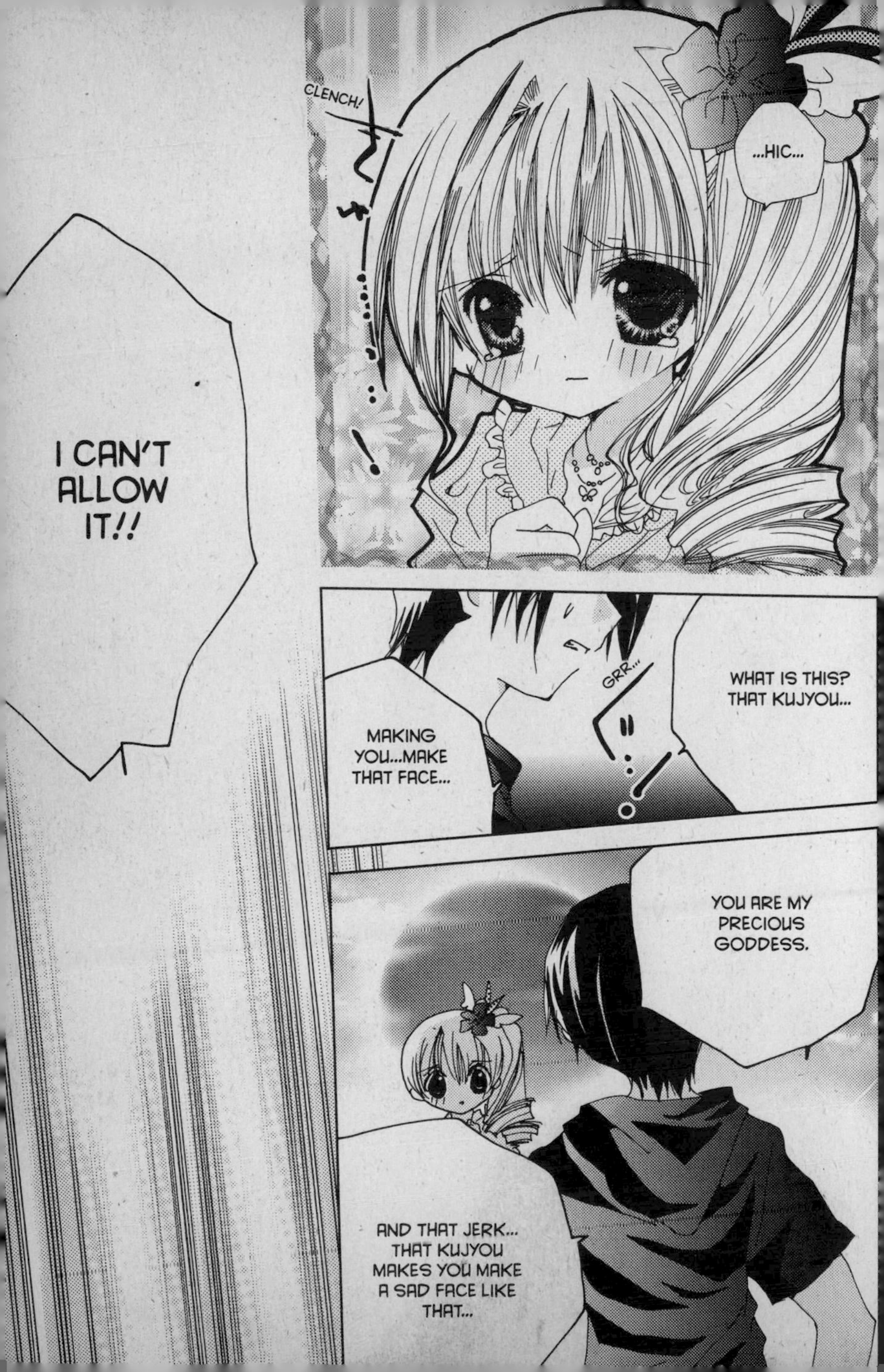
...HIC...
CLENCH!
WHAT IS THIS? THAT KUJYOU...
GRR...
MAKING YOU...MAKE THAT FACE...
YOU ARE MY PRECIOUS GODDESS.
AND THAT JERK... THAT KUJYOU MAKES YOU MAKE A SAD FACE LIKE THAT...
I CAN'T ALLOW IT!!

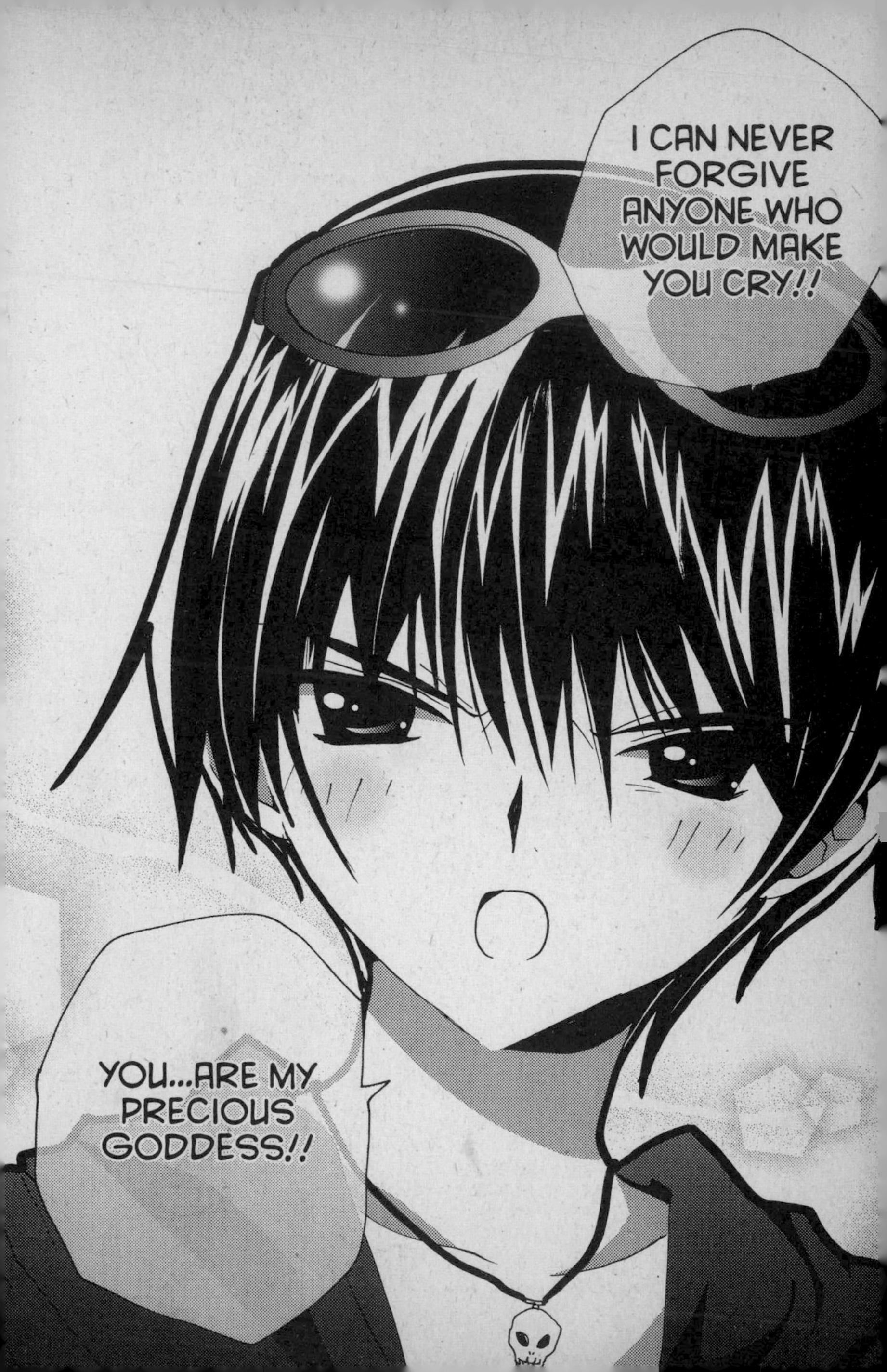
I CAN NEVER FORGIVE ANYONE WHO WOULD MAKE YOU CRY!!
YOU...ARE MY PRECIOUS GODDESS!!

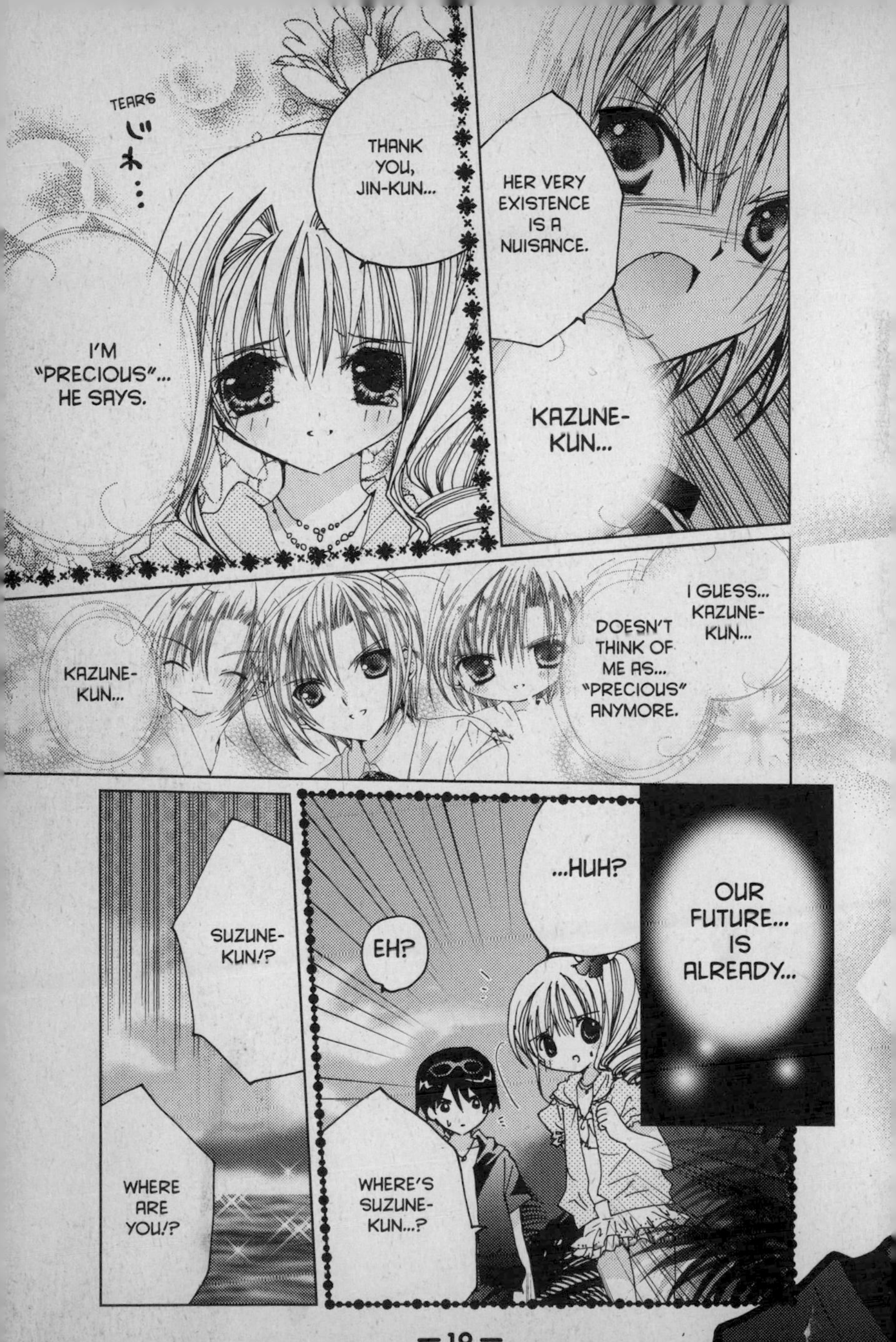
HER VERY EXISTENCE IS A NUISANCE.
KAZUNE-KUN...
THANK YOU, JIN-KUN...
TEARS
じわ…
I'M "PRECIOUS"... HE SAYS.
I GUESS... KAZUNE-KUN...
DOESN'T THINK OF ME AS... "PRECIOUS" ANYMORE.
KAZUNE-KUN...
OUR FUTURE... IS ALREADY...
...HUH?
EH?
WHERE'S SUZUNE-KUN...?
SUZUNE-KUN!?
WHERE ARE YOU!?

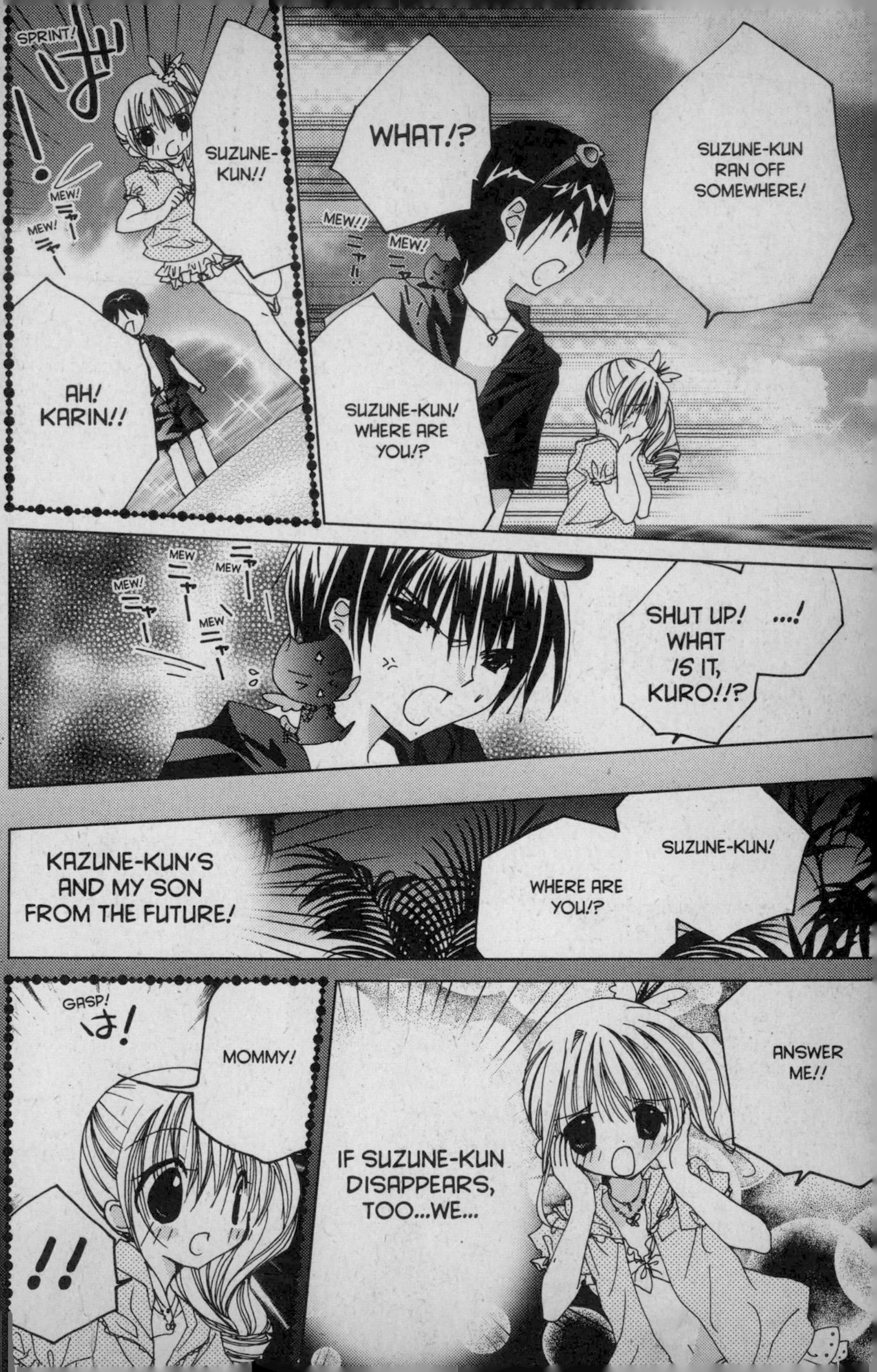
SUZUNE-KUN RAN OFF SOMEWHERE!
WHAT!?
MEW!! ニャー!!
MEW! ニャー
SUZUNE-KUN! WHERE ARE YOU!?
SUZUNE-KUN!!
SPRINT! ば!
MEW! ニャー
MEW! ニャー
AH! KARIN!!
...!
SHUT UP! WHAT IS IT, KURO!!?
MEW ニャー
MEW ニャー
MEW! ニャー
MEW ニャー
SUZUNE-KUN!
WHERE ARE YOU!?
KAZUNE-KUN'S AND MY SON FROM THE FUTURE!
ANSWER ME!!
IF SUZUNE-KUN DISAPPEARS, TOO...WE...
MOMMY!
GASP! は!
!!

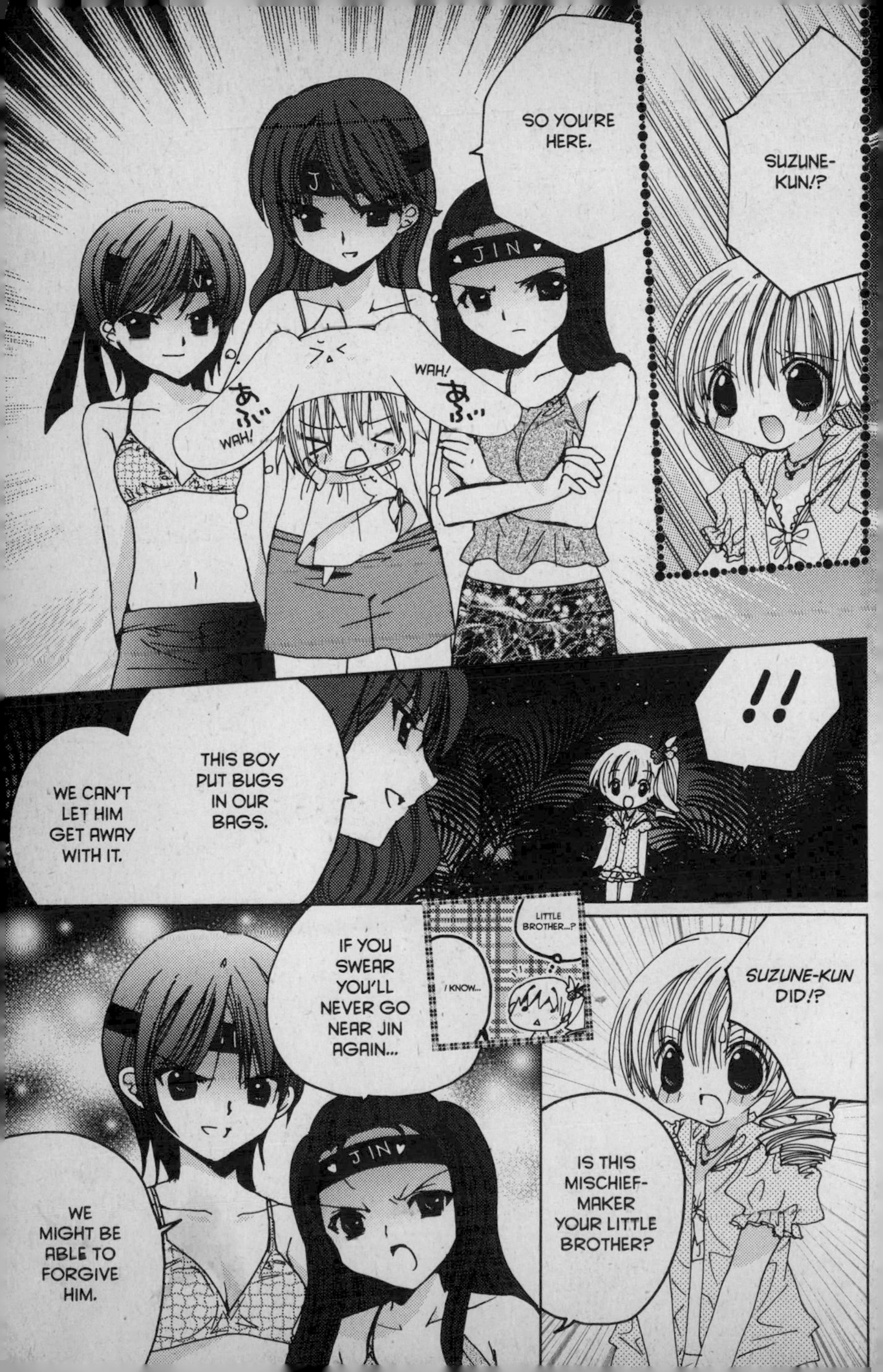
SUZUNE-KUN!?
SO YOU'RE HERE.
JIN
WAH!
あぶ
WAH!
あぶ
!!
THIS BOY PUT BUGS IN OUR BAGS.
WE CAN'T LET HIM GET AWAY WITH IT.
SUZUNE-KUN DID!?
IS THIS MISCHIEF-MAKER YOUR LITTLE BROTHER?
LITTLE BROTHER...?
I KNOW...
IF YOU SWEAR YOU'LL NEVER GO NEAR JIN AGAIN...
JIN
WE MIGHT BE ABLE TO FORGIVE HIM.

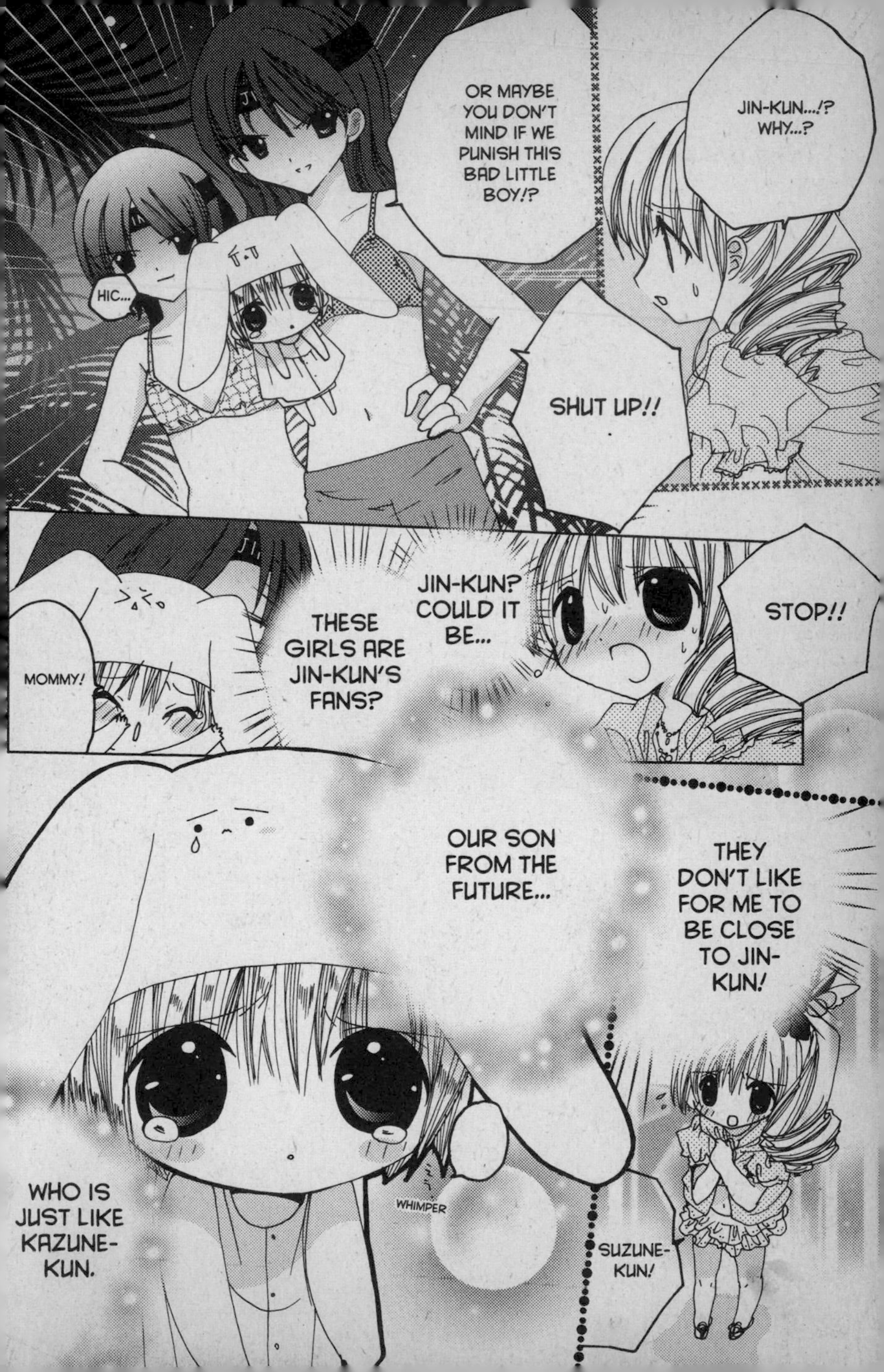
JIN-KUN...!? WHY...?
SHUT UP!!
OR MAYBE YOU DON'T MIND IF WE PUNISH THIS BAD LITTLE BOY!?
HIC...
STOP!!
JIN-KUN? COULD IT BE...
THESE GIRLS ARE JIN-KUN'S FANS?
MOMMY!
THEY DON'T LIKE FOR ME TO BE CLOSE TO JIN-KUN!
SUZUNE-KUN!
OUR SON FROM THE FUTURE...
WHO IS JUST LIKE KAZUNE-KUN.
WHIMPER

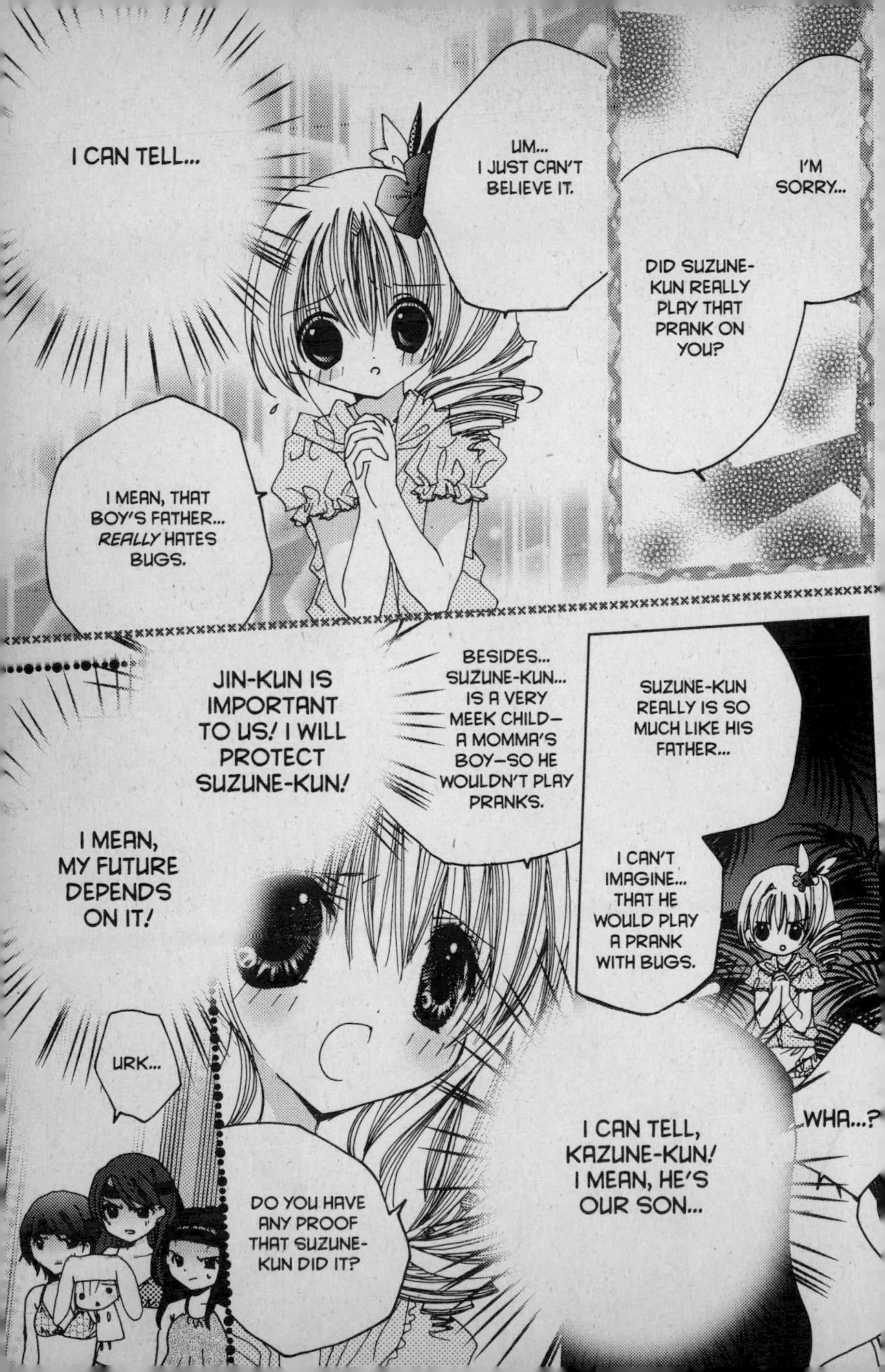
I'M SORRY...
DID SUZUNE-KUN REALLY PLAY THAT PRANK ON YOU?
UM... I JUST CAN'T BELIEVE IT.
I CAN TELL...
I MEAN, THAT BOY'S FATHER... *REALLY* HATES BUGS.
SUZUNE-KUN REALLY IS SO MUCH LIKE HIS FATHER...
I CAN'T IMAGINE... THAT HE WOULD PLAY A PRANK WITH BUGS.
BESIDES... SUZUNE-KUN... IS A VERY MEEK CHILD—A MOMMA'S BOY—SO HE WOULDN'T PLAY PRANKS.
JIN-KUN IS IMPORTANT TO US! I WILL PROTECT SUZUNE-KUN!
I MEAN, MY FUTURE DEPENDS ON IT!
WHA...?
I CAN TELL, KAZUNE-KUN! I MEAN, HE'S OUR SON...
DO YOU HAVE ANY PROOF THAT SUZUNE-KUN DID IT?
URK...

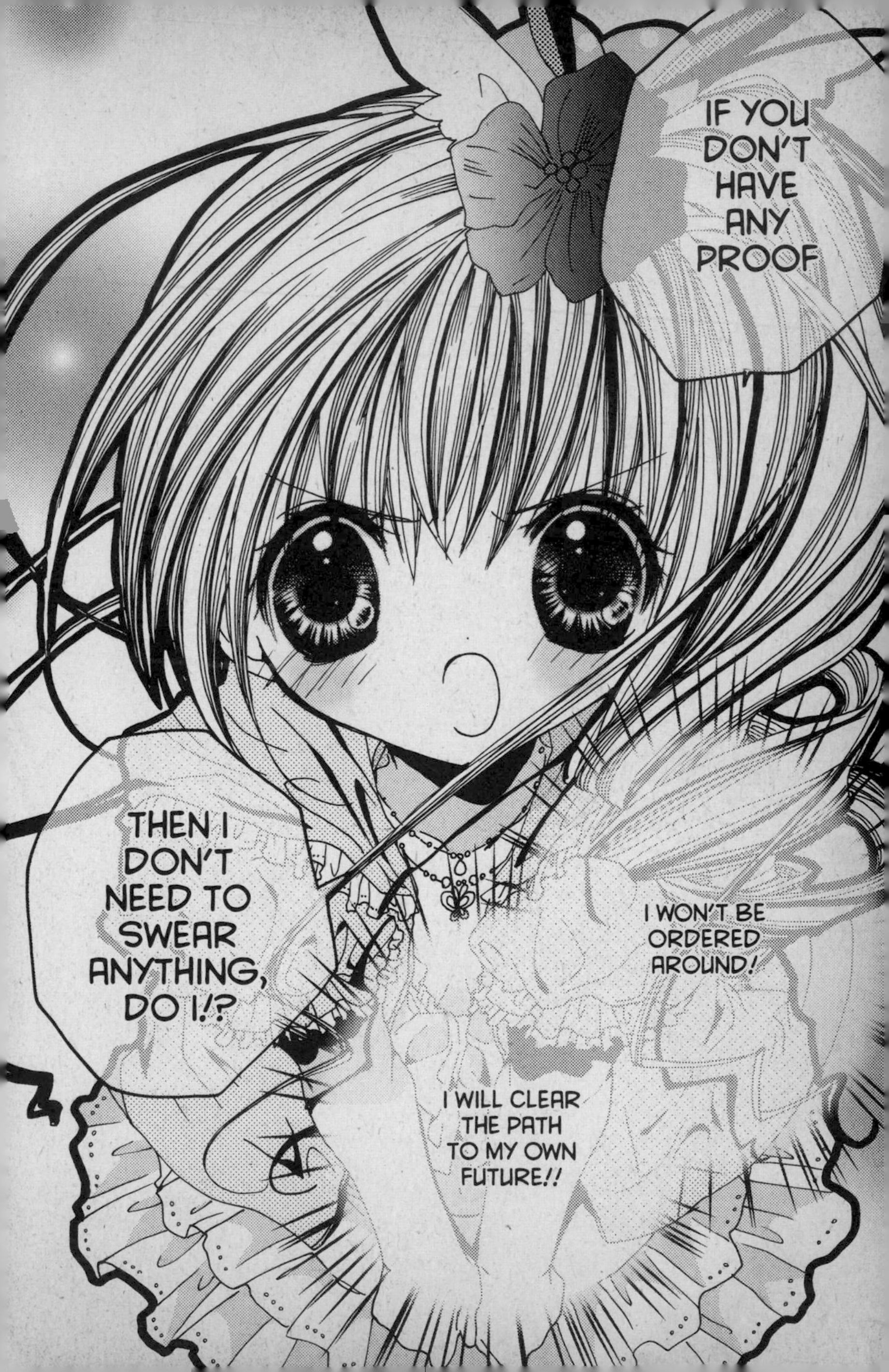
IF YOU DON'T HAVE ANY PROOF
THEN I DON'T NEED TO SWEAR ANYTHING, DO I!?
I WON'T BE ORDERED AROUND!
I WILL CLEAR THE PATH TO MY OWN FUTURE!!

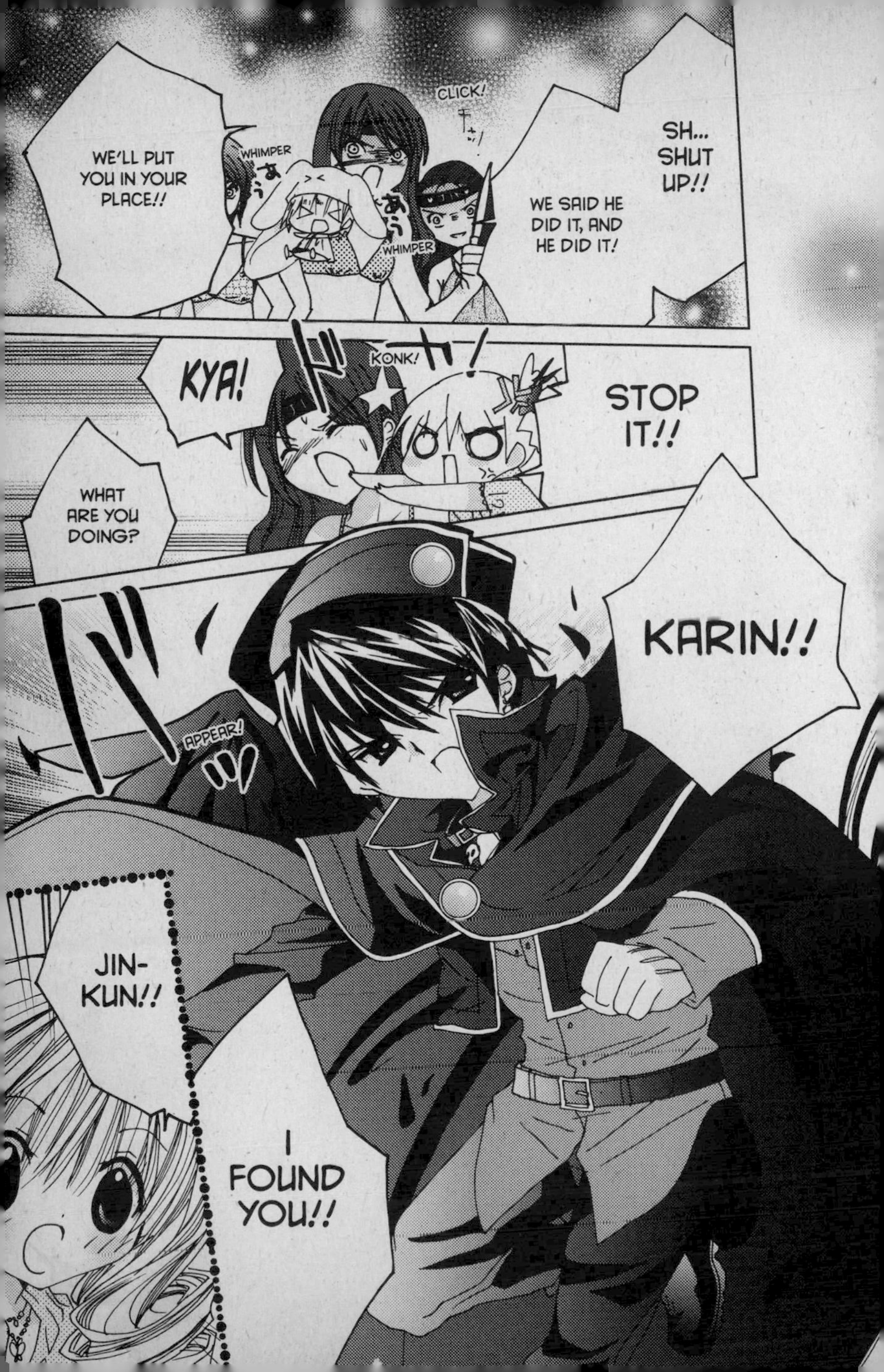
SH... SHUT UP!!
CLICK!
WE SAID HE DID IT, AND HE DID IT!
WHIMPER
WHIMPER
WE'LL PUT YOU IN YOUR PLACE!!
STOP IT!!
KONK!
KYA!
WHAT ARE YOU DOING?
KARIN!!
APPEAR!
JIN-KUN!!
I FOUND YOU!!

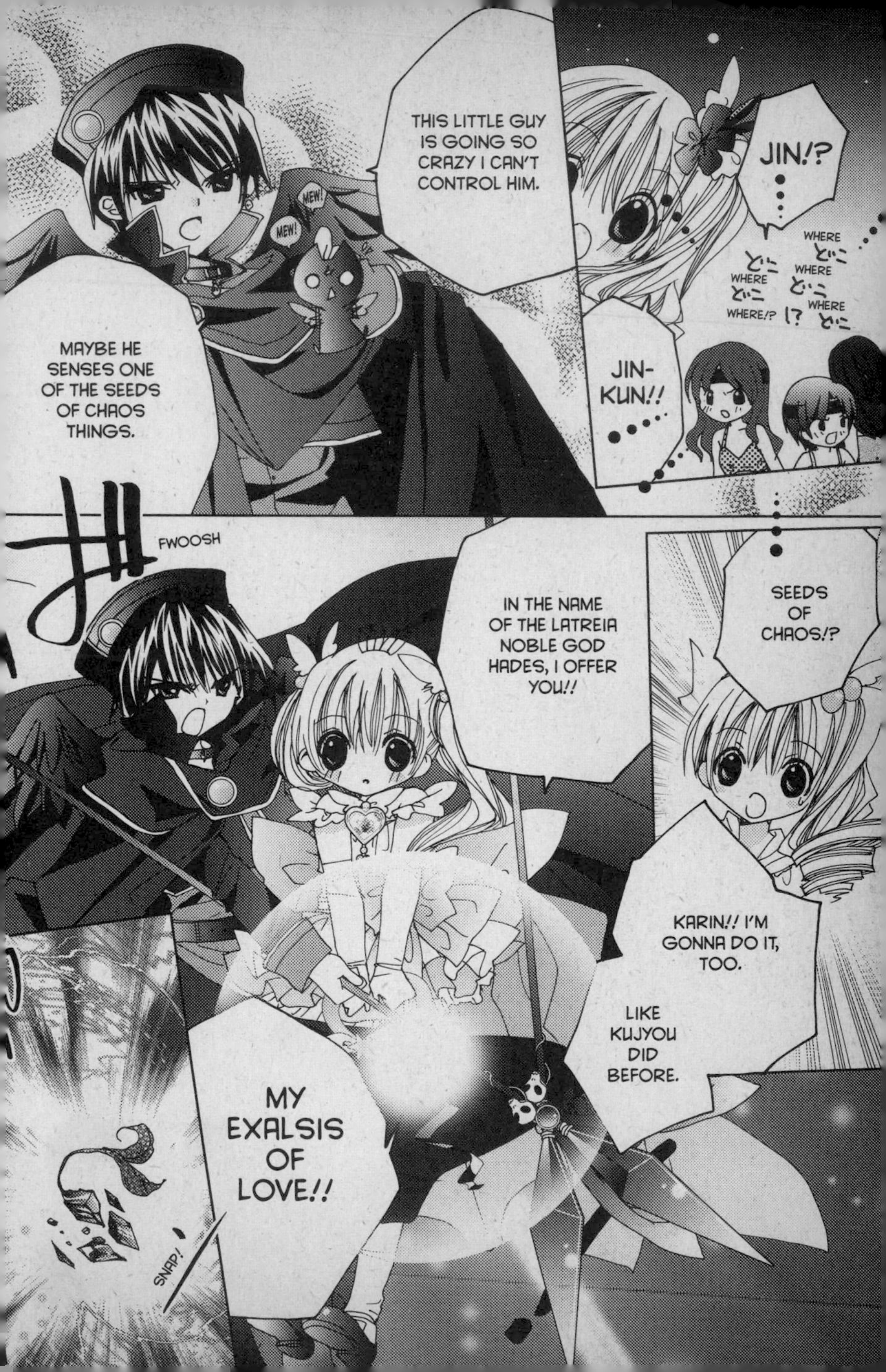
JIN!?
WHERE どこ
WHERE どこ
WHERE どこ
WHERE どこ
WHERE!? !?
JIN-KUN!!
THIS LITTLE GUY IS GOING SO CRAZY I CAN'T CONTROL HIM.
MEW!
MEW!
MAYBE HE SENSES ONE OF THE SEEDS OF CHAOS THINGS.
SEEDS OF CHAOS!?
KARIN!! I'M GONNA DO IT, TOO.
LIKE KUJYOU DID BEFORE.
FWOOSH
IN THE NAME OF THE LATREIA NOBLE GOD HADES, I OFFER YOU!!
MY EXALSIS OF LOVE!!
SNAP!

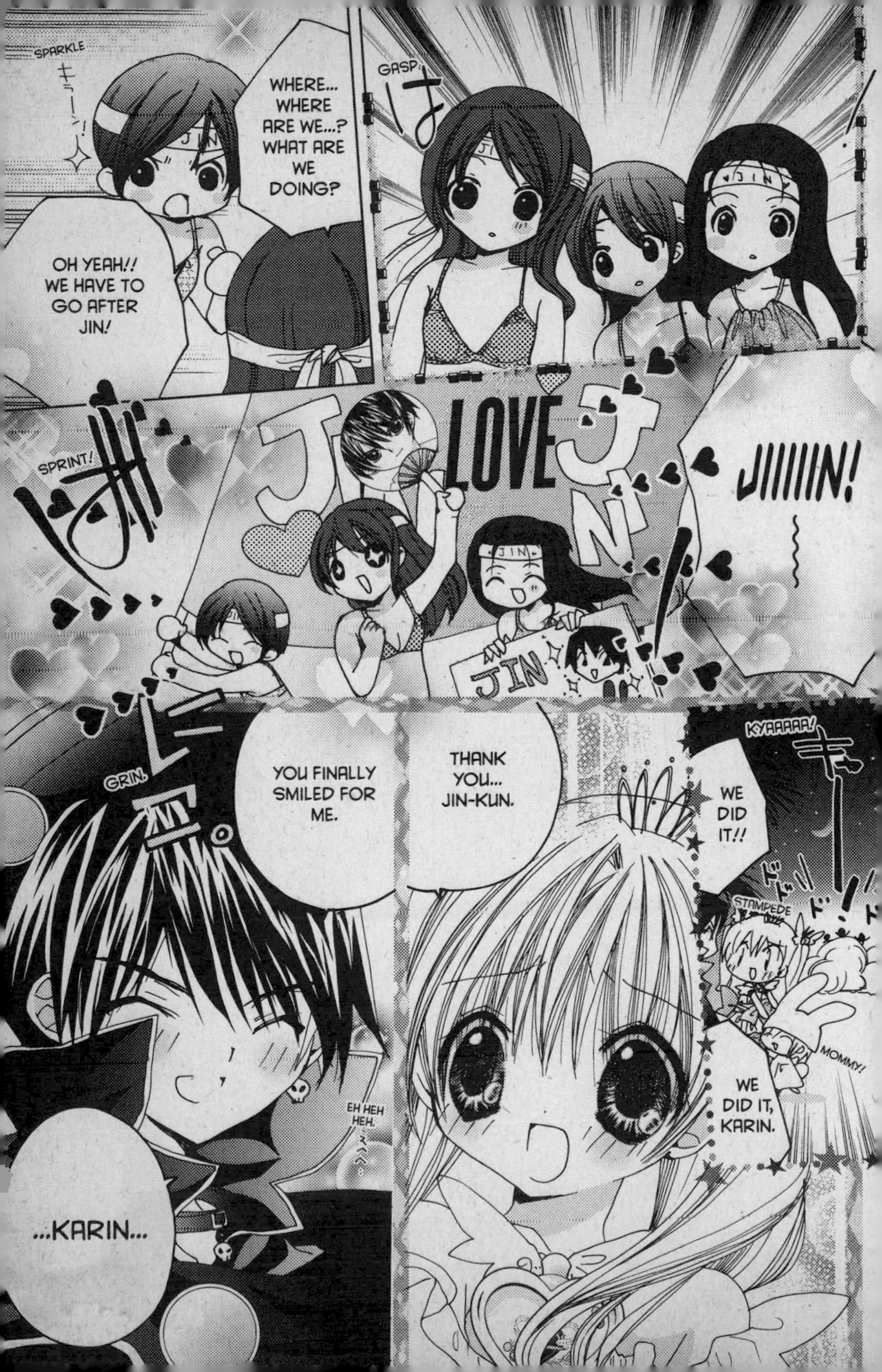
GASP
SPARKLE
WHERE... WHERE ARE WE...? WHAT ARE WE DOING?
OH YEAH!! WE HAVE TO GO AFTER JIN!
JIIIIIN!
LOVE JIN
JIN
SPRINT!
KYAAAAA!
WE DID IT!!
STAMPEDE
MOMMY!
WE DID IT, KARIN.
THANK YOU... JIN-KUN.
YOU FINALLY SMILED FOR ME.
GRIN.
EH HEH HEH.
...KARIN...

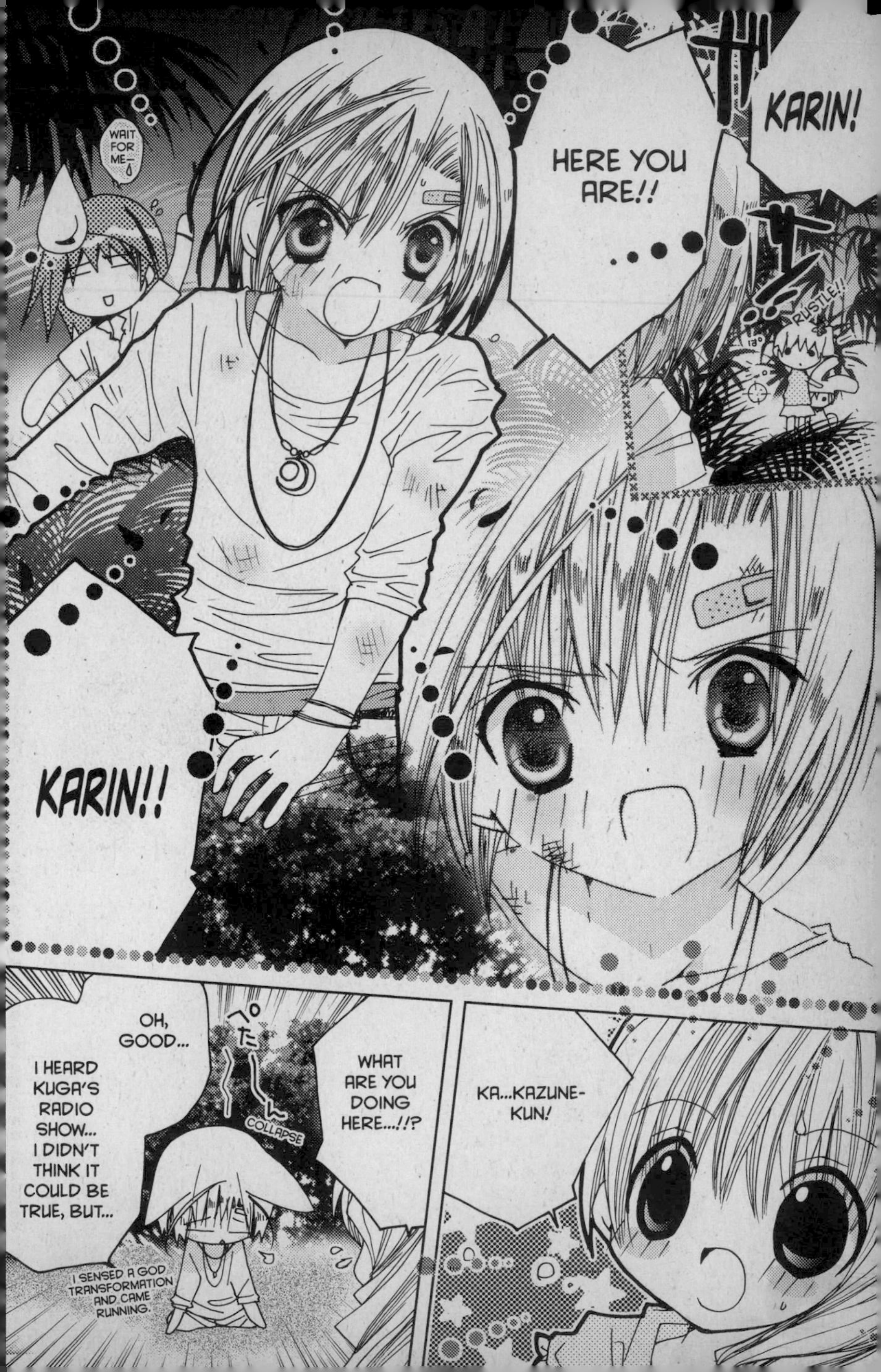
KARIN!
HERE YOU ARE!!
RUSTLE!!
WAIT FOR ME—
KARIN!!
KA...KAZUNE-KUN!
WHAT ARE YOU DOING HERE...!?
OH, GOOD...
I HEARD KUGA'S RADIO SHOW... I DIDN'T THINK IT COULD BE TRUE, BUT...
COLLAPSE
I SENSED A GOD TRANSFORMATION AND CAME RUNNING.

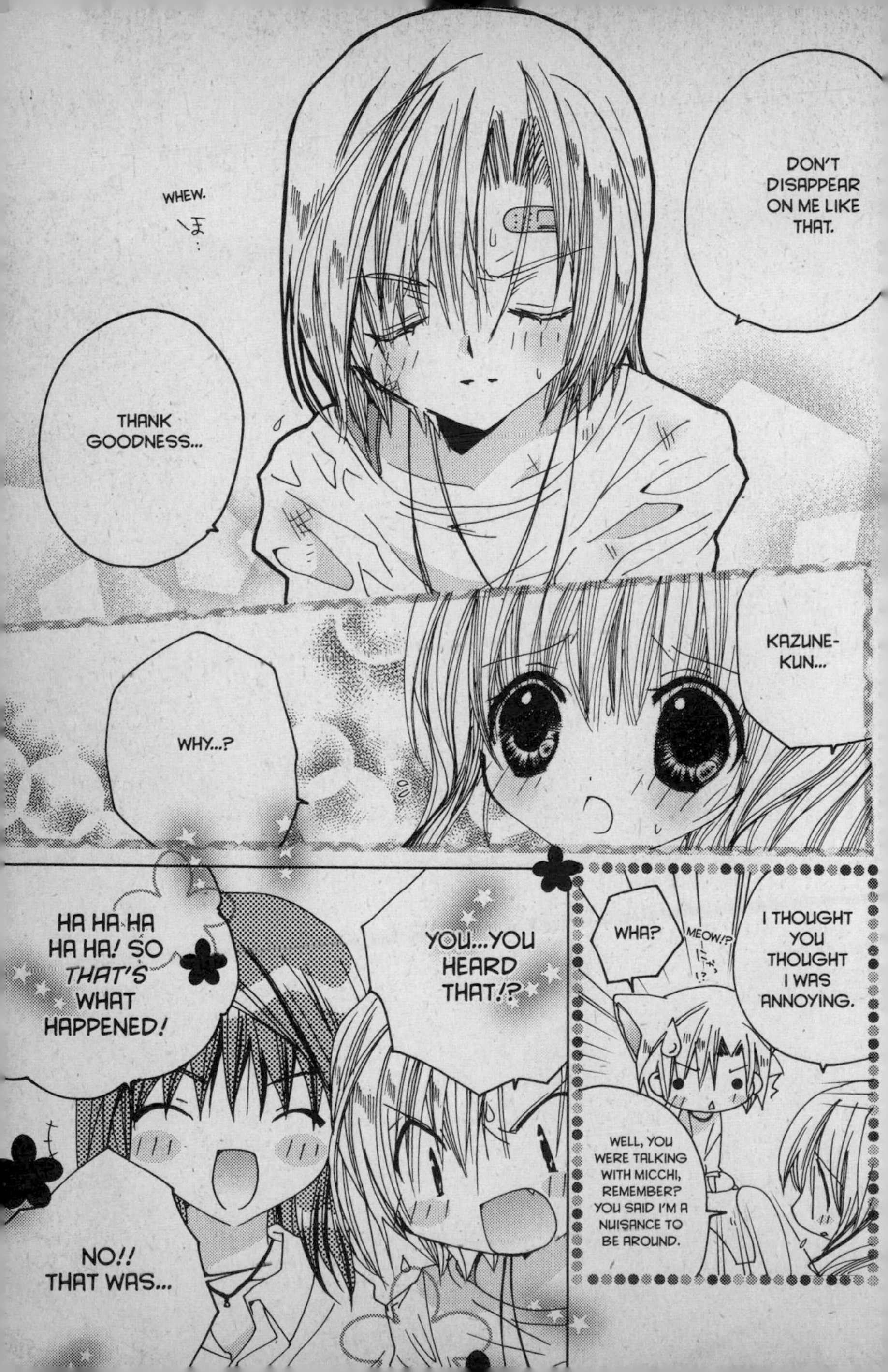
DON'T DISAPPEAR ON ME LIKE THAT.
WHEW.
THANK GOODNESS...
KAZUNE-KUN...
WHY...?
I THOUGHT YOU THOUGHT I WAS ANNOYING.
WHA?
MEOW!?
WELL, YOU WERE TALKING WITH MICCHI, REMEMBER? YOU SAID I'M A NUISANCE TO BE AROUND.
YOU...YOU HEARD THAT!?
HA HA HA HA HA! SO *THAT'S* WHAT HAPPENED!
NO!! THAT WAS...

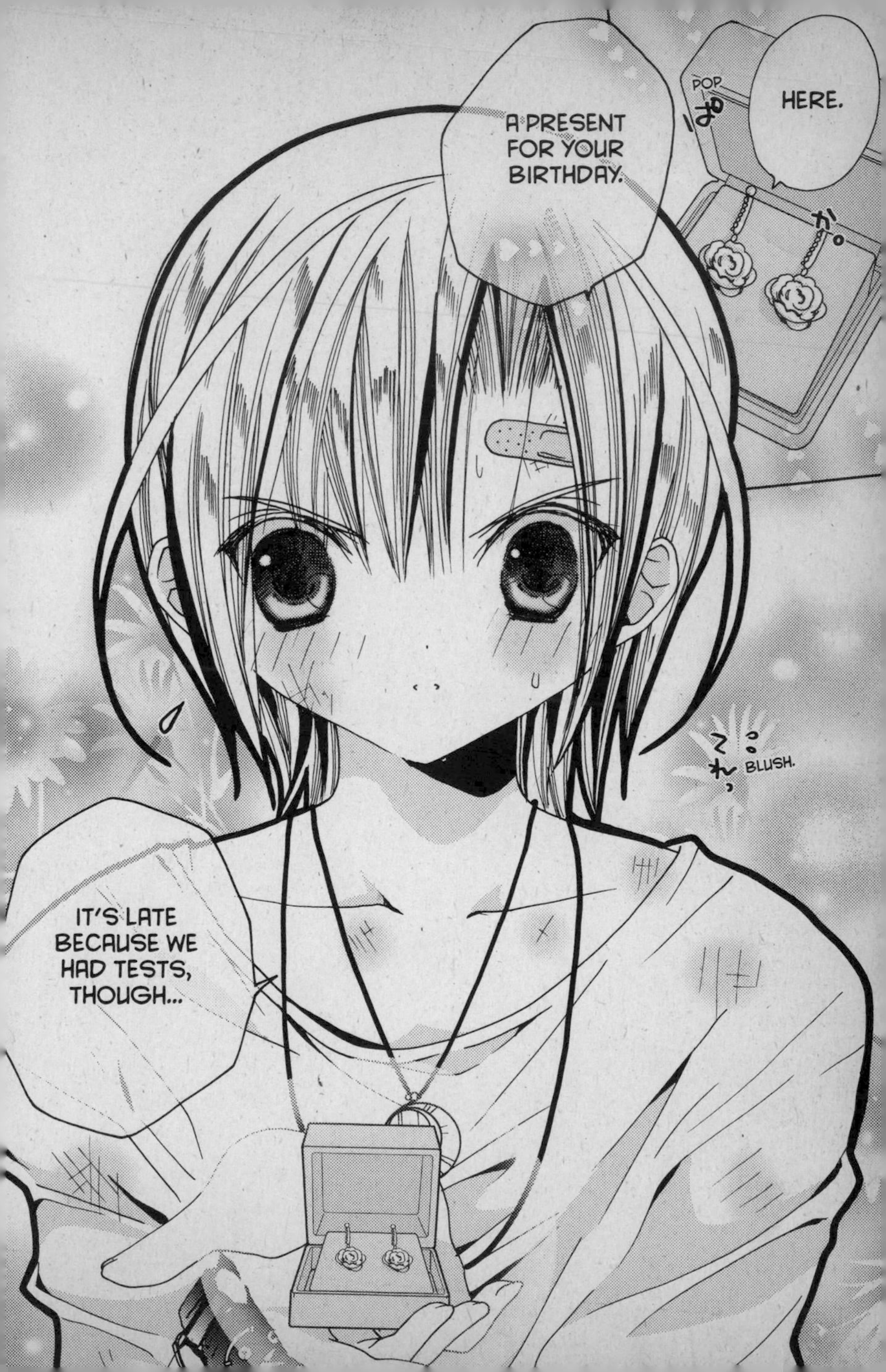
HERE.
POP
ぱ
A PRESENT FOR YOUR BIRTHDAY.
かぱ
BLUSH.
IT'S LATE BECAUSE WE HAD TESTS, THOUGH...

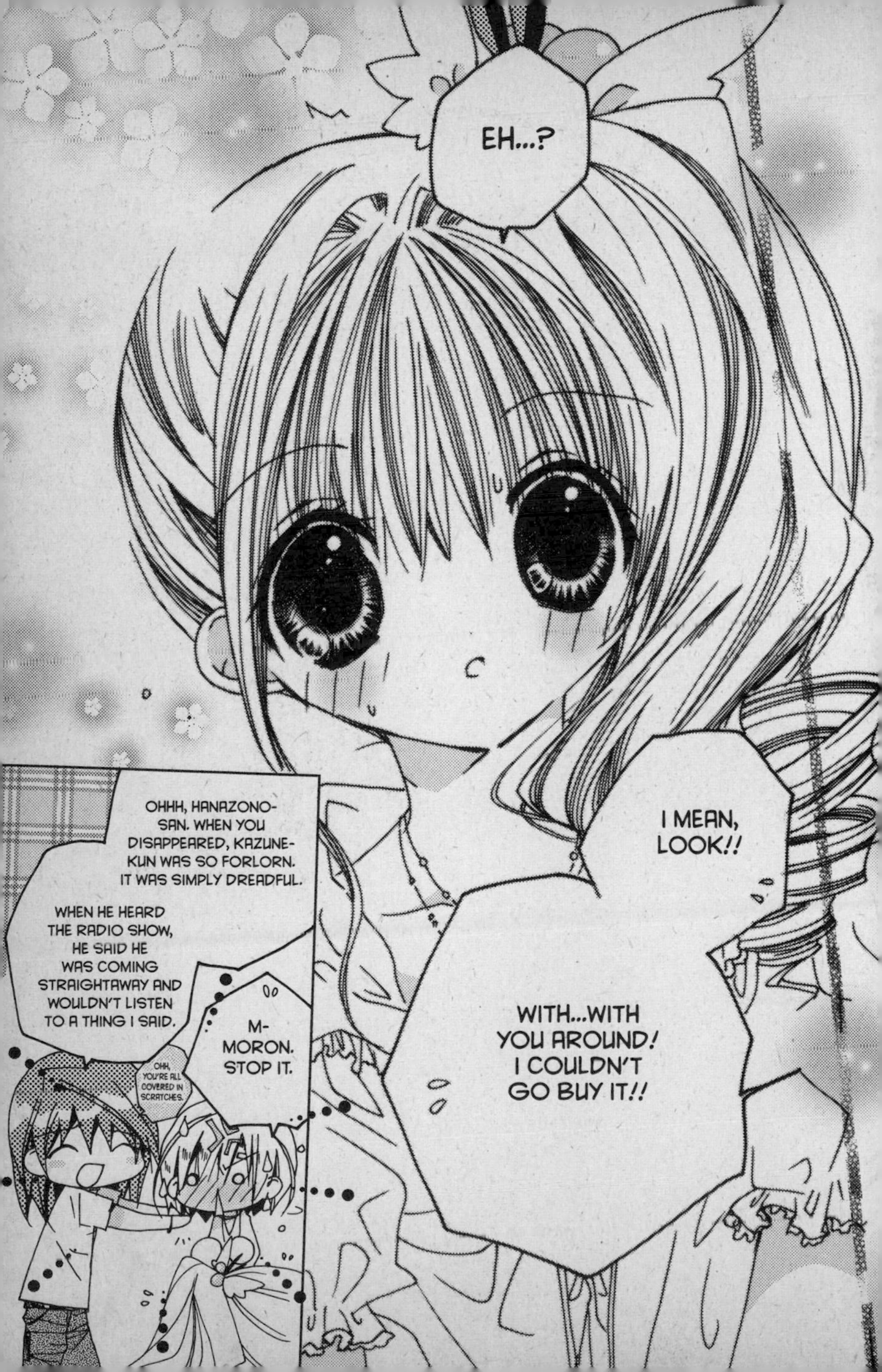
EH...?
I MEAN, LOOK!!
WITH...WITH YOU AROUND! I COULDN'T GO BUY IT!!
OHHH, HANAZONO-SAN. WHEN YOU DISAPPEARED, KAZUNE-KUN WAS SO FORLORN. IT WAS SIMPLY DREADFUL.
WHEN HE HEARD THE RADIO SHOW, HE SAID HE WAS COMING STRAIGHTAWAY AND WOULDN'T LISTEN TO A THING I SAID.
M-MORON. STOP IT.
OHH, YOU'RE ALL COVERED IN SCRATCHES.

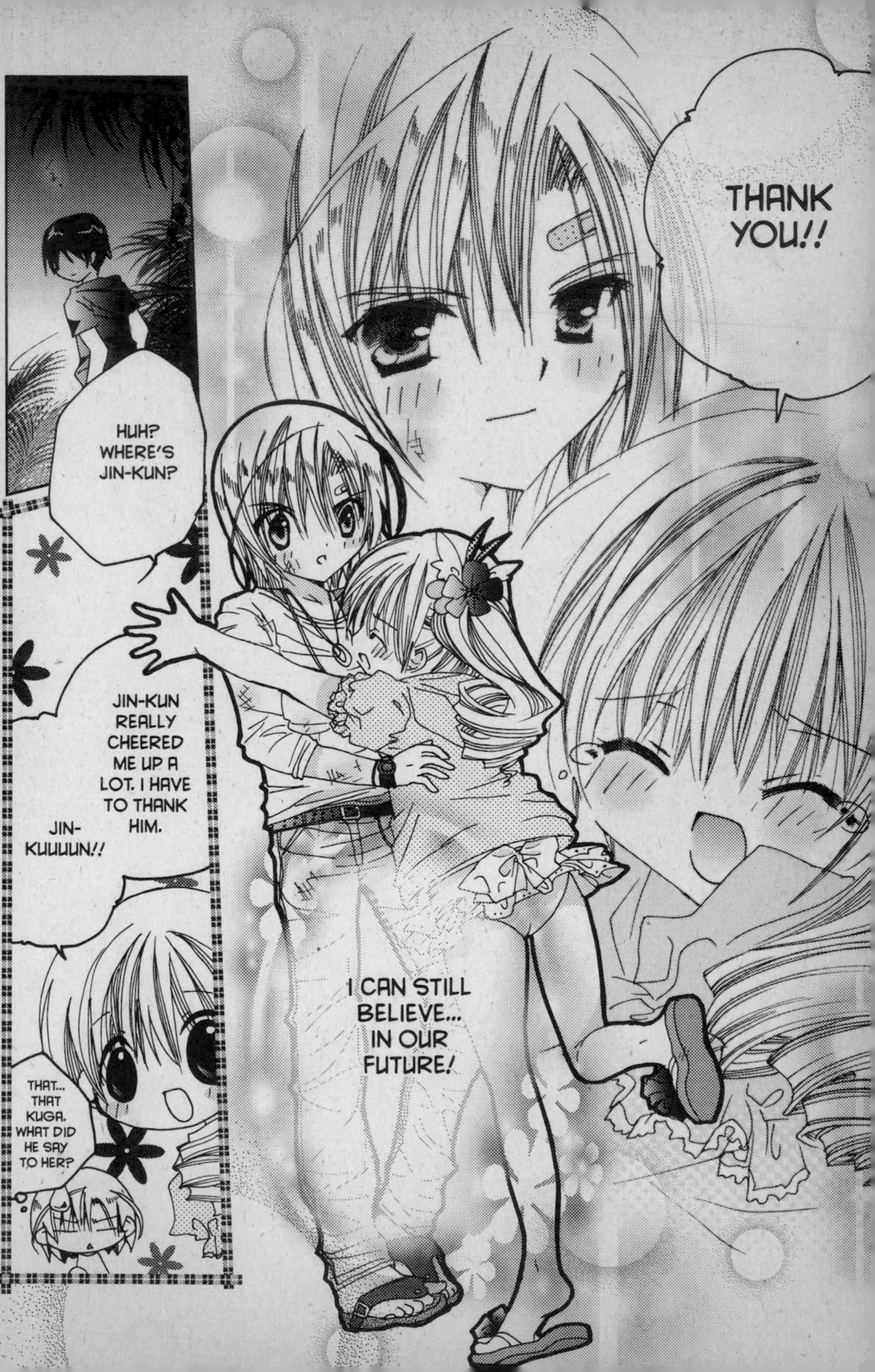
THANK YOU!!
I CAN STILL BELIEVE... IN OUR FUTURE!
HUH? WHERE'S JIN-KUN?
JIN-KUN REALLY CHEERED ME UP A LOT. I HAVE TO THANK HIM.
JIN-KUUUUN!!
THAT... THAT KUGA. WHAT DID HE SAY TO HER?

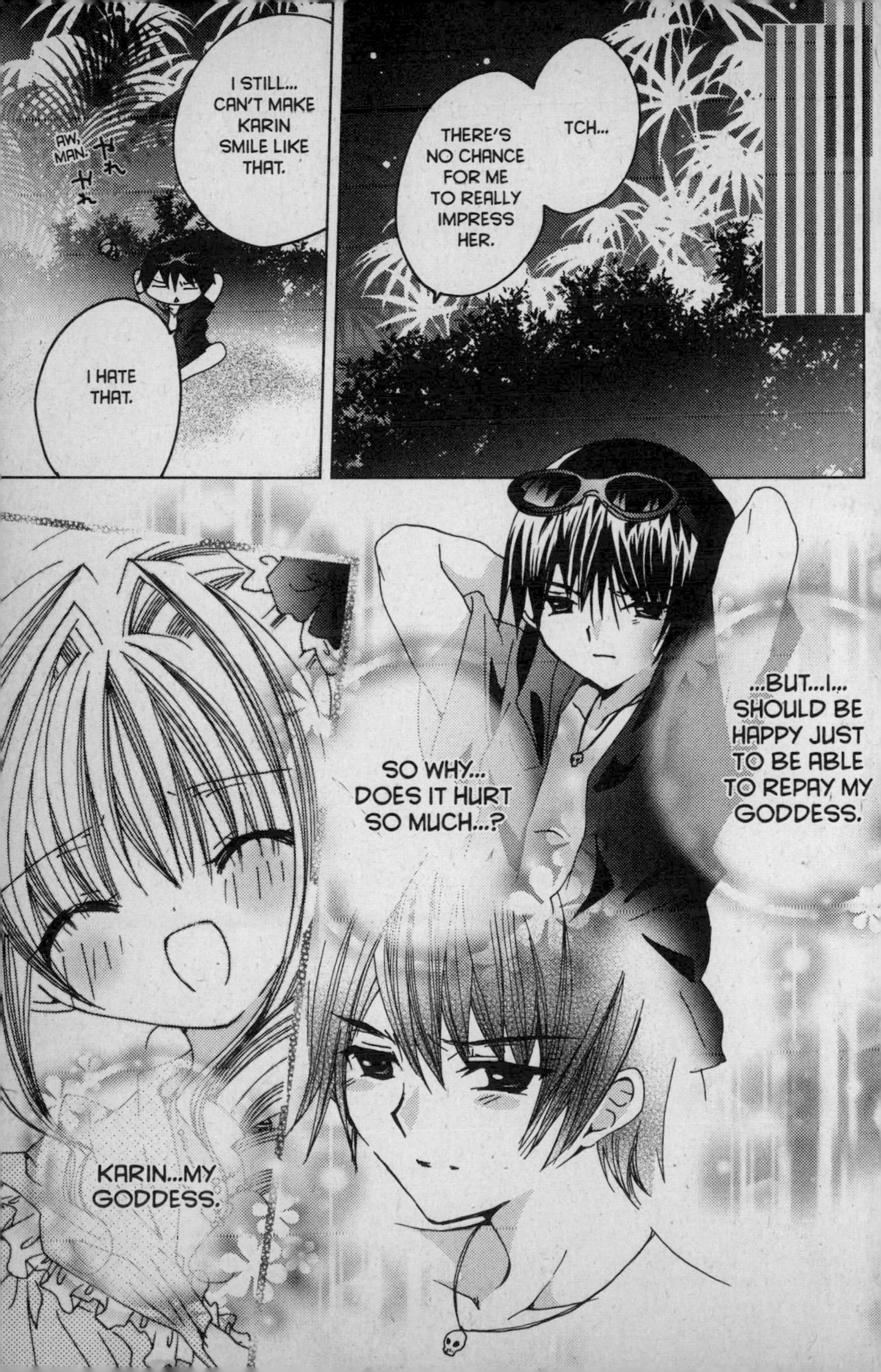
TCH...
THERE'S NO CHANCE FOR ME TO REALLY IMPRESS HER.
I STILL... CAN'T MAKE KARIN SMILE LIKE THAT.
AW, MAN.
I HATE THAT.
...BUT...I... SHOULD BE HAPPY JUST TO BE ABLE TO REPAY MY GODDESS.
SO WHY... DOES IT HURT SO MUCH...?
KARIN...MY GODDESS.

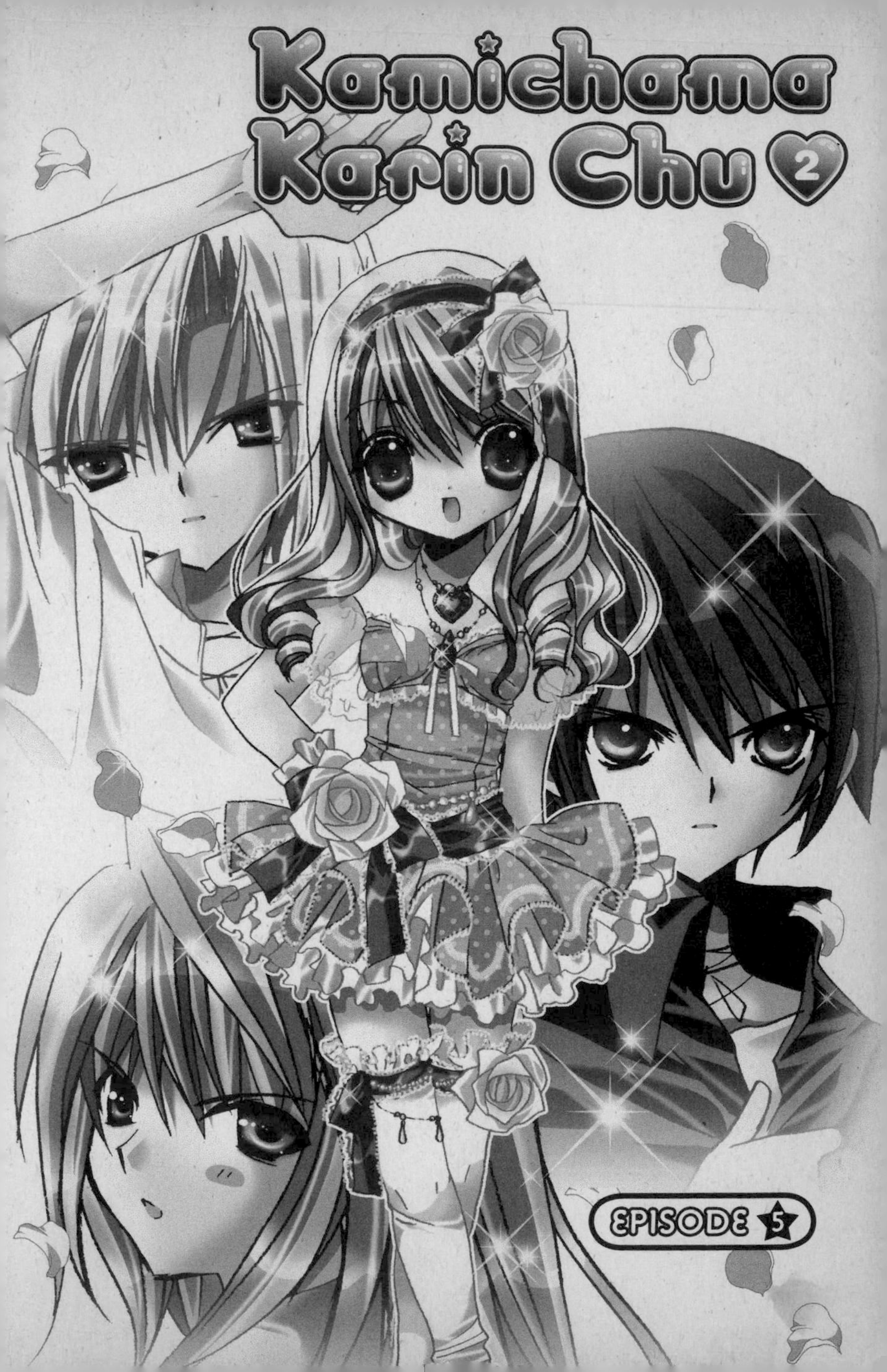
Kamichama Karin Chu 2
EPISODE 5

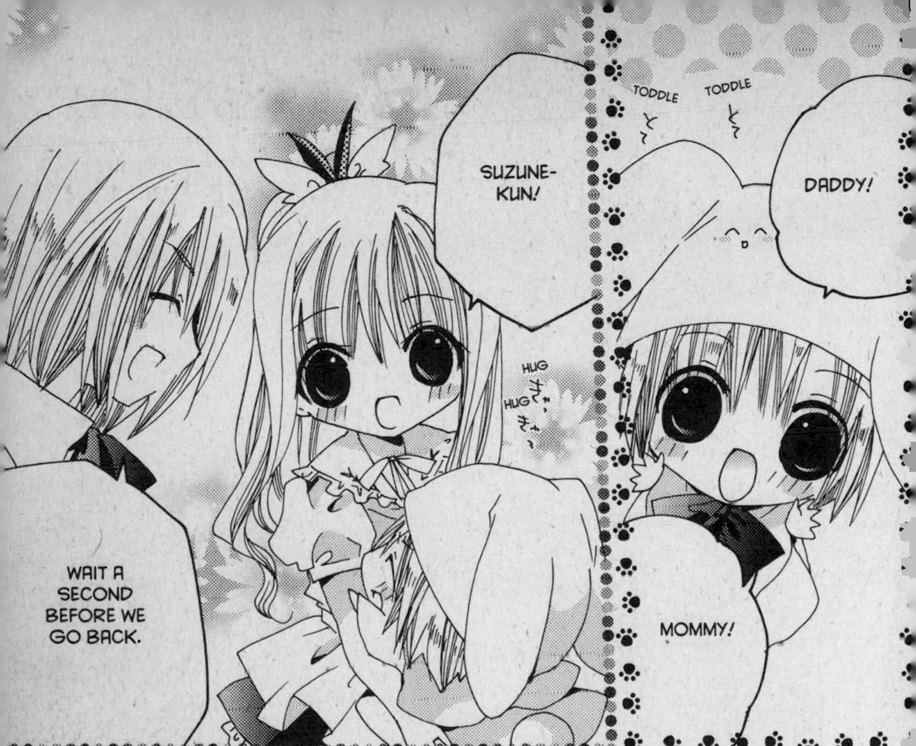
TODDLE
TODDLE
DADDY!
MOMMY!
SUZUNE-KUN!
HUG
HUG
WAIT A SECOND BEFORE WE GO BACK.

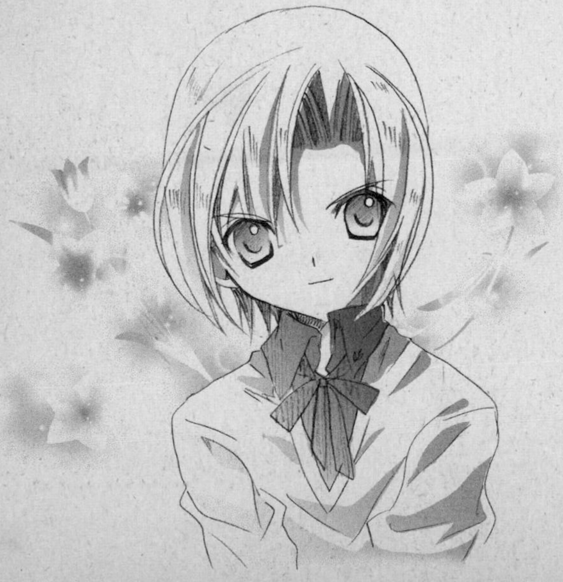

CHARACTER MINI-INTRODUCTION

•

KAZUNE KUJYOU

BORN FEBRUARY 1

AQUARIUS, AGE 13, BLOOD TYPE A

FOR MORE DETAILS, SEE THE SPECIAL EDITION.

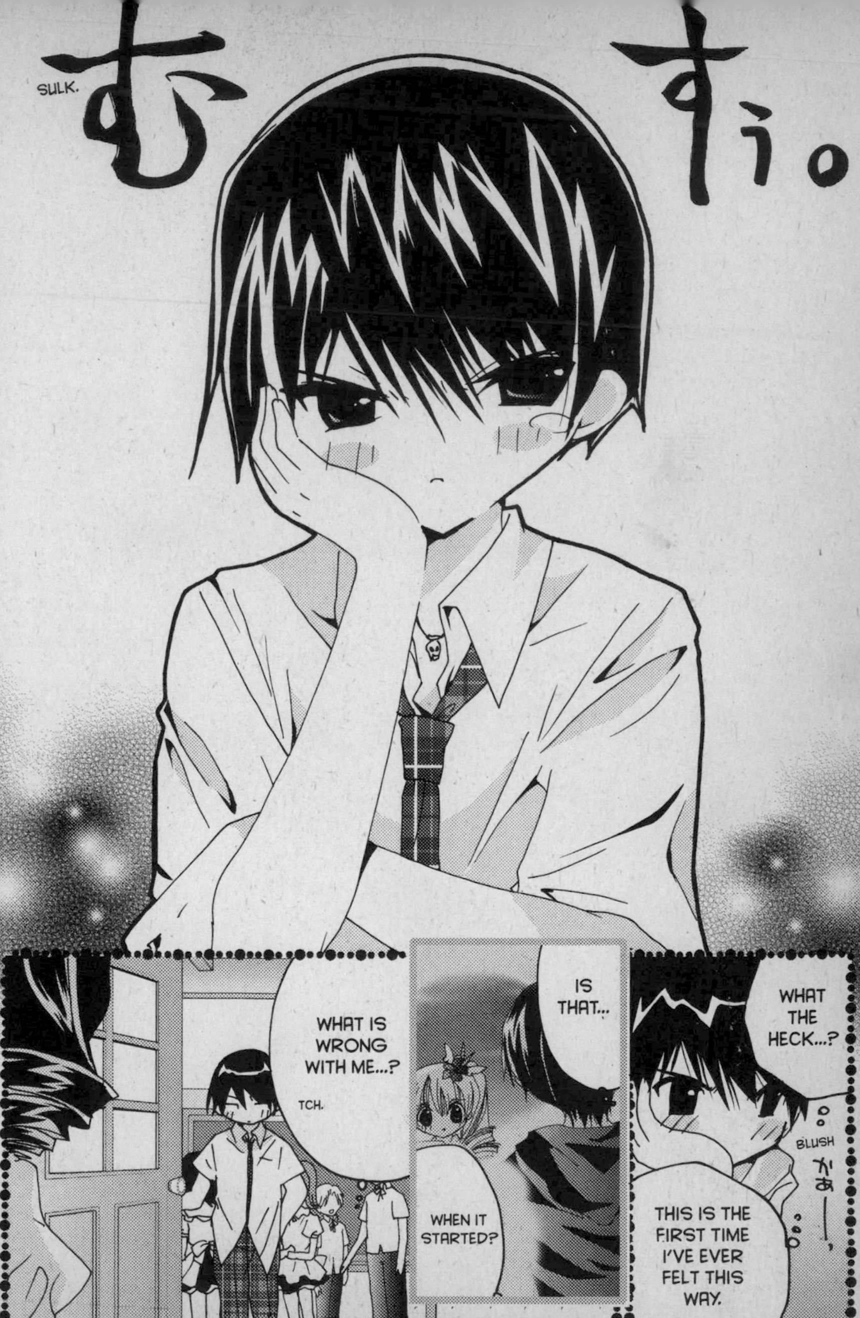
むすっ。
SULK.
WHAT THE HECK...?
BLUSH
かぁー
THIS IS THE FIRST TIME I'VE EVER FELT THIS WAY.
IS THAT...
WHEN IT STARTED?
WHAT IS WRONG WITH ME...?
TCH.

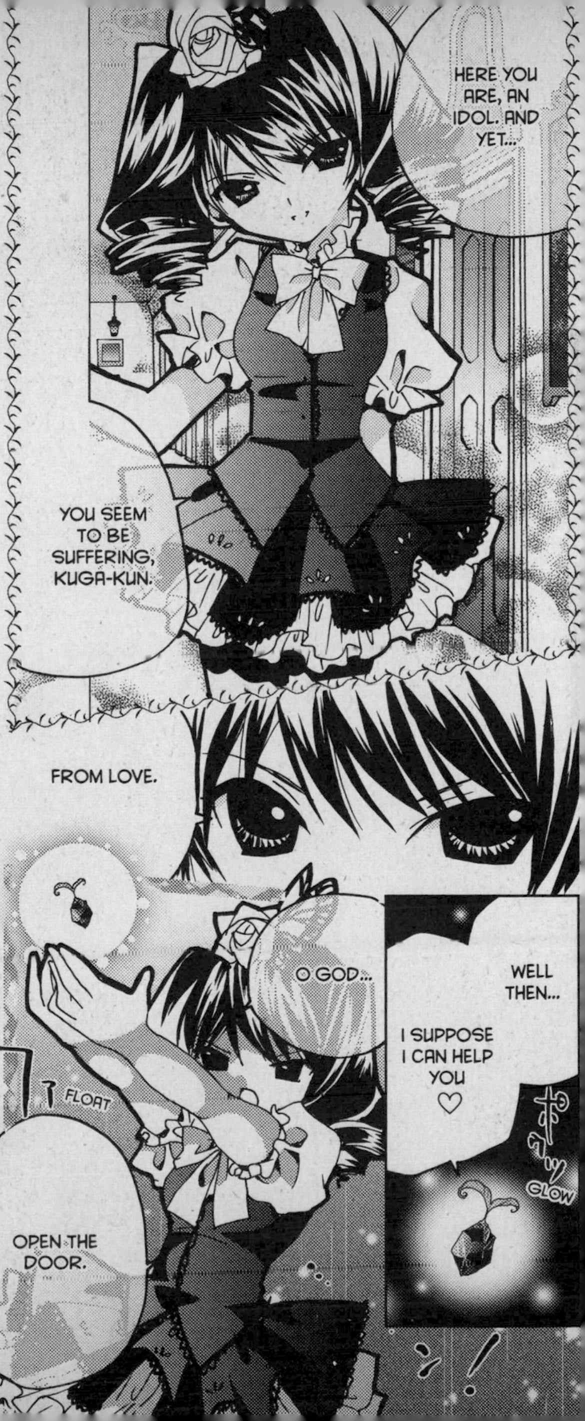
HERE YOU ARE, AN IDOL. AND YET...
YOU SEEM TO BE SUFFERING, KUGA-KUN.
FROM LOVE.
WELL THEN...
I SUPPOSE I CAN HELP YOU ♡
GLOW
O GOD...
FLOAT
OPEN THE DOOR.
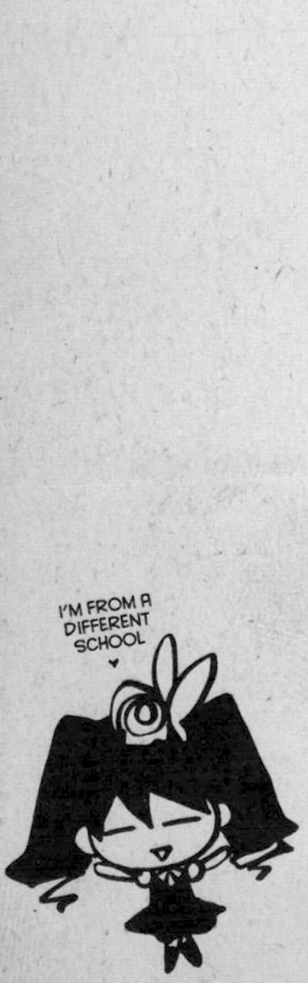
I'M FROM A DIFFERENT SCHOOL ♥

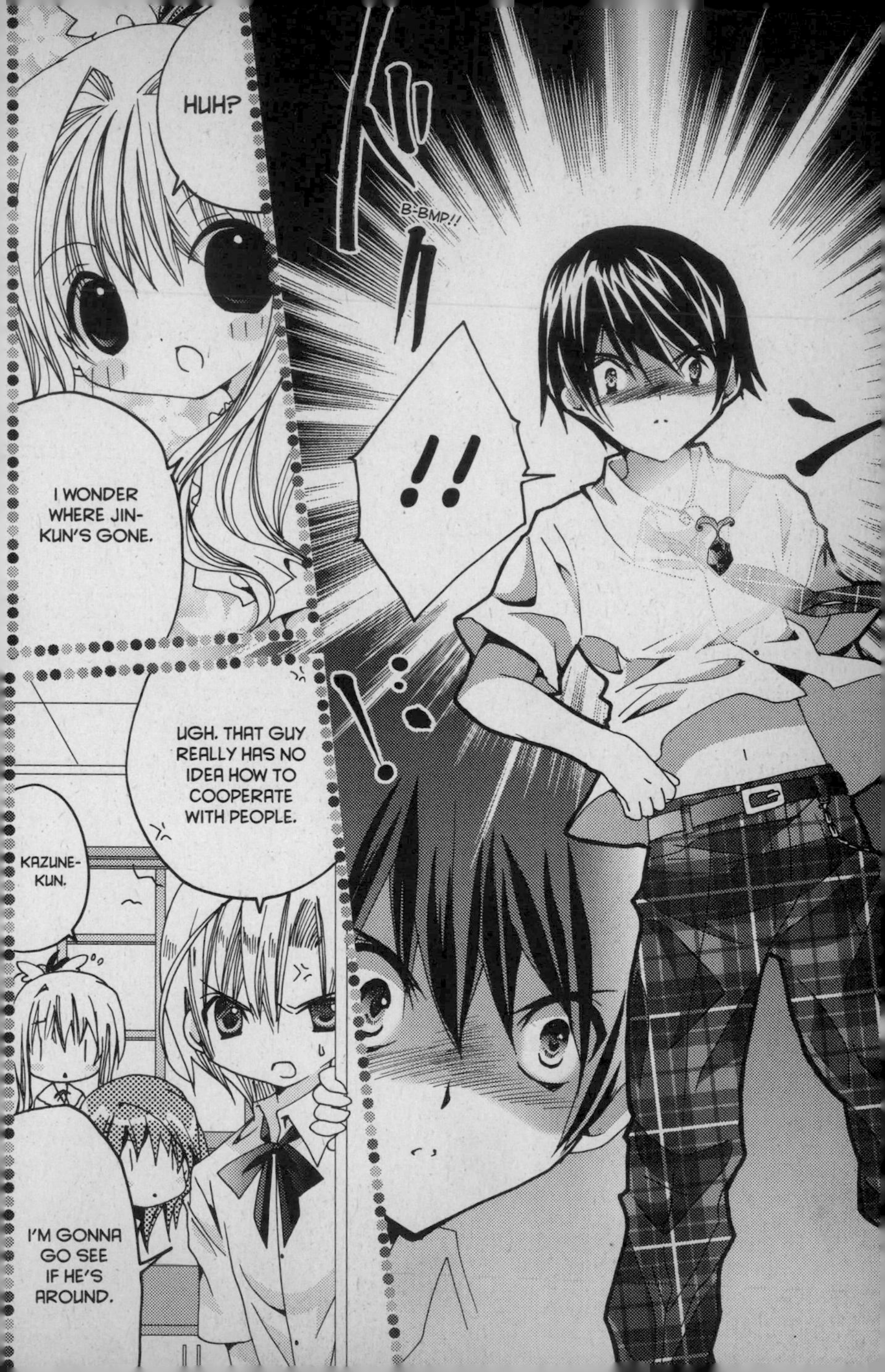
B-BMP!!
!!
HUH?
I WONDER WHERE JIN-KUN'S GONE.
UGH. THAT GUY REALLY HAS NO IDEA HOW TO COOPERATE WITH PEOPLE.
KAZUNE-KUN.
I'M GONNA GO SEE IF HE'S AROUND.

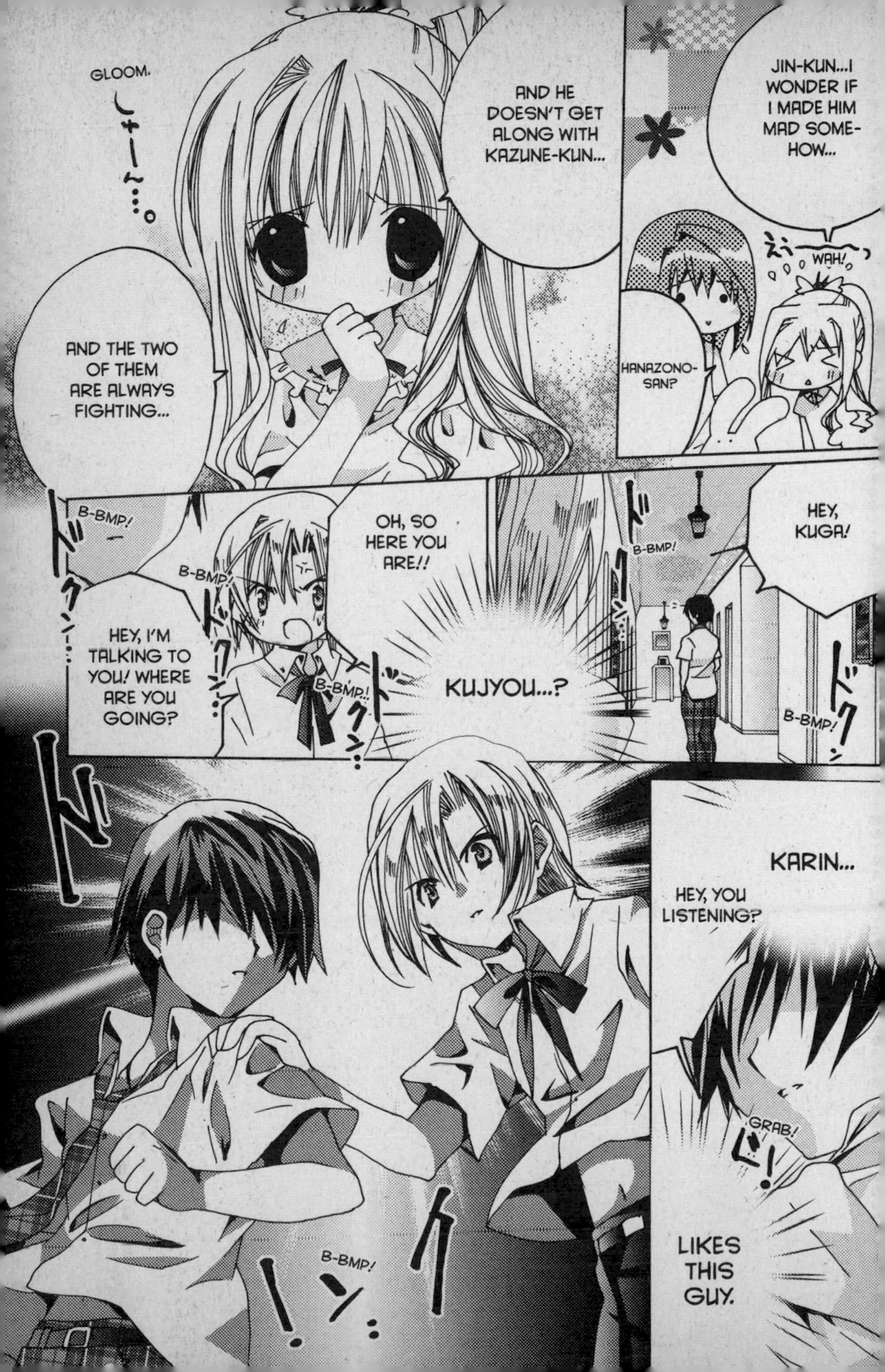
JIN-KUN...I WONDER IF I MADE HIM MAD SOMEHOW...
えぇ〜
WAH!
HANAZONO-SAN?
AND HE DOESN'T GET ALONG WITH KAZUNE-KUN...
GLOOM.
しゃーん…。
AND THE TWO OF THEM ARE ALWAYS FIGHTING...
HEY, KUGA!
B-BMP!
B-BMP!
KUJYOU...?
OH, SO HERE YOU ARE!!
B-BMP!
B-BMP!
HEY, I'M TALKING TO YOU! WHERE ARE YOU GOING?
B-BMP!
KARIN...
HEY, YOU LISTENING?
GRAB!
LIKES THIS GUY.
B-BMP!

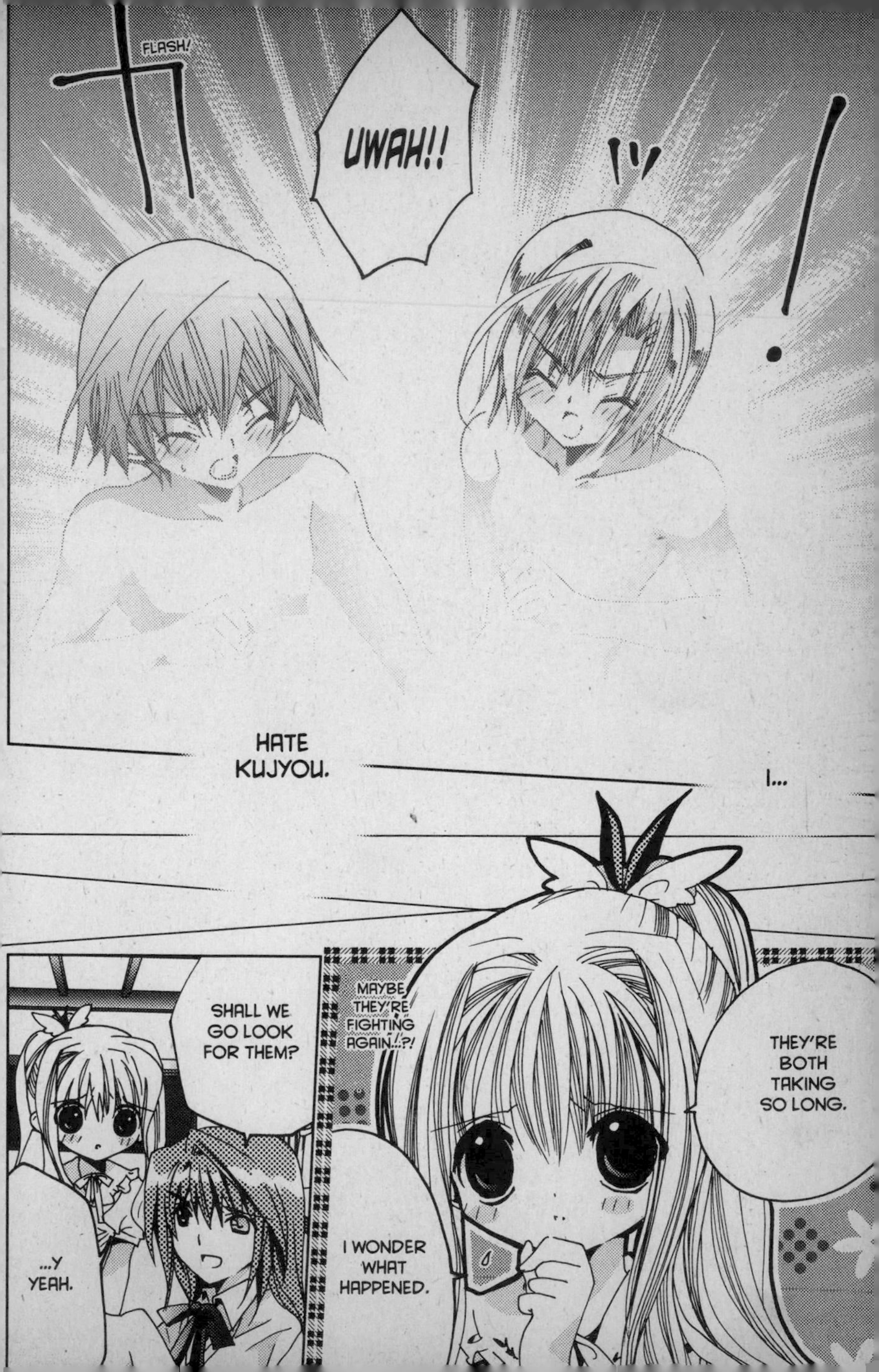
UWAH!!
FLASH!
I...
HATE KUJYOU.
THEY'RE BOTH TAKING SO LONG.
MAYBE THEY'RE FIGHTING AGAIN...?!
I WONDER WHAT HAPPENED.
SHALL WE GO LOOK FOR THEM?
...Y YEAH.

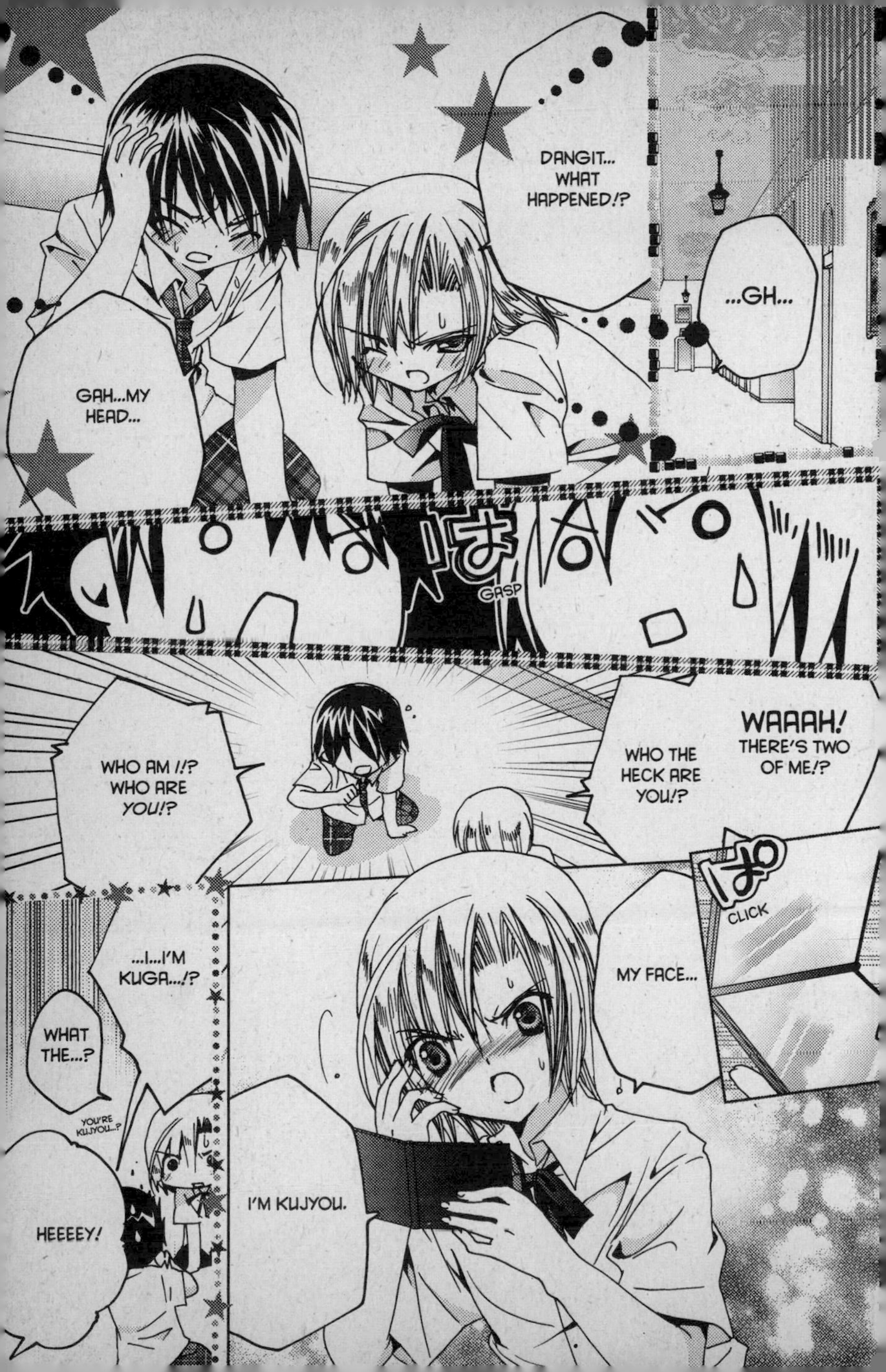
...GH...
DANGIT... WHAT HAPPENED!?
GAH...MY HEAD...
GASP
WAAAH! THERE'S TWO OF ME!?
WHO THE HECK ARE YOU!?
WHO AM I!? WHO ARE YOU!?
CLICK
MY FACE...
I'M KUJYOU.
...I...I'M KUGA...!?
WHAT THE...?
YOU'RE KUJYOU...?
HEEEEY!

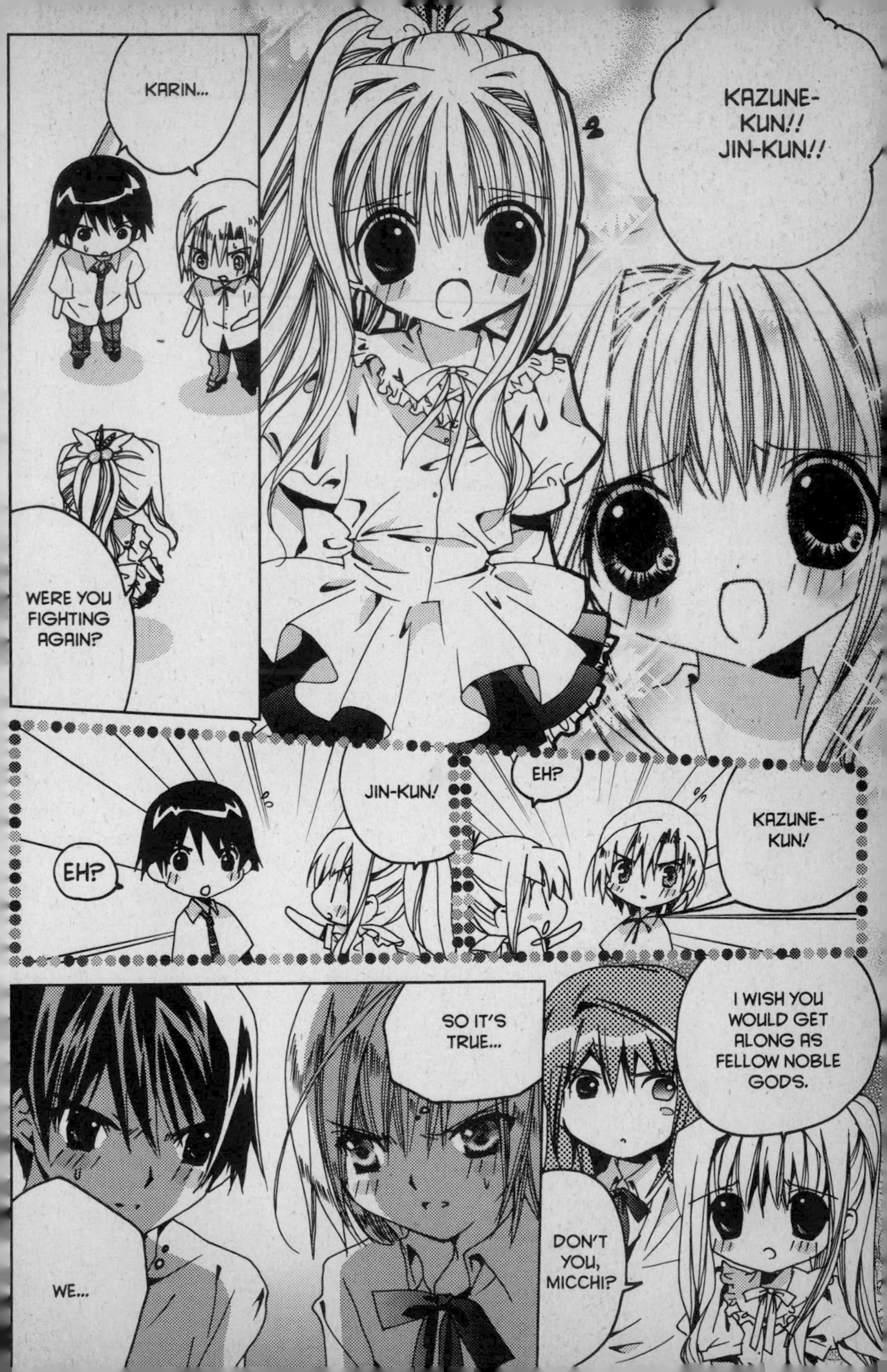
KAZUNE-KUN!! JIN-KUN!!
KARIN...
WERE YOU FIGHTING AGAIN?
KAZUNE-KUN!
EH?
JIN-KUN!
EH?
I WISH YOU WOULD GET ALONG AS FELLOW NOBLE GODS.
DON'T YOU, MICCHI?
SO IT'S TRUE...
WE...

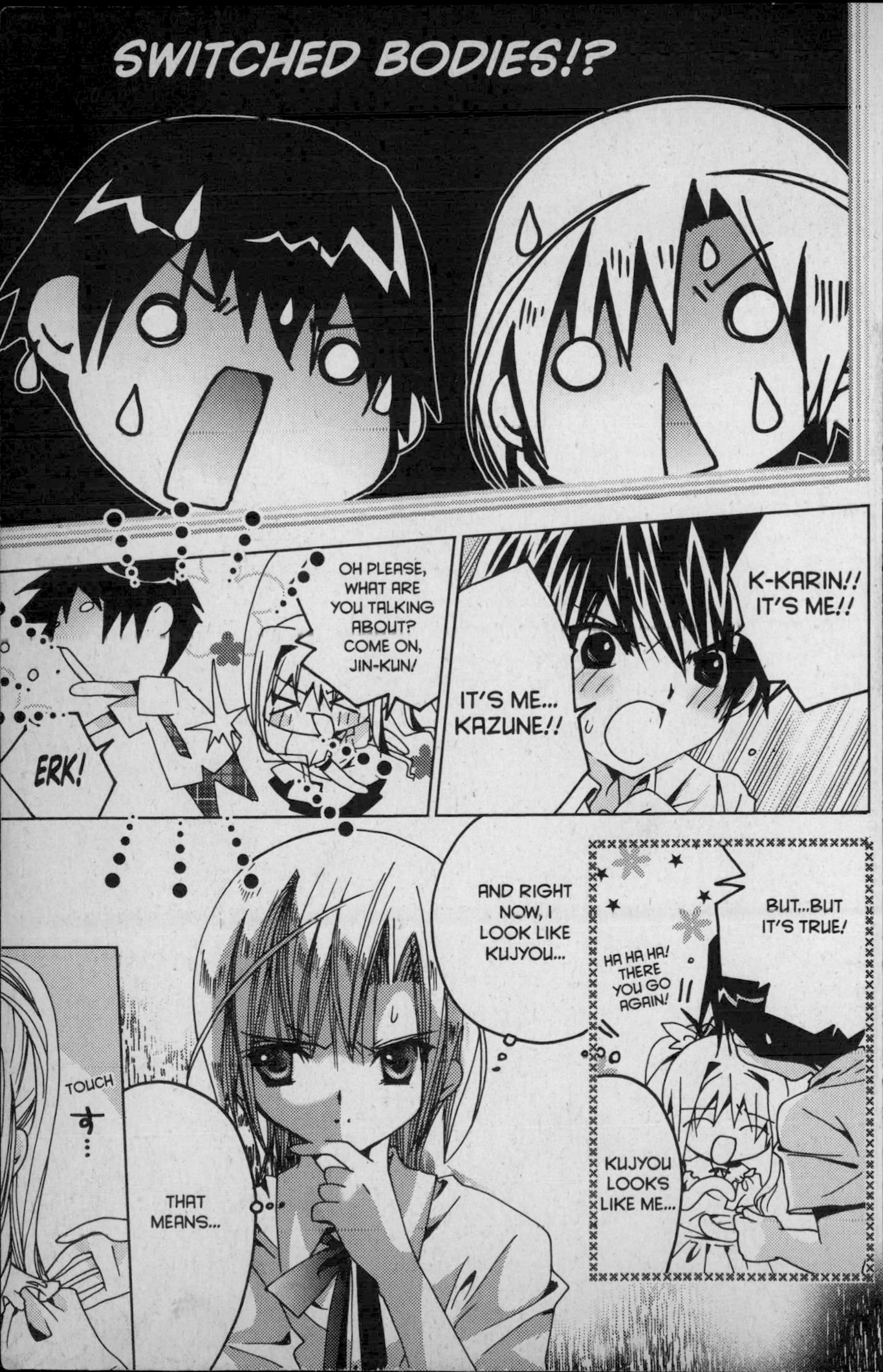
SWITCHED BODIES!?
K-KARIN!! IT'S ME!!
IT'S ME... KAZUNE!!
OH PLEASE, WHAT ARE YOU TALKING ABOUT? COME ON, JIN-KUN!
ERK!
BUT...BUT IT'S TRUE!
HA HA HA! THERE YOU GO AGAIN!
KUJYOU LOOKS LIKE ME...
AND RIGHT NOW, I LOOK LIKE KUJYOU...
TOUCH
す...
THAT MEANS...

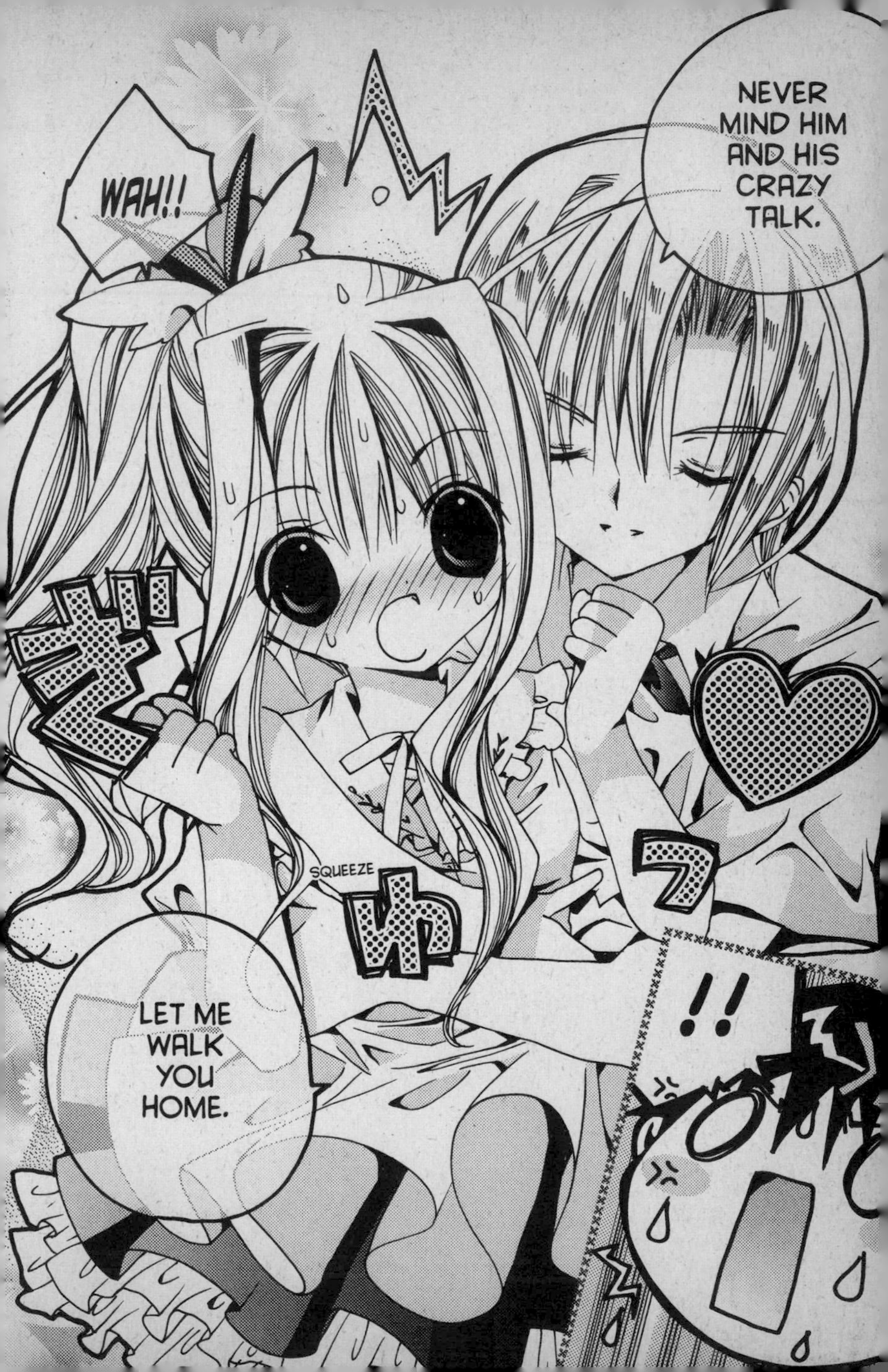
NEVER MIND HIM AND HIS CRAZY TALK.
WAH!!
SQUEEZE
!!
LET ME WALK YOU HOME.

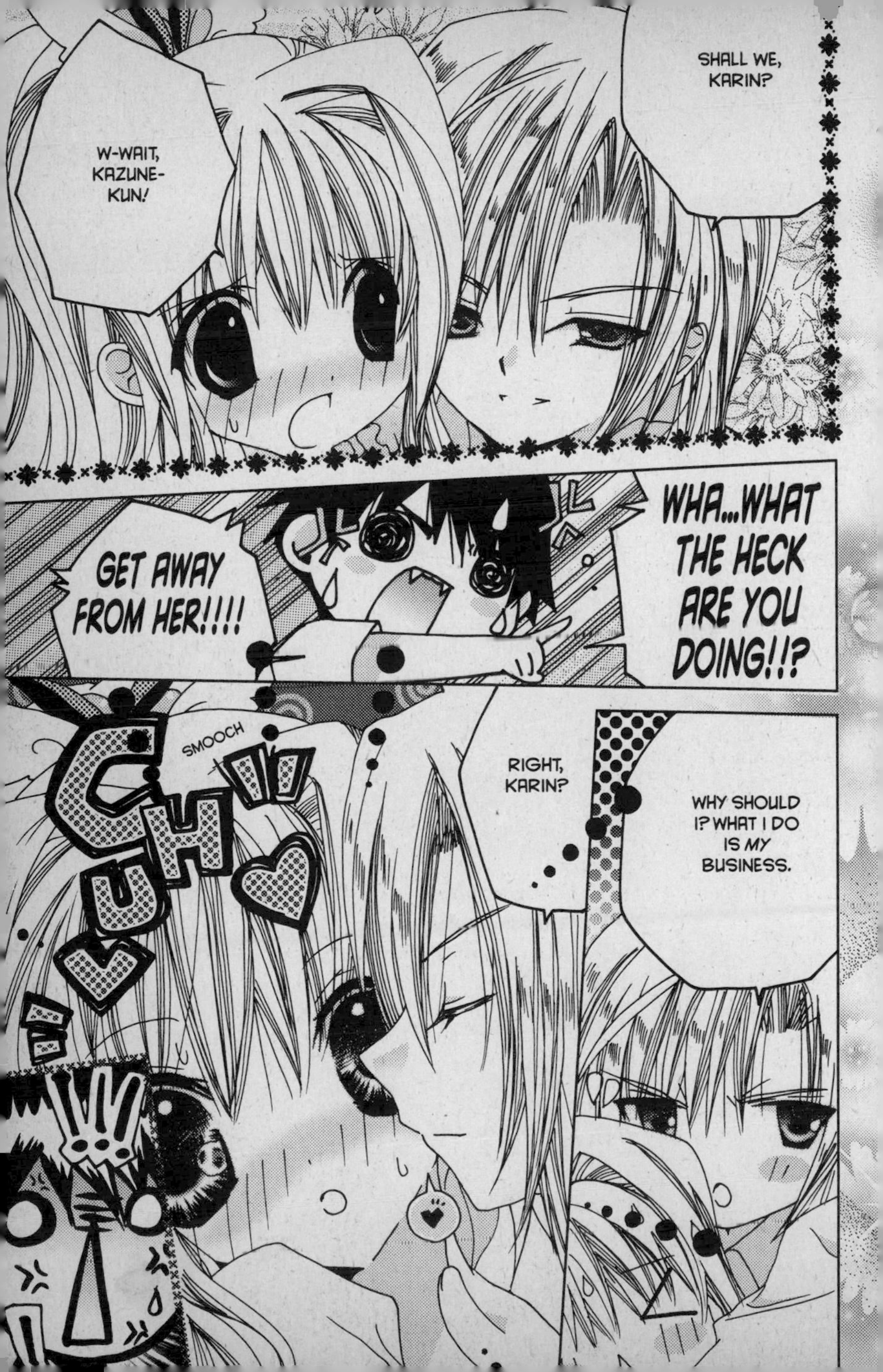

SHALL WE, KARIN?
W-WAIT, KAZUNE-KUN!
WHA...WHAT THE HECK ARE YOU DOING!!?
GET AWAY FROM HER!!!!
WHY SHOULD I? WHAT I DO IS MY BUSINESS.
RIGHT, KARIN?
SMOOCH

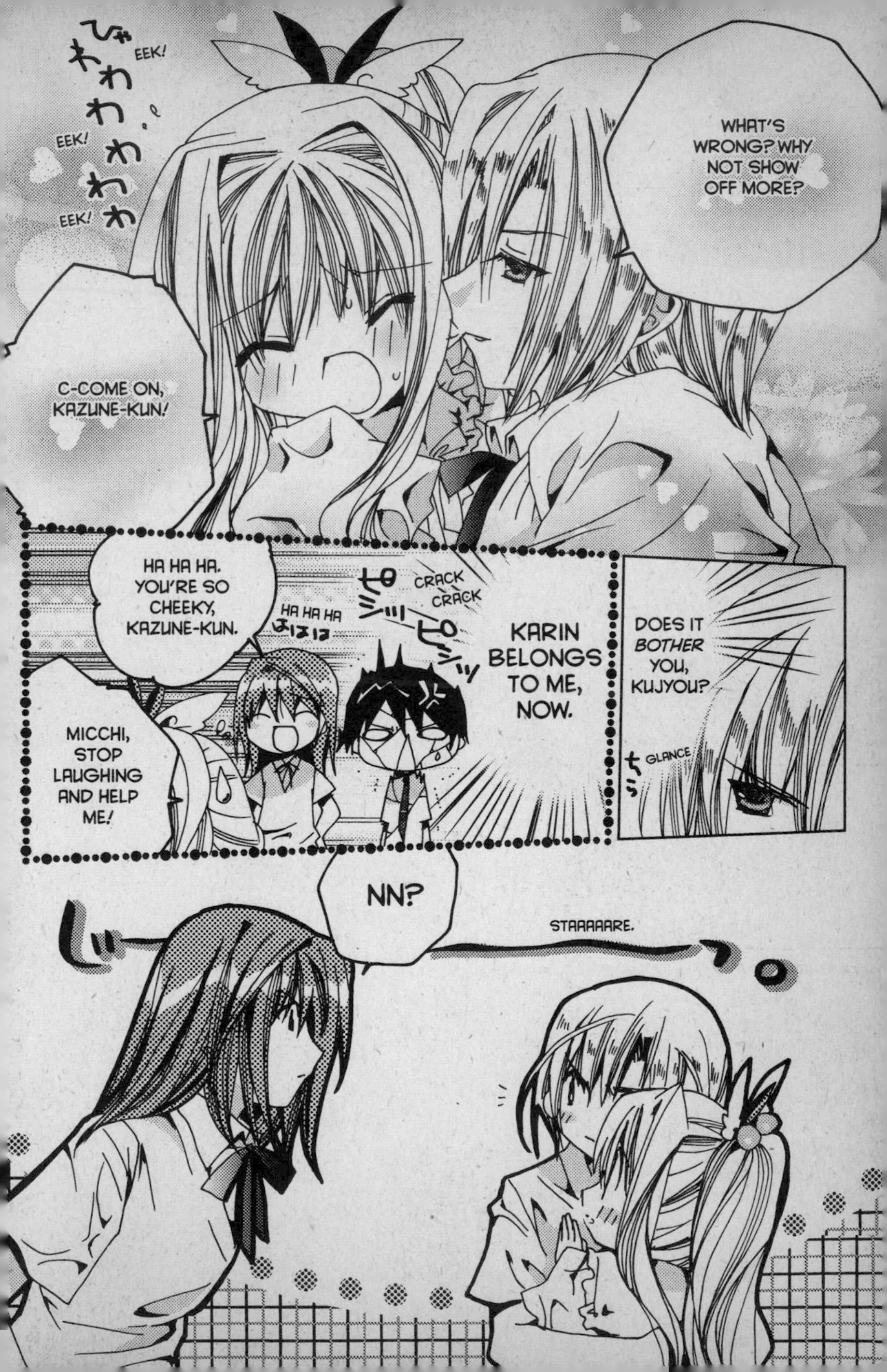

WHAT'S WRONG? WHY NOT SHOW OFF MORE?
ひゃわわわわわ
EEK!
EEK!
EEK!
C-COME ON, KAZUNE-KUN!
DOES IT BOTHER YOU, KUJYOU?
ちら
GLANCE
KARIN BELONGS TO ME, NOW.
ピシッピシッ
CRACK CRACK
HA HA HA
ははは
HA HA HA. YOU'RE SO CHEEKY, KAZUNE-KUN.
MICCHI, STOP LAUGHING AND HELP ME!
NN?
じーっ。
STARAAAARE.

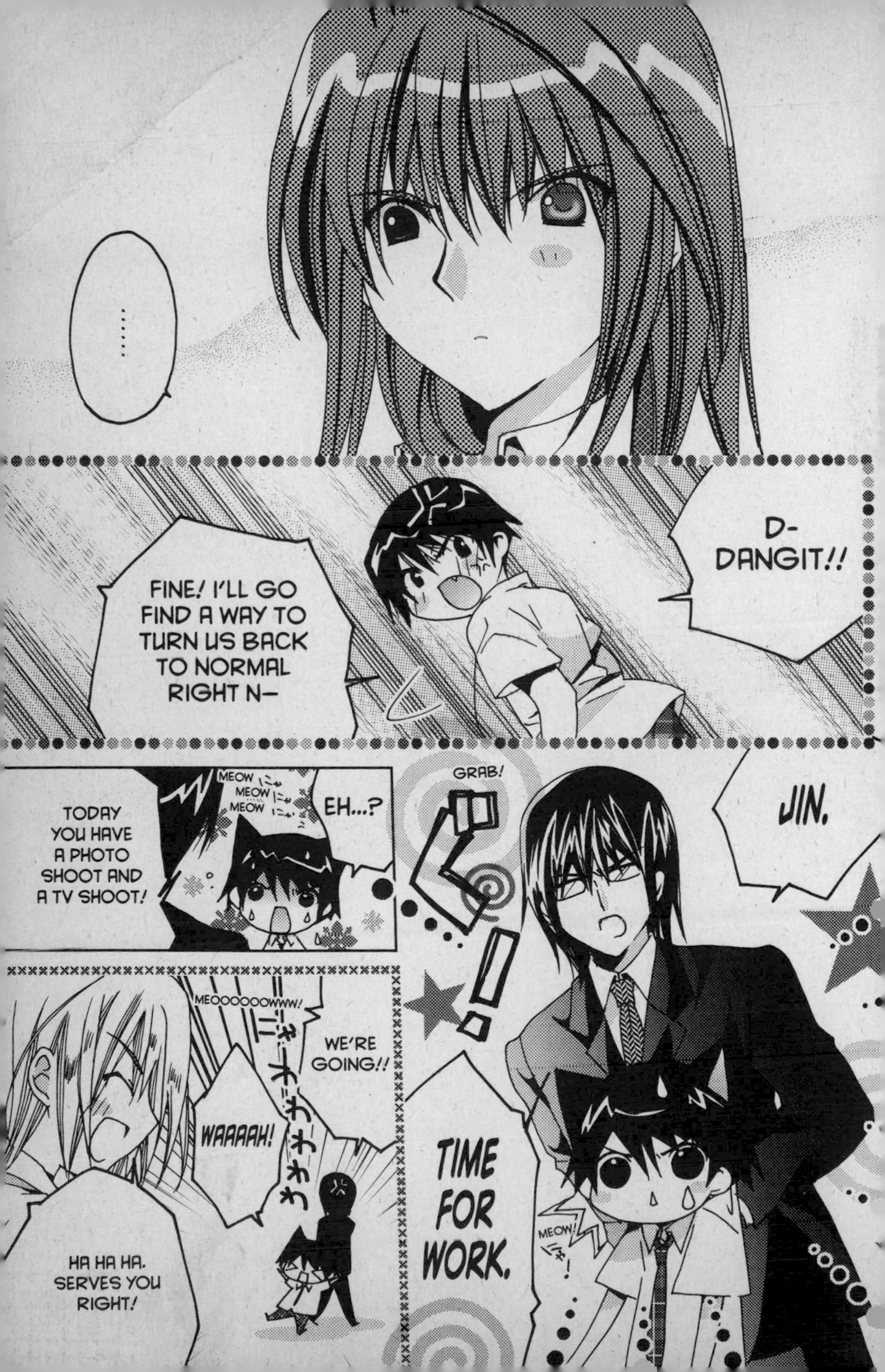
......
D- DANGIT!!
FINE! I'LL GO FIND A WAY TO TURN US BACK TO NORMAL RIGHT N—
JIN.
GRAB!
TIME FOR WORK.
MEOW! にゃ!
EH...?
MEOW にゃ MEOW にゃ MEOW にゃ
TODAY YOU HAVE A PHOTO SHOOT AND A TV SHOOT!
WE'RE GOING!!
MEOOOOOOWWW! にゃー
WAAAAH! わーわわわ
HA HA HA. SERVES YOU RIGHT!

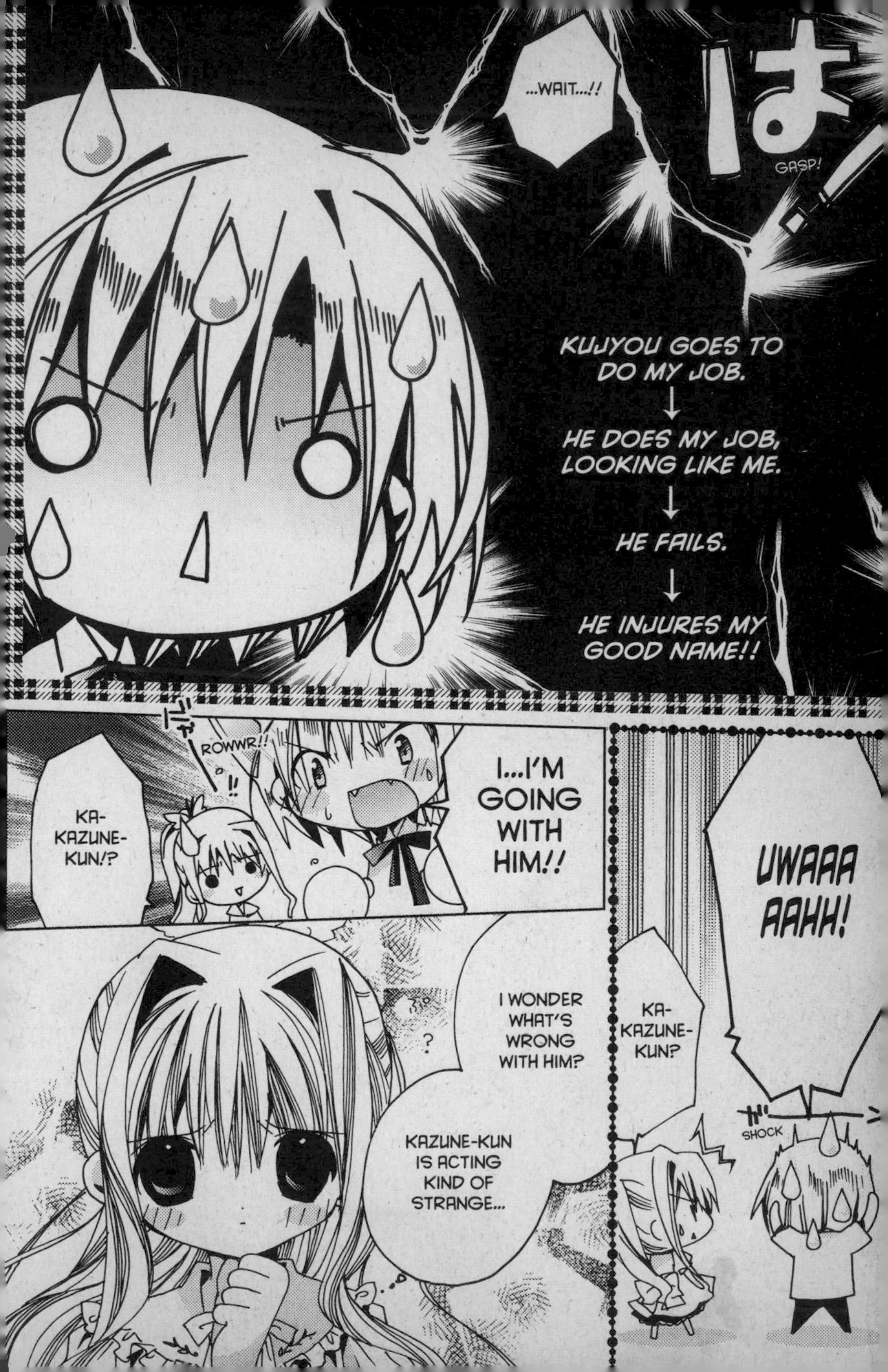
は!
GASP!
...WAIT...!!
KUJYOU GOES TO DO MY JOB.
↓
HE DOES MY JOB, LOOKING LIKE ME.
↓
HE FAILS.
↓
HE INJURES MY GOOD NAME!!
UWAAA AAHH!
KA-KAZUNE-KUN?
SHOCK
I...I'M GOING WITH HIM!!
ROWWR!!
!!
KA-KAZUNE-KUN!?
?
I WONDER WHAT'S WRONG WITH HIM?
KAZUNE-KUN IS ACTING KIND OF STRANGE...

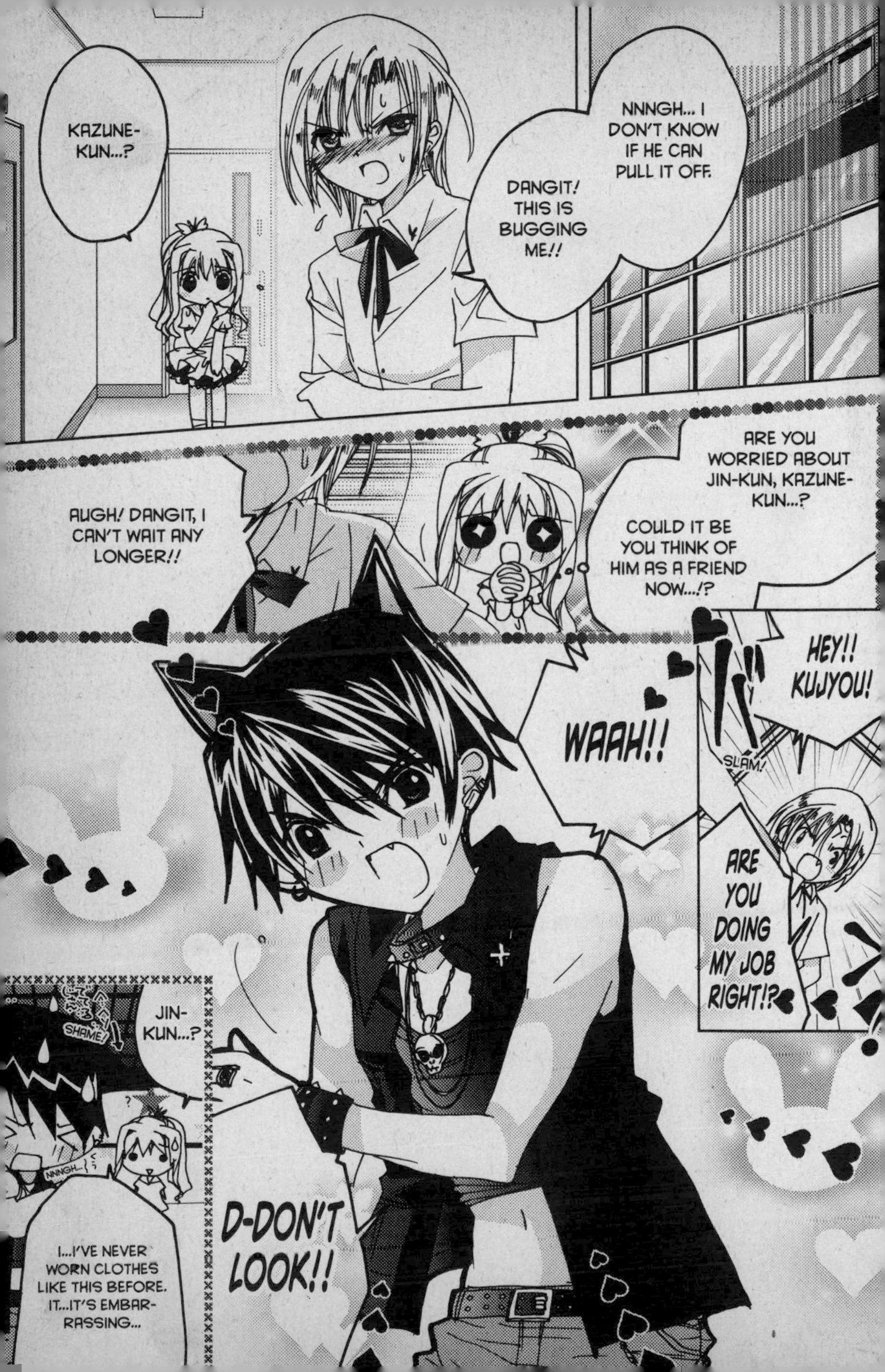
NNNGH... I DON'T KNOW IF HE CAN PULL IT OFF.
DANGIT! THIS IS BUGGING ME!!
KAZUNE-KUN...?
ARE YOU WORRIED ABOUT JIN-KUN, KAZUNE-KUN...?
COULD IT BE YOU THINK OF HIM AS A FRIEND NOW...!?
AUGH! DANGIT, I CAN'T WAIT ANY LONGER!!
HEY!! KUJYOU!
SLAM!
ARE YOU DOING MY JOB RIGHT!?
WAAH!!
D-DON'T LOOK!!
JIN-KUN...?
SHAME!
NNNGH...
I...I'VE NEVER WORN CLOTHES LIKE THIS BEFORE. IT...IT'S EMBARRASSING...

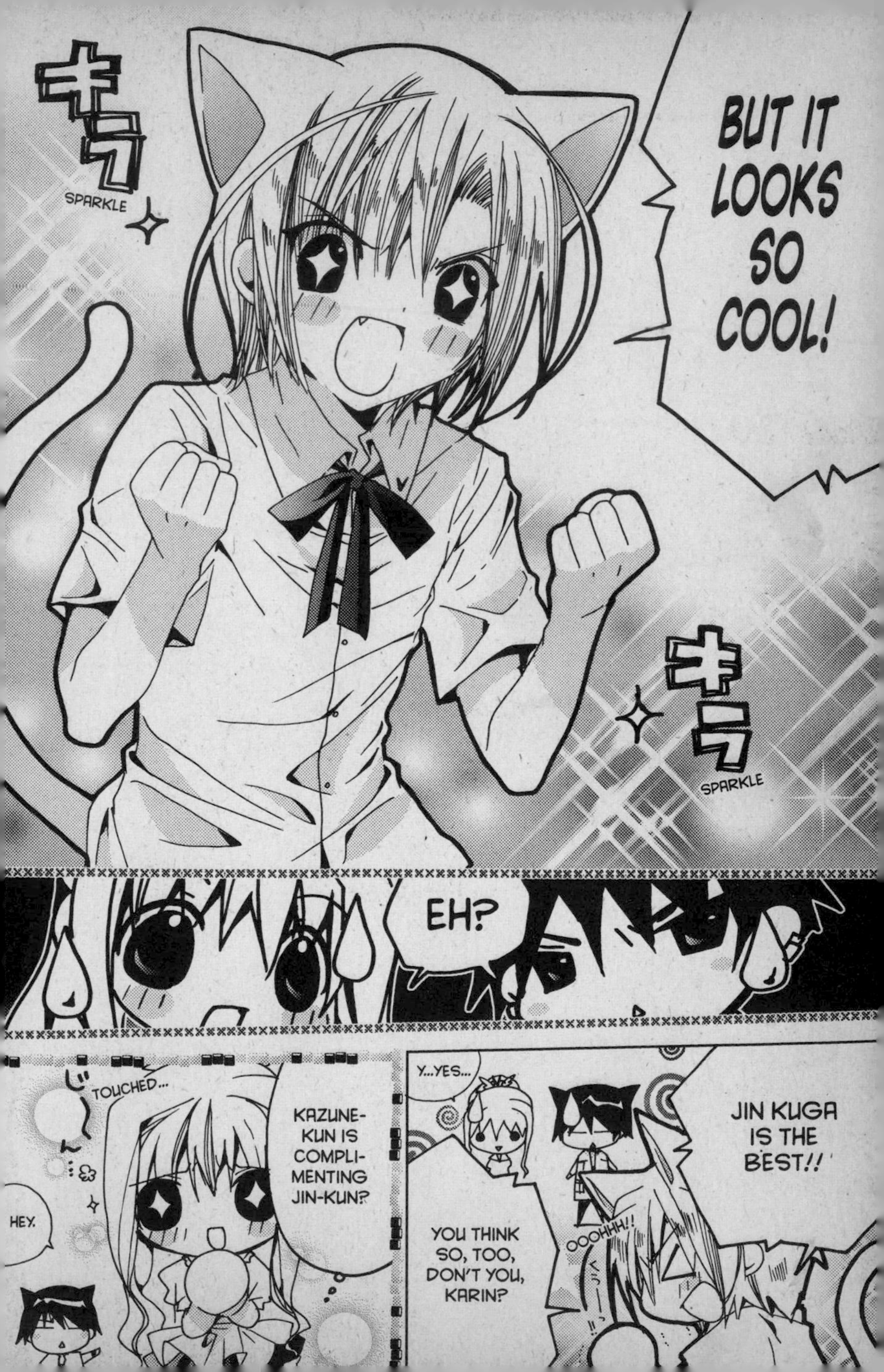
BUT IT LOOKS SO COOL!
キラ
SPARKLE
キラ
SPARKLE
EH?
JIN KUGA IS THE BEST!!
Y...YES...
OOOHHH!!
YOU THINK SO, TOO, DON'T YOU, KARIN?
KAZUNE-KUN IS COMPLIMENTING JIN-KUN?
じ～ん
TOUCHED...
HEY.

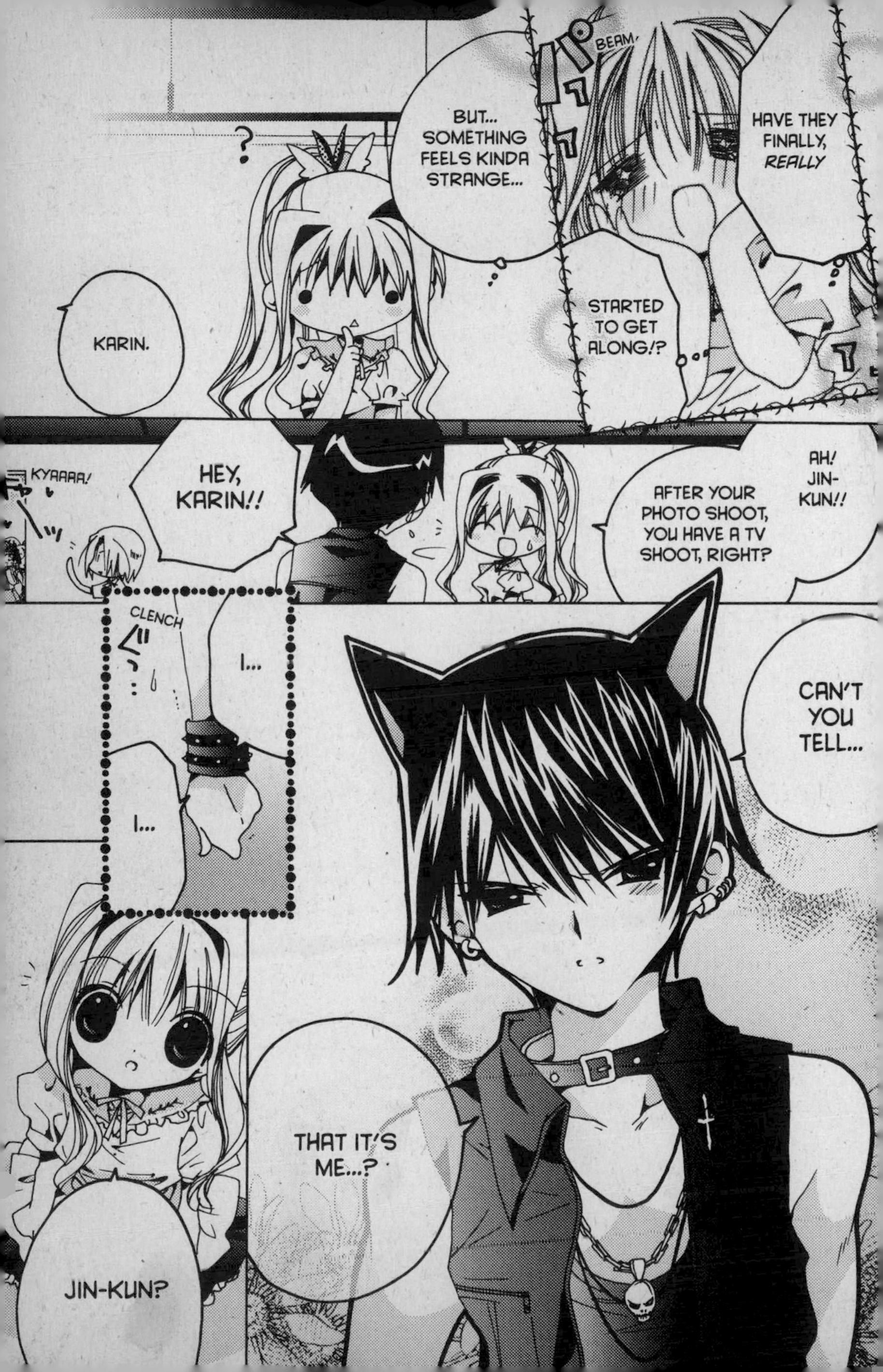
BEAM
HAVE THEY FINALLY, *REALLY*
STARTED TO GET ALONG!?
BUT... SOMETHING FEELS KINDA STRANGE...
?
KARIN.
AH! JIN-KUN!!
AFTER YOUR PHOTO SHOOT, YOU HAVE A TV SHOOT, RIGHT?
HEY, KARIN!!
KYAAAA!
CAN'T YOU TELL...
CLENCH
I...
I...
THAT IT'S ME...?
JIN-KUN?

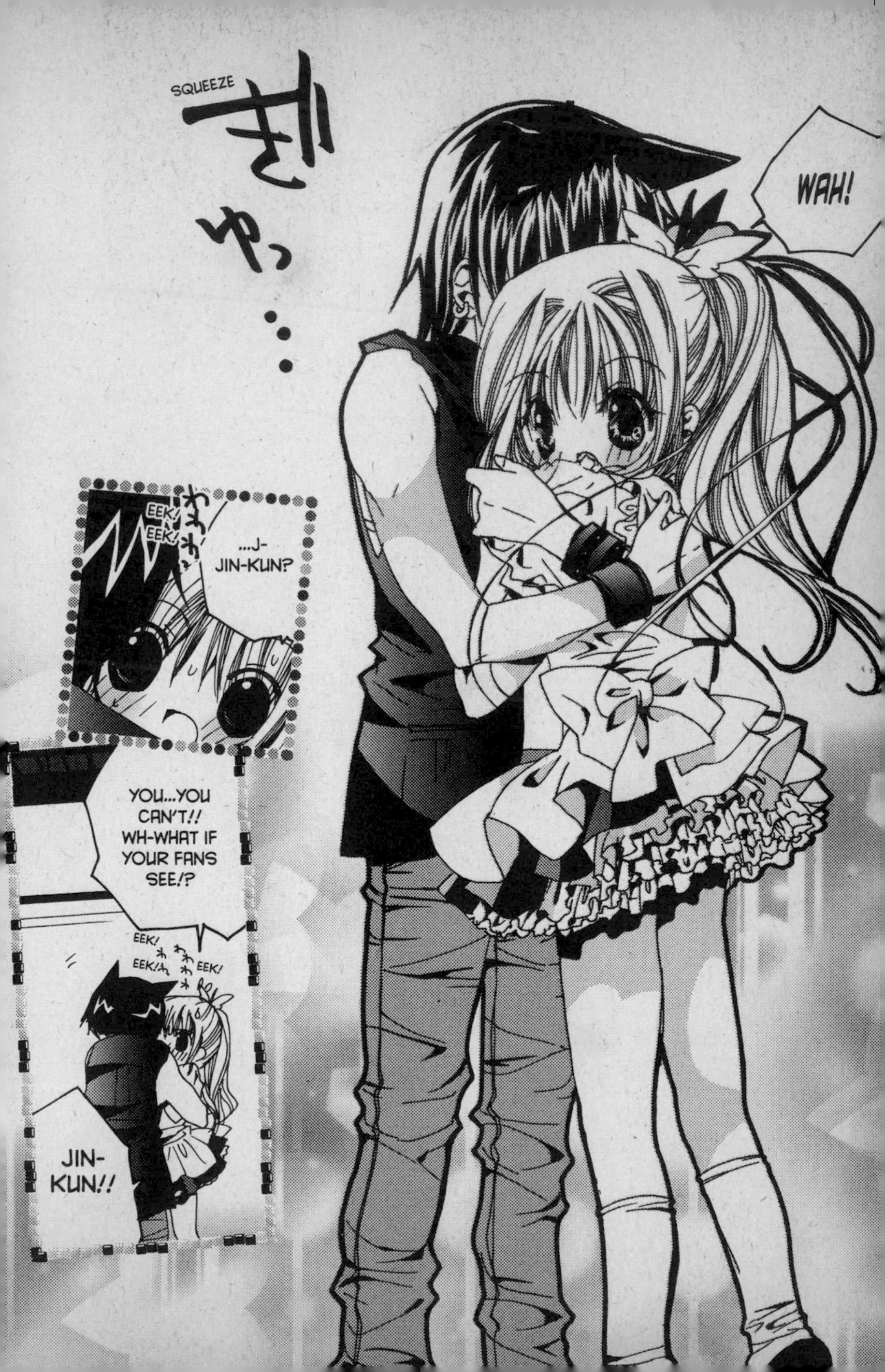
SQUEEZE
ぎゅっ…
WAH!
EEK! EEK!
...J- JIN-KUN?
YOU...YOU CAN'T!! WH-WHAT IF YOUR FANS SEE!?
EEK! EEK! EEK!
JIN-KUN!!

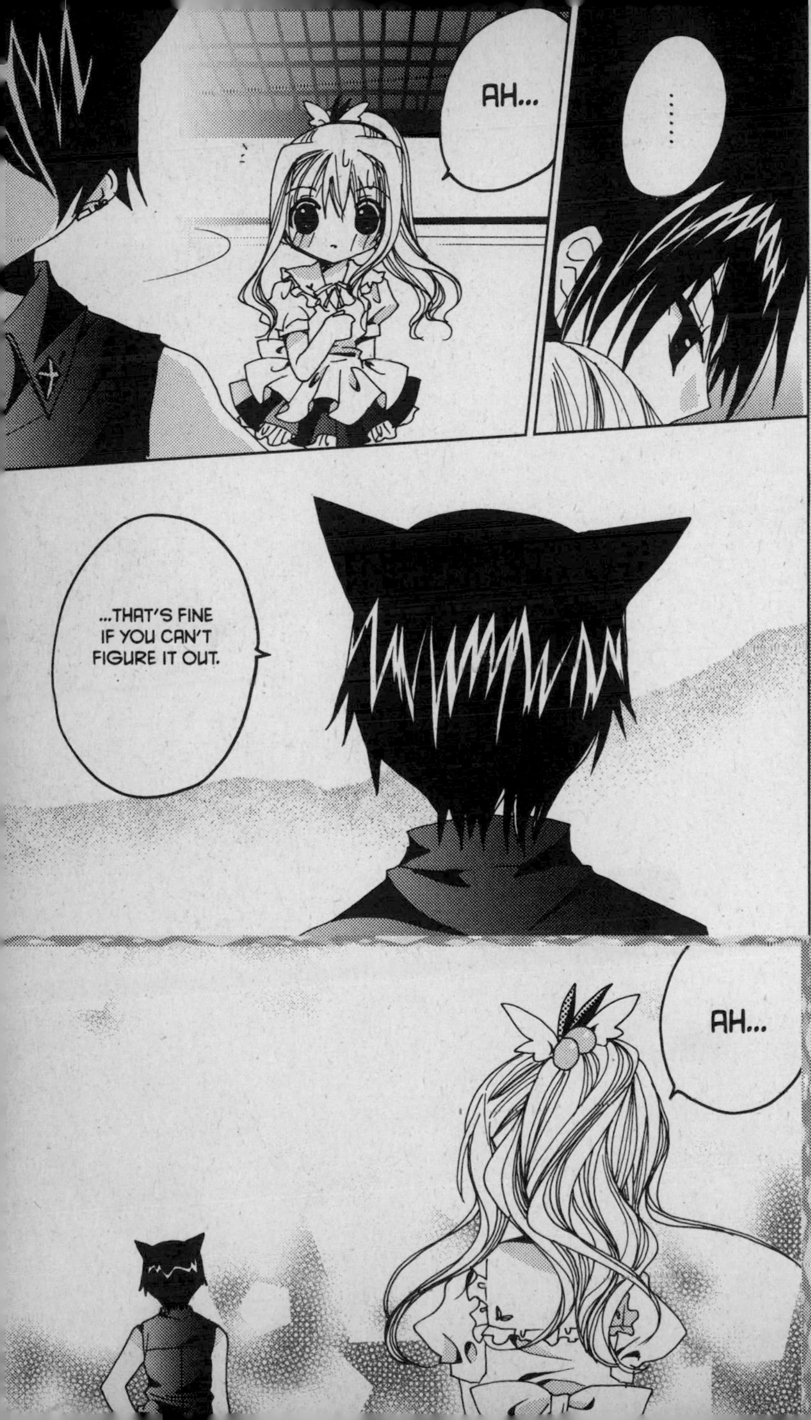
......
AH...
...THAT'S FINE IF YOU CAN'T FIGURE IT OUT.
AH...

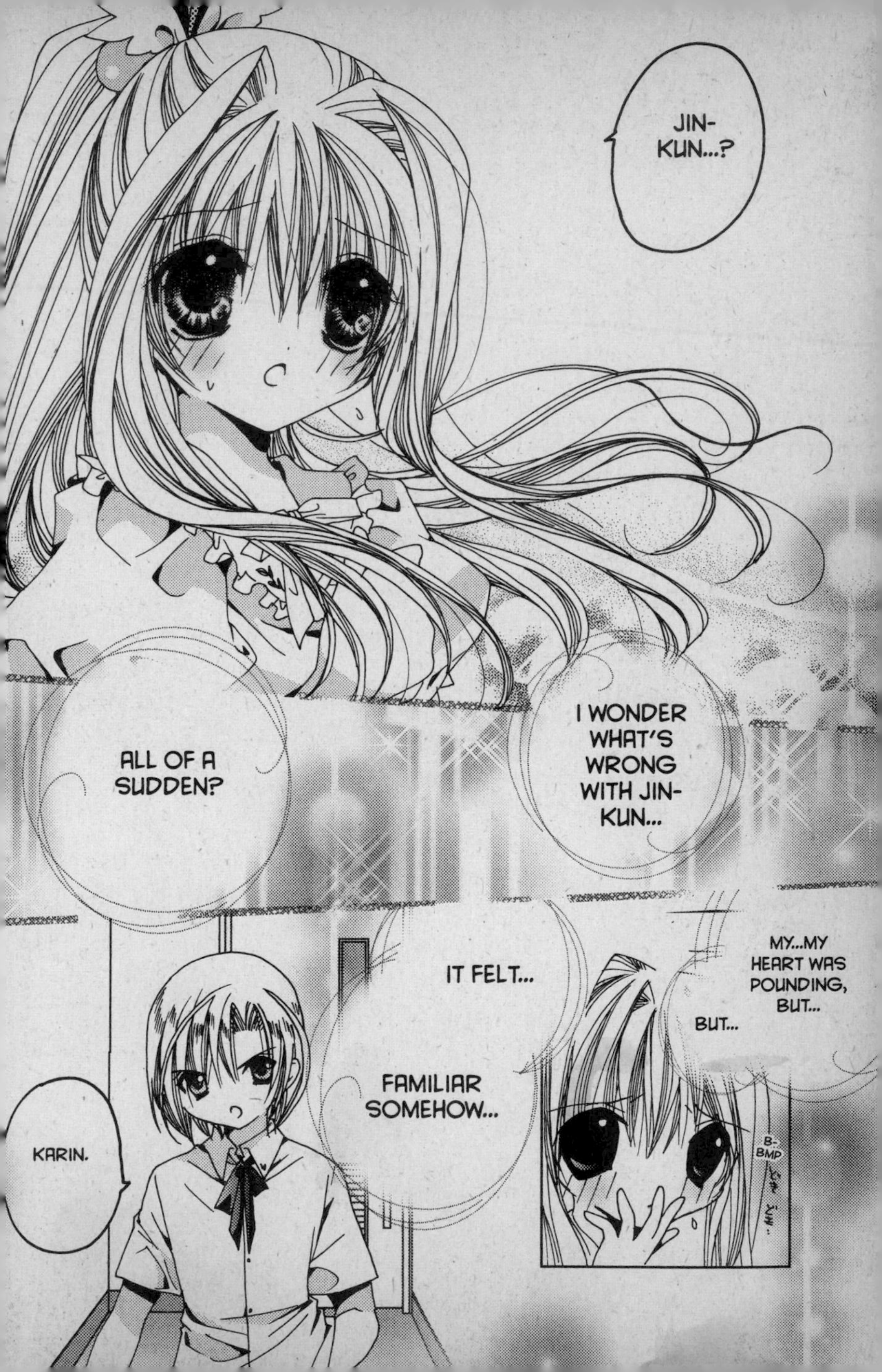
JIN-KUN...?
I WONDER WHAT'S WRONG WITH JIN-KUN...
ALL OF A SUDDEN?
MY...MY HEART WAS POUNDING, BUT...
BUT...
B-BMP
IT FELT...
FAMILIAR SOMEHOW...
KARIN.

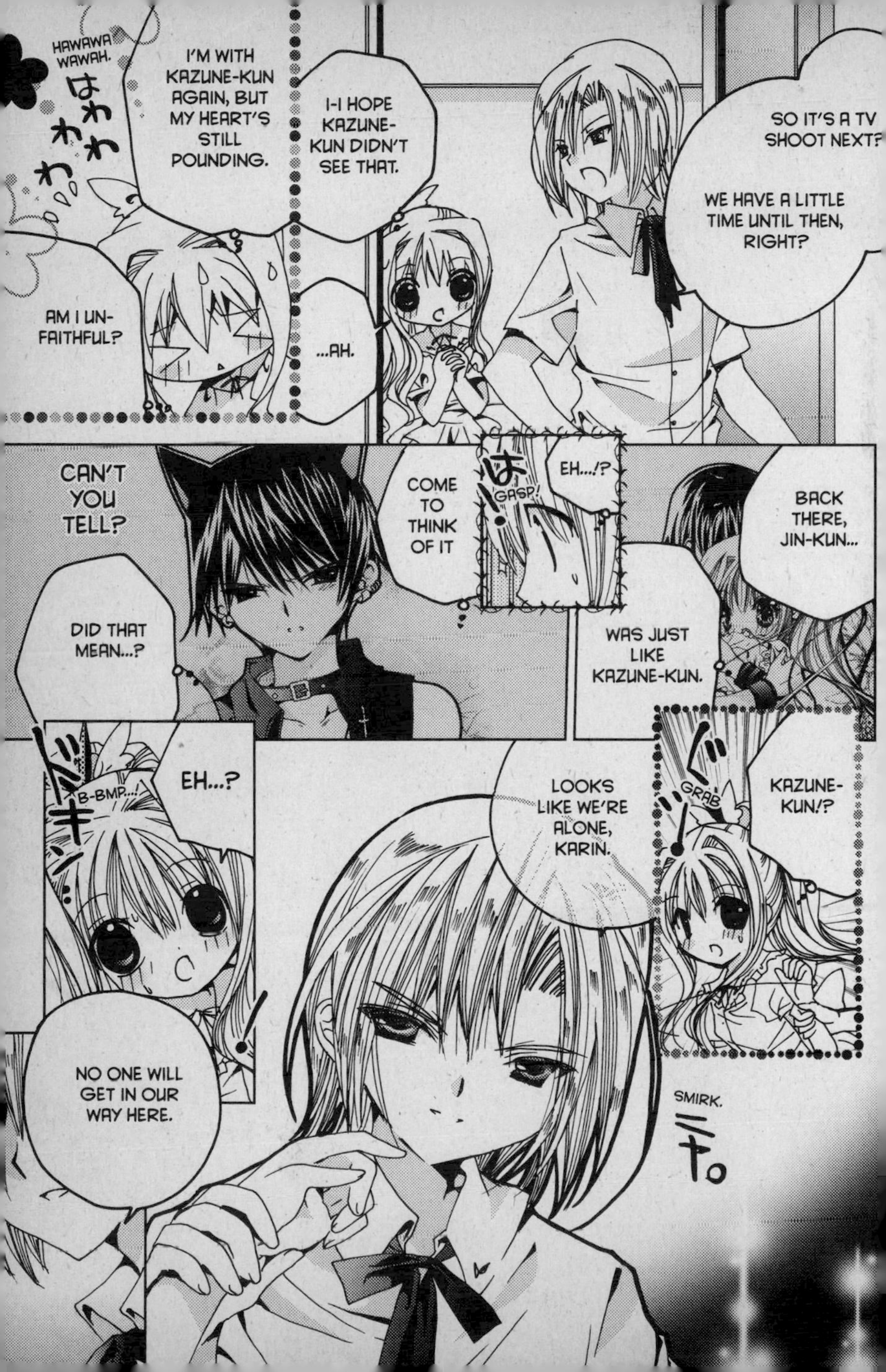
SO IT'S A TV SHOOT NEXT?
WE HAVE A LITTLE TIME UNTIL THEN, RIGHT?
...AH.
I-I HOPE KAZUNE-KUN DIDN'T SEE THAT.
I'M WITH KAZUNE-KUN AGAIN, BUT MY HEART'S STILL POUNDING.
HAWAWA WAWAH.
はわわわわ
AM I UN-FAITHFUL?
BACK THERE, JIN-KUN...
WAS JUST LIKE KAZUNE-KUN.
EH...!?
GASP!
COME TO THINK OF IT
CAN'T YOU TELL?
DID THAT MEAN...?
GRAB
KAZUNE-KUN!?
LOOKS LIKE WE'RE ALONE, KARIN.
SMIRK.
EH...?
B-BMP...!
NO ONE WILL GET IN OUR WAY HERE.

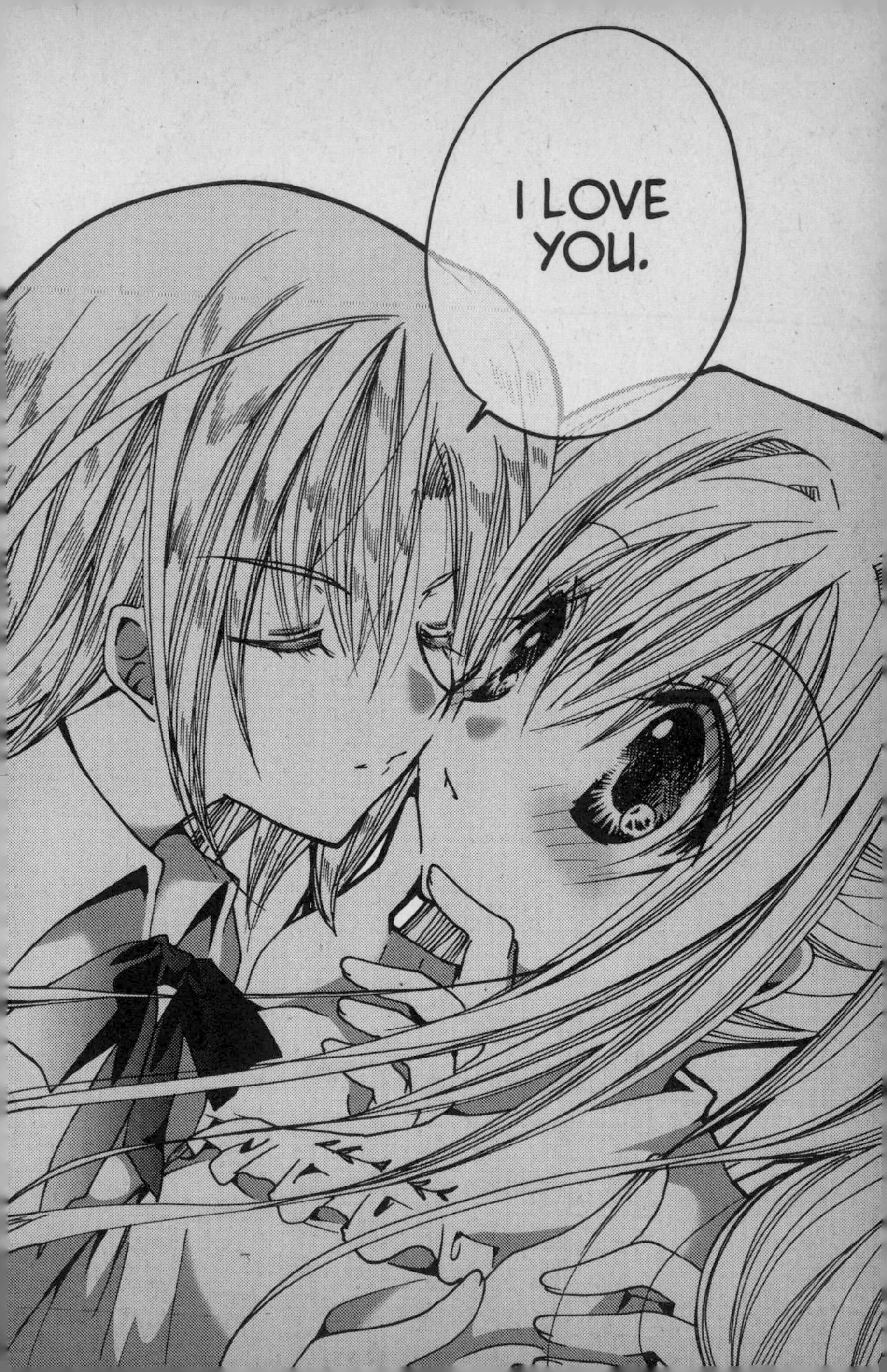
I LOVE YOU.

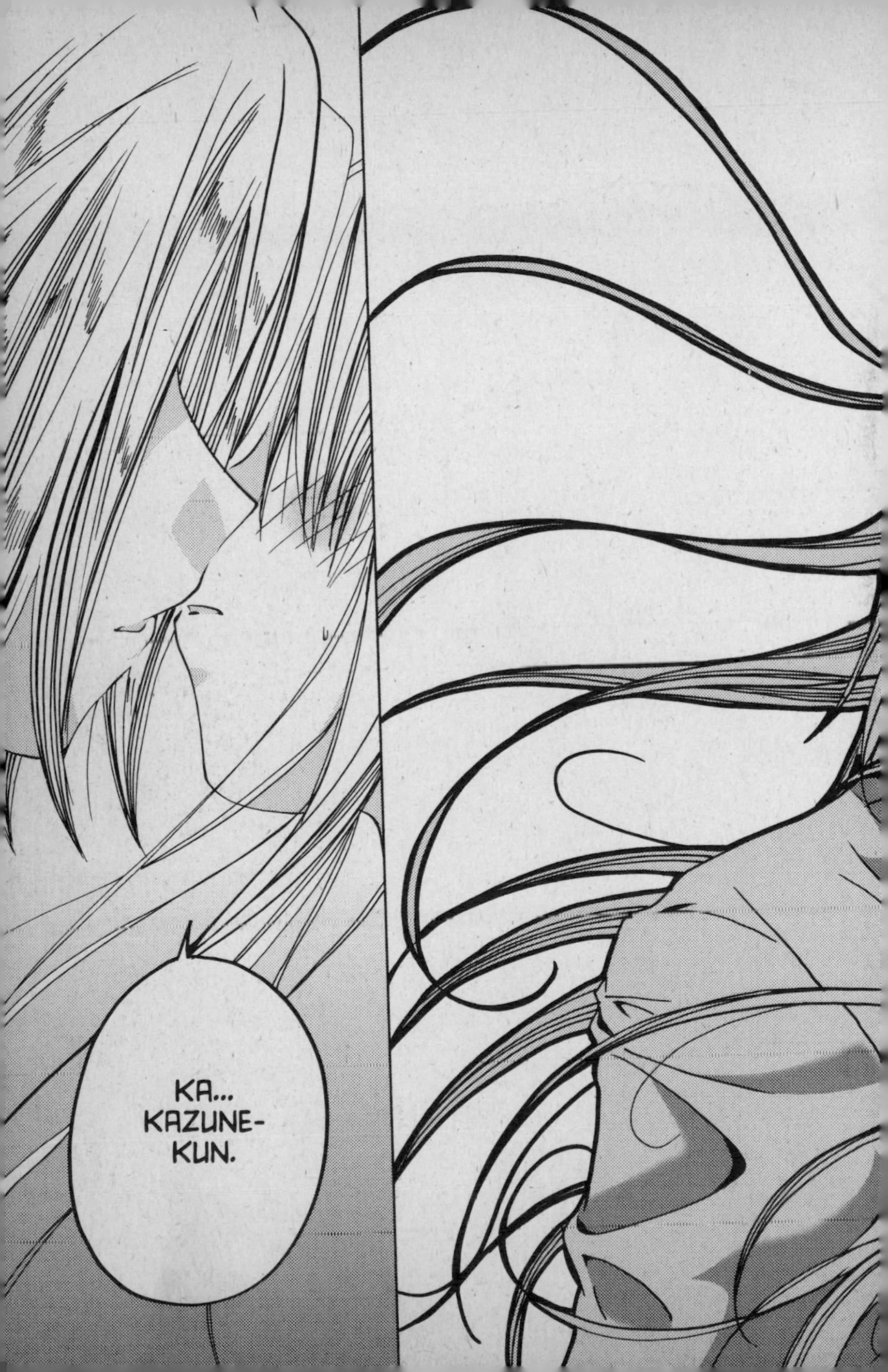
KA... KAZUNE-KUN.

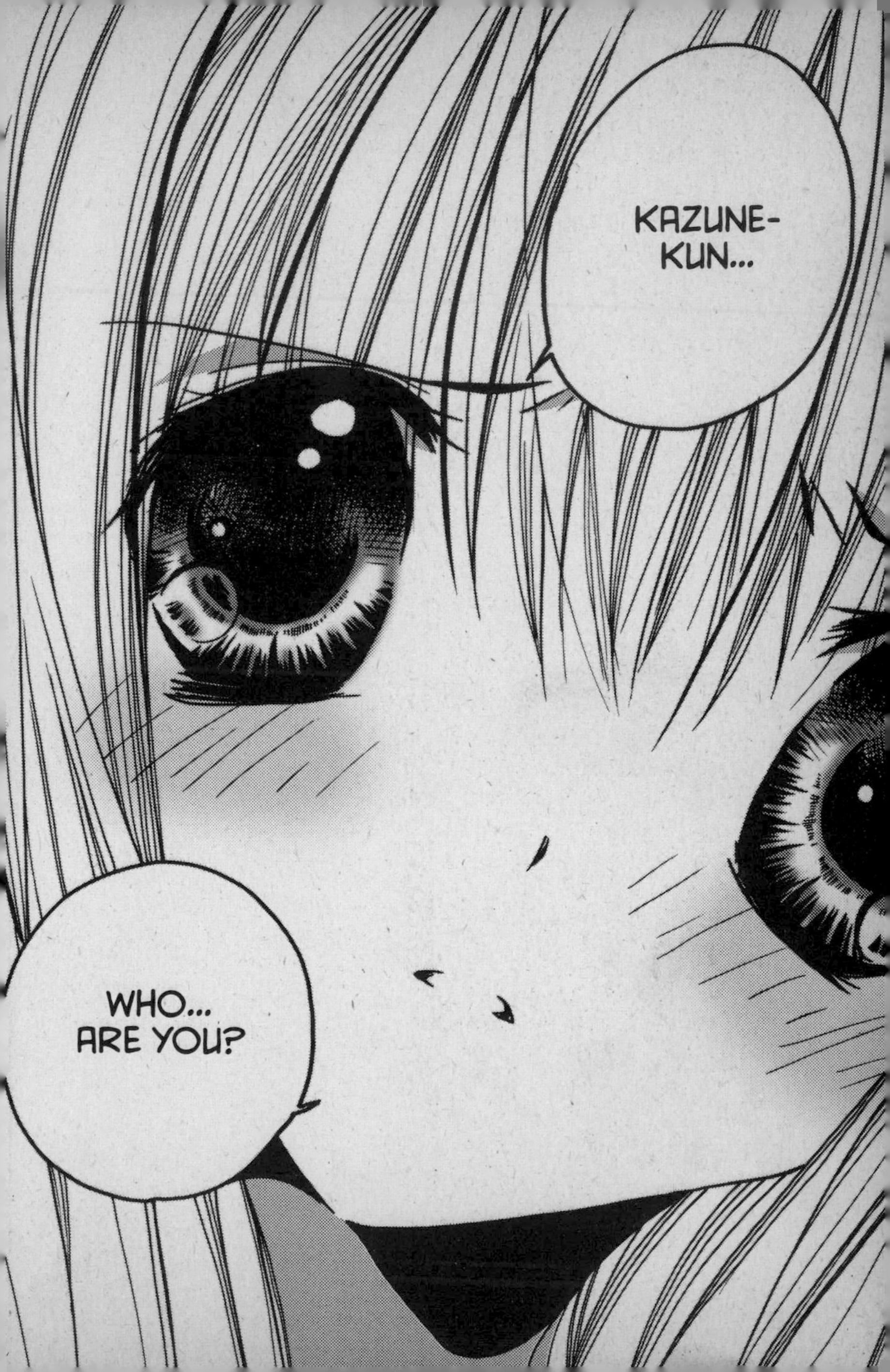
KAZUNE-KUN...
WHO... ARE YOU?

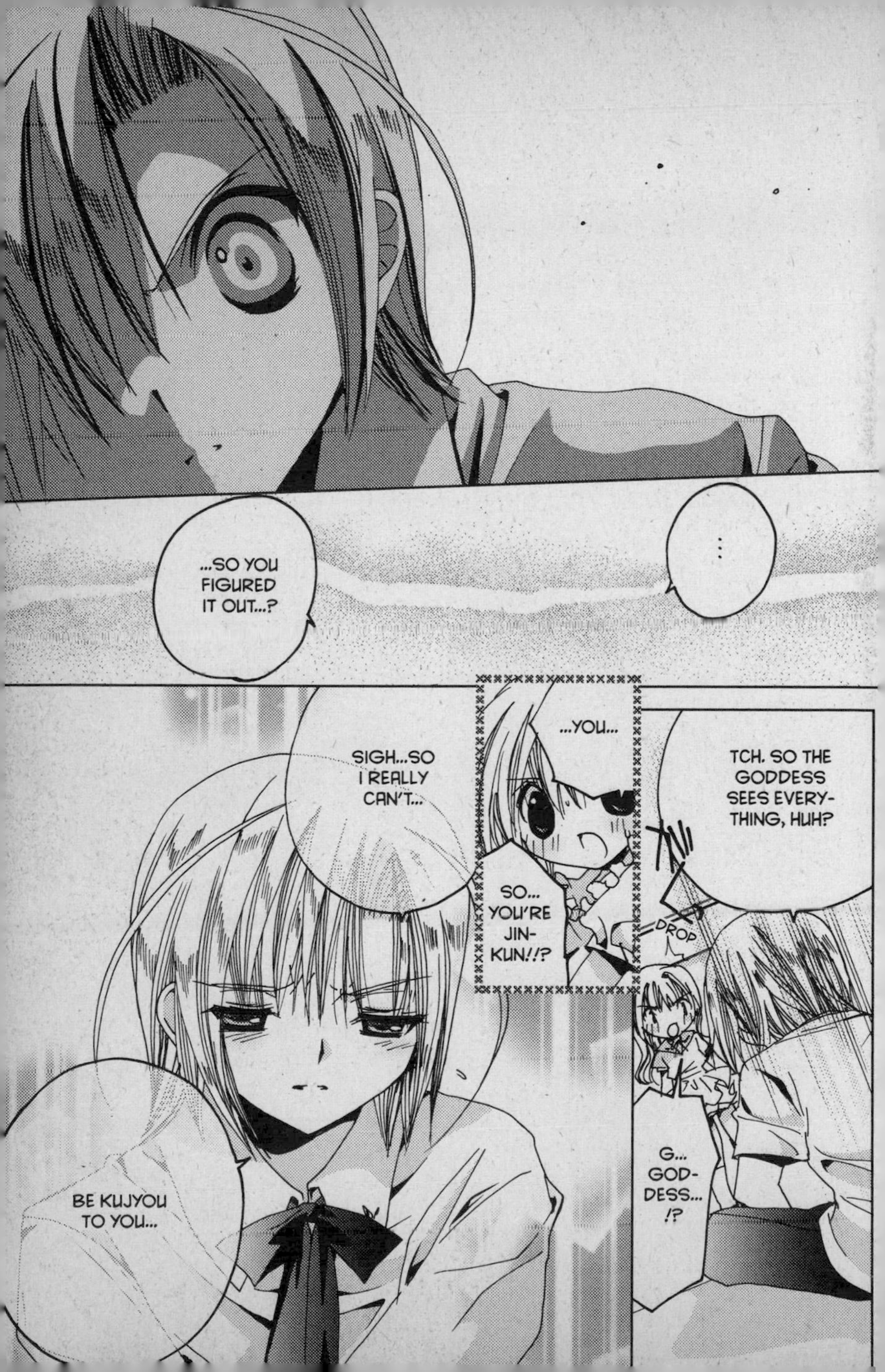
...
...SO YOU FIGURED IT OUT...?
TCH. SO THE GODDESS SEES EVERY-THING, HUH?
DROP
G... GOD-DESS...!?
...YOU...
SO... YOU'RE JIN-KUN!!?
SIGH...SO I REALLY CAN'T...
BE KUJYOU TO YOU...

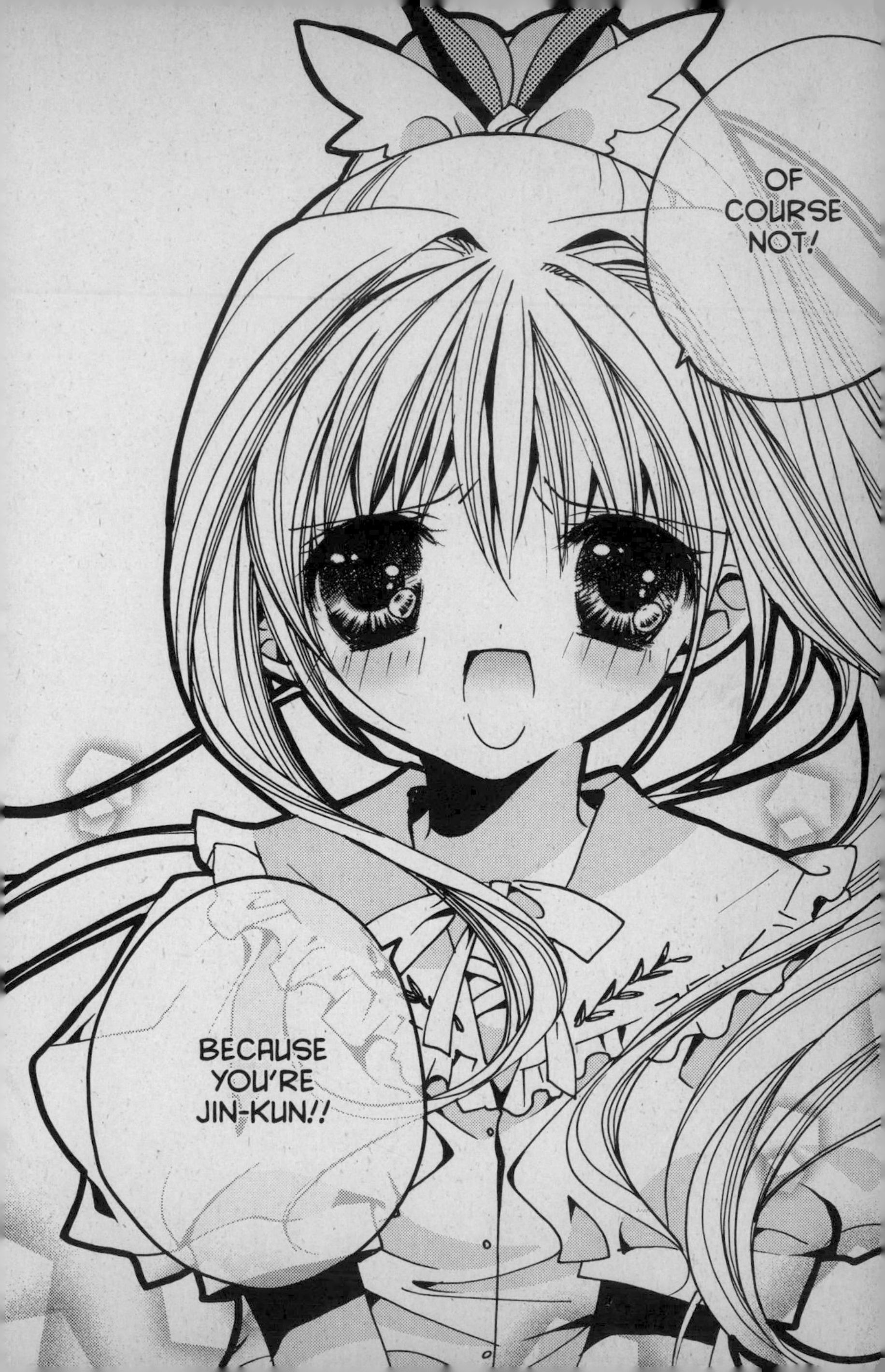
OF COURSE NOT!
BECAUSE YOU'RE JIN-KUN!!

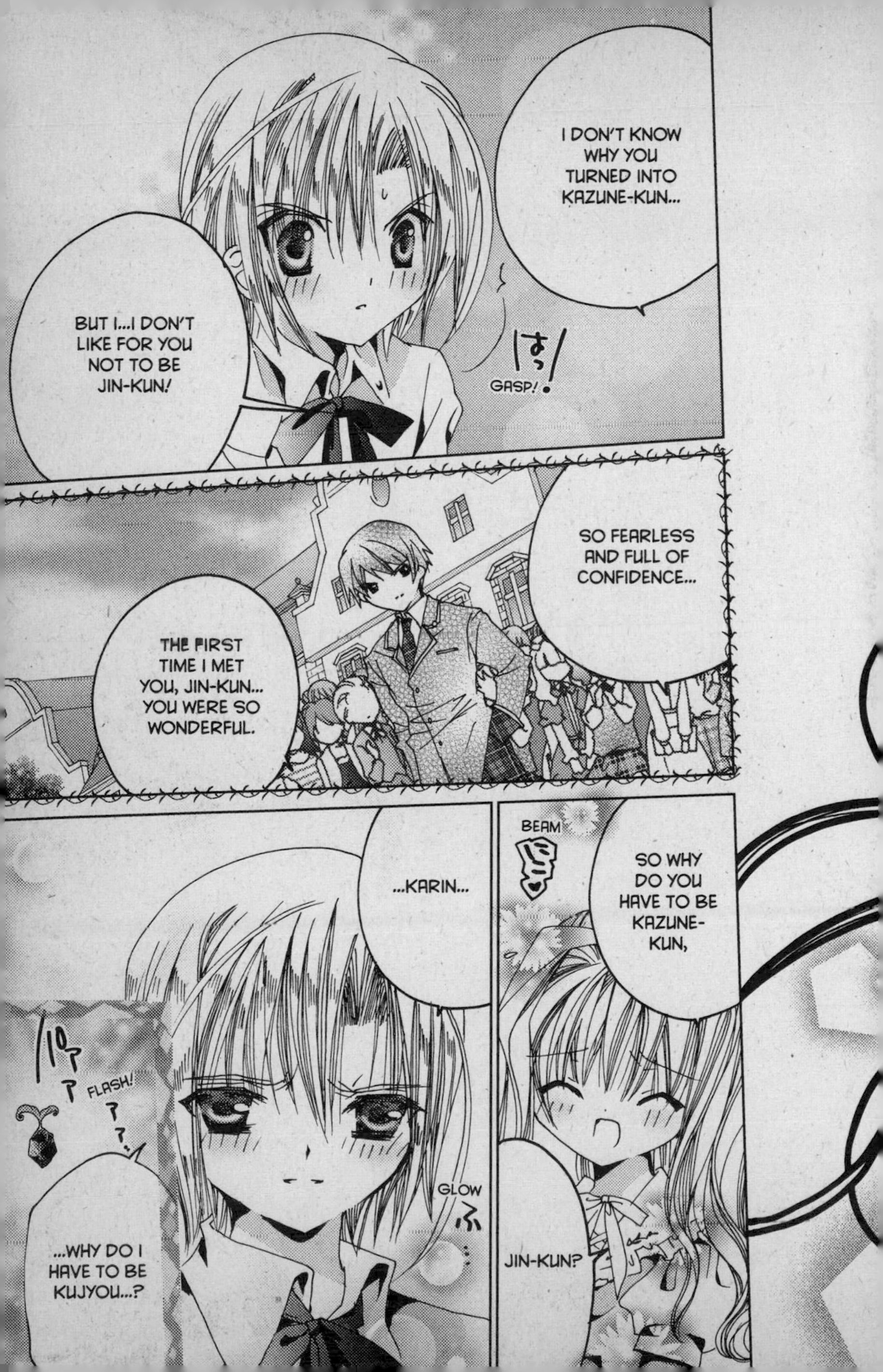
I DON'T KNOW WHY YOU TURNED INTO KAZUNE-KUN...
GASP!
BUT I...I DON'T LIKE FOR YOU NOT TO BE JIN-KUN!
SO FEARLESS AND FULL OF CONFIDENCE...
THE FIRST TIME I MET YOU, JIN-KUN... YOU WERE SO WONDERFUL.
BEAM
SO WHY DO YOU HAVE TO BE KAZUNE-KUN,
JIN-KUN?
...KARIN...
FLASH!
GLOW
...WHY DO I HAVE TO BE KUJYOU...?

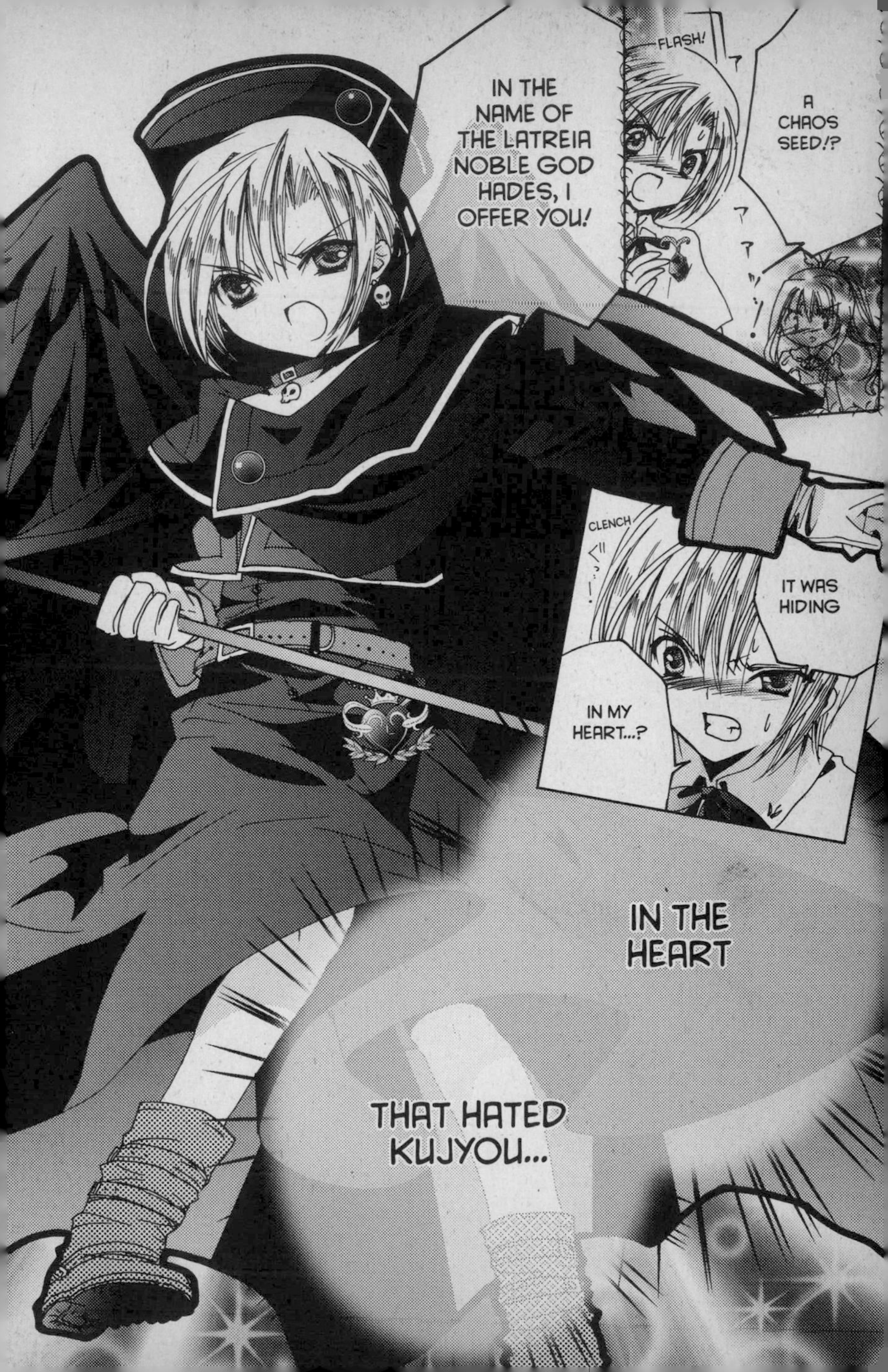
FLASH!
A CHAOS SEED!?
IN THE NAME OF THE LATREIA NOBLE GOD HADES, I OFFER YOU!
CLENCH
IT WAS HIDING
IN MY HEART...?
IN THE HEART
THAT HATED KUJYOU...

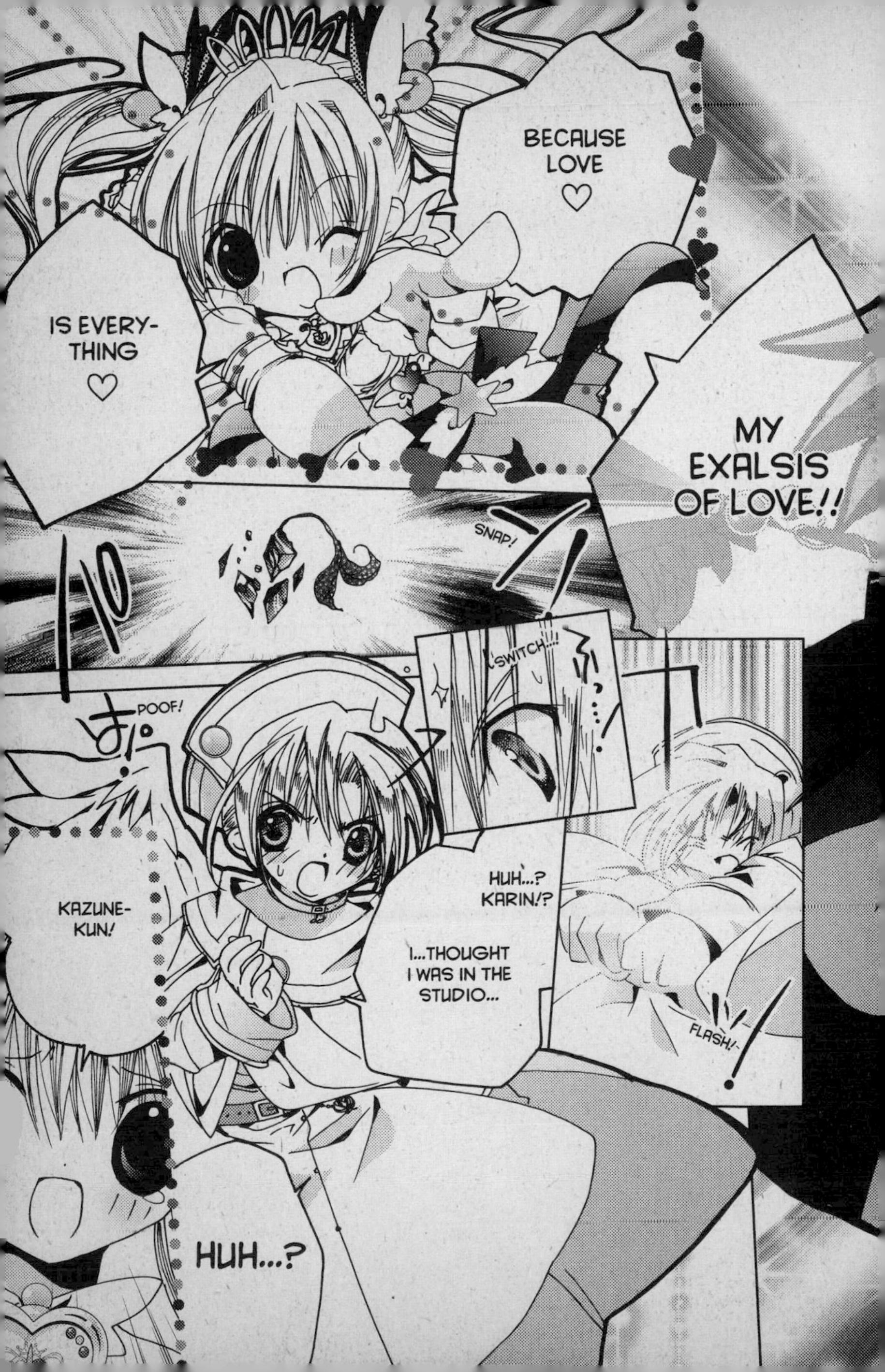
BECAUSE LOVE ♡
IS EVERY-THING ♡
MY EXALSIS OF LOVE!!
SNAP!
FLASH!
SWITCH!!!
POOF!
HUH...? KARIN!?
I...THOUGHT I WAS IN THE STUDIO...
KAZUNE-KUN!
HUH...?

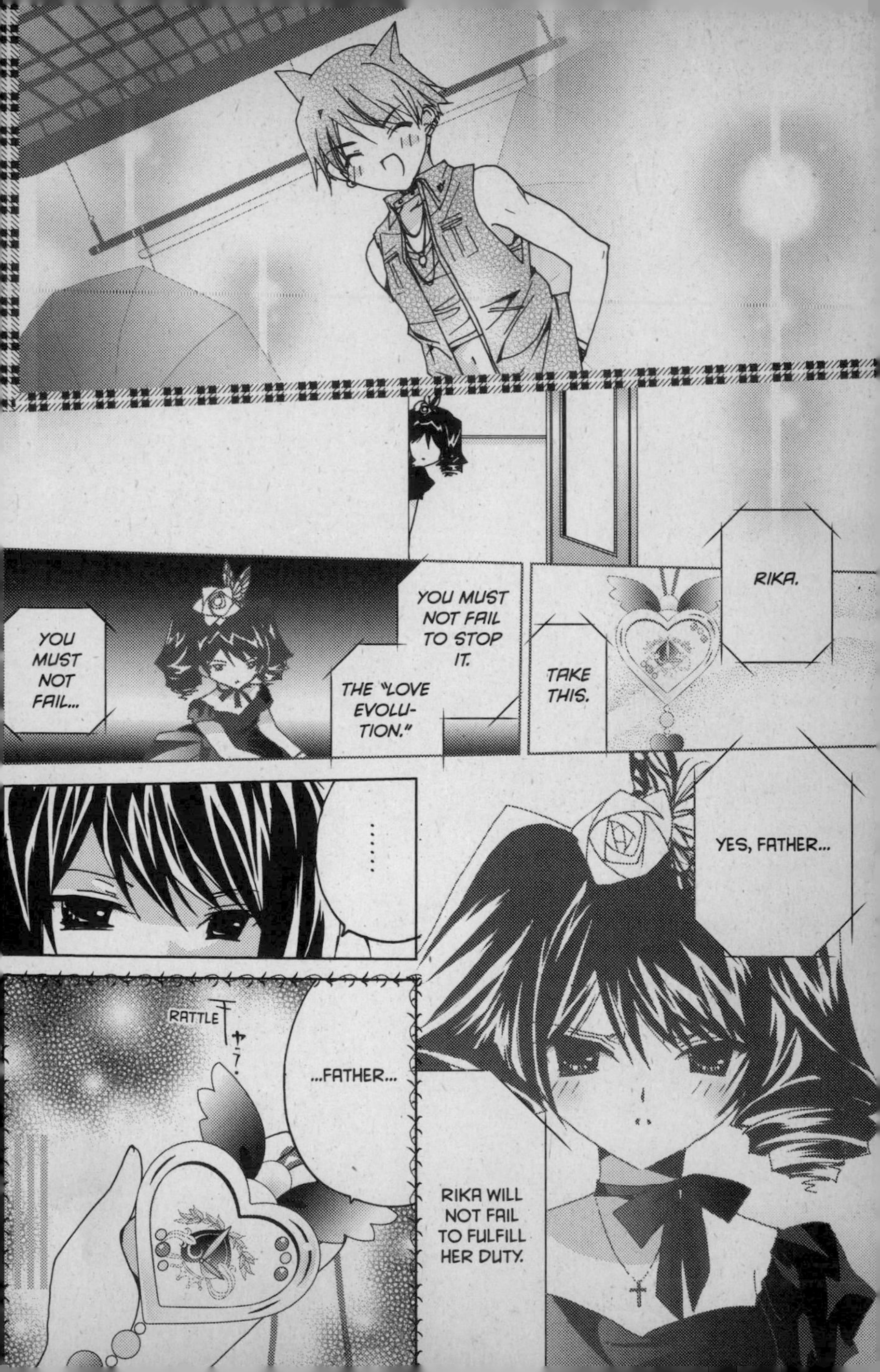
RIKA.
TAKE THIS.
YOU MUST NOT FAIL TO STOP IT.
THE "LOVE EVOLUTION."
YOU MUST NOT FAIL...
YES, FATHER...
RIKA WILL NOT FAIL TO FULFILL HER DUTY.
......
RATTLE
...FATHER...

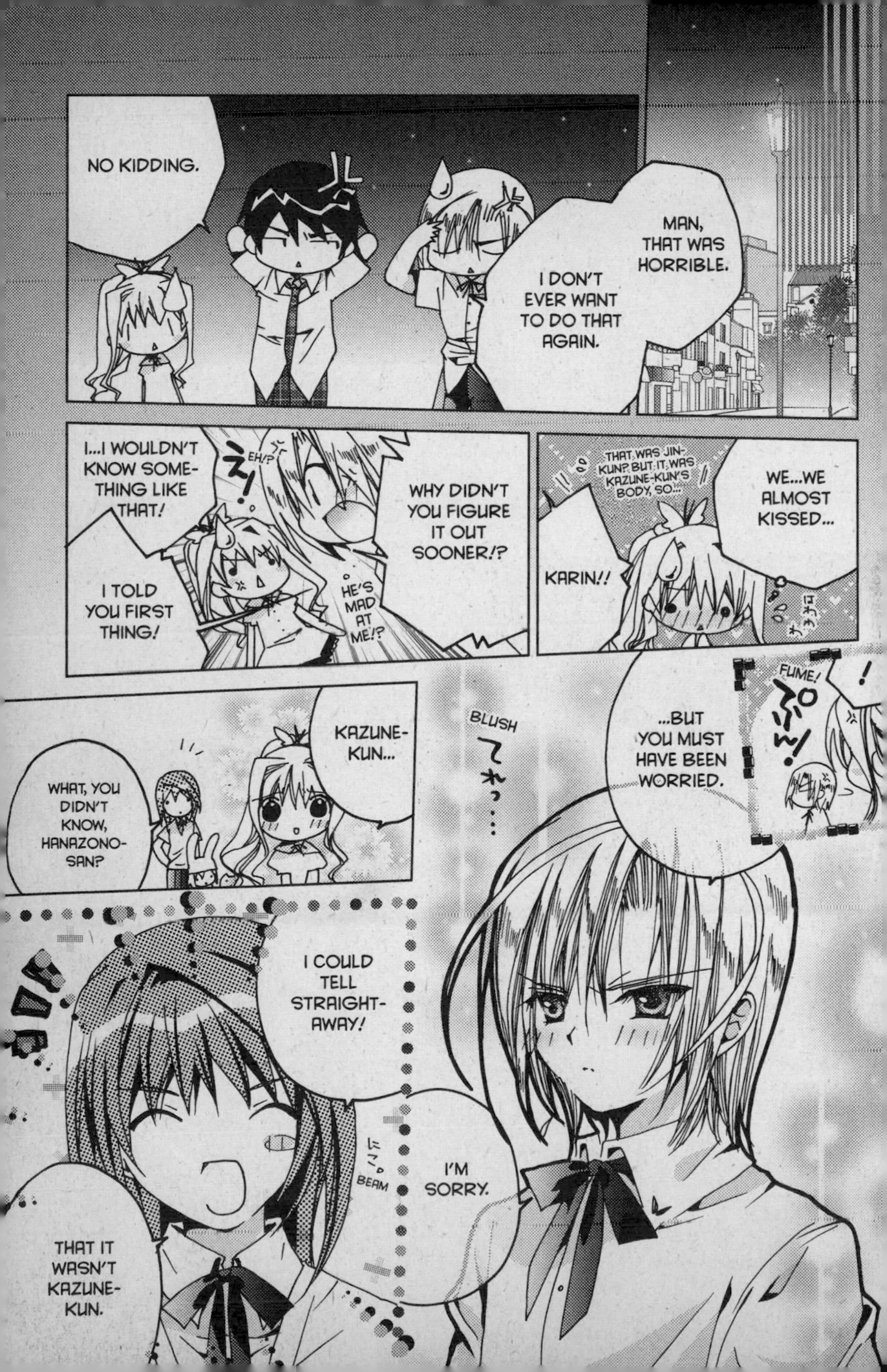
MAN, THAT WAS HORRIBLE.
I DON'T EVER WANT TO DO THAT AGAIN.
NO KIDDING.
WE...WE ALMOST KISSED...
THAT WAS JIN-KUN? BUT IT WAS KAZUNE-KUN'S BODY, SO...
KARIN!!
WHY DIDN'T YOU FIGURE IT OUT SOONER!?
EH!?
I...I WOULDN'T KNOW SOMETHING LIKE THAT!
HE'S MAD AT ME!?
I TOLD YOU FIRST THING!
FUME!
...BUT YOU MUST HAVE BEEN WORRIED.
BLUSH
I'M SORRY.
KAZUNE-KUN...
WHAT, YOU DIDN'T KNOW, HANAZONO-SAN?
I COULD TELL STRAIGHTAWAY!
BEAM
THAT IT WASN'T KAZUNE-KUN.

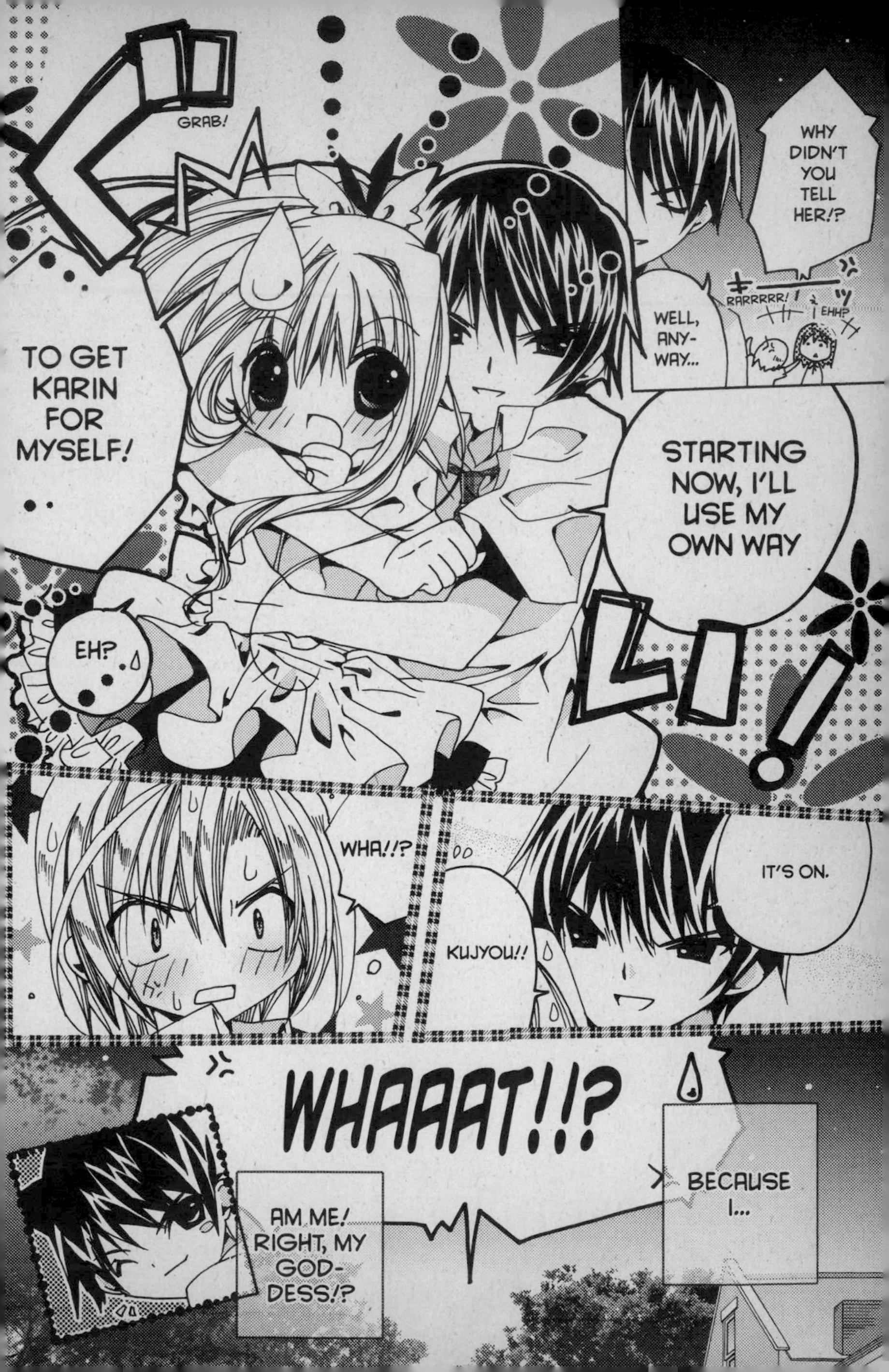
WHY DIDN'T YOU TELL HER!?
RARRRRR!
EHH?
WELL, ANY-WAY...
STARTING NOW, I'LL USE MY OWN WAY
LI!
TO GET KARIN FOR MYSELF!
GRAB!
EH?
IT'S ON.
KUJYOU!!
WHA!!?
BECAUSE I...
WHAAAT!!?
AM ME! RIGHT, MY GOD-DESS!?

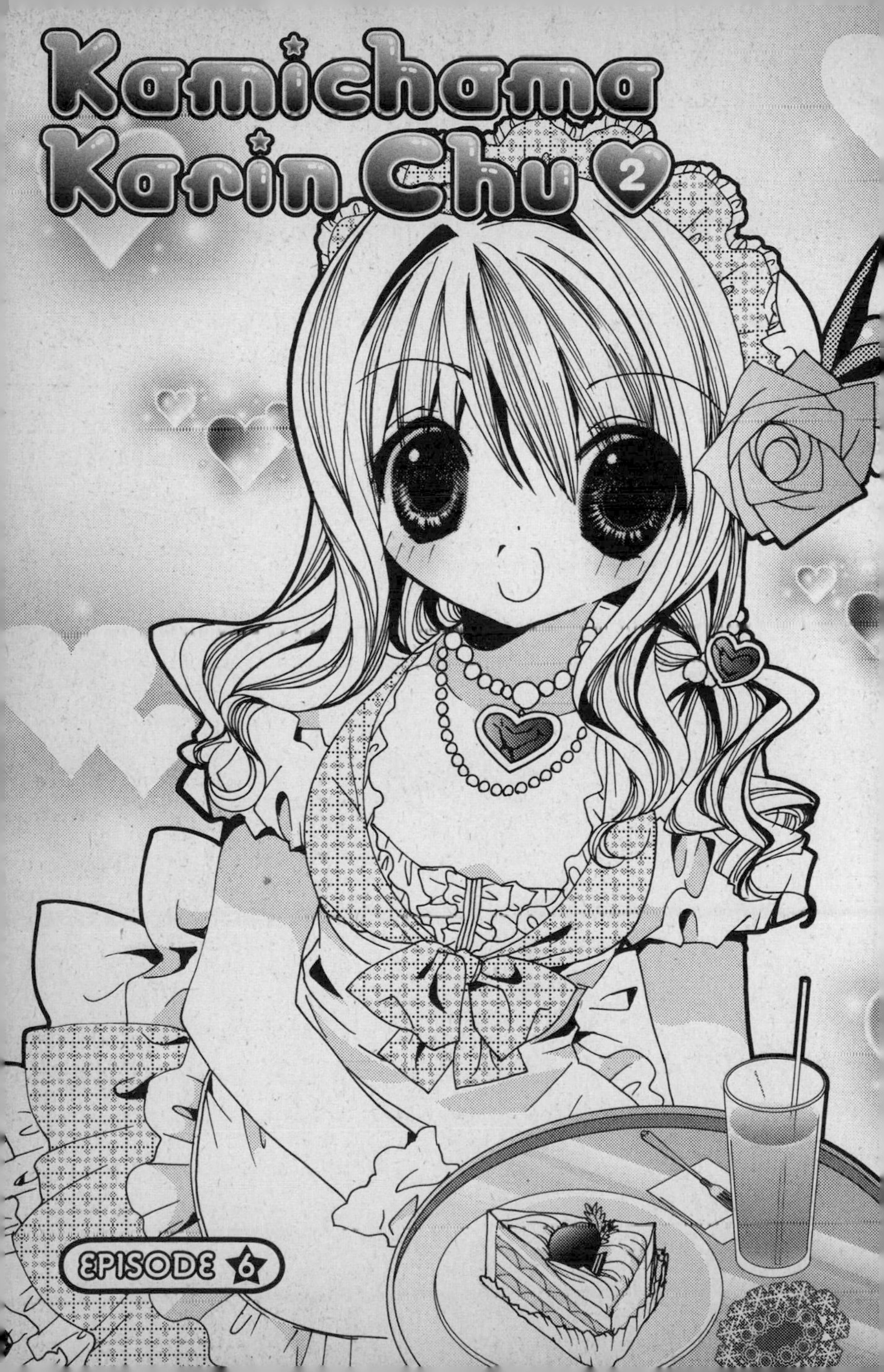
Kamichama Karin Chu 2
EPISODE 6

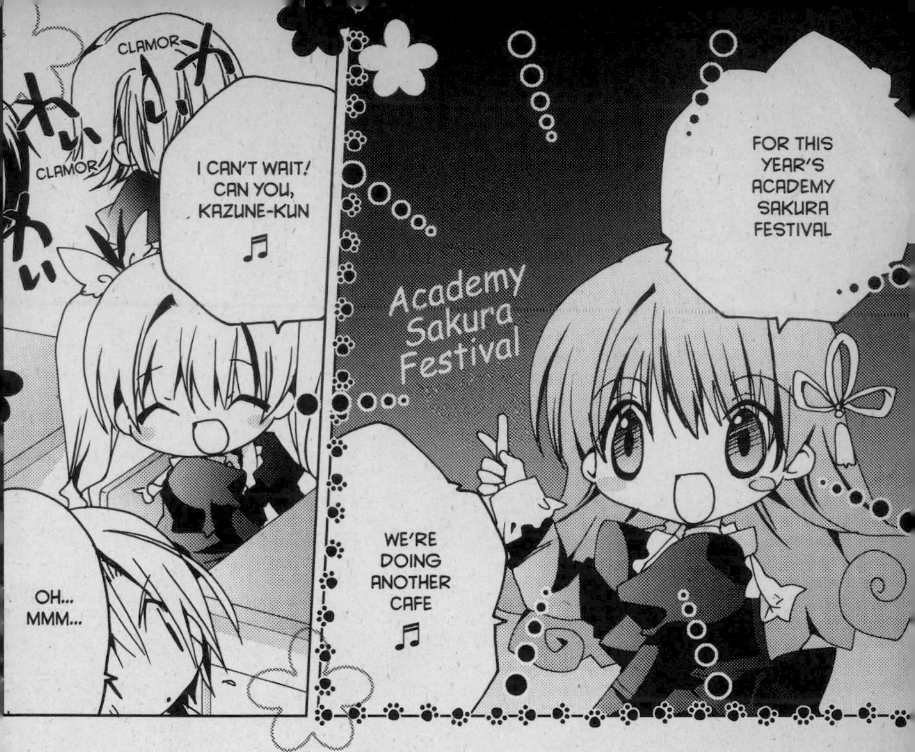
FOR THIS YEAR'S ACADEMY SAKURA FESTIVAL
Academy Sakura Festival
WE'RE DOING ANOTHER CAFE ♫
I CAN'T WAIT! CAN YOU, KAZUNE-KUN ♫
CLAMOR
CLAMOR
OH... MMM...

I WISH I COULD DO A CAFE...

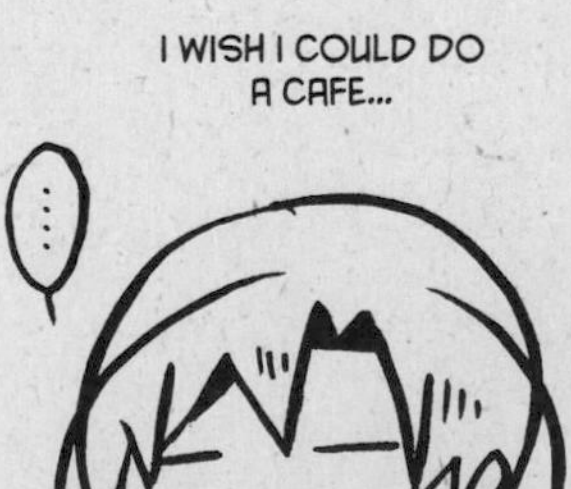
.....

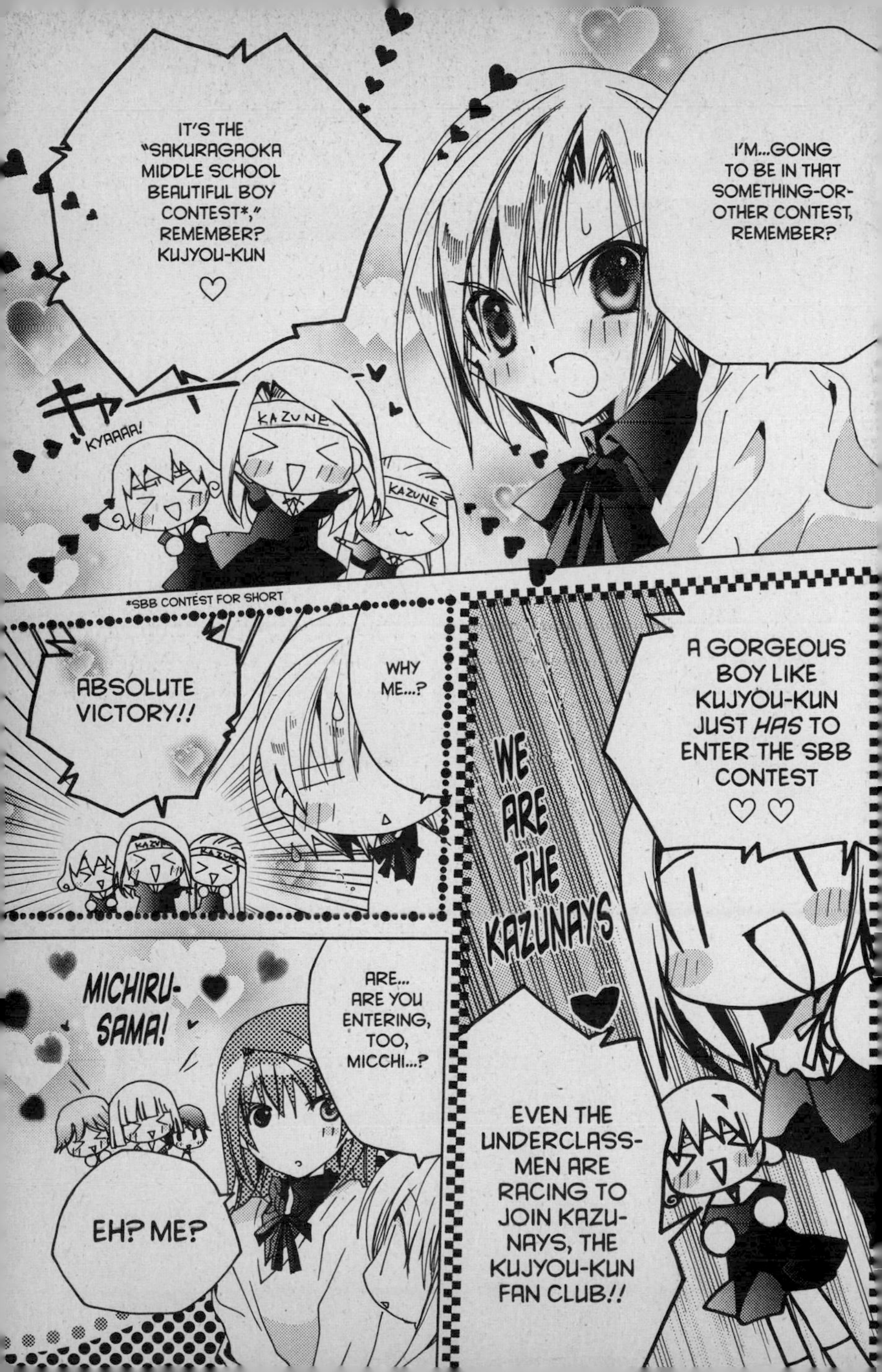
I'M...GOING TO BE IN THAT SOMETHING-OR-OTHER CONTEST, REMEMBER?
IT'S THE "SAKURAGAOKA MIDDLE SCHOOL BEAUTIFUL BOY CONTEST*," REMEMBER? KUJYOU-KUN ♡
キャ
KYAAAA!
KAZUNE
KAZUNE
*SBB CONTEST FOR SHORT
A GORGEOUS BOY LIKE KUJYOU-KUN JUST *HAS* TO ENTER THE SBB CONTEST ♡ ♡
WE ARE THE KAZUNAYS
EVEN THE UNDERCLASSMEN ARE RACING TO JOIN KAZUNAYS, THE KUJYOU-KUN FAN CLUB!!
WHY ME...?
ABSOLUTE VICTORY!!
ARE... ARE YOU ENTERING, TOO, MICCHI...?
MICHIRU-SAMA!
EH? ME?

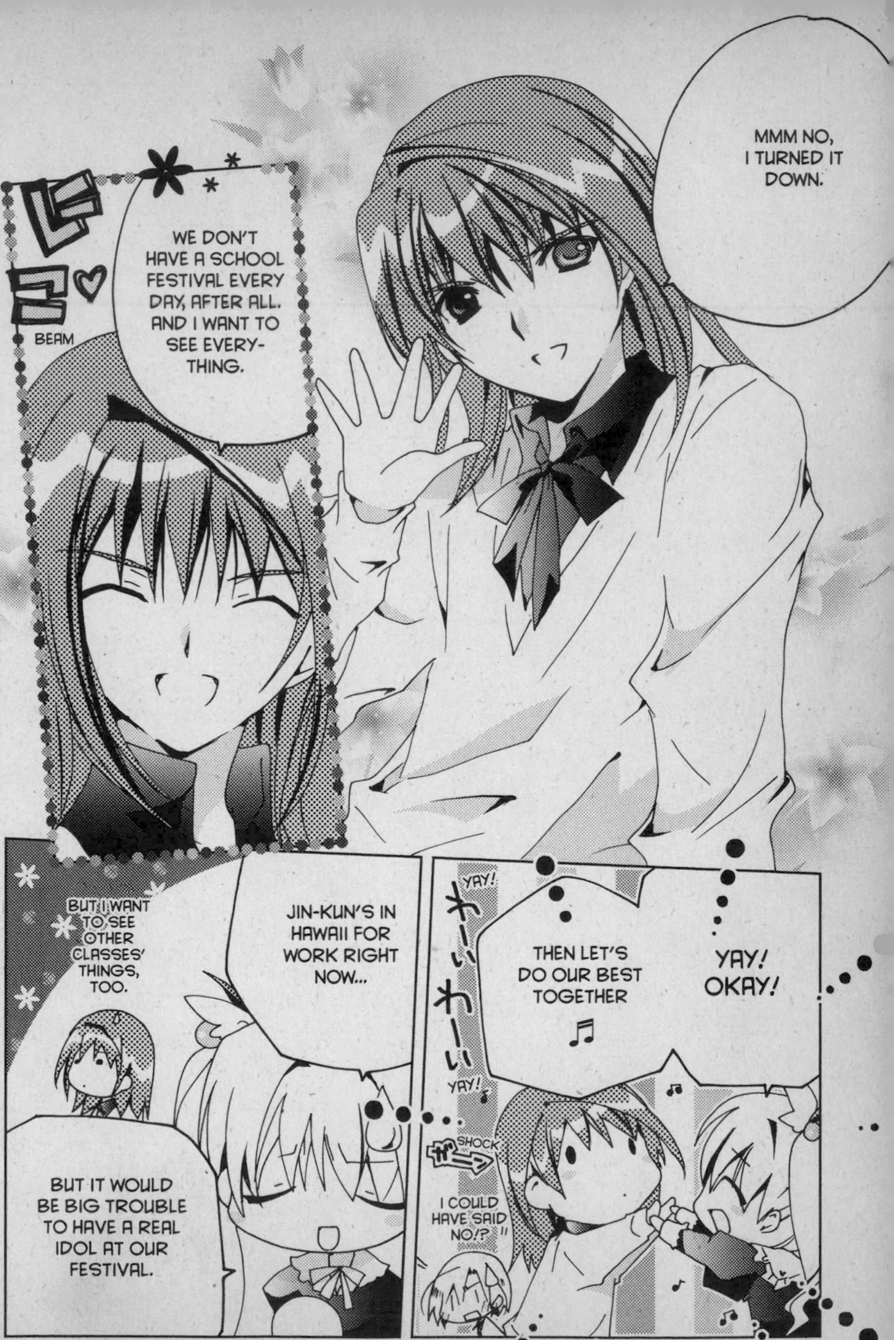
MMM NO, I TURNED IT DOWN.
BEAM
WE DON'T HAVE A SCHOOL FESTIVAL EVERY DAY, AFTER ALL. AND I WANT TO SEE EVERY-THING.
YAY! OKAY!
THEN LET'S DO OUR BEST TOGETHER ♫
YAY!
YAY!
SHOCK
I COULD HAVE SAID NO!? !!
JIN-KUN'S IN HAWAII FOR WORK RIGHT NOW...
BUT I WANT TO SEE OTHER CLASSES' THINGS, TOO.
BUT IT WOULD BE BIG TROUBLE TO HAVE A REAL IDOL AT OUR FESTIVAL.

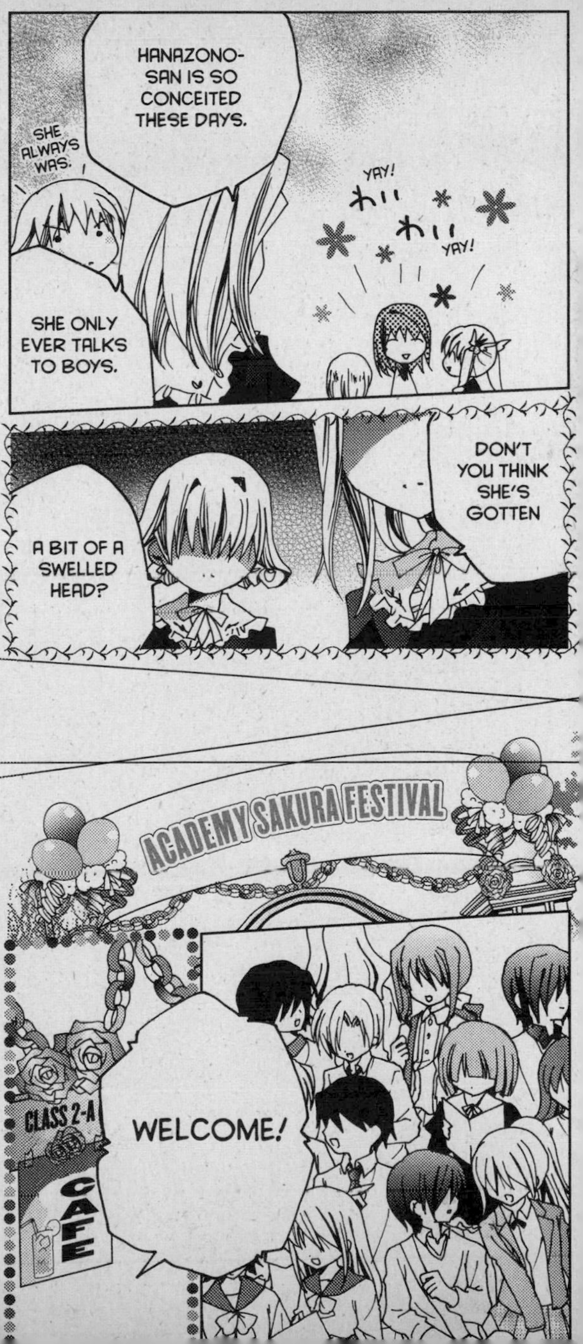
YAY!
わい
わい
YAY!
HANAZONO-SAN IS SO CONCEITED THESE DAYS.
SHE ALWAYS WAS.
SHE ONLY EVER TALKS TO BOYS.
DON'T YOU THINK SHE'S GOTTEN
A BIT OF A SWELLED HEAD?
ACADEMY SAKURA FESTIVAL
CLASS 2-A
CAFE
WELCOME!

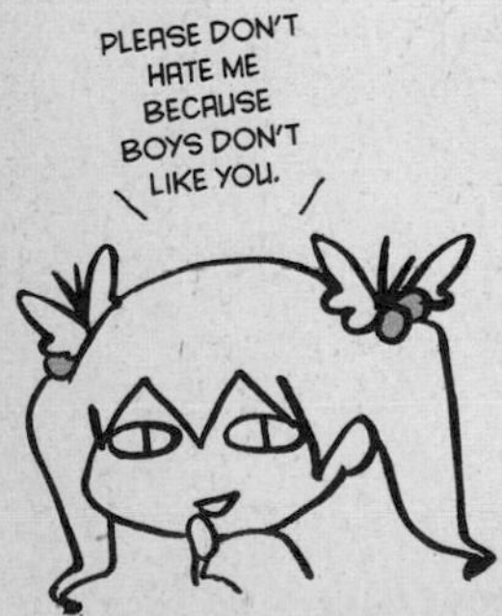
PLEASE DON'T HATE ME BECAUSE BOYS DON'T LIKE YOU.

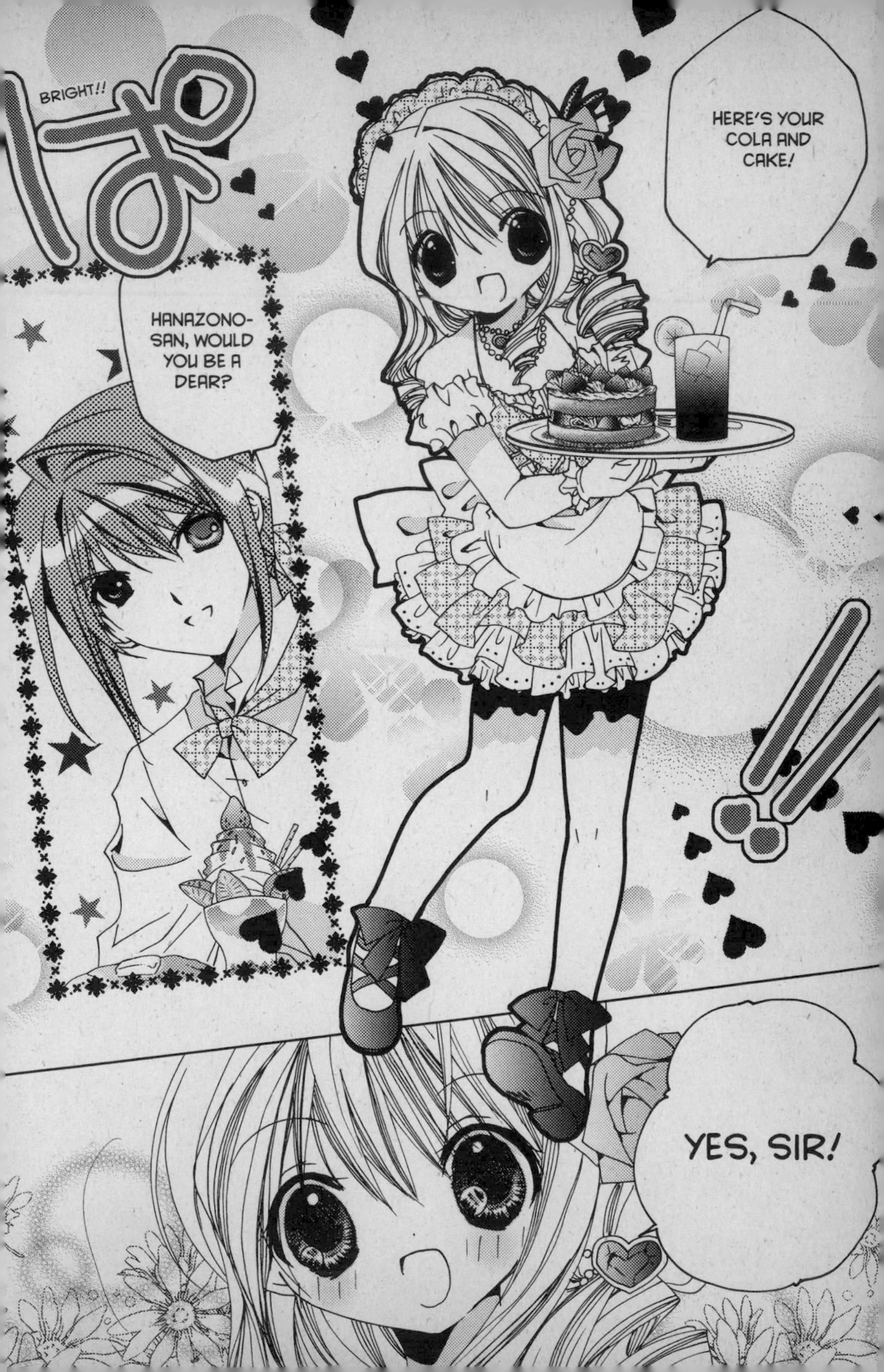
HERE'S YOUR COLA AND CAKE!
BRIGHT!!
HANAZONO-SAN, WOULD YOU BE A DEAR?
YES, SIR!

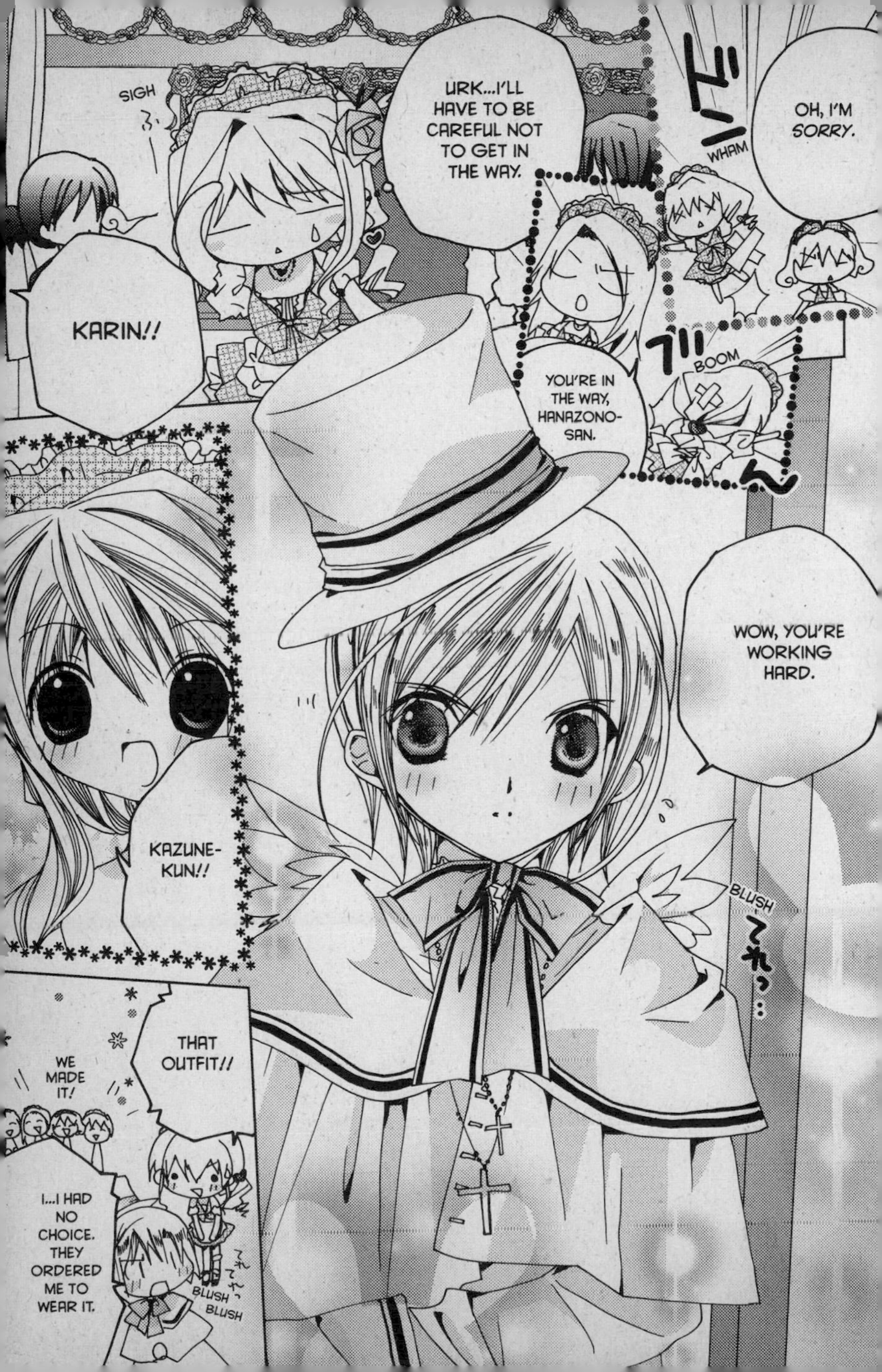
URK...I'LL HAVE TO BE CAREFUL NOT TO GET IN THE WAY.
WHAM
OH, I'M SORRY.
YOU'RE IN THE WAY, HANAZONO-SAN.
BOOM
SIGH
KARIN!!
WOW, YOU'RE WORKING HARD.
BLUSH
KAZUNE-KUN!!
THAT OUTFIT!!
WE MADE IT!
I...I HAD NO CHOICE. THEY ORDERED ME TO WEAR IT.
BLUSH BLUSH

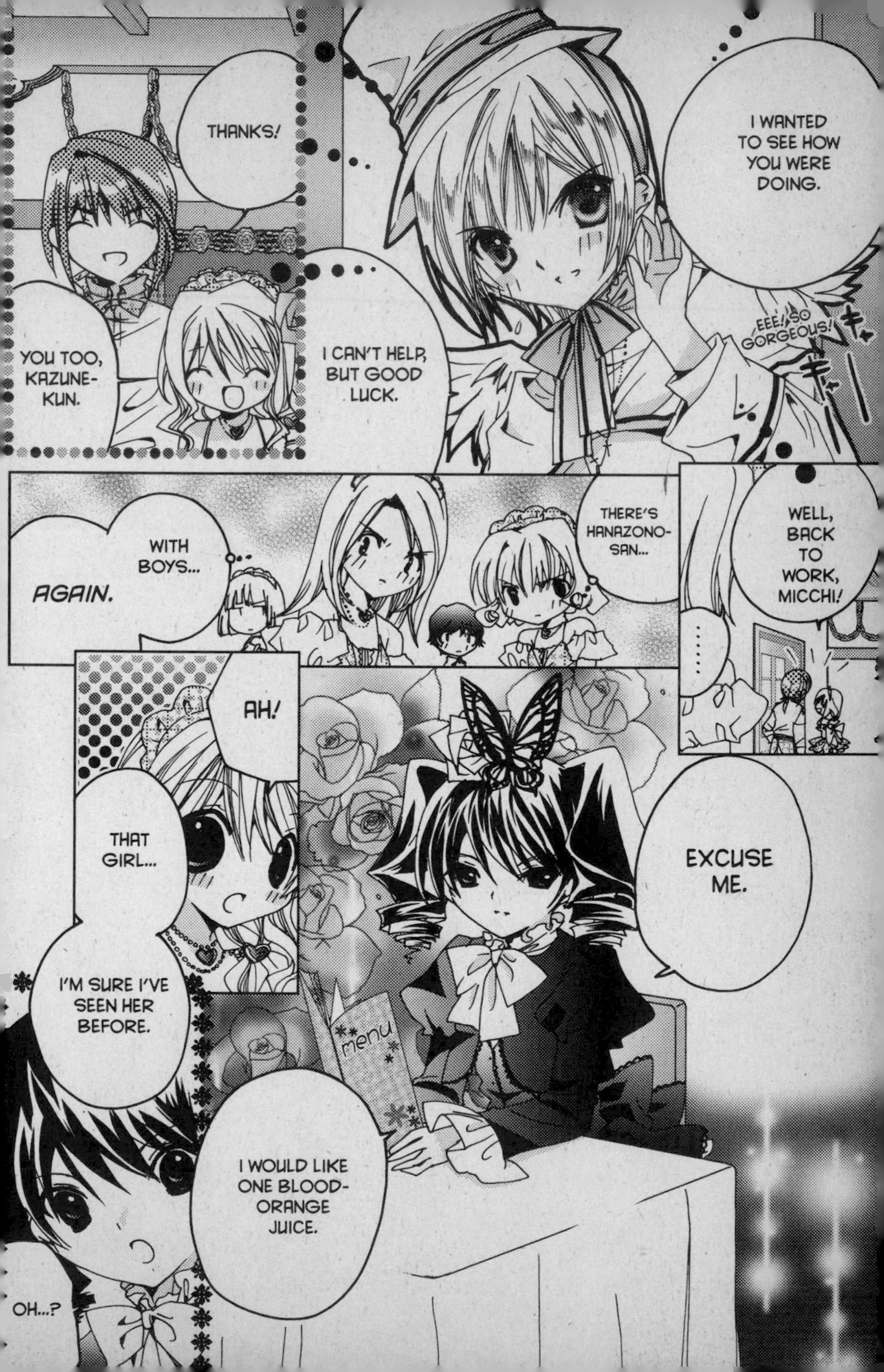
I WANTED TO SEE HOW YOU WERE DOING.
EEE! SO GORGEOUS!
...
I CAN'T HELP, BUT GOOD LUCK.
THANKS!
YOU TOO, KAZUNE-KUN.
WELL, BACK TO WORK, MICCHI!
......
THERE'S HANAZONO-SAN...
WITH BOYS...
AGAIN.
EXCUSE ME.
I WOULD LIKE ONE BLOOD-ORANGE JUICE.
menu
AH!
THAT GIRL...
I'M SURE I'VE SEEN HER BEFORE.
OH...?

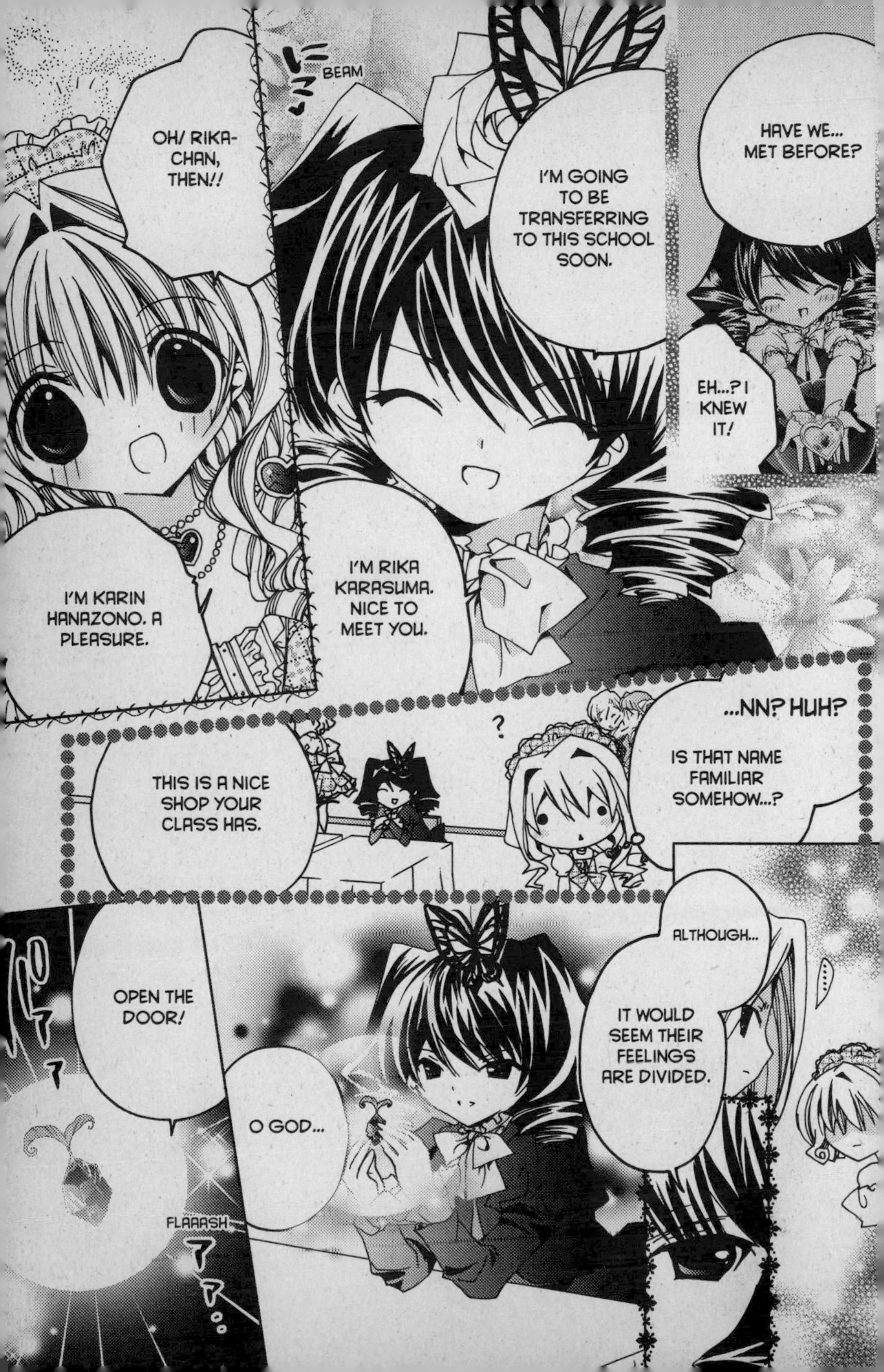
HAVE WE... MET BEFORE?
EH...? I KNEW IT!
BEAM
I'M GOING TO BE TRANSFERRING TO THIS SCHOOL SOON.
I'M RIKA KARASUMA. NICE TO MEET YOU.
OH! RIKA-CHAN, THEN!!
I'M KARIN HANAZONO. A PLEASURE.
...NN? HUH?
IS THAT NAME FAMILIAR SOMEHOW...?
THIS IS A NICE SHOP YOUR CLASS HAS.
ALTHOUGH...
IT WOULD SEEM THEIR FEELINGS ARE DIVIDED.
O GOD...
OPEN THE DOOR!
FLAAASH

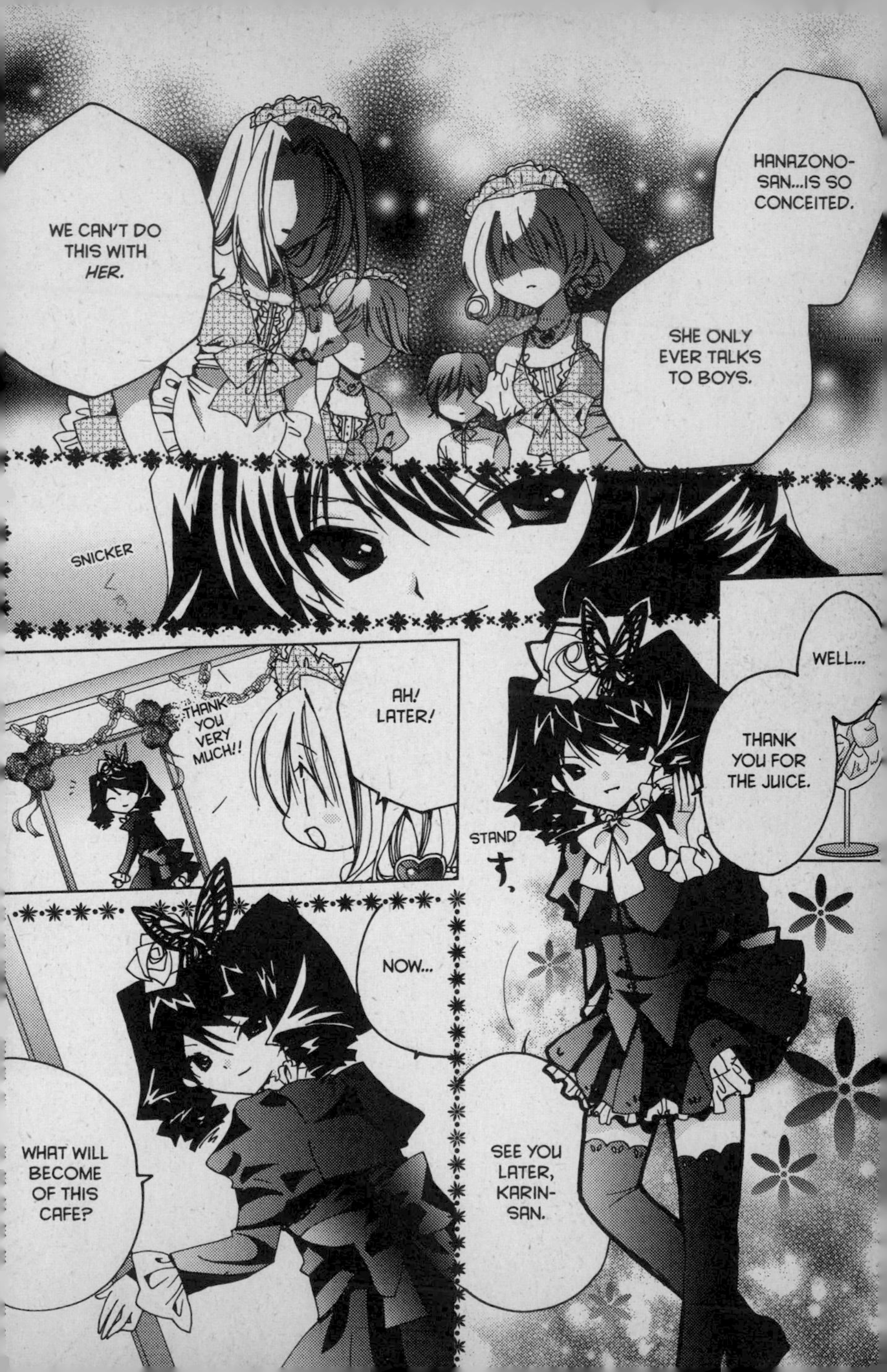
HANAZONO-SAN...IS SO CONCEITED.
SHE ONLY EVER TALKS TO BOYS.
WE CAN'T DO THIS WITH *HER*.
SNICKER
WELL...
THANK YOU FOR THE JUICE.
STAND
す
SEE YOU LATER, KARIN-SAN.
AH! LATER!
THANK YOU VERY MUCH!!
NOW...
WHAT WILL BECOME OF THIS CAFE?

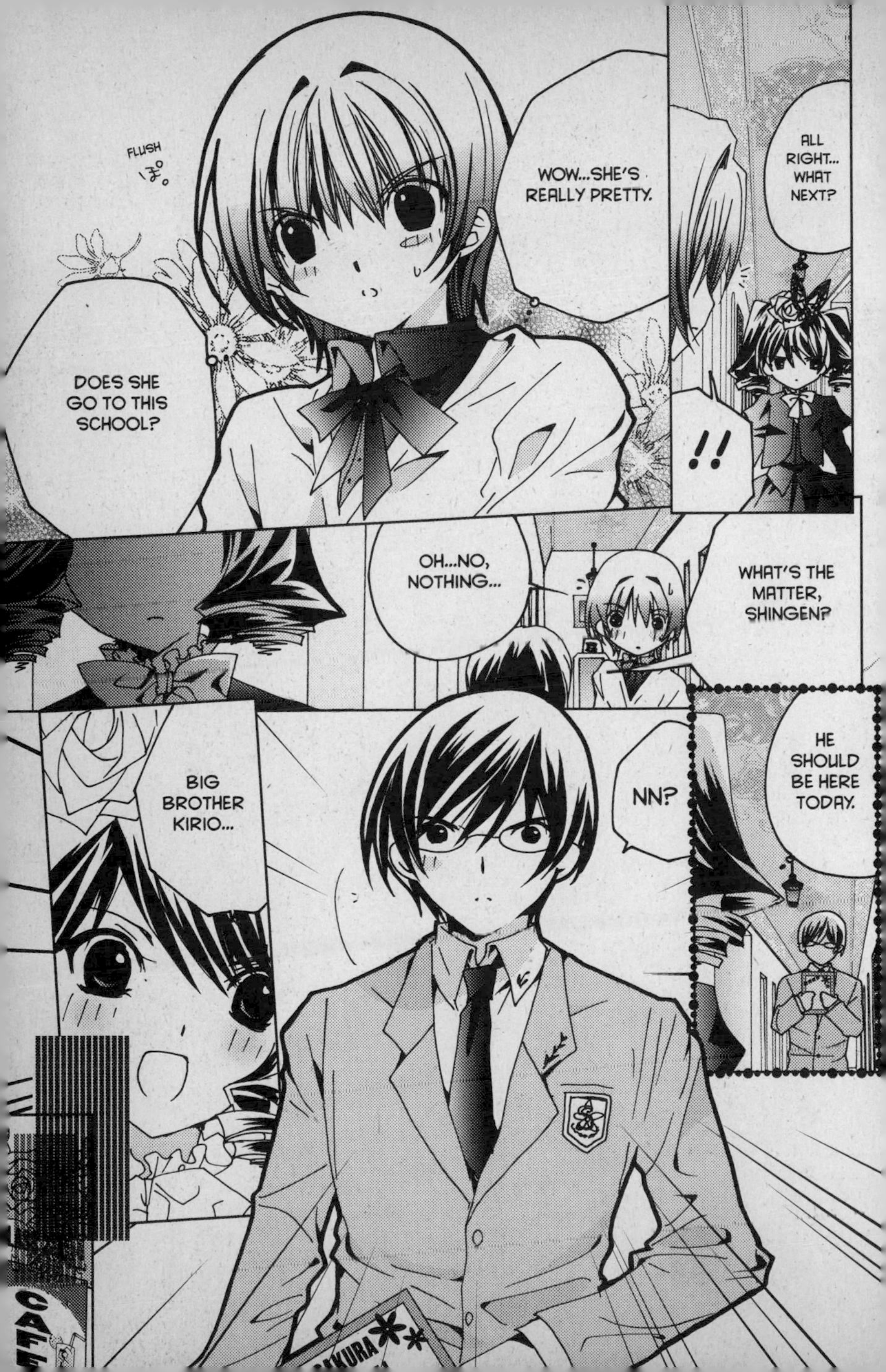
ALL RIGHT... WHAT NEXT?
!!
WOW...SHE'S REALLY PRETTY.
FLUSH
ぽ。
DOES SHE GO TO THIS SCHOOL?
WHAT'S THE MATTER, SHINGEN?
OH...NO, NOTHING...
HE SHOULD BE HERE TODAY.
NN?
BIG BROTHER KIRIO...

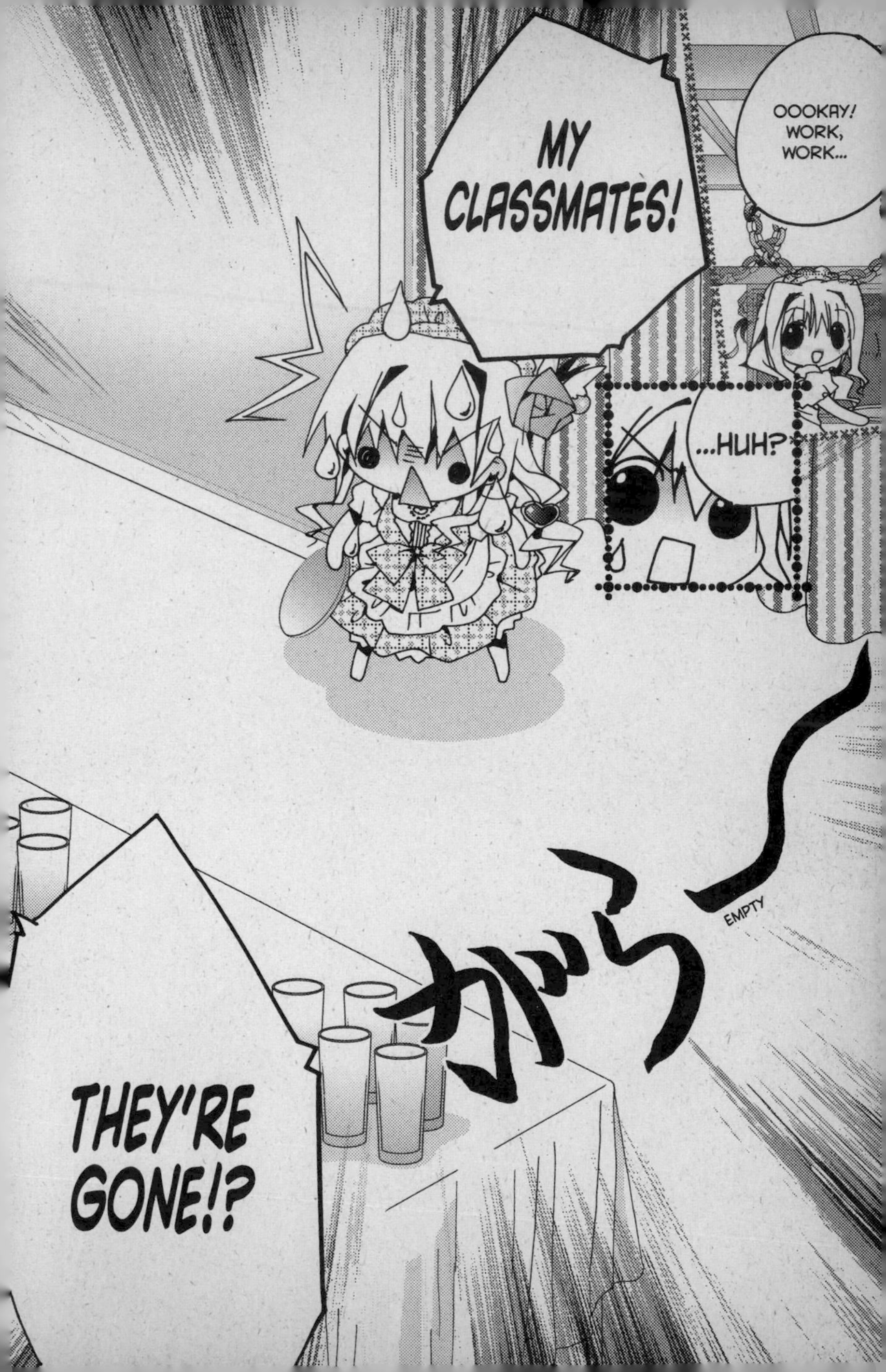
OOOKAY! WORK, WORK...
MY CLASSMATES!
...HUH?
EMPTY
THEY'RE GONE!?

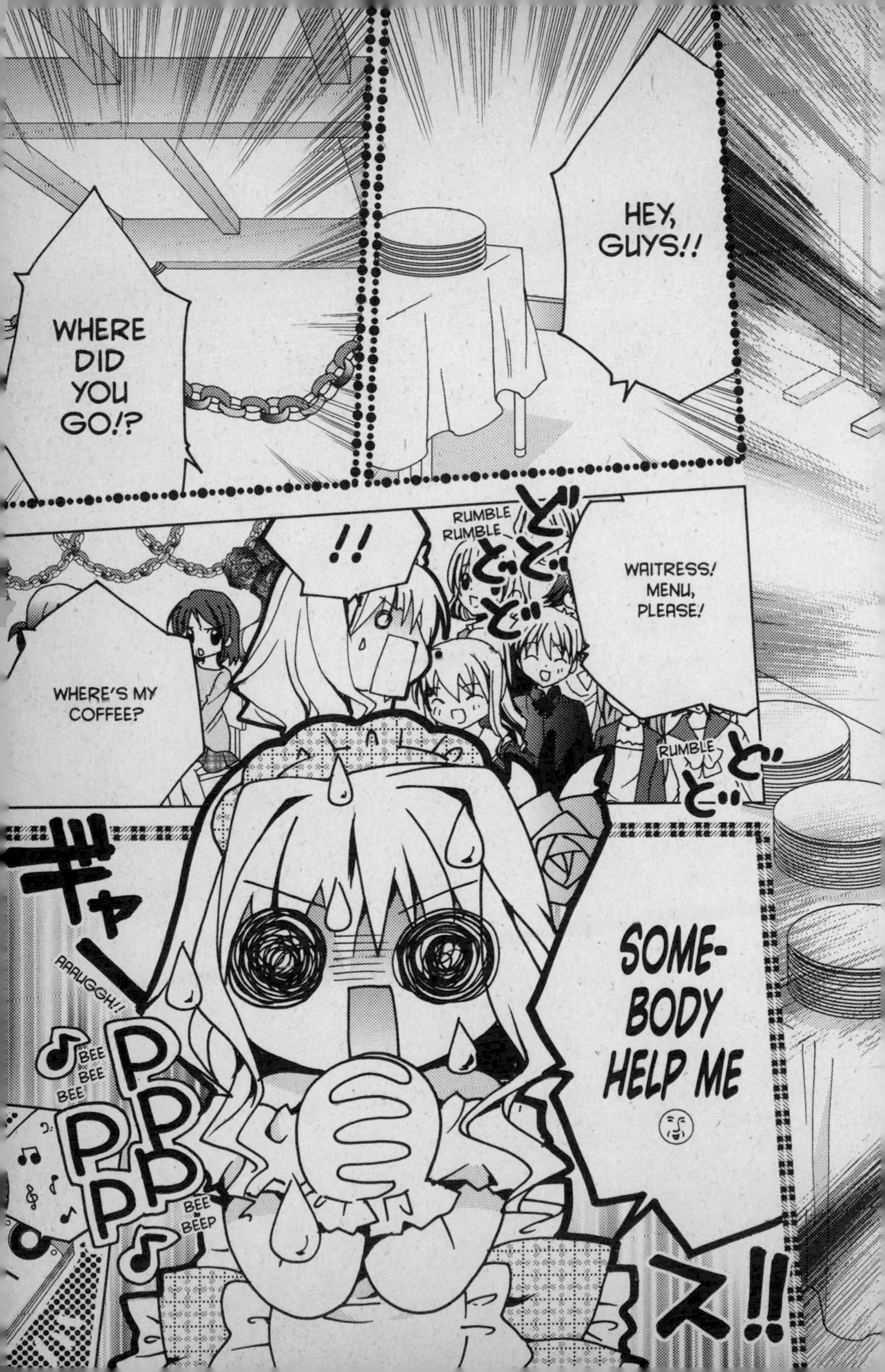
HEY, GUYS!!
WHERE DID YOU GO!?
WAITRESS! MENU, PLEASE!
RUMBLE RUMBLE
!!
WHERE'S MY COFFEE?
RUMBLE
SOME-BODY HELP ME
AAAUGGH!!
BEE BEE BEE
BEE BEEP

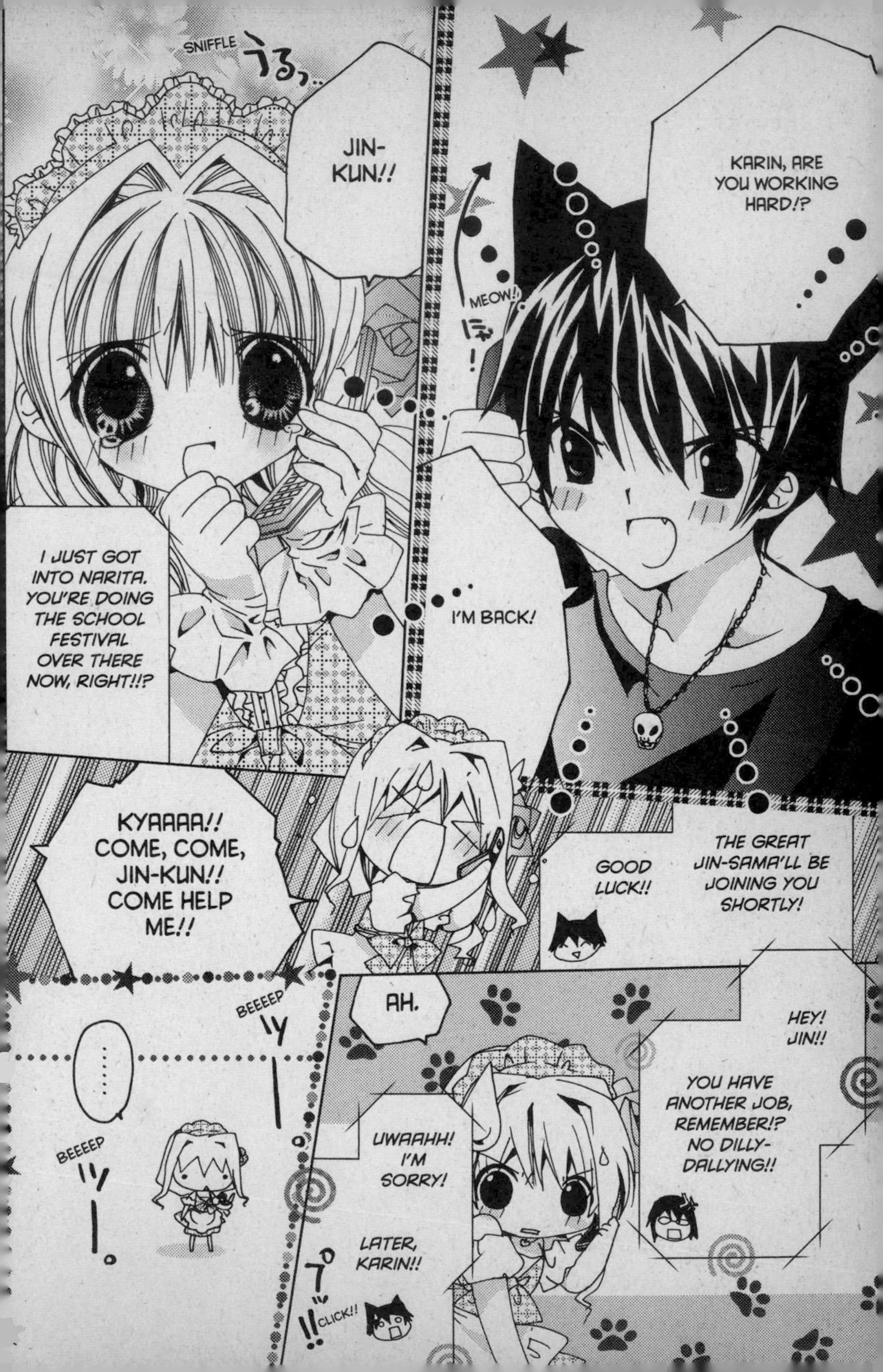
KARIN, ARE YOU WORKING HARD!?
MEOW!
にゃ!
I'M BACK!
SNIFFLE
うるっ...
JIN-KUN!!
I JUST GOT INTO NARITA. YOU'RE DOING THE SCHOOL FESTIVAL OVER THERE NOW, RIGHT!!?
THE GREAT JIN-SAMA'LL BE JOINING YOU SHORTLY!
GOOD LUCK!!
KYAAAA!! COME, COME, JIN-KUN!! COME HELP ME!!
HEY! JIN!!
YOU HAVE ANOTHER JOB, REMEMBER!? NO DILLY-DALLYING!!
AH.
UWAAHH! I'M SORRY!
LATER, KARIN!!
ブツ!!
CLICK!!
BEEEEP
ツー。
......
BEEEEP
ツー。

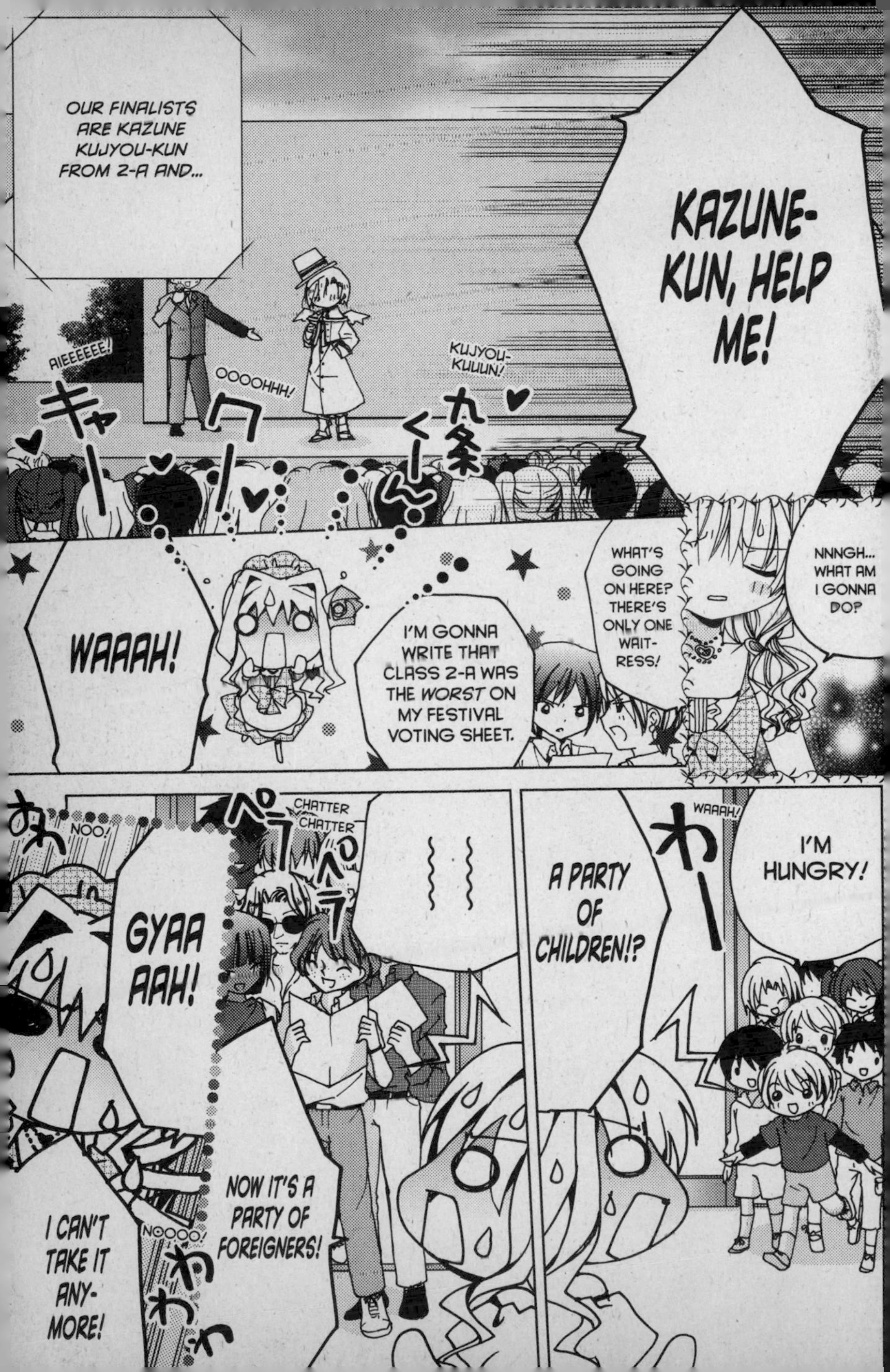
KAZUNE-KUN, HELP ME!
OUR FINALISTS ARE KAZUNE KUJYOU-KUN FROM 2-A AND...
KUJYOU-KUUUN!
九条くーん
OOOOHHH!
ワー
AIEEEEEE!
キャー
NNNGH... WHAT AM I GONNA DO?
WHAT'S GOING ON HERE? THERE'S ONLY ONE WAITRESS!
I'M GONNA WRITE THAT CLASS 2-A WAS THE *WORST* ON MY FESTIVAL VOTING SHEET.
WAAAH!
I'M HUNGRY!
WAAAH!
わー
A PARTY OF CHILDREN!?
......
CHATTER CHATTER
ぺらぺら
NOO!
GYAA AAH!
NOW IT'S A PARTY OF FOREIGNERS!
NOOOO!
I CAN'T TAKE IT ANY-MORE!

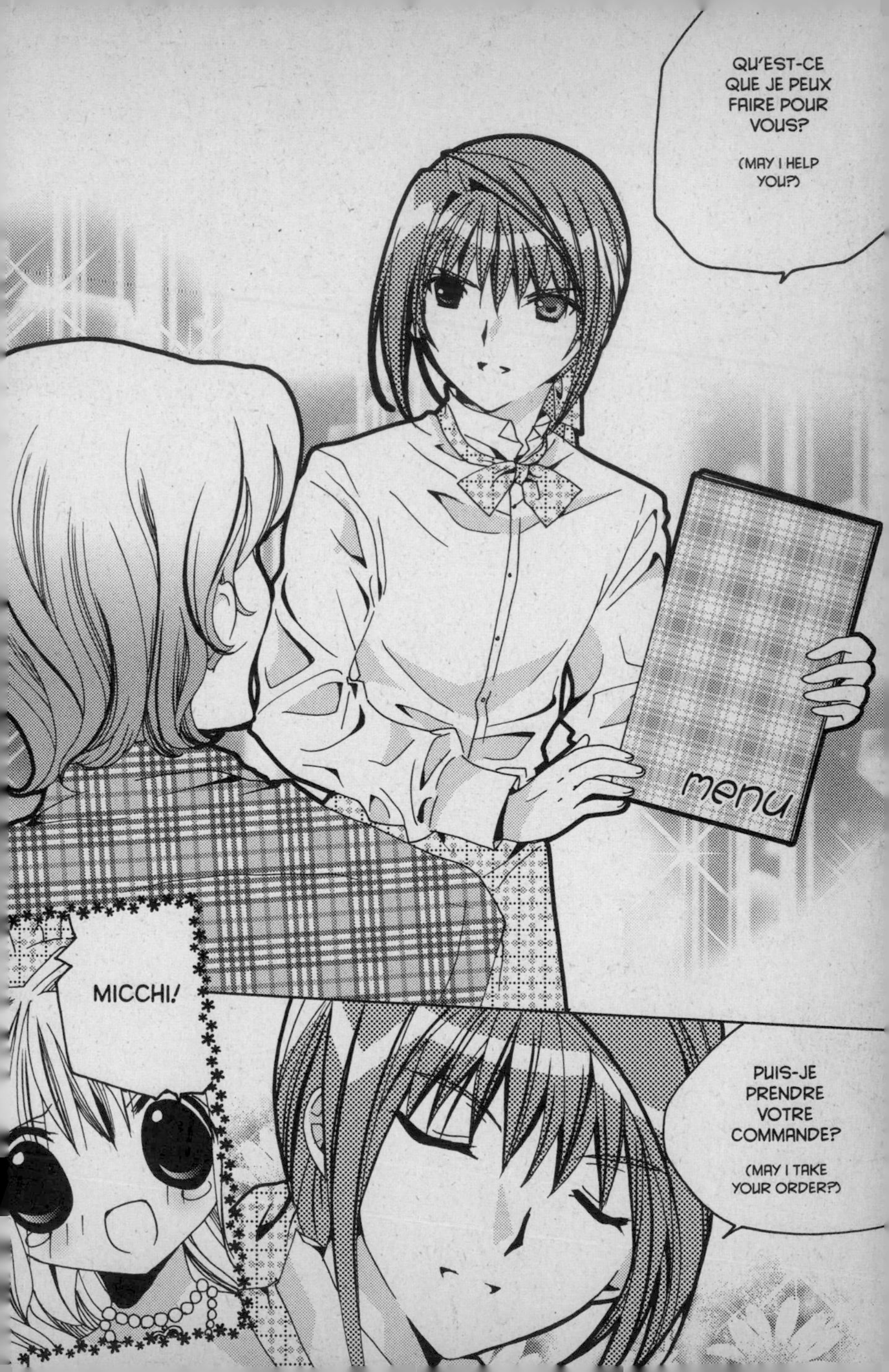
QU'EST-CE QUE JE PEUX FAIRE POUR VOUS?
(MAY I HELP YOU?)
menu
PUIS-JE PRENDRE VOTRE COMMANDE?
(MAY I TAKE YOUR ORDER?)
MICCHI!

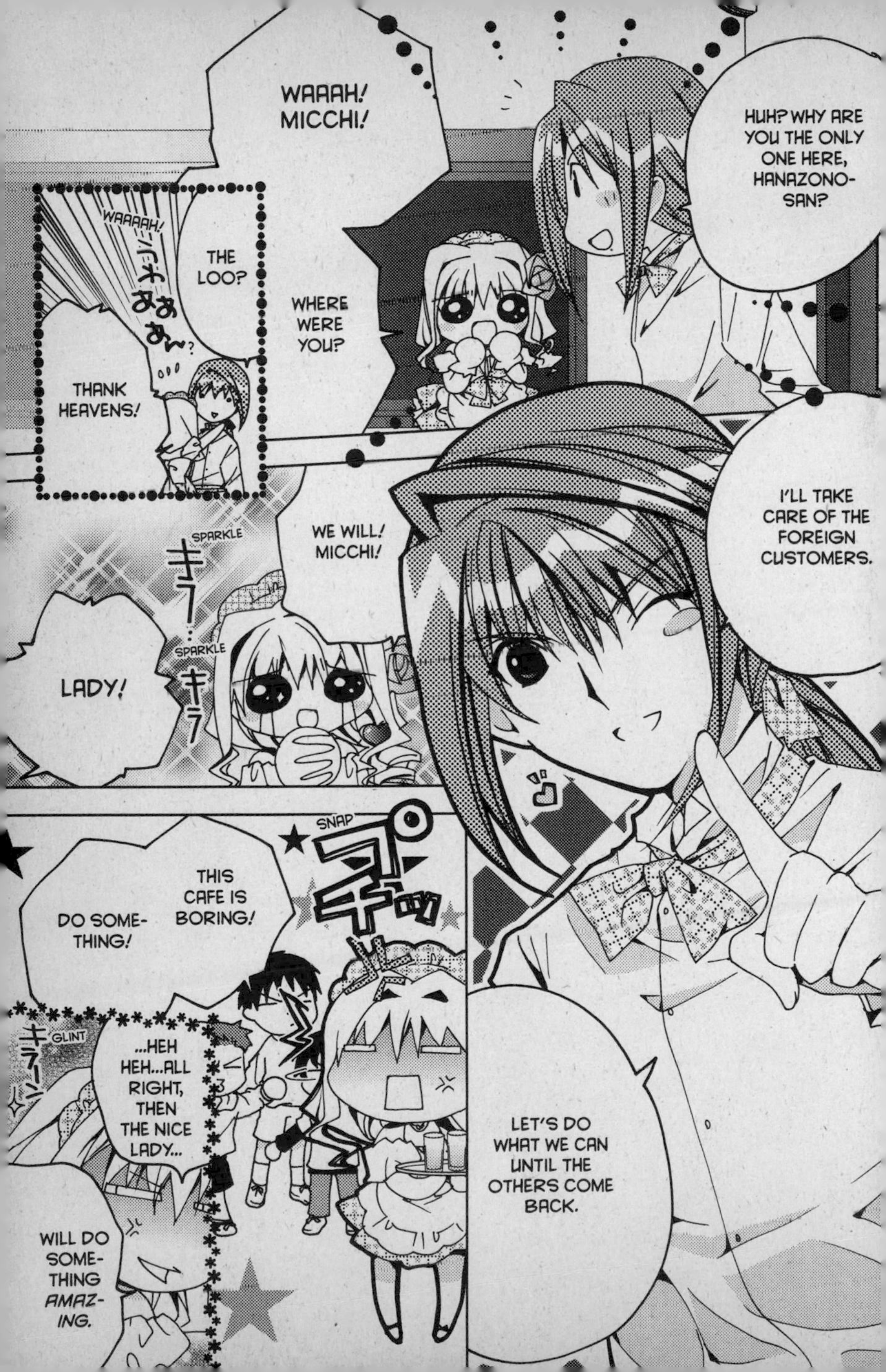
HUH? WHY ARE YOU THE ONLY ONE HERE, HANAZONO-SAN?
WAAAH! MICCHI!
WHERE WERE YOU?
WAAAAH!
THE LOO?
THANK HEAVENS!
I'LL TAKE CARE OF THE FOREIGN CUSTOMERS.
LET'S DO WHAT WE CAN UNTIL THE OTHERS COME BACK.
WE WILL! MICCHI!
SPARKLE
SPARKLE
LADY!
SNAP
THIS CAFE IS BORING!
DO SOME-THING!
GLINT
...HEH HEH...ALL RIGHT, THEN THE NICE LADY...
WILL DO SOME-THING AMAZ-ING.

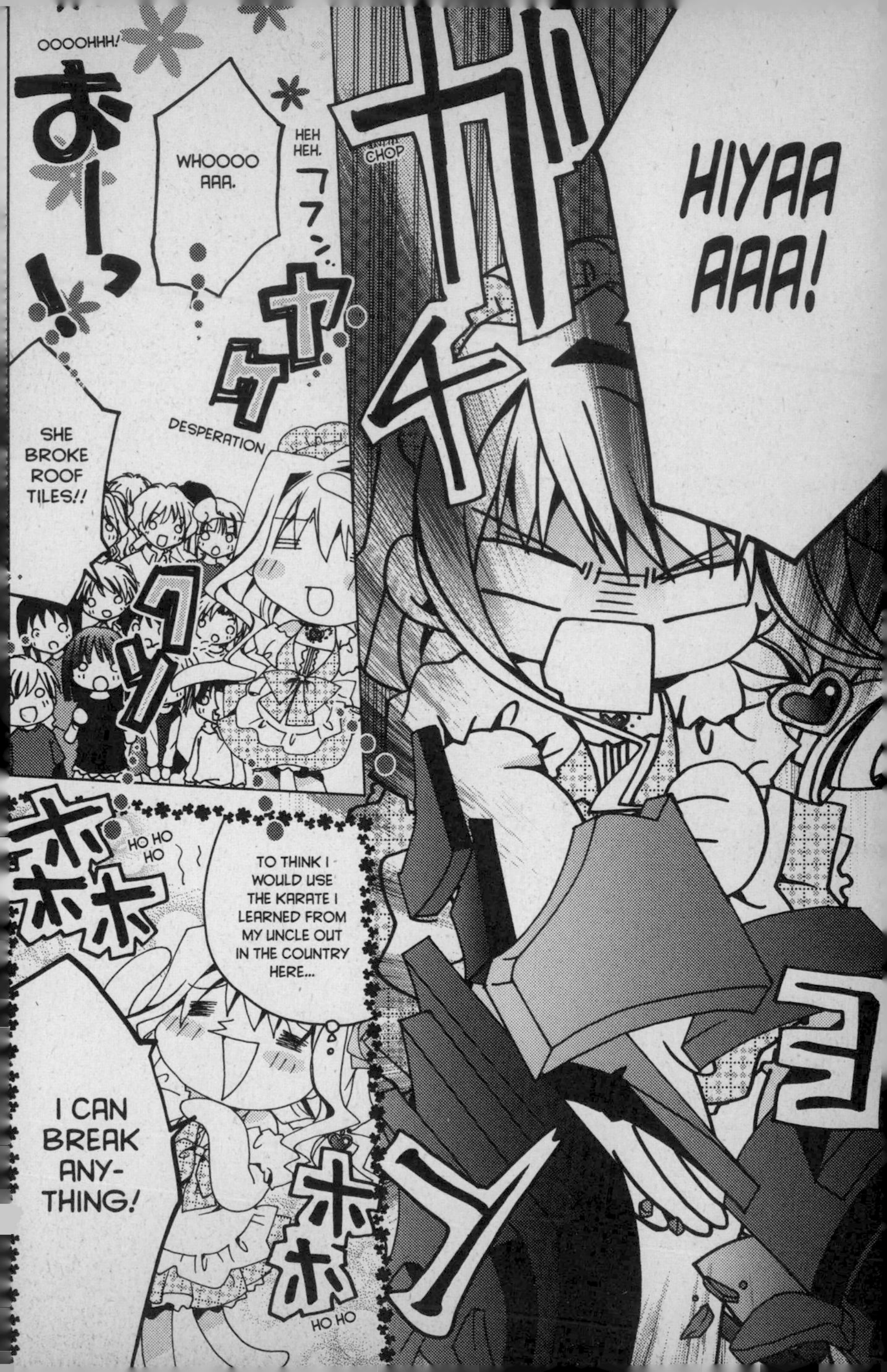
HIYAA AAA!
CHOP
HEH HEH.
WHOOOO AAA.
OOOOHHH!
DESPERATION
SHE BROKE ROOF TILES!!
TO THINK I WOULD USE THE KARATE I LEARNED FROM MY UNCLE OUT IN THE COUNTRY HERE...
HO HO HO
I CAN BREAK ANY-THING!
HO HO

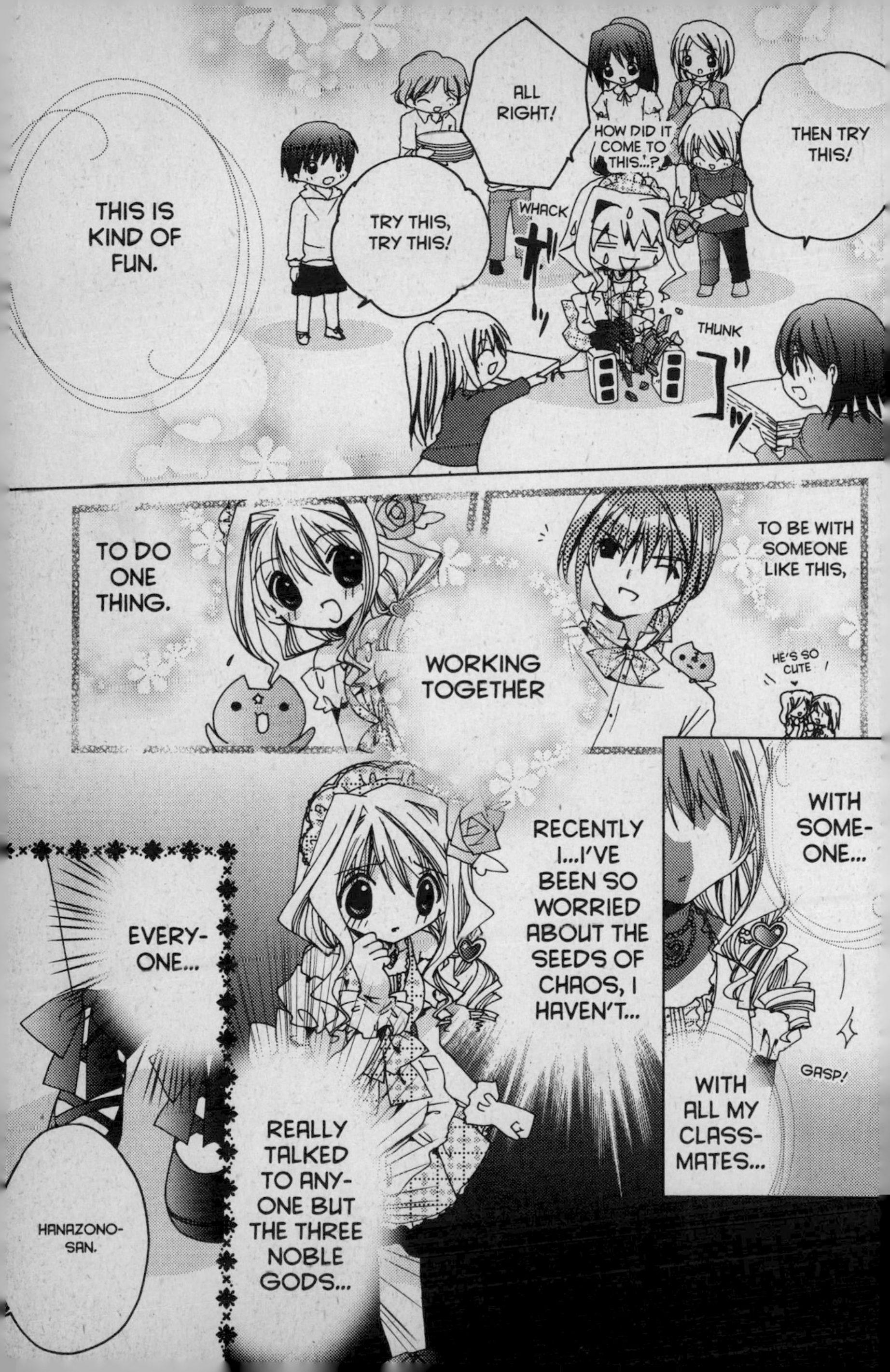
THEN TRY THIS!
HOW DID IT COME TO THIS...?
ALL RIGHT!
WHACK
THUNK
TRY THIS, TRY THIS!
THIS IS KIND OF FUN.
TO BE WITH SOMEONE LIKE THIS,
HE'S SO CUTE!
WORKING TOGETHER
TO DO ONE THING.
WITH SOME-ONE...
GASP!
WITH ALL MY CLASS-MATES...
RECENTLY I...I'VE BEEN SO WORRIED ABOUT THE SEEDS OF CHAOS, I HAVEN'T...
REALLY TALKED TO ANY-ONE BUT THE THREE NOBLE GODS...
EVERY-ONE...
HANAZONO-SAN.

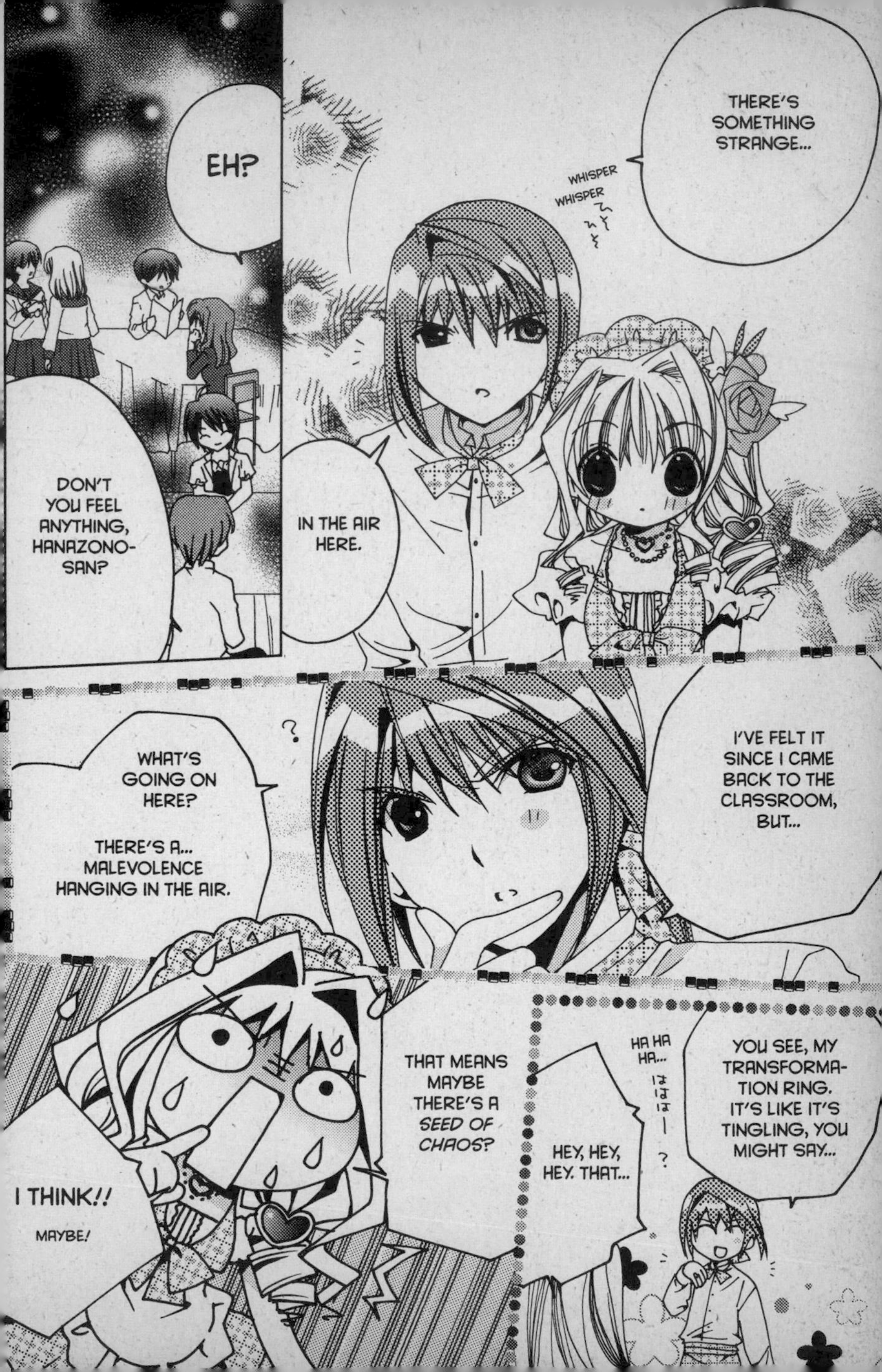
THERE'S SOMETHING STRANGE...
WHISPER WHISPER
ひそひそ
IN THE AIR HERE.
EH?
DON'T YOU FEEL ANYTHING, HANAZONO-SAN?
I'VE FELT IT SINCE I CAME BACK TO THE CLASSROOM, BUT...
?
WHAT'S GOING ON HERE?
THERE'S A... MALEVOLENCE HANGING IN THE AIR.
YOU SEE, MY TRANSFORMATION RING. IT'S LIKE IT'S TINGLING, YOU MIGHT SAY...
HA HA HA...
はははー
HEY, HEY, HEY. THAT...
?
THAT MEANS MAYBE THERE'S A *SEED OF CHAOS*?
I THINK!!
MAYBE!

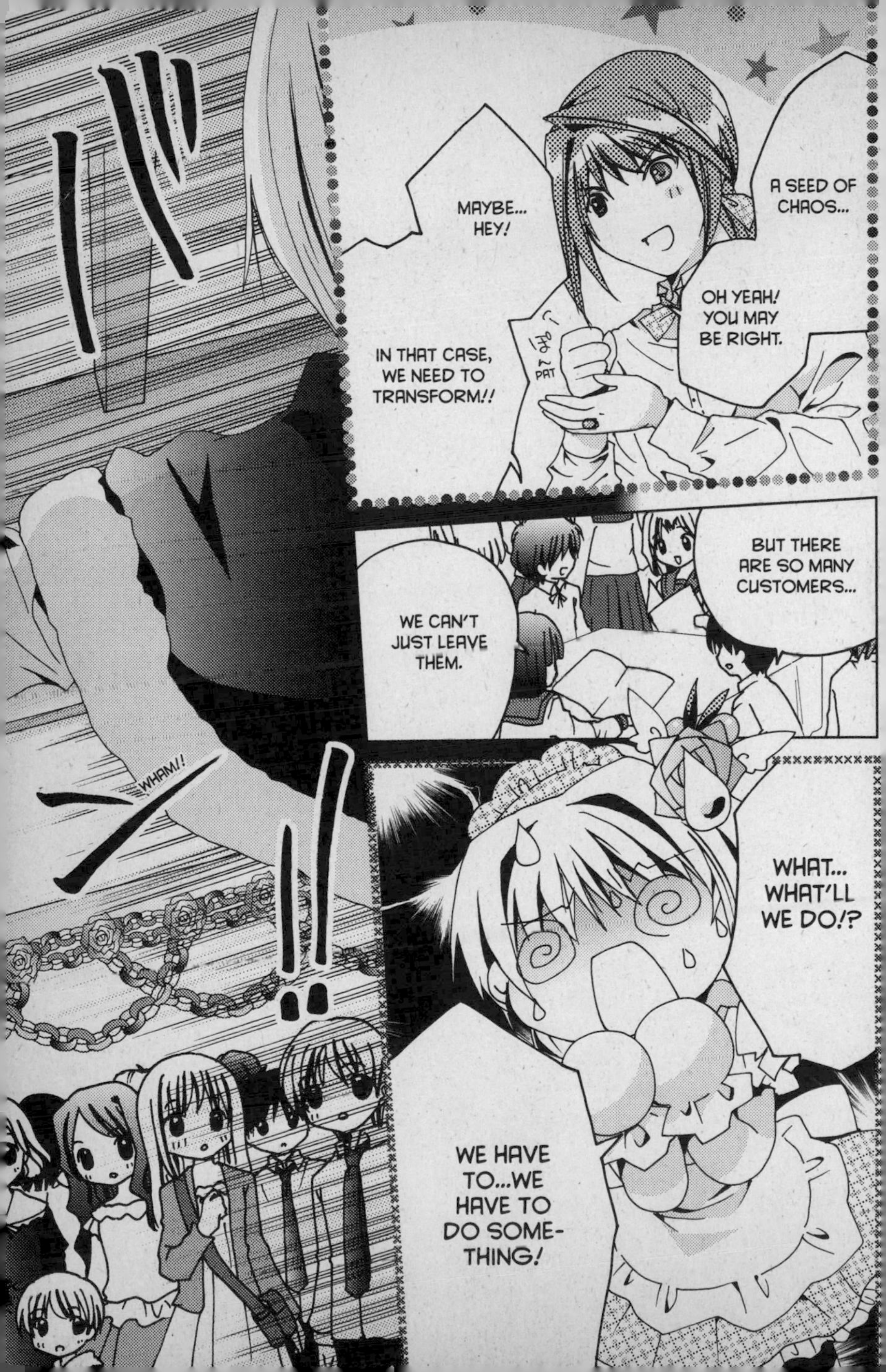
A SEED OF CHAOS...
OH YEAH! YOU MAY BE RIGHT.
PAT
MAYBE... HEY!
IN THAT CASE, WE NEED TO TRANSFORM!!
BUT THERE ARE SO MANY CUSTOMERS...
WE CAN'T JUST LEAVE THEM.
WHAT... WHAT'LL WE DO!?
WE HAVE TO...WE HAVE TO DO SOME-THING!
WHAM!
!!

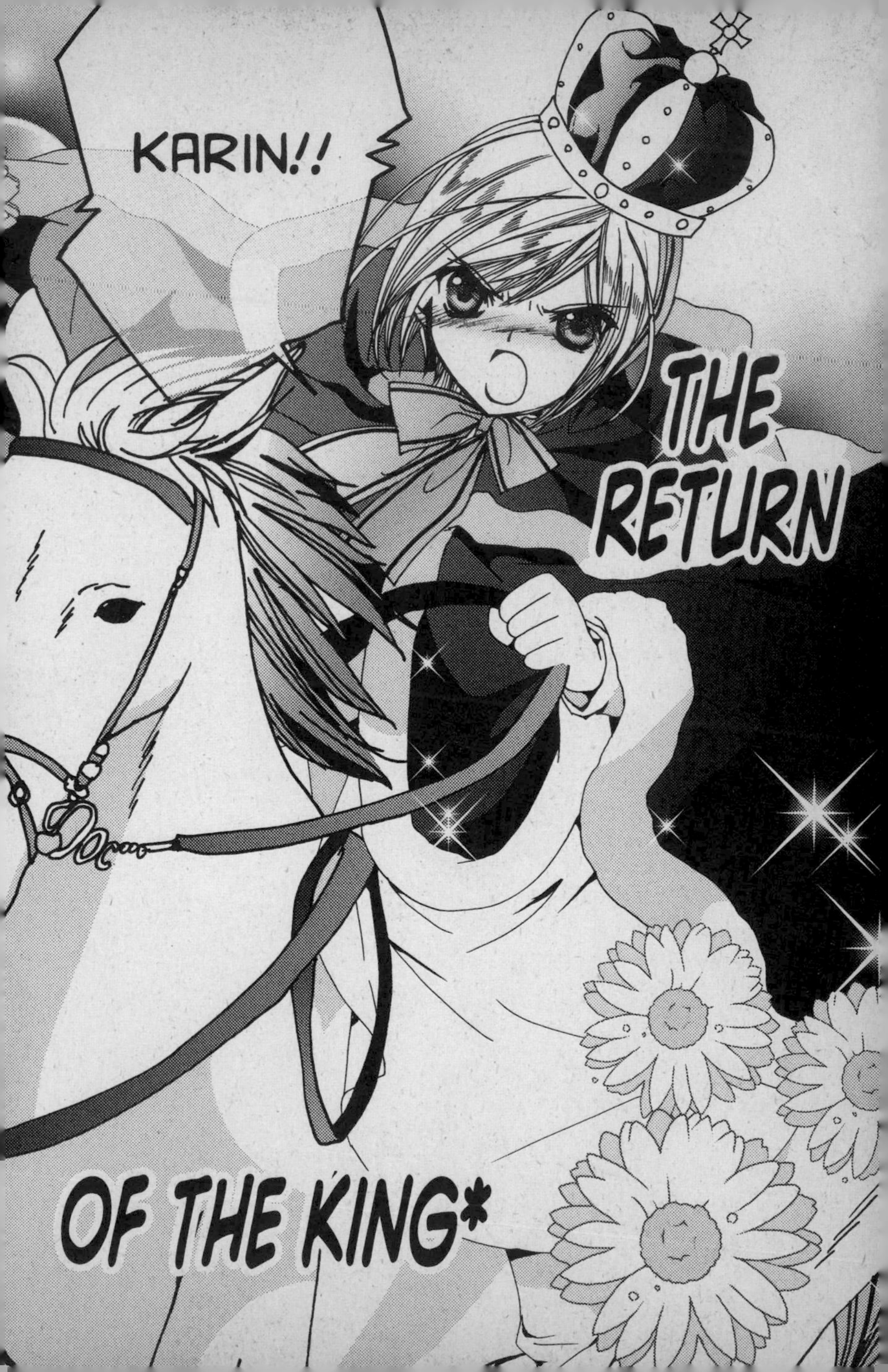
KARIN!!
THE RETURN
OF THE KING*

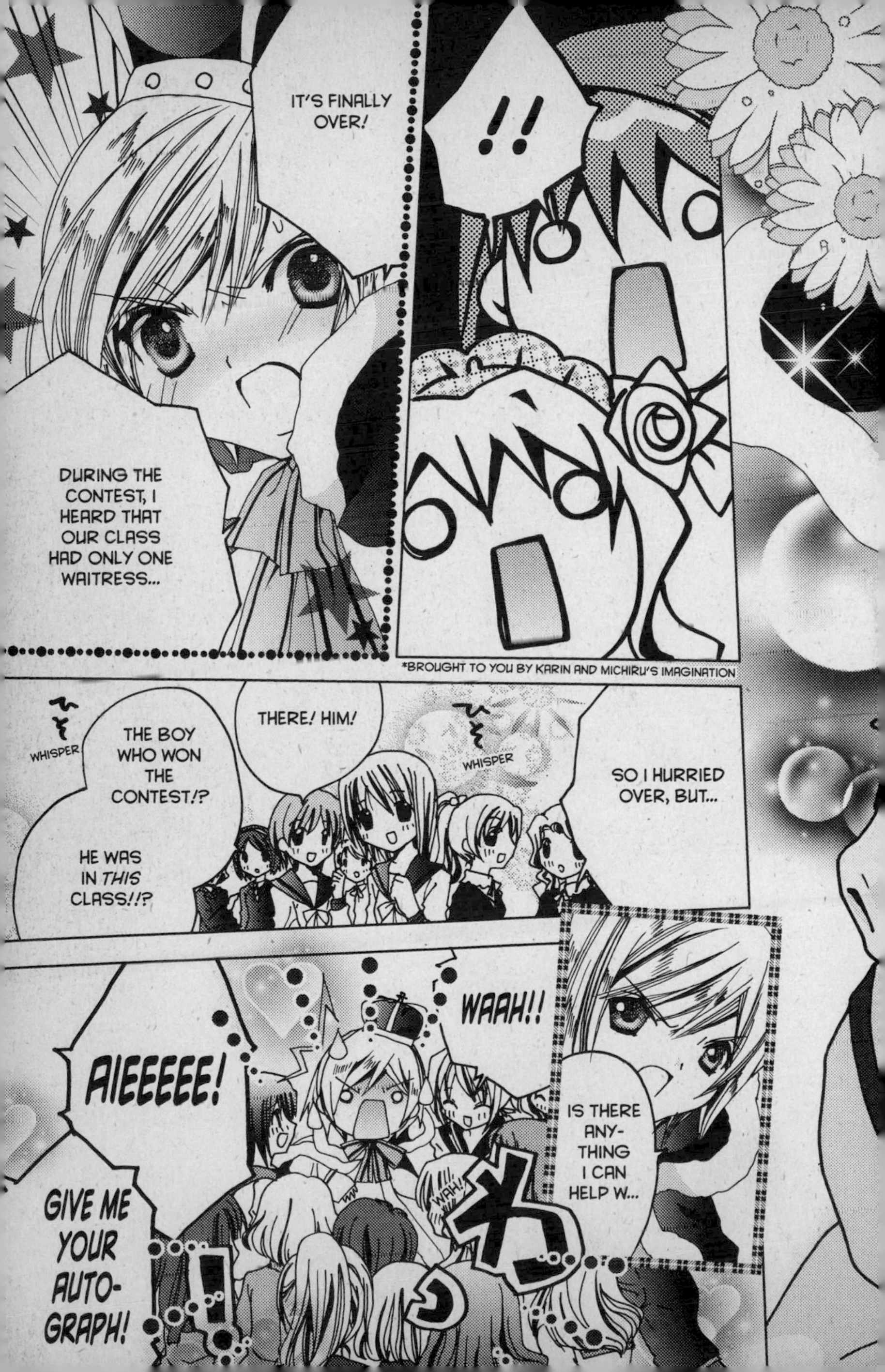
!!
*BROUGHT TO YOU BY KARIN AND MICHIRU'S IMAGINATION
IT'S FINALLY OVER!
DURING THE CONTEST, I HEARD THAT OUR CLASS HAD ONLY ONE WAITRESS...
SO I HURRIED OVER, BUT...
WHISPER
THERE! HIM!
WHISPER
THE BOY WHO WON THE CONTEST!?
HE WAS IN *THIS* CLASS!!?
IS THERE ANY-THING I CAN HELP W...
WAAH!!
WAH!
AIEEEEE!
GIVE ME YOUR AUTO-GRAPH!

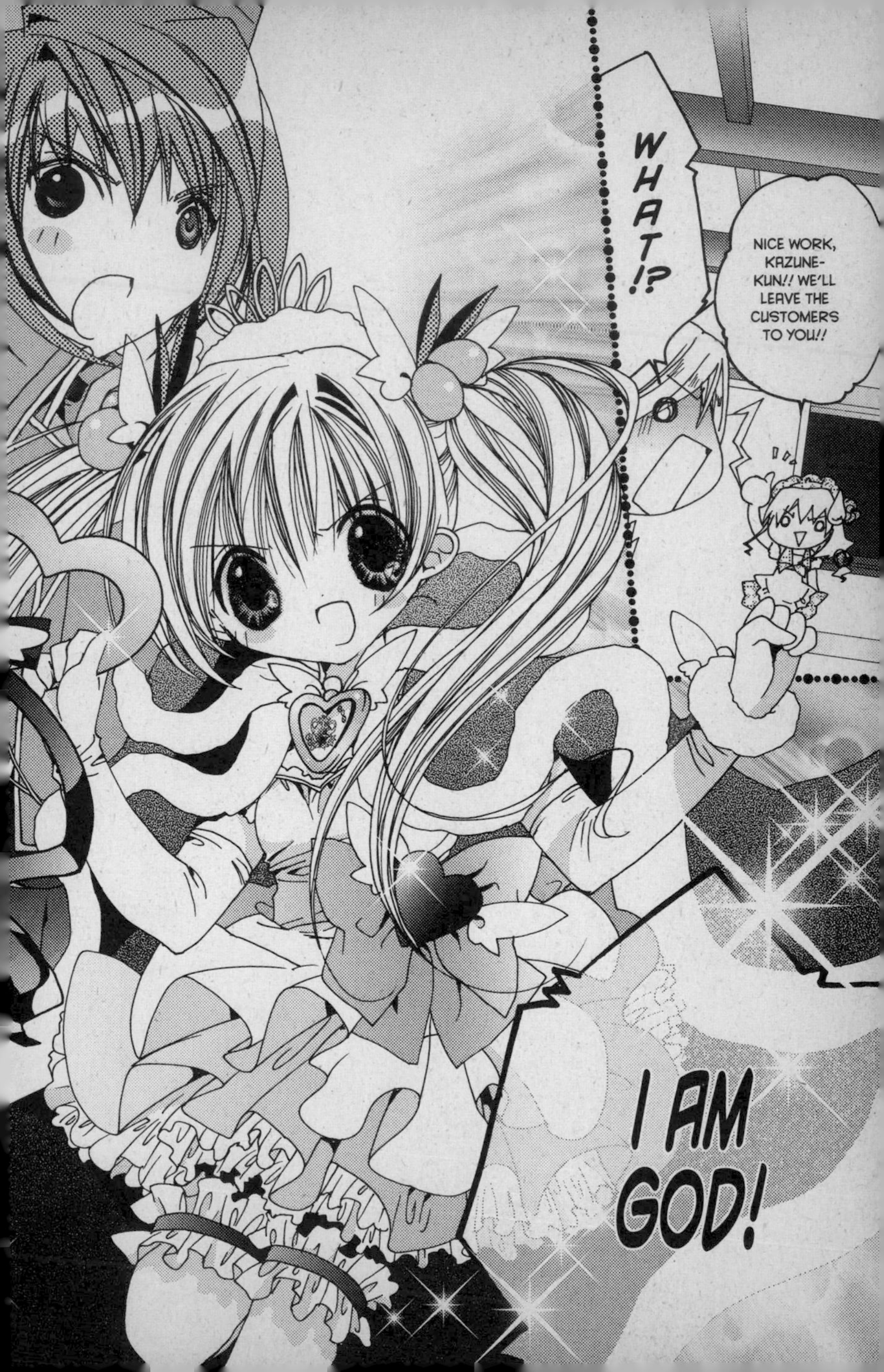
NICE WORK, KAZUNE-KUN!! WE'LL LEAVE THE CUSTOMERS TO YOU!!
WHAT!?
I AM GOD!

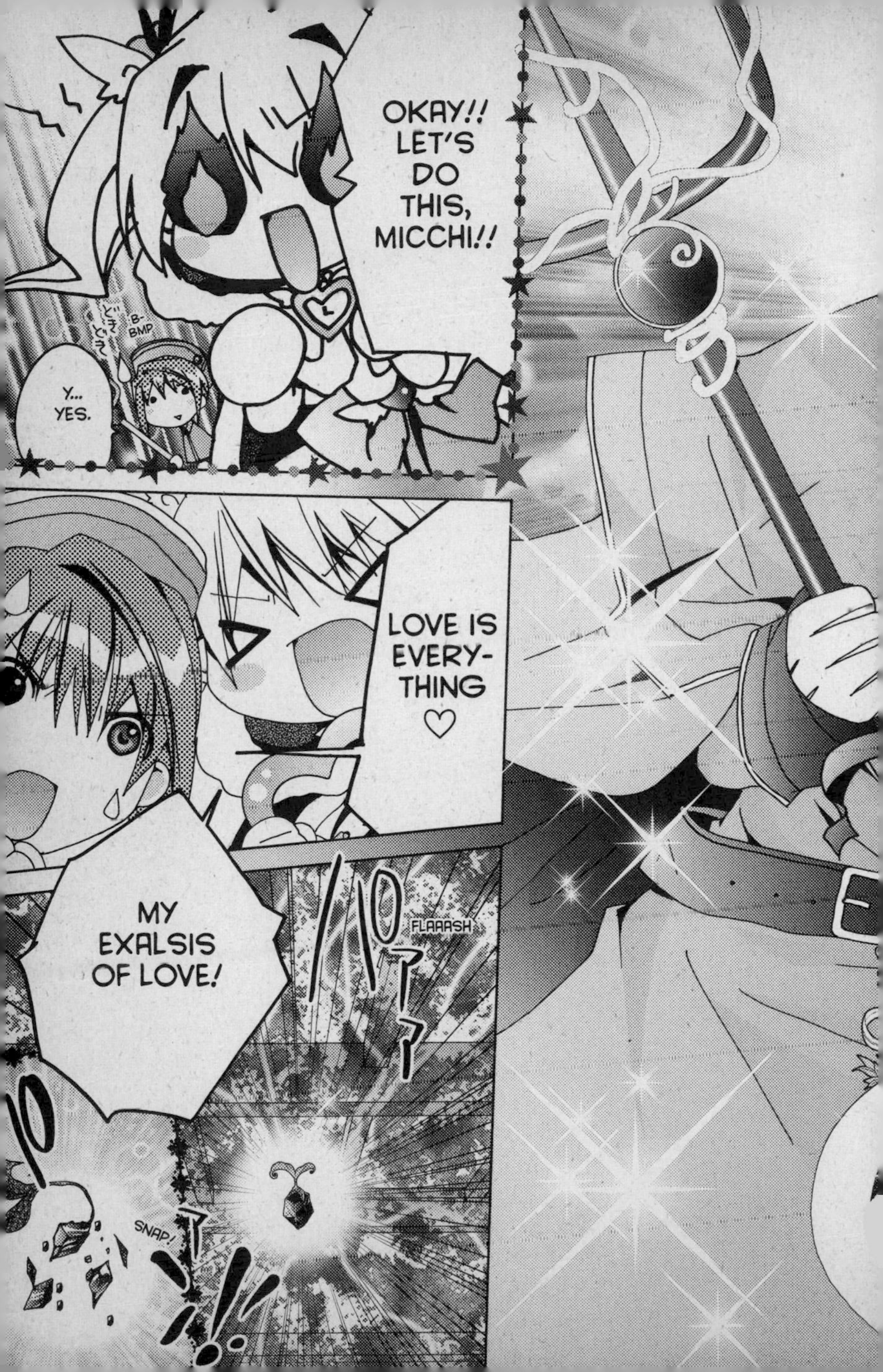
OKAY!! LET'S DO THIS, MICCHI!!
B-BMP
Y... YES.
LOVE IS EVERY-THING ♡
MY EXALSIS OF LOVE!
FLAAASH
SNAP!

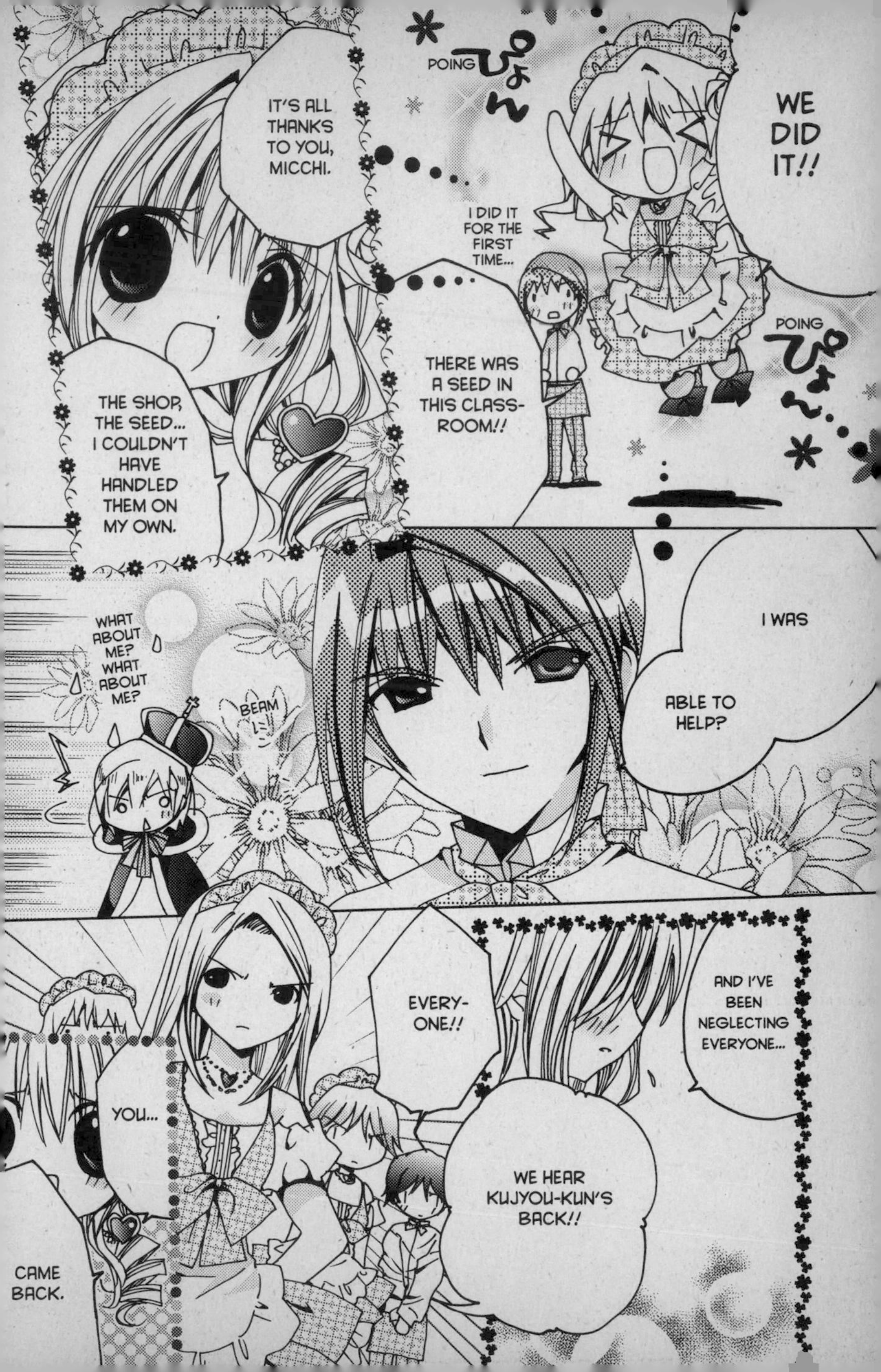

WE DID IT!!
POING ぴょん
I DID IT FOR THE FIRST TIME...
THERE WAS A SEED IN THIS CLASS-ROOM!!
POING ぴょん
IT'S ALL THANKS TO YOU, MICCHI.
THE SHOP, THE SEED... I COULDN'T HAVE HANDLED THEM ON MY OWN.
I WAS
ABLE TO HELP?
WHAT ABOUT ME? WHAT ABOUT ME?
BEAM
AND I'VE BEEN NEGLECTING EVERYONE...
EVERY-ONE!!
WE HEAR KUJYOU-KUN'S BACK!!
YOU...
CAME BACK.

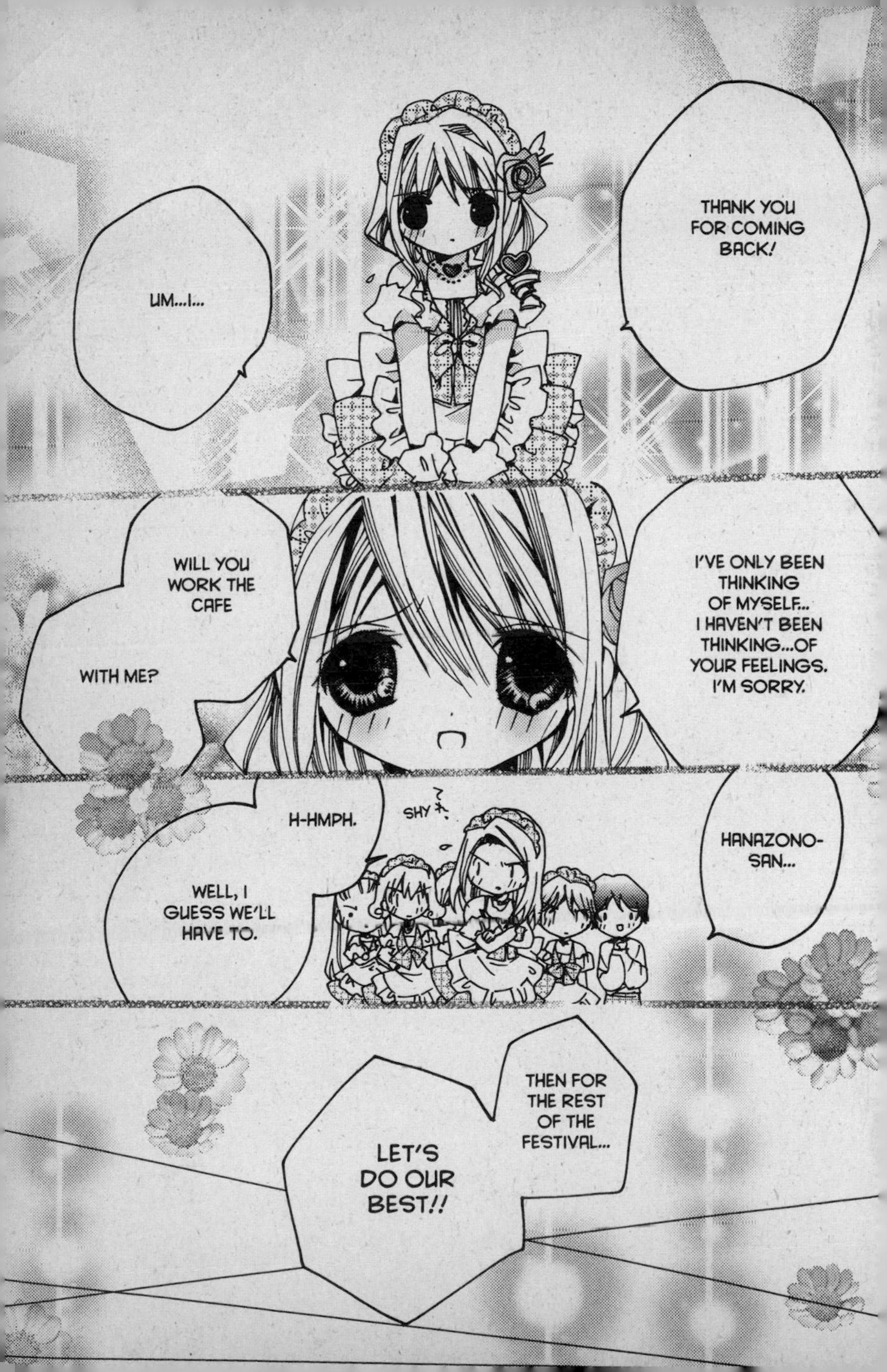
THANK YOU FOR COMING BACK!
UM...I...
I'VE ONLY BEEN THINKING OF MYSELF... I HAVEN'T BEEN THINKING...OF YOUR FEELINGS. I'M SORRY.
WILL YOU WORK THE CAFE
WITH ME?
HANAZONO-SAN...
SHY
H-HMPH.
WELL, I GUESS WE'LL HAVE TO.
THEN FOR THE REST OF THE FESTIVAL...
LET'S DO OUR BEST!!

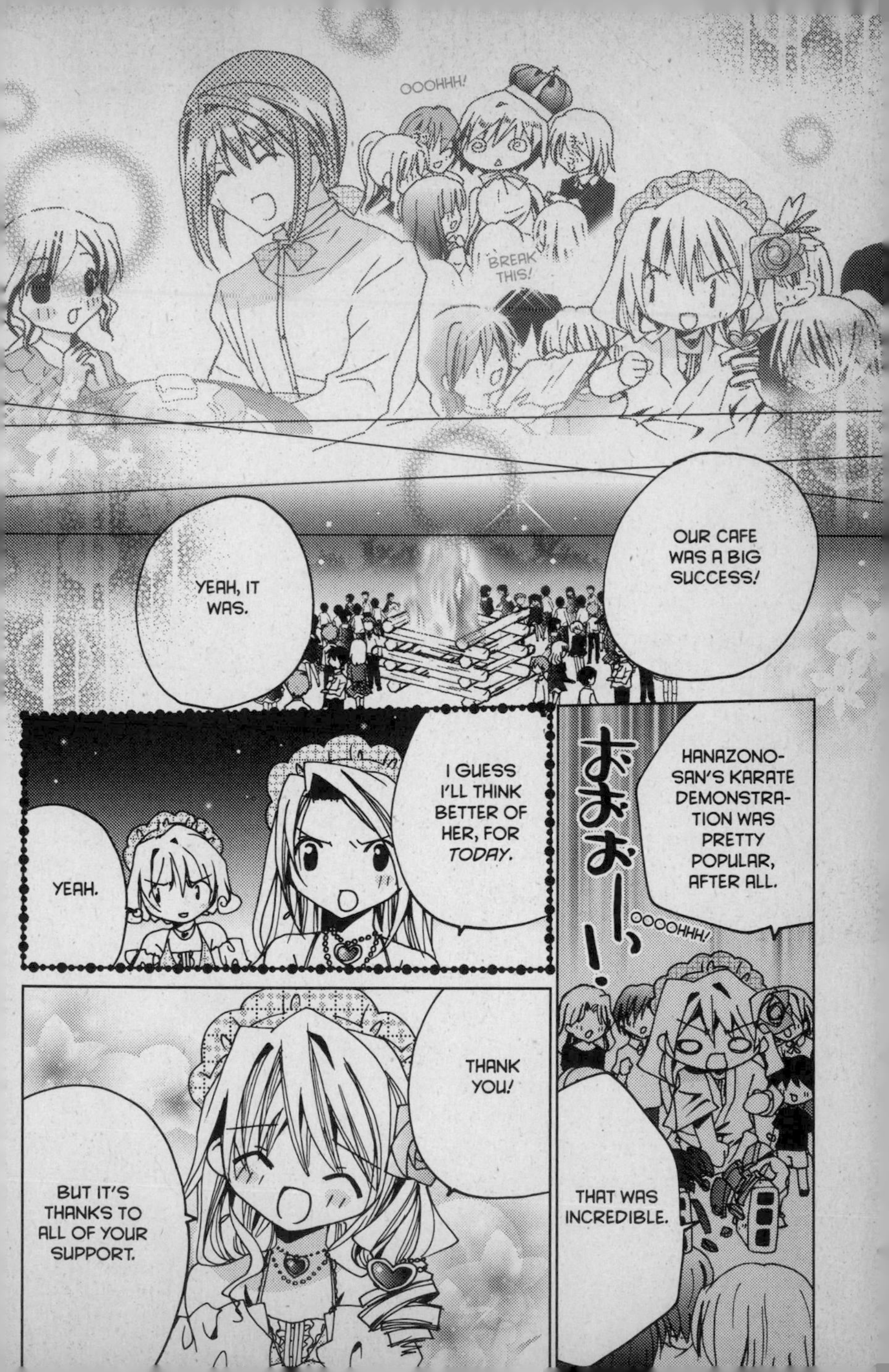
OOOHHH!
BREAK THIS!
OUR CAFE WAS A BIG SUCCESS!
YEAH, IT WAS.
HANAZONO-SAN'S KARATE DEMONSTRATION WAS PRETTY POPULAR, AFTER ALL.
OOOOHHH!
THAT WAS INCREDIBLE.
I GUESS I'LL THINK BETTER OF HER, FOR *TODAY*.
YEAH.
THANK YOU!
BUT IT'S THANKS TO ALL OF YOUR SUPPORT.

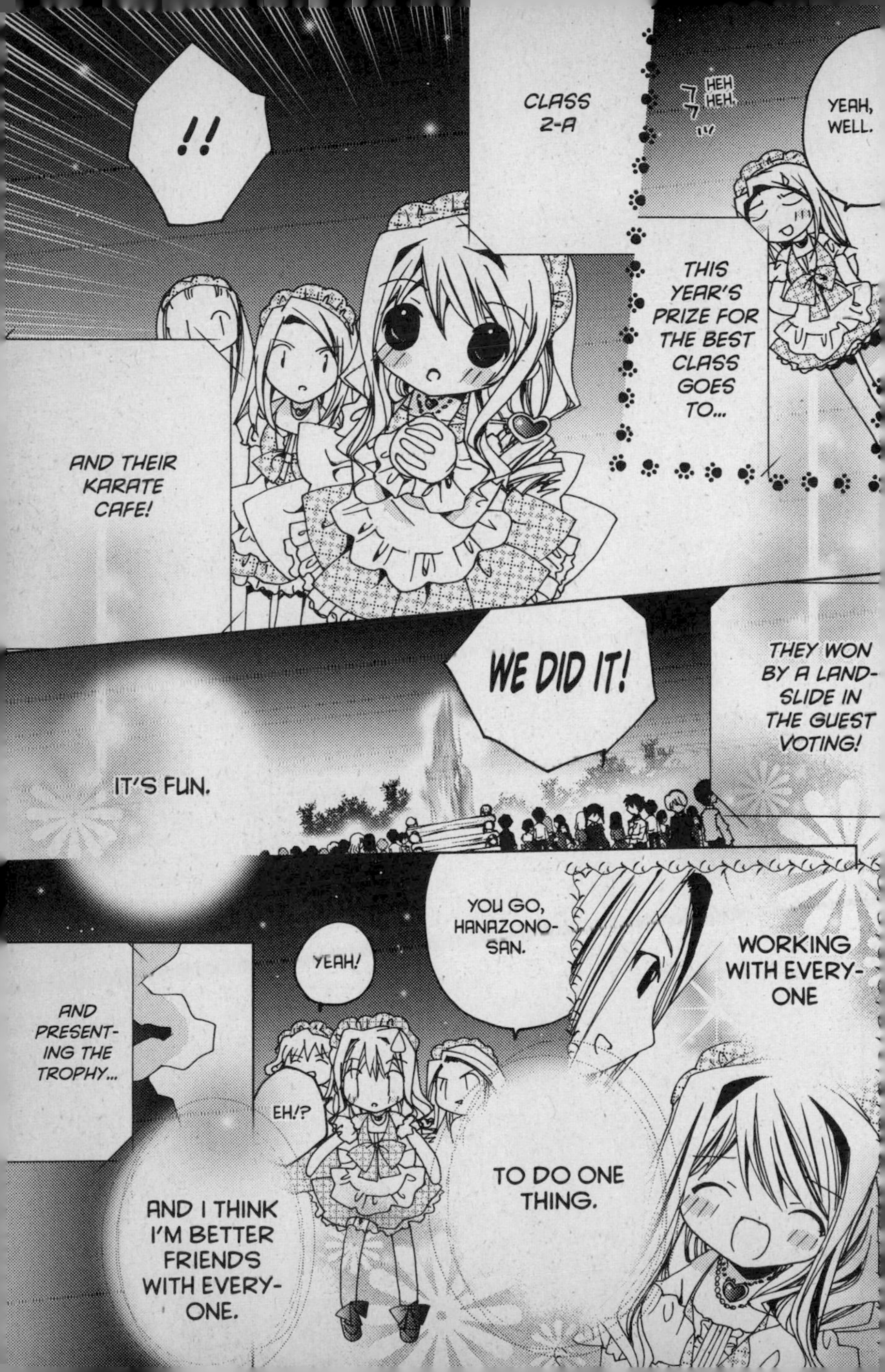
YEAH, WELL.
HEH HEH.
THIS YEAR'S PRIZE FOR THE BEST CLASS GOES TO...
CLASS 2-A
AND THEIR KARATE CAFE!
!!
THEY WON BY A LAND-SLIDE IN THE GUEST VOTING!
WE DID IT!
IT'S FUN.
WORKING WITH EVERY-ONE
YOU GO, HANAZONO-SAN.
TO DO ONE THING.
YEAH!
EH!?
AND I THINK I'M BETTER FRIENDS WITH EVERY-ONE.
AND PRESENT-ING THE TROPHY...

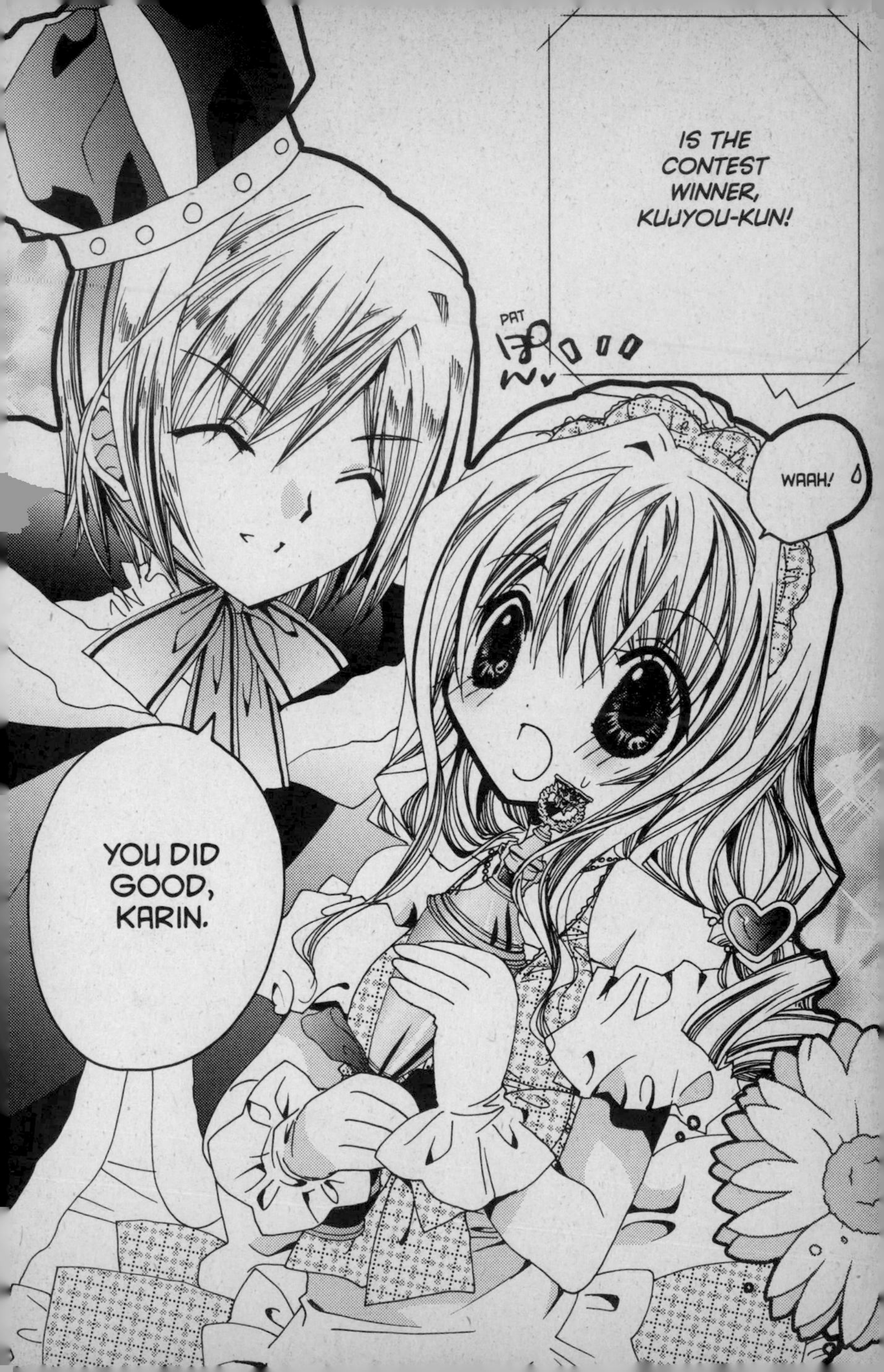
IS THE CONTEST WINNER, KUJYOU-KUN!
PAT
ぽんっ
WAAH!
YOU DID GOOD, KARIN.

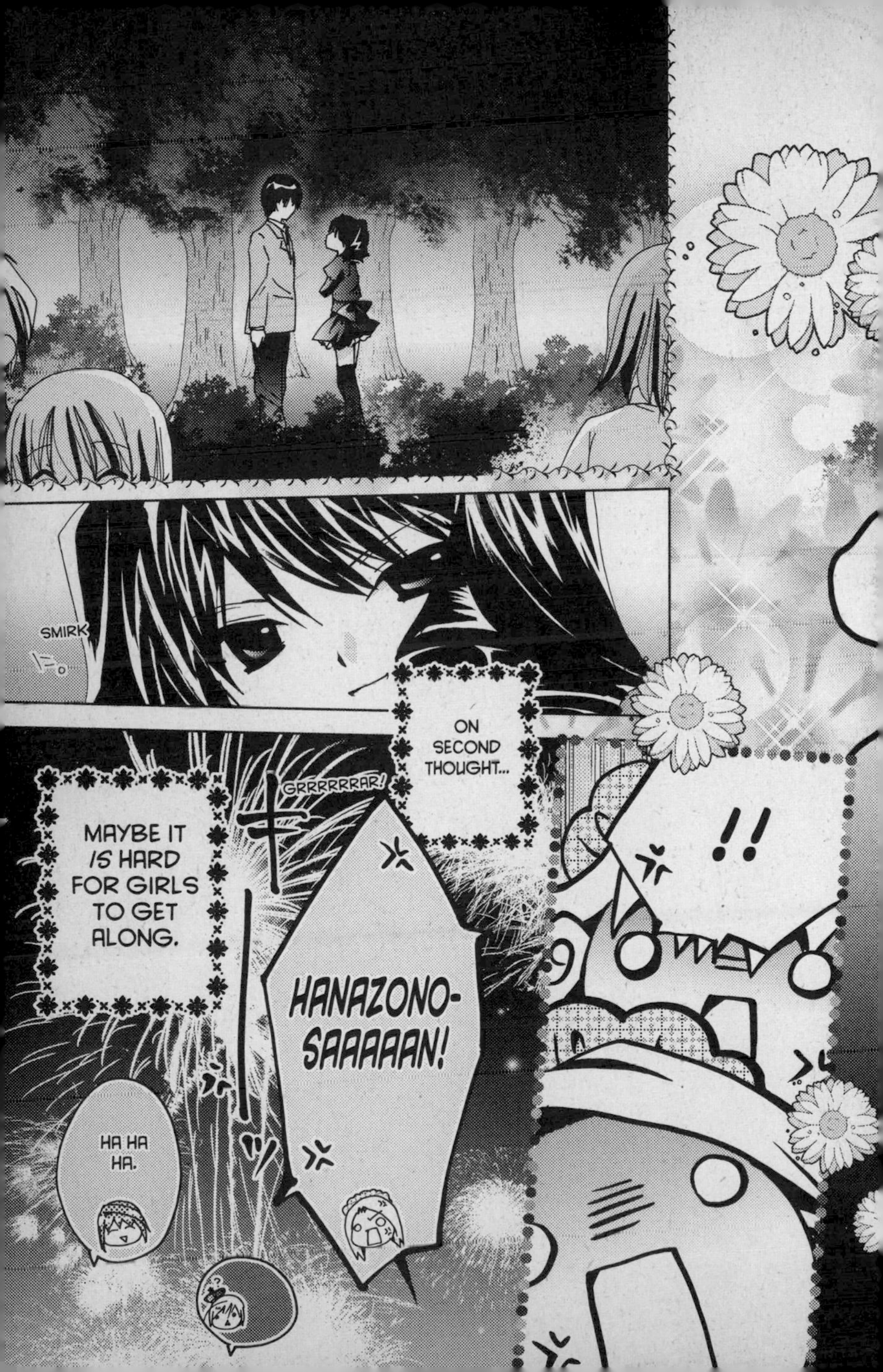
SMIRK
ON SECOND THOUGHT...
MAYBE IT IS HARD FOR GIRLS TO GET ALONG.
!!
GRRRRRRAR!
HANAZONO-SAAAAAN!
HA HA HA.

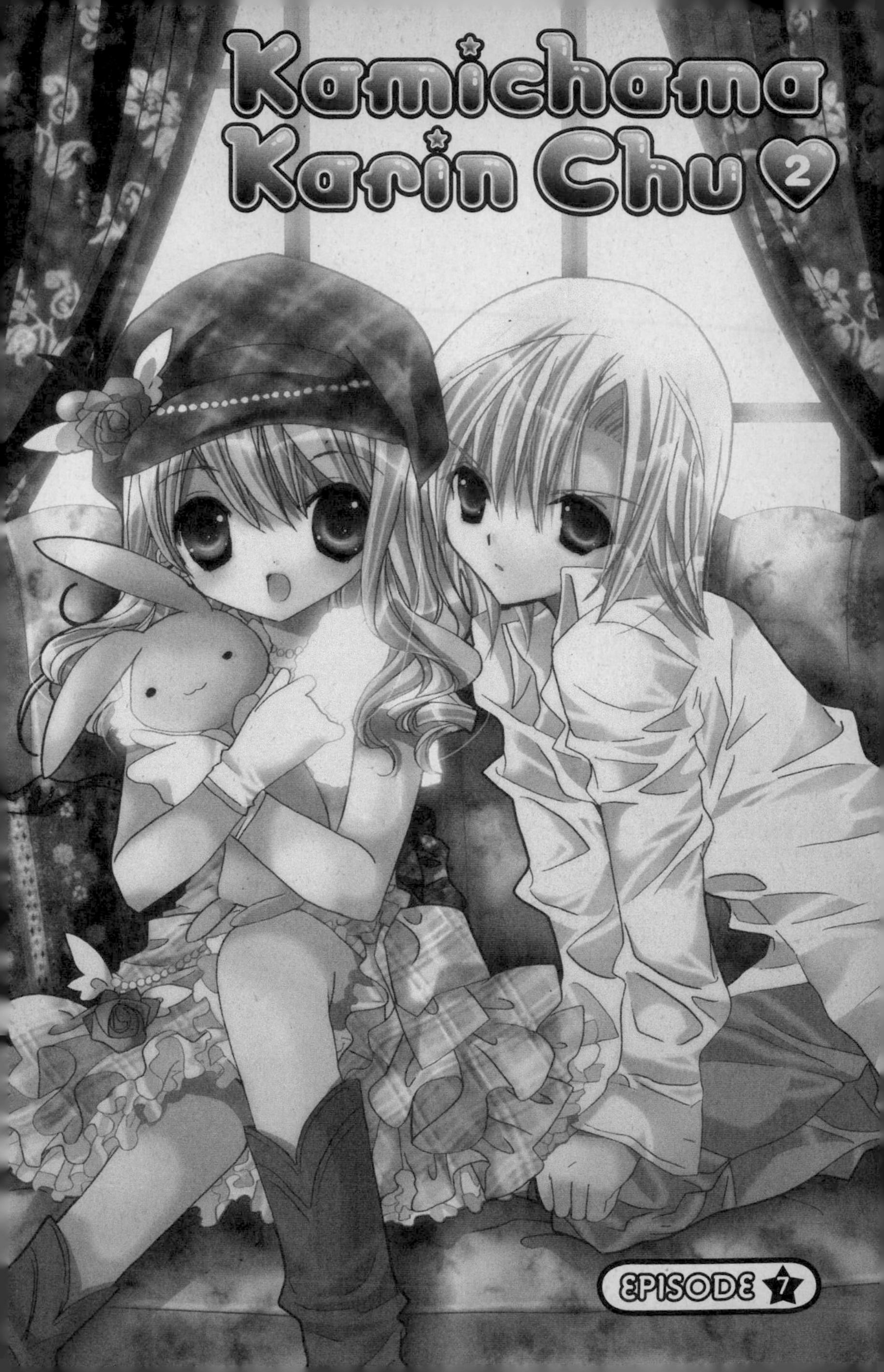
Kamichama Karin Chu 2
EPISODE 7

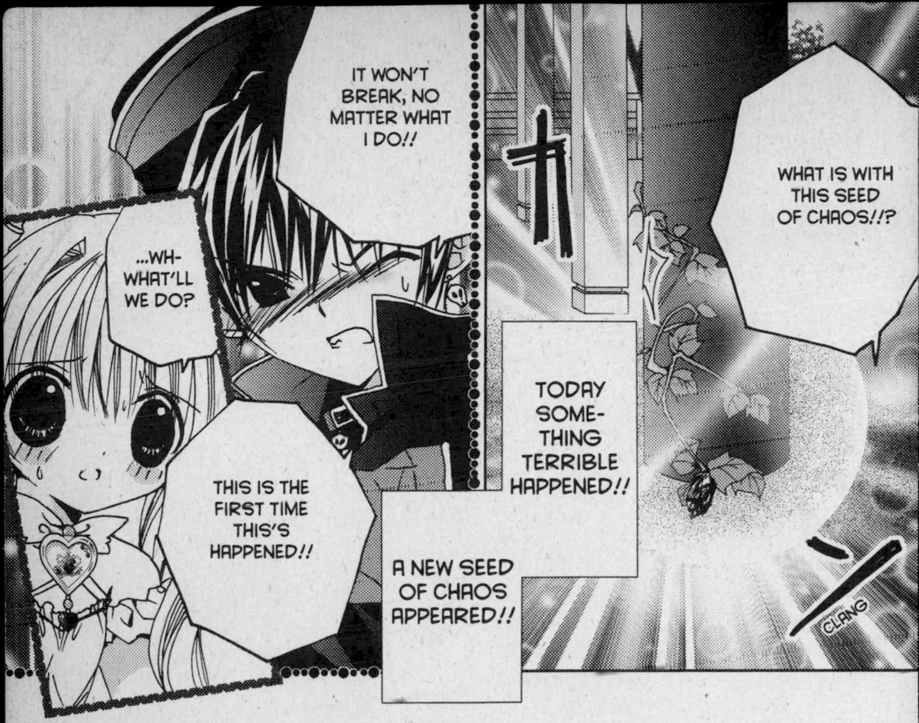
WHAT IS WITH THIS SEED OF CHAOS!!?
CLANG
TODAY SOMETHING TERRIBLE HAPPENED!!
A NEW SEED OF CHAOS APPEARED!!
IT WON'T BREAK, NO MATTER WHAT I DO!!
...WH-WHAT'LL WE DO?
THIS IS THE FIRST TIME THIS'S HAPPENED!!

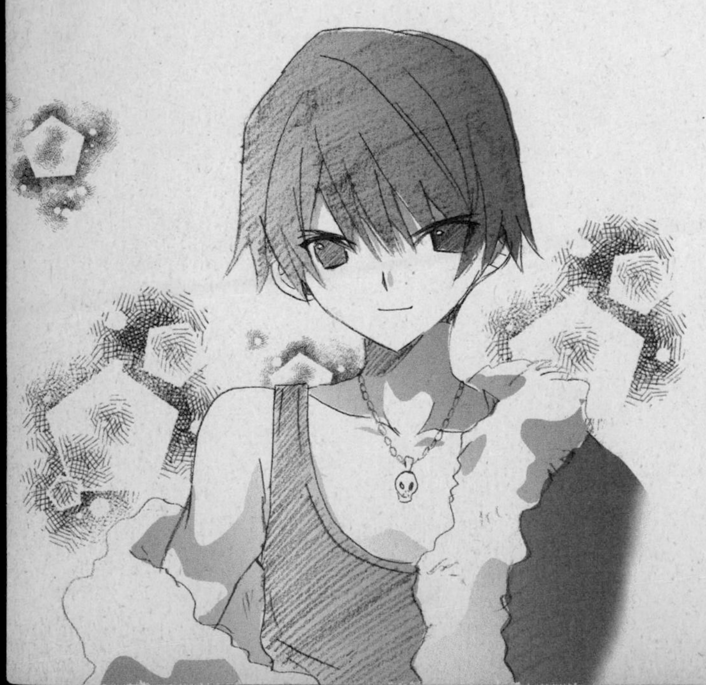

I DREW JIN-KUN.

•

HE'S AN IDOL WITH A WILD PERSONALITY, AND HE'S A *LITTLE* BIT OF A PERVERT, BUT HE'S SUPER-OBEDIENT TO KARIN-CHAN, AND IT'S REALLY FUN TO WRITE AND DRAW HIM.

HIS SOMEWHAT CHILDISH TRAITS ARE HEARTWARMING AND ENDEARING...OR SO I THINK...BUT WHAT DO YOU THINK??

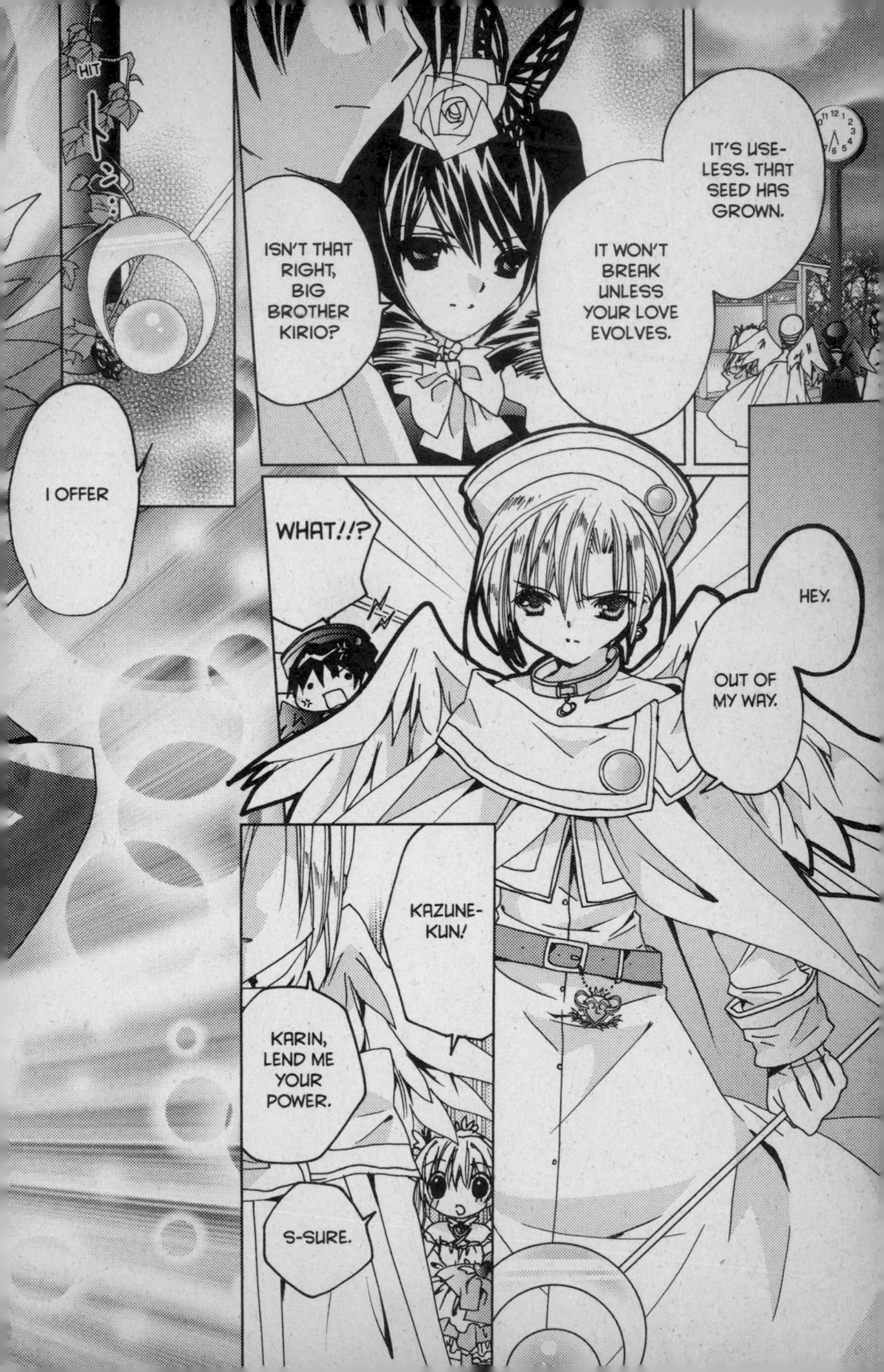
IT'S USE-LESS. THAT SEED HAS GROWN.
IT WON'T BREAK UNLESS YOUR LOVE EVOLVES.
ISN'T THAT RIGHT, BIG BROTHER KIRIO?
HIT
HEY.
OUT OF MY WAY.
WHAT!!?
KAZUNE-KUN!
KARIN, LEND ME YOUR POWER.
S-SURE.
I OFFER

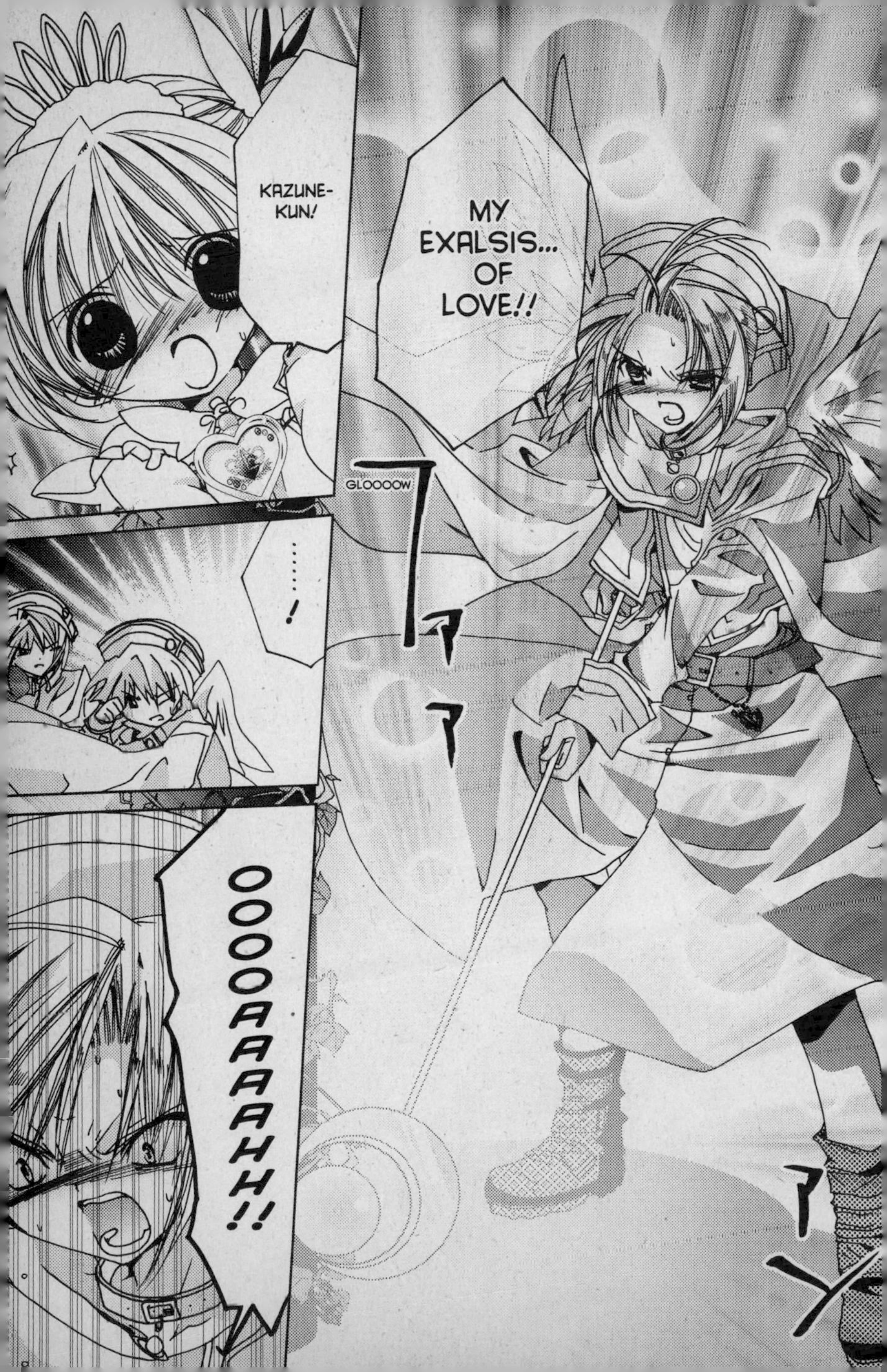
MY EXALSIS... OF LOVE!!
GLOOOOW
KAZUNE-KUN!
......!
OOOOAAAAHH!!

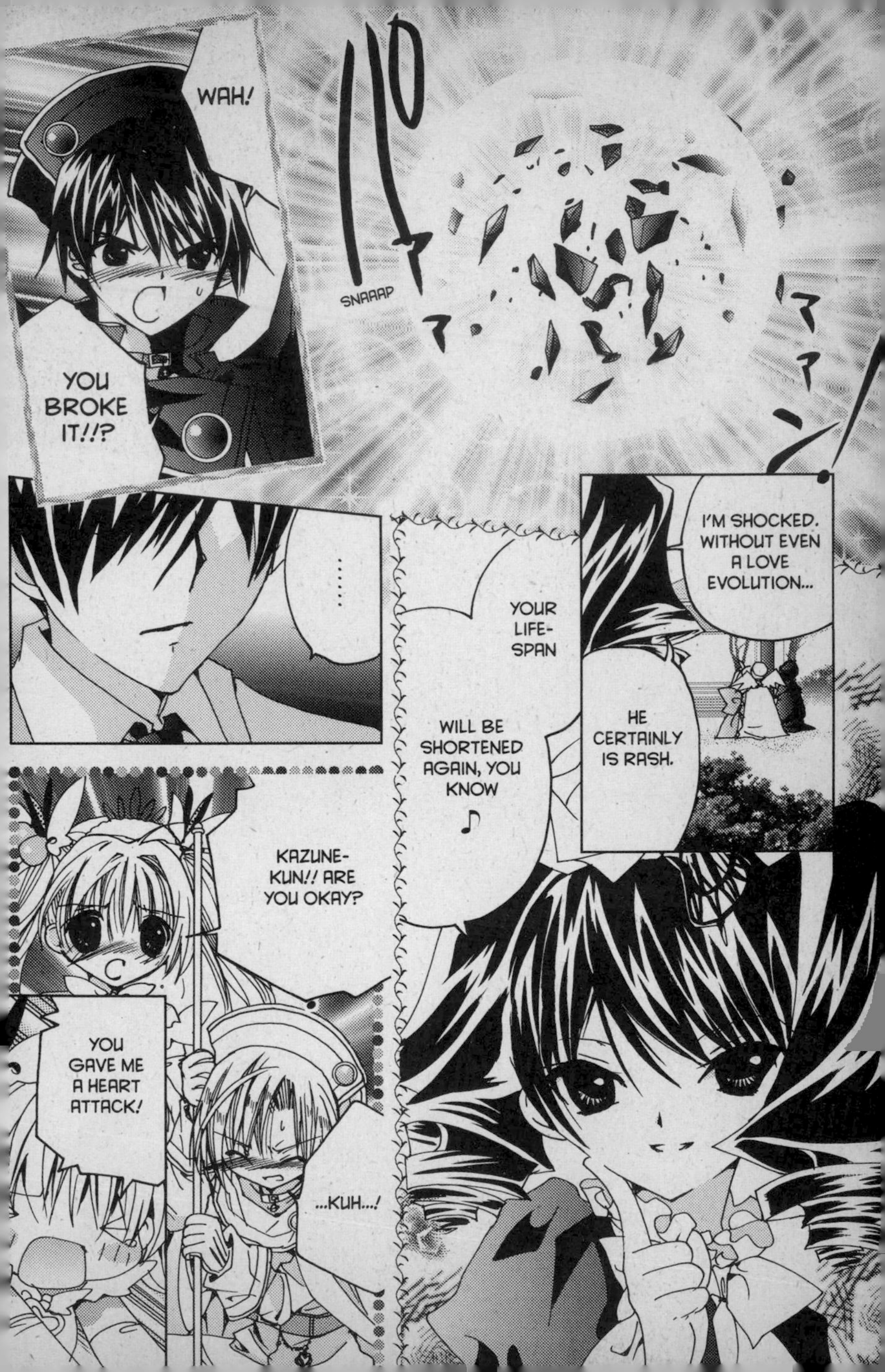
SNAAAP
WAH!
YOU BROKE IT!!?
I'M SHOCKED. WITHOUT EVEN A LOVE EVOLUTION...
HE CERTAINLY IS RASH.
YOUR LIFE-SPAN
WILL BE SHORTENED AGAIN, YOU KNOW ♪
......
KAZUNE-KUN!! ARE YOU OKAY?
YOU GAVE ME A HEART ATTACK!
...KUH...!

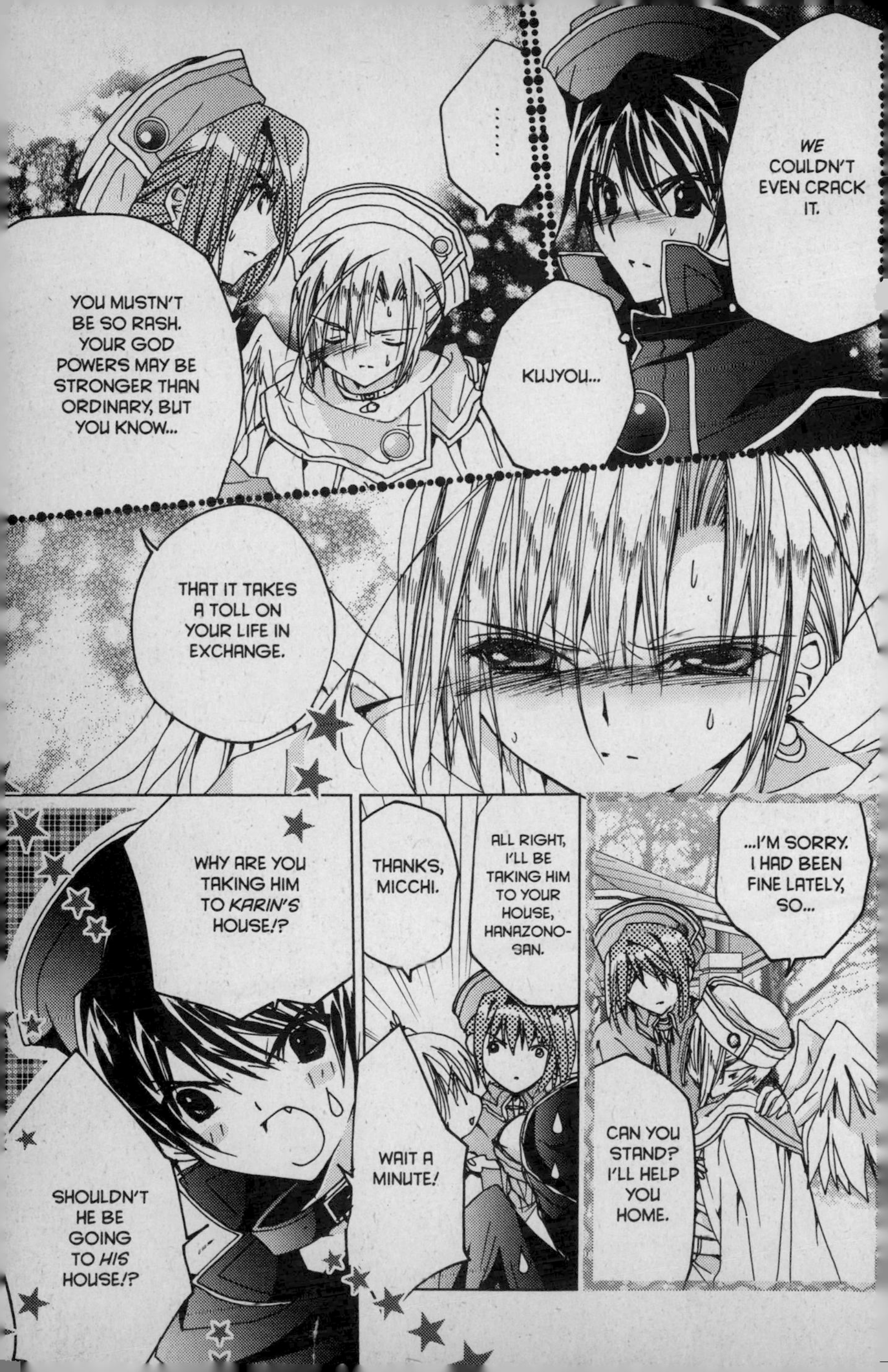
WE COULDN'T EVEN CRACK IT.
......
KUJYOU...
YOU MUSTN'T BE SO RASH. YOUR GOD POWERS MAY BE STRONGER THAN ORDINARY, BUT YOU KNOW...
THAT IT TAKES A TOLL ON YOUR LIFE IN EXCHANGE.
...I'M SORRY. I HAD BEEN FINE LATELY, SO...
CAN YOU STAND? I'LL HELP YOU HOME.
ALL RIGHT, I'LL BE TAKING HIM TO YOUR HOUSE, HANAZONO-SAN.
THANKS, MICCHI.
WAIT A MINUTE!
WHY ARE YOU TAKING HIM TO *KARIN'S* HOUSE!?
SHOULDN'T HE BE GOING TO *HIS* HOUSE!?

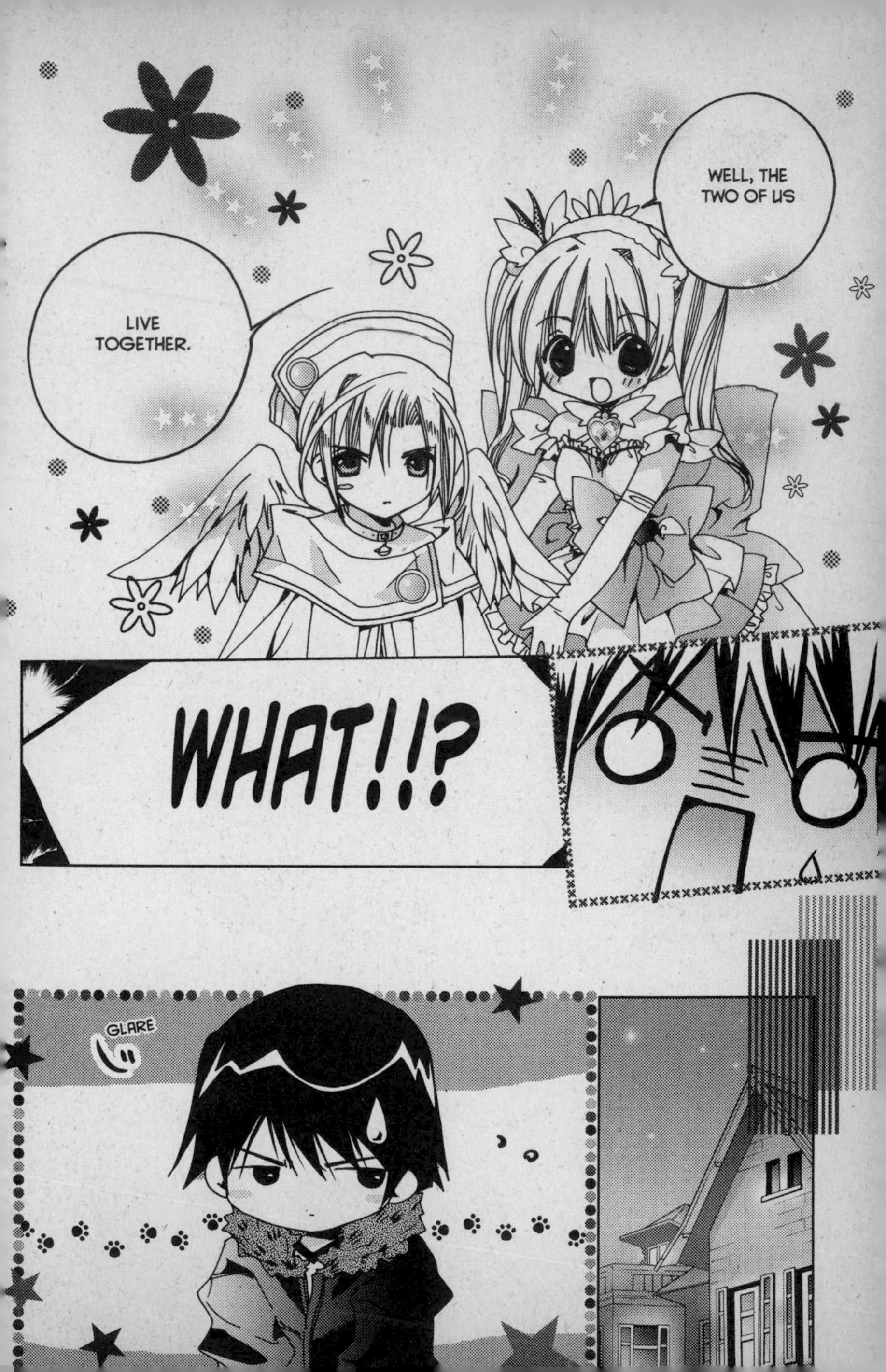
WELL, THE TWO OF US
LIVE TOGETHER.
WHAT!!?
GLARE

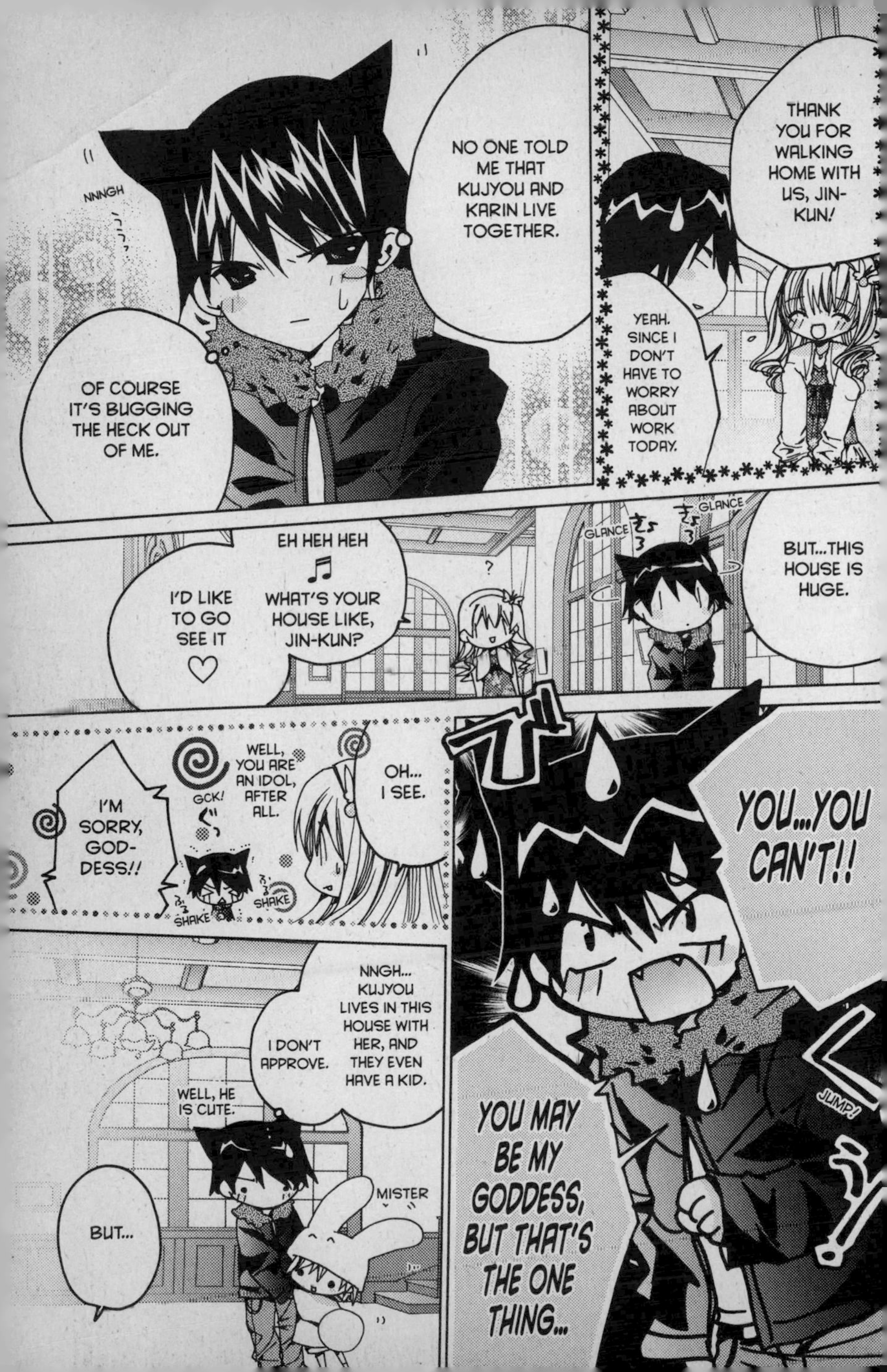
THANK YOU FOR WALKING HOME WITH US, JIN-KUN!
YEAH. SINCE I DON'T HAVE TO WORRY ABOUT WORK TODAY.
NO ONE TOLD ME THAT KUJYOU AND KARIN LIVE TOGETHER.
NNNGH
OF COURSE IT'S BUGGING THE HECK OUT OF ME.
BUT...THIS HOUSE IS HUGE.
GLANCE
GLANCE
?
EH HEH HEH ♫ WHAT'S YOUR HOUSE LIKE, JIN-KUN?
I'D LIKE TO GO SEE IT ♡
YOU...YOU CAN'T!!
JUMP!
YOU MAY BE MY GODDESS, BUT THAT'S THE ONE THING...
OH... I SEE.
WELL, YOU ARE AN IDOL, AFTER ALL.
GCK!
I'M SORRY, GODDESS!!
SHAKE
SHAKE
NNGH... KUJYOU LIVES IN THIS HOUSE WITH HER, AND THEY EVEN HAVE A KID.
I DON'T APPROVE.
WELL, HE IS CUTE.
MISTER
BUT...

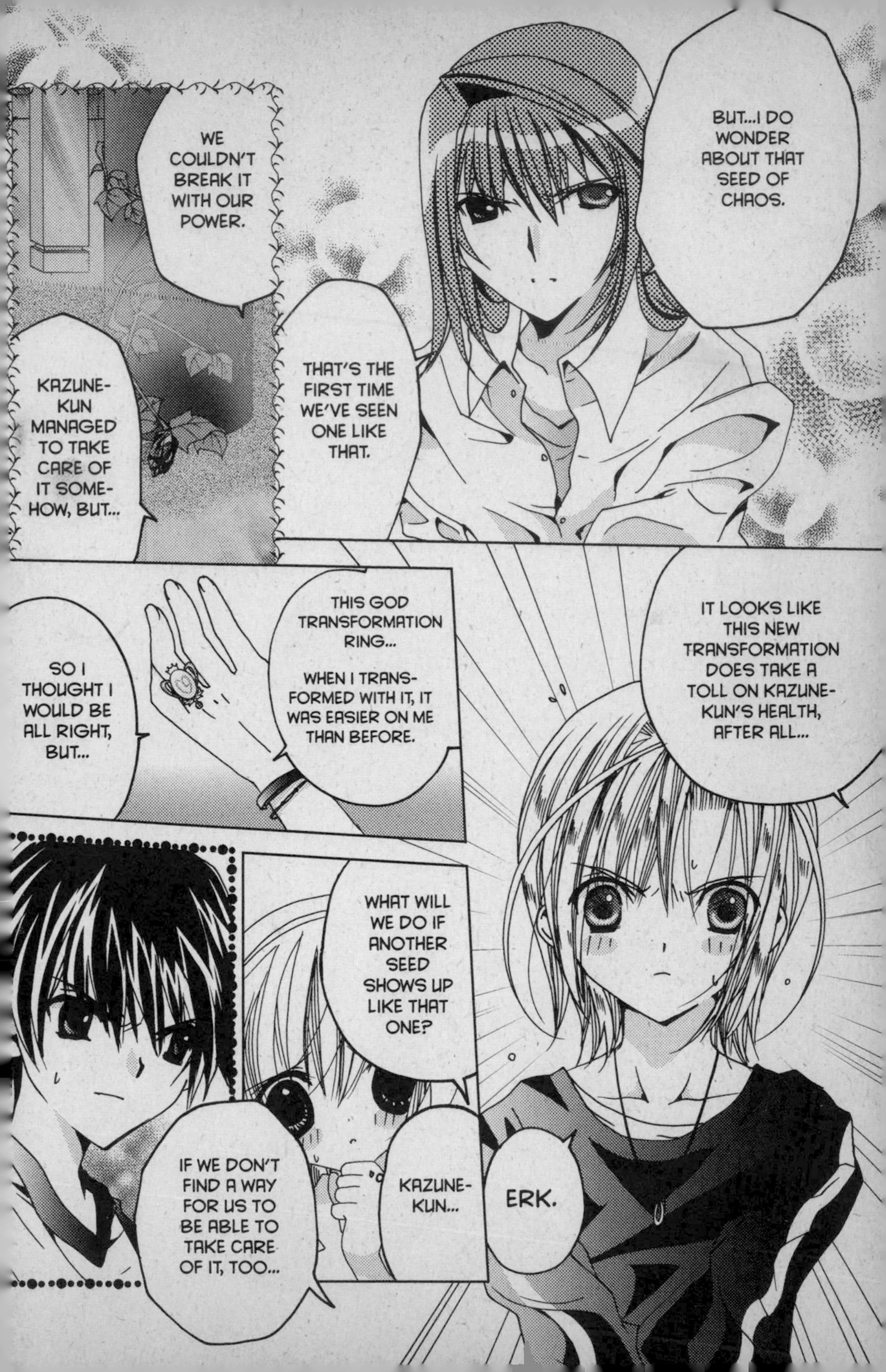
BUT...I DO WONDER ABOUT THAT SEED OF CHAOS.
THAT'S THE FIRST TIME WE'VE SEEN ONE LIKE THAT.
WE COULDN'T BREAK IT WITH OUR POWER.
KAZUNE-KUN MANAGED TO TAKE CARE OF IT SOME-HOW, BUT...
IT LOOKS LIKE THIS NEW TRANSFORMATION DOES TAKE A TOLL ON KAZUNE-KUN'S HEALTH, AFTER ALL...
ERK.
THIS GOD TRANSFORMATION RING... WHEN I TRANS-FORMED WITH IT, IT WAS EASIER ON ME THAN BEFORE.
SO I THOUGHT I WOULD BE ALL RIGHT, BUT...
WHAT WILL WE DO IF ANOTHER SEED SHOWS UP LIKE THAT ONE?
KAZUNE-KUN...
IF WE DON'T FIND A WAY FOR US TO BE ABLE TO TAKE CARE OF IT, TOO...

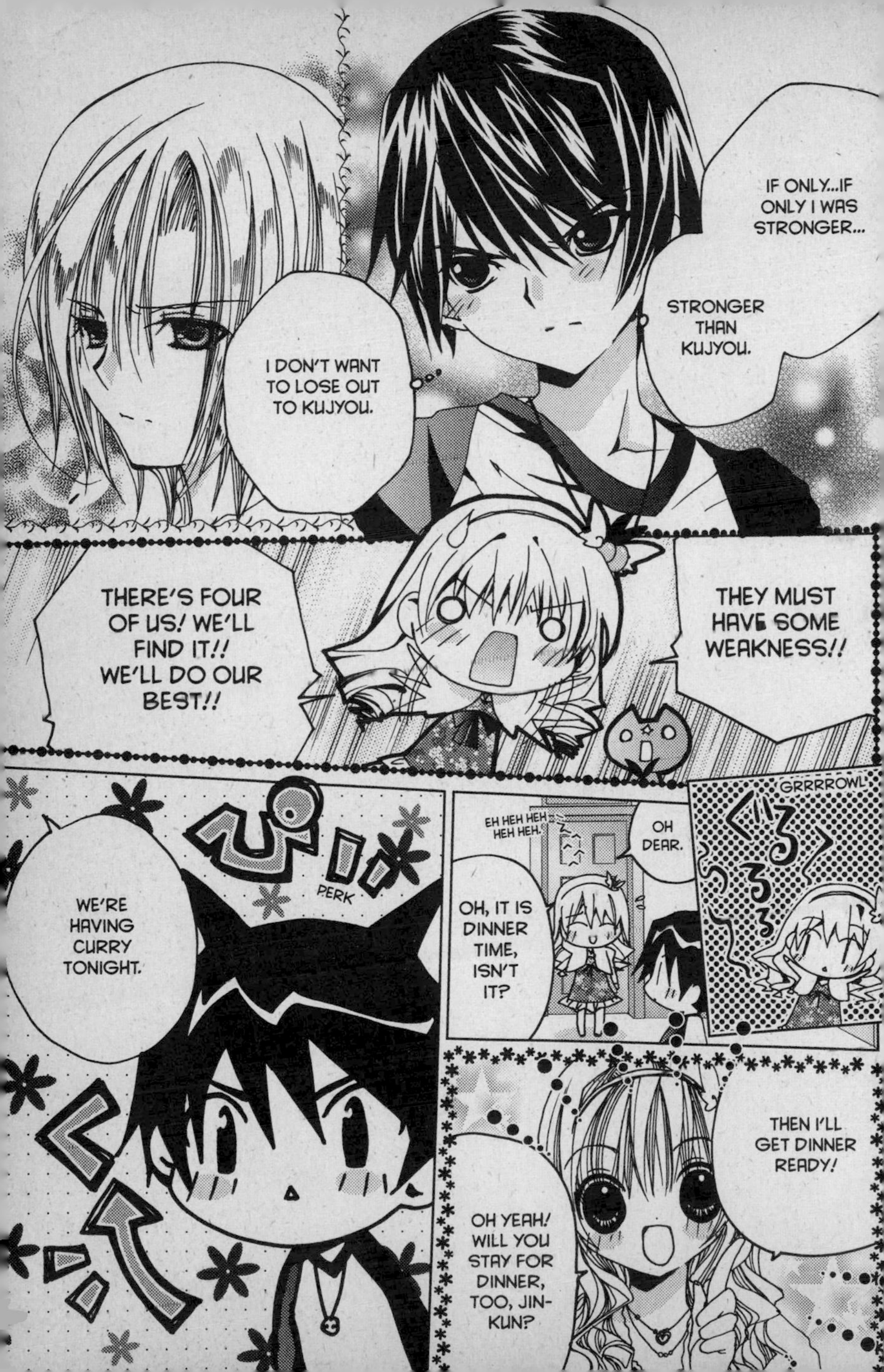
IF ONLY...IF ONLY I WAS STRONGER...
STRONGER THAN KUJYOU.
I DON'T WANT TO LOSE OUT TO KUJYOU.
THEY MUST HAVE SOME WEAKNESS!!
THERE'S FOUR OF US! WE'LL FIND IT!! WE'LL DO OUR BEST!!
GRRRROWL
OH DEAR.
EH HEH HEH HEH HEH.
OH, IT IS DINNER TIME, ISN'T IT?
THEN I'LL GET DINNER READY!
OH YEAH! WILL YOU STAY FOR DINNER, TOO, JIN-KUN?
PERK
WE'RE HAVING CURRY TONIGHT.

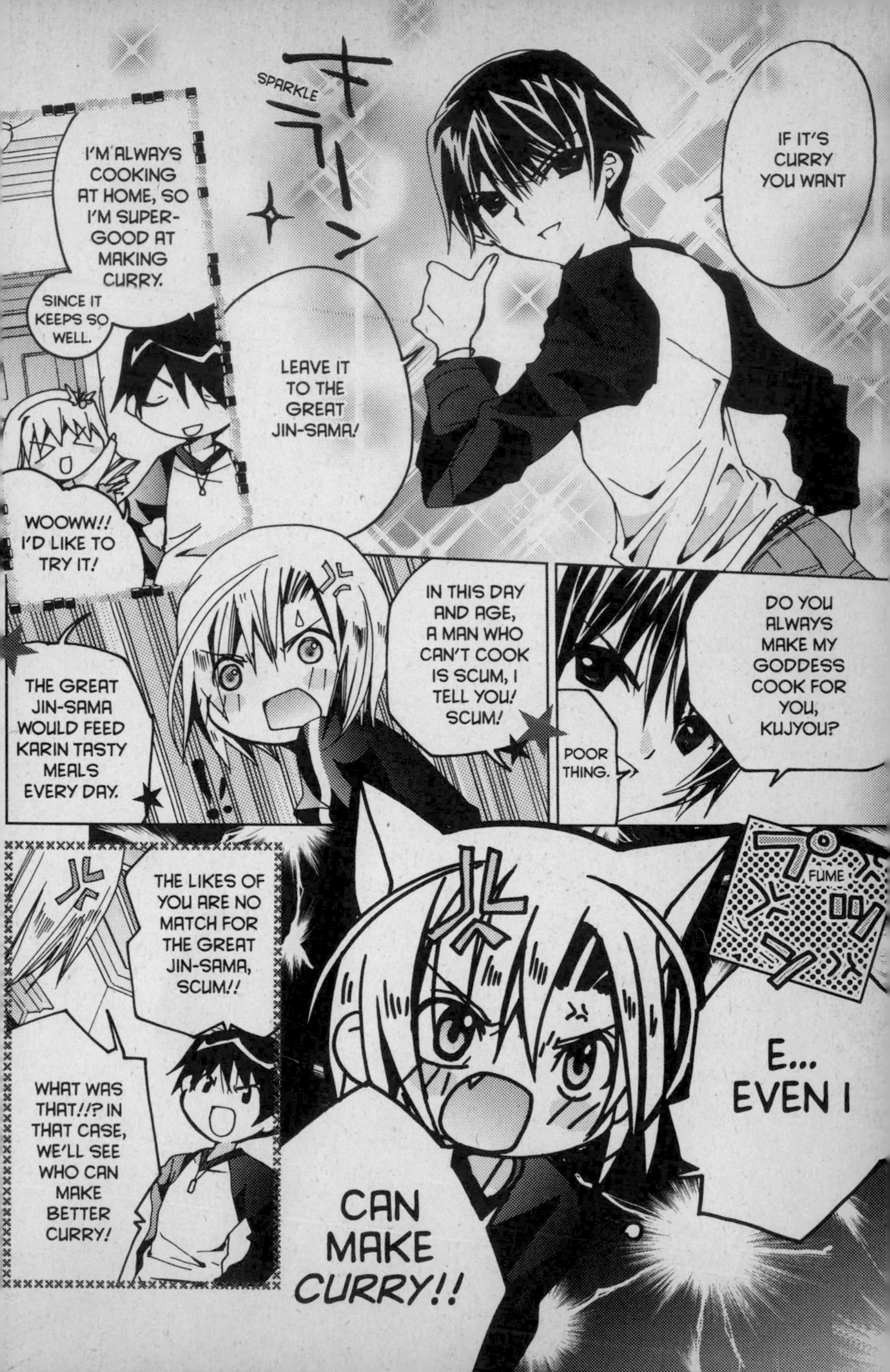
IF IT'S CURRY YOU WANT
SPARKLE
LEAVE IT TO THE GREAT JIN-SAMA!
I'M ALWAYS COOKING AT HOME, SO I'M SUPER-GOOD AT MAKING CURRY.
SINCE IT KEEPS SO WELL.
WOOWW!! I'D LIKE TO TRY IT!
DO YOU ALWAYS MAKE MY GODDESS COOK FOR YOU, KUJYOU?
POOR THING.
IN THIS DAY AND AGE, A MAN WHO CAN'T COOK IS SCUM, I TELL YOU! SCUM!
THE GREAT JIN-SAMA WOULD FEED KARIN TASTY MEALS EVERY DAY.
FUME
E... EVEN I
CAN MAKE CURRY!!
THE LIKES OF YOU ARE NO MATCH FOR THE GREAT JIN-SAMA, SCUM!!
WHAT WAS THAT!!? IN THAT CASE, WE'LL SEE WHO CAN MAKE BETTER CURRY!

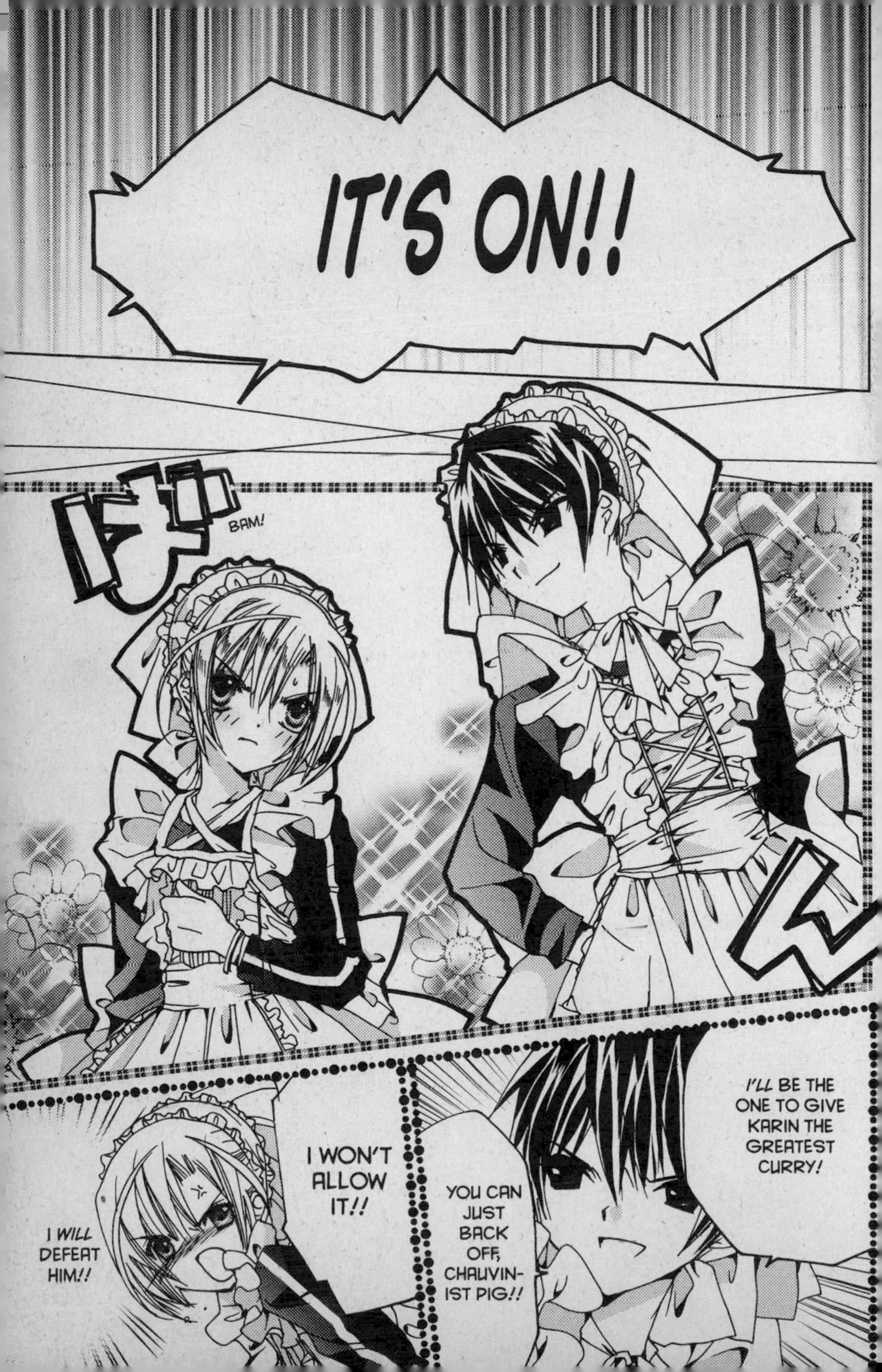
IT'S ON!!
BAM!
I'LL BE THE ONE TO GIVE KARIN THE GREATEST CURRY!
YOU CAN JUST BACK OFF, CHAUVIN-IST PIG!!
I WON'T ALLOW IT!!
I WILL DEFEAT HIM!!

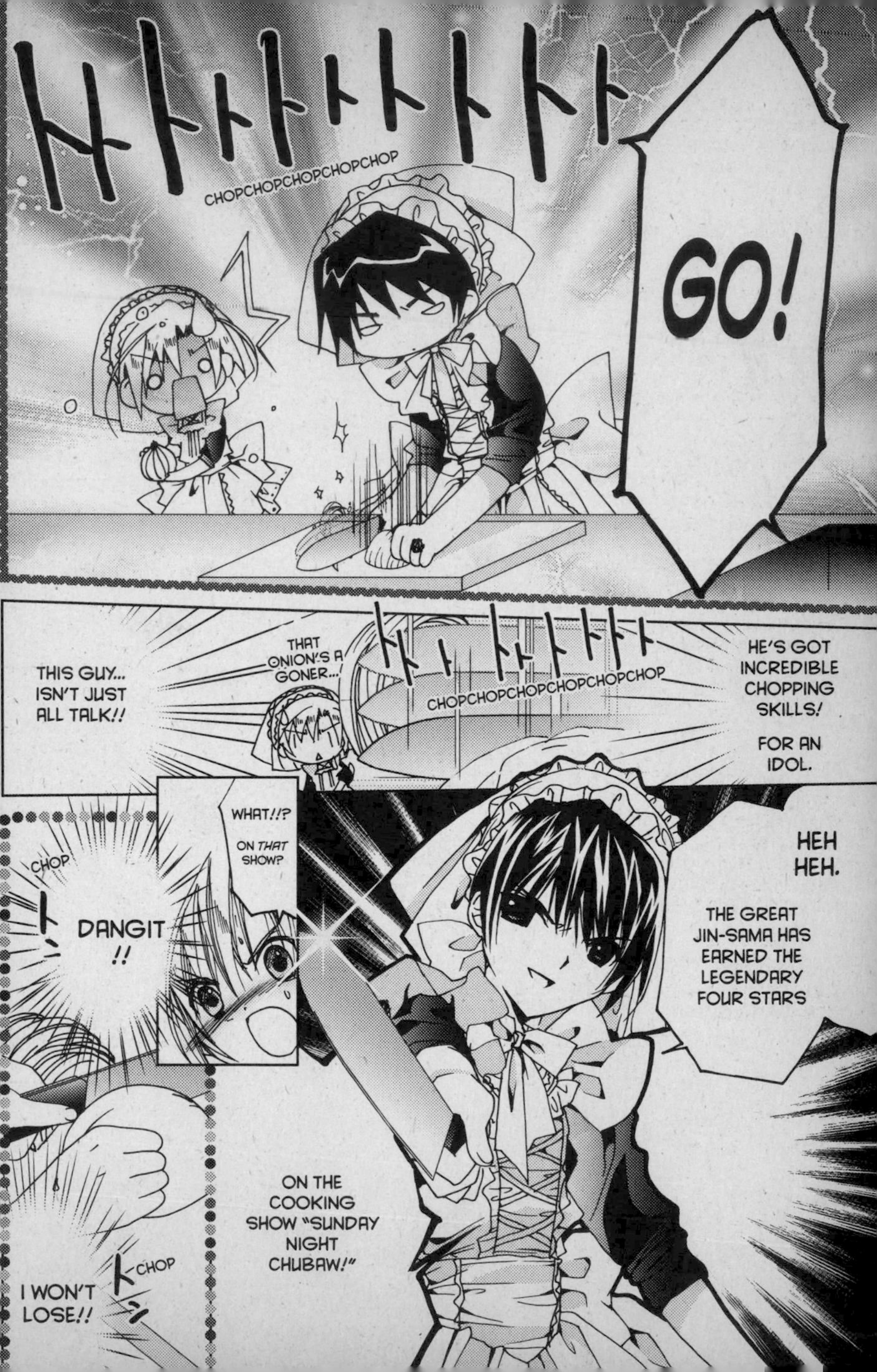
GO!
CHOPCHOPCHOPCHOPCHOP
HE'S GOT INCREDIBLE CHOPPING SKILLS!
FOR AN IDOL.
CHOPCHOPCHOPCHOPCHOPCHOP
THAT ONION'S A GONER...
THIS GUY... ISN'T JUST ALL TALK!!
HEH HEH.
THE GREAT JIN-SAMA HAS EARNED THE LEGENDARY FOUR STARS
ON THE COOKING SHOW "SUNDAY NIGHT CHUBAW!"
WHAT!!?
ON *THAT* SHOW?
CHOP
DANGIT!!
CHOP
I WON'T LOSE!!

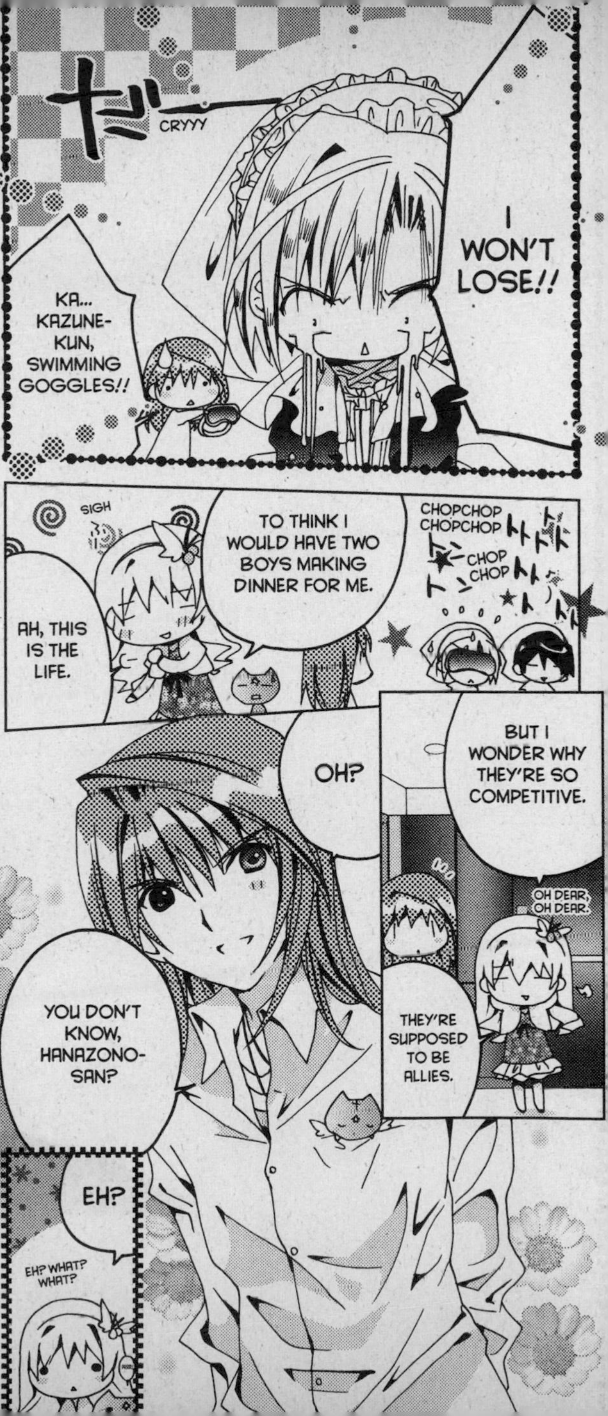
I WON'T LOSE!!
CRYYY
KA... KAZUNE-KUN, SWIMMING GOGGLES!!
CHOPCHOP CHOPCHOP
CHOP CHOP
TO THINK I WOULD HAVE TWO BOYS MAKING DINNER FOR ME.
SIGH
AH, THIS IS THE LIFE.
BUT I WONDER WHY THEY'RE SO COMPETITIVE.
OH DEAR, OH DEAR.
THEY'RE SUPPOSED TO BE ALLIES.
OH?
YOU DON'T KNOW, HANAZONO-SAN?
EH?
EH? WHAT? WHAT?

HELLO! THIS IS KOGE-DONBO. THANK YOU VERY MUCH FOR BUYING *KAMICHAMA KARIN CHU* TWO!!

WHILE VOLUME ONE WAS THE STORY UP UNTIL THE THREE NOBLE GODS ARE GATHERED, VOLUME TWO IS THE STORY AFTER THAT! WE'LL KEEP GOING, MAKING A RACKET AND BUSTLING ABOUT, AND WITH A BIT OF A "THERE'S MYSTERY, TOO!?" FEEL, SO PLEASE ENJOY!! AND ABOUT *THAT PERSON* FROM THE LAST SERIES... HE APPEARS IN THE EXTRA STORY FROM THE LAST SERIES THAT SHOWS UP AT THE END OF THIS BOOK. IF HE SAW IT, HE WOULD BE A LITTLE HEARTBROKEN AFTER HE FINALLY APPEARED IN SUCH A COOL WAY IN CHU...MAYBE.... WELL, I WOULD.

...AND SO, I HAD FUN DRAWING THE THREE BOYS AND KARIN-CHAN FOR VOLUME TWO!! SO IF YOU ALL ENJOY IT TOO, I WILL BE *VERY* HAPPY! HAPPY TIMES 100!

WELL THEN, I WILL BE SUPER HAPPY IF WE MEET AGAIN IN VOLUME THREE!

♥

IT'S ALSO GOING TO BE AN ANIME! PLEASE ENJOY THAT, TOO!

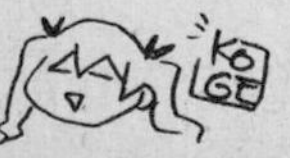
KOGE

DECEMBER 7, 2006
KOGE-DONBO

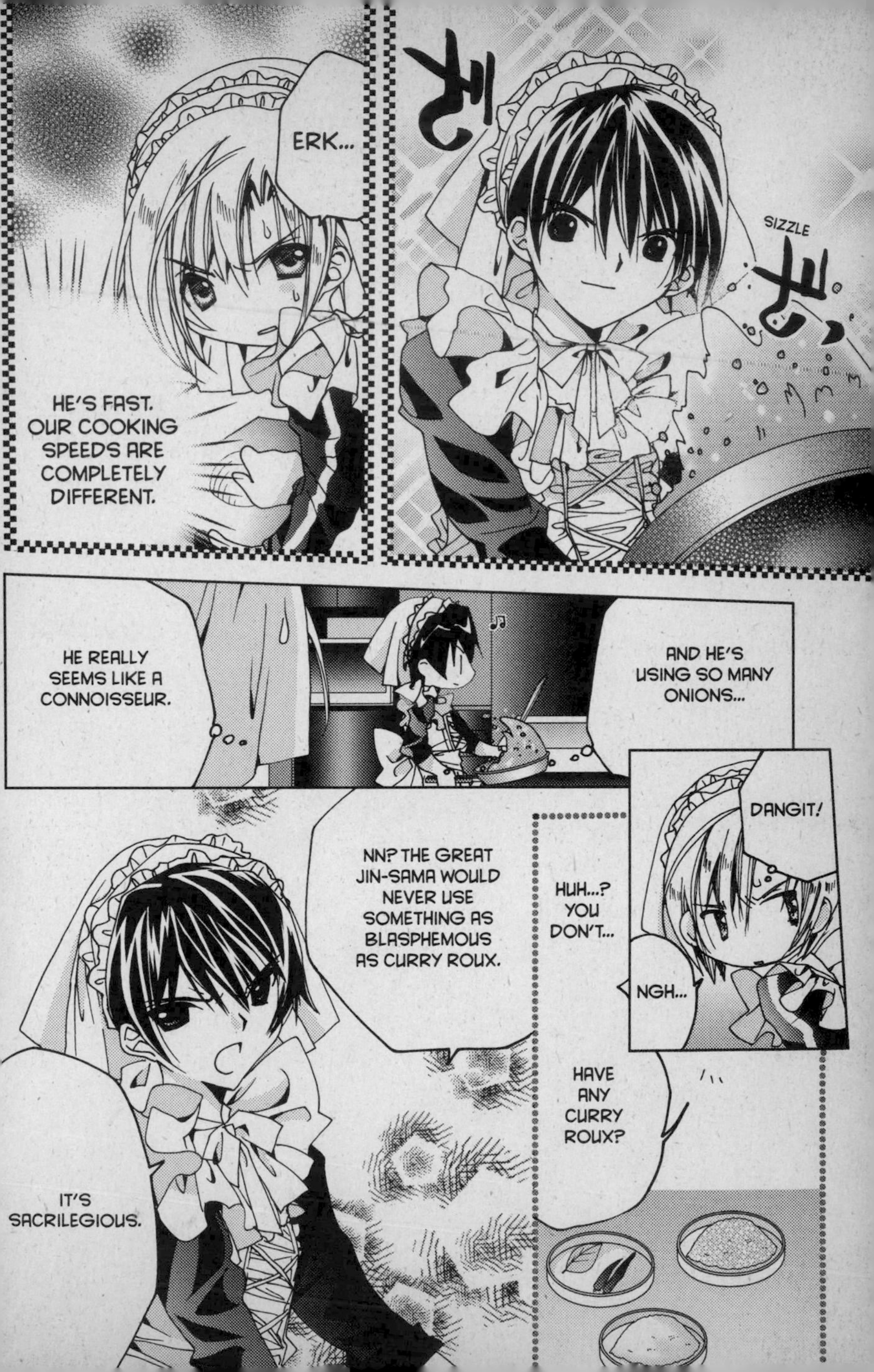
SIZZLE
ERK...
HE'S FAST. OUR COOKING SPEEDS ARE COMPLETELY DIFFERENT.
AND HE'S USING SO MANY ONIONS...
HE REALLY SEEMS LIKE A CONNOISSEUR.
DANGIT!
NGH...
HUH...? YOU DON'T...
HAVE ANY CURRY ROUX?
NN? THE GREAT JIN-SAMA WOULD NEVER USE SOMETHING AS BLASPHEMOUS AS CURRY ROUX.
IT'S SACRILEGIOUS.

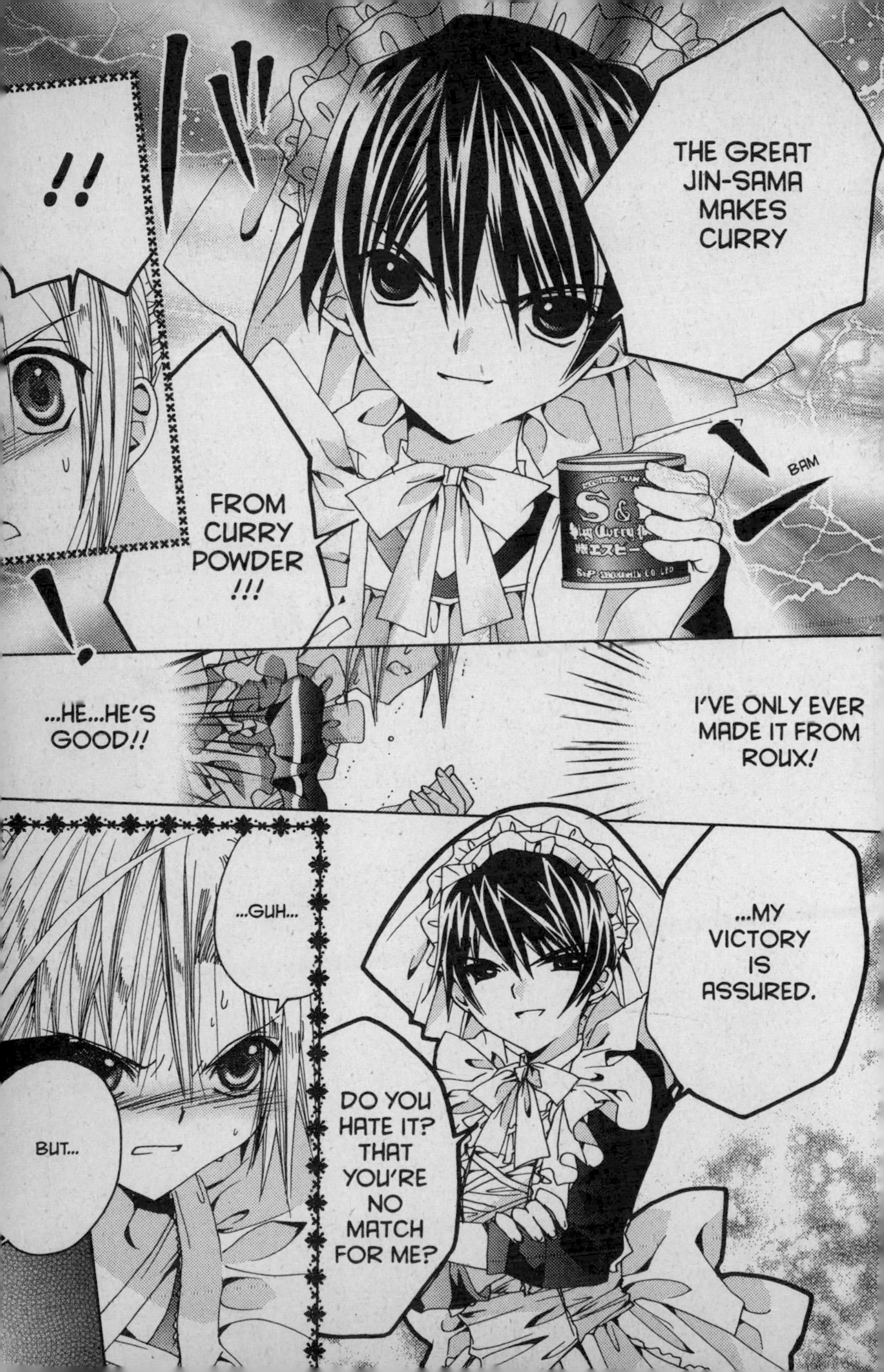
THE GREAT JIN-SAMA MAKES CURRY
FROM CURRY POWDER !!!
BAM
!!
!
I'VE ONLY EVER MADE IT FROM ROUX!
...HE...HE'S GOOD!!
...MY VICTORY IS ASSURED.
DO YOU HATE IT? THAT YOU'RE NO MATCH FOR ME?
...GUH...
BUT...

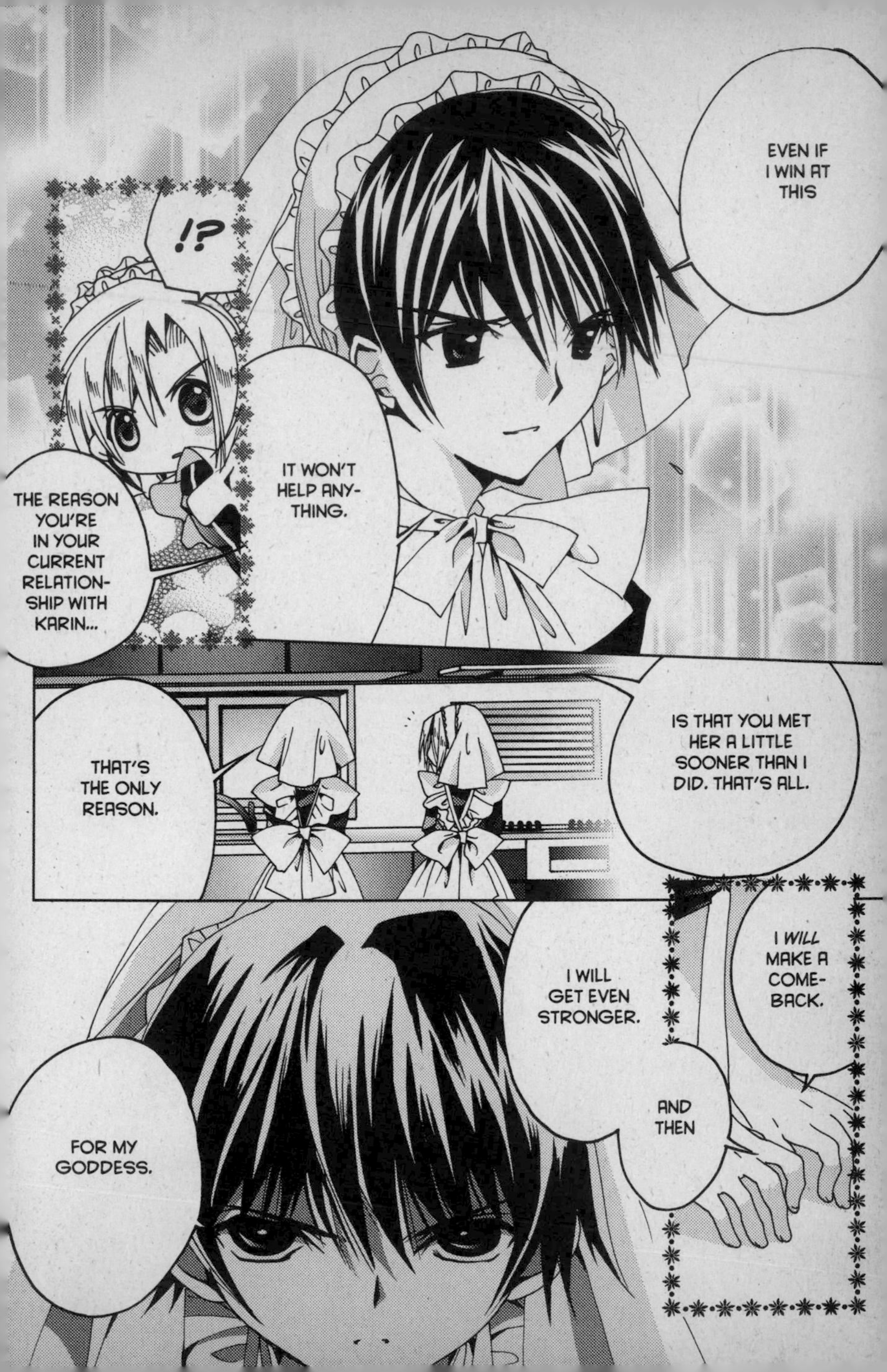
EVEN IF I WIN AT THIS
IT WON'T HELP ANY-THING.
!?
THE REASON YOU'RE IN YOUR CURRENT RELATION-SHIP WITH KARIN...
IS THAT YOU MET HER A LITTLE SOONER THAN I DID. THAT'S ALL.
THAT'S THE ONLY REASON.
I *WILL* MAKE A COME-BACK.
I WILL GET EVEN STRONGER.
AND THEN
FOR MY GODDESS.

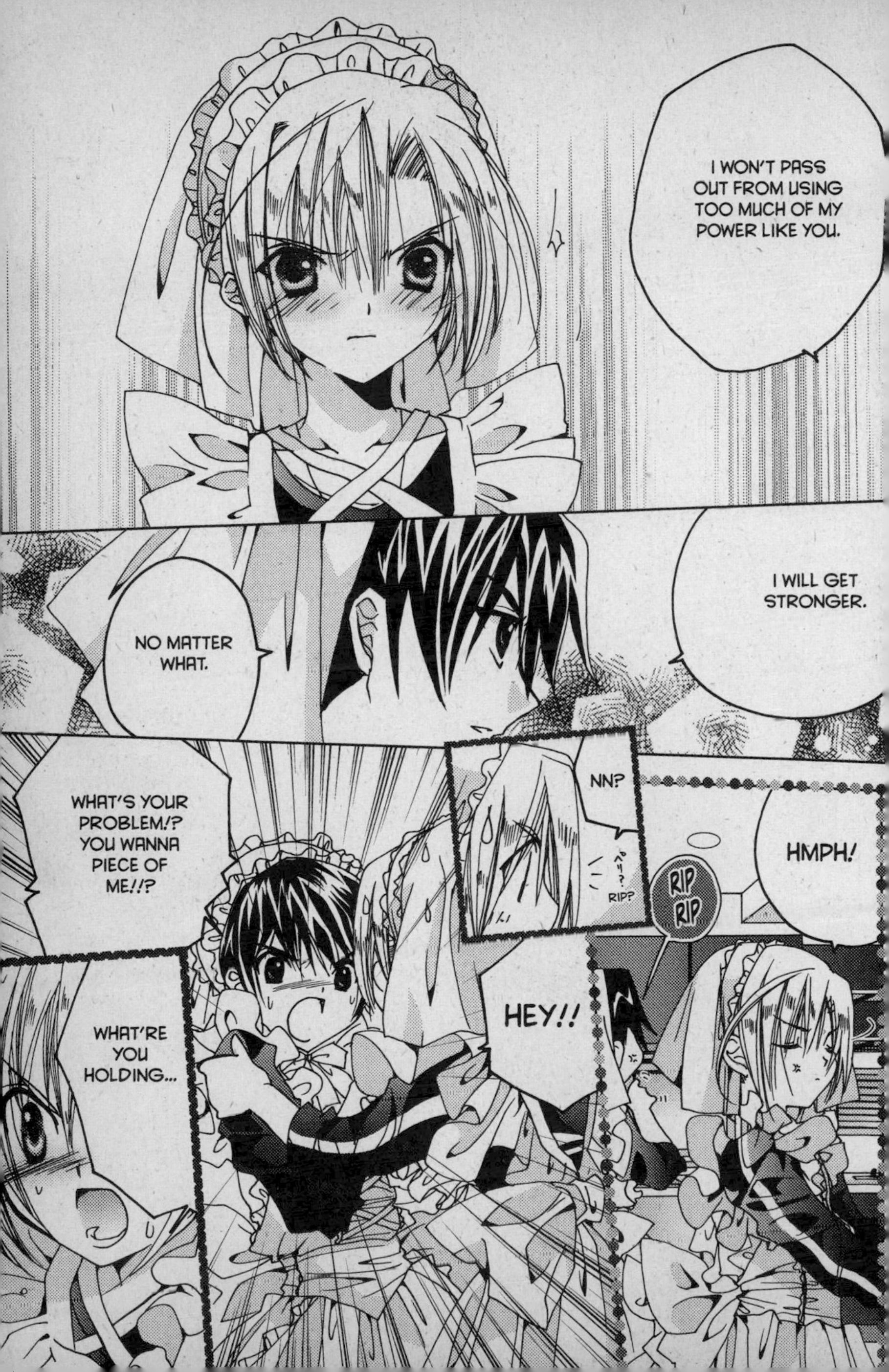
I WON'T PASS OUT FROM USING TOO MUCH OF MY POWER LIKE YOU.
I WILL GET STRONGER.
NO MATTER WHAT.
HMPH!
RIP RIP
NN?
RIP?
HEY!!
WHAT'S YOUR PROBLEM!? YOU WANNA PIECE OF ME!!?
WHAT'RE YOU HOLDING...

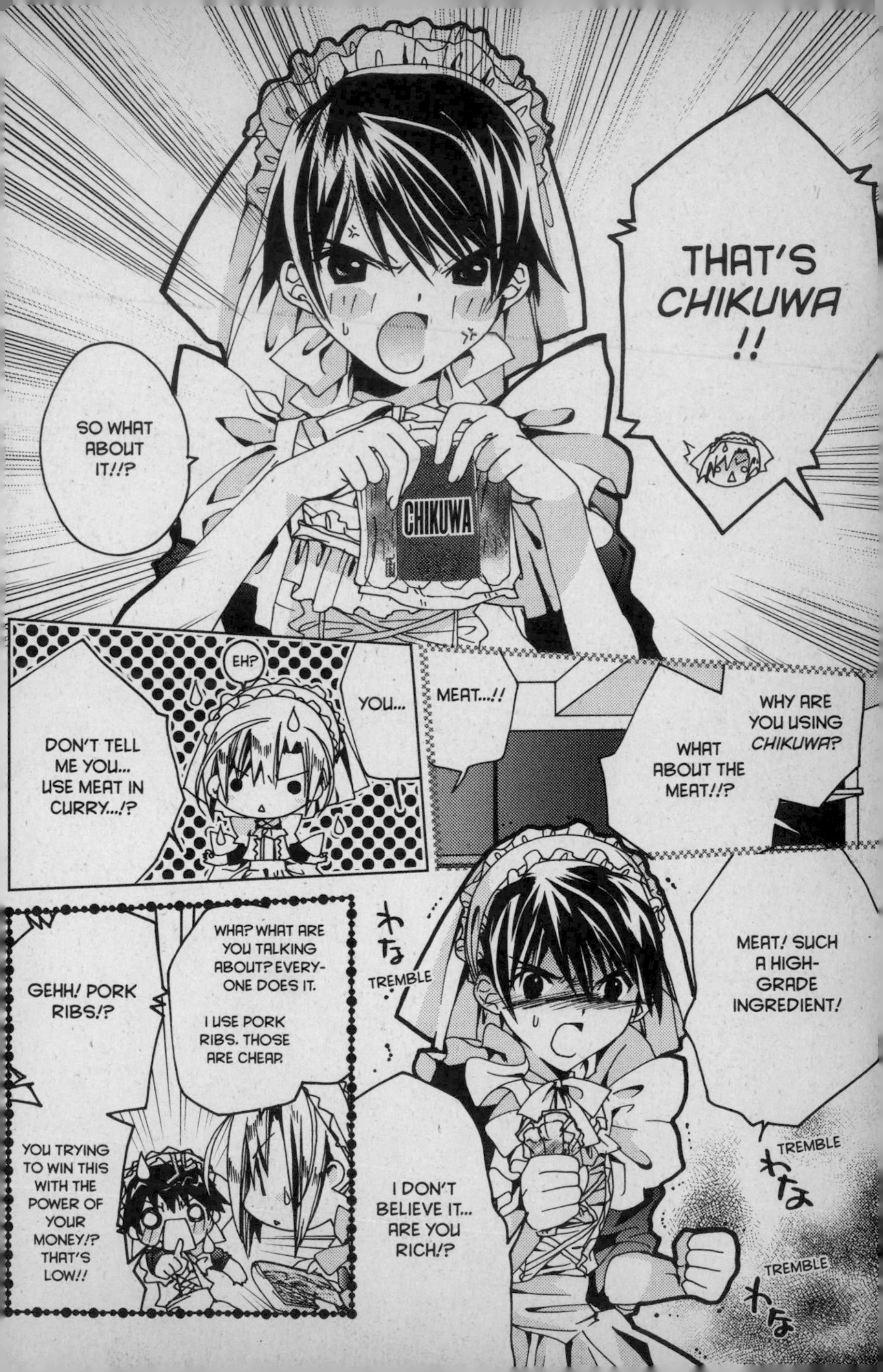
THAT'S CHIKUWA!!
CHIKUWA
SO WHAT ABOUT IT!!?
WHY ARE YOU USING CHIKUWA?
WHAT ABOUT THE MEAT!!?
MEAT...!!
EH?
YOU...
DON'T TELL ME YOU... USE MEAT IN CURRY...!?
MEAT! SUCH A HIGH-GRADE INGREDIENT!
わな
TREMBLE
わな
TREMBLE
わな
TREMBLE
I DON'T BELIEVE IT... ARE YOU RICH!?
WHA? WHAT ARE YOU TALKING ABOUT? EVERY-ONE DOES IT.
I USE PORK RIBS. THOSE ARE CHEAP.
GEHH! PORK RIBS!?
YOU TRYING TO WIN THIS WITH THE POWER OF YOUR MONEY!? THAT'S LOW!!

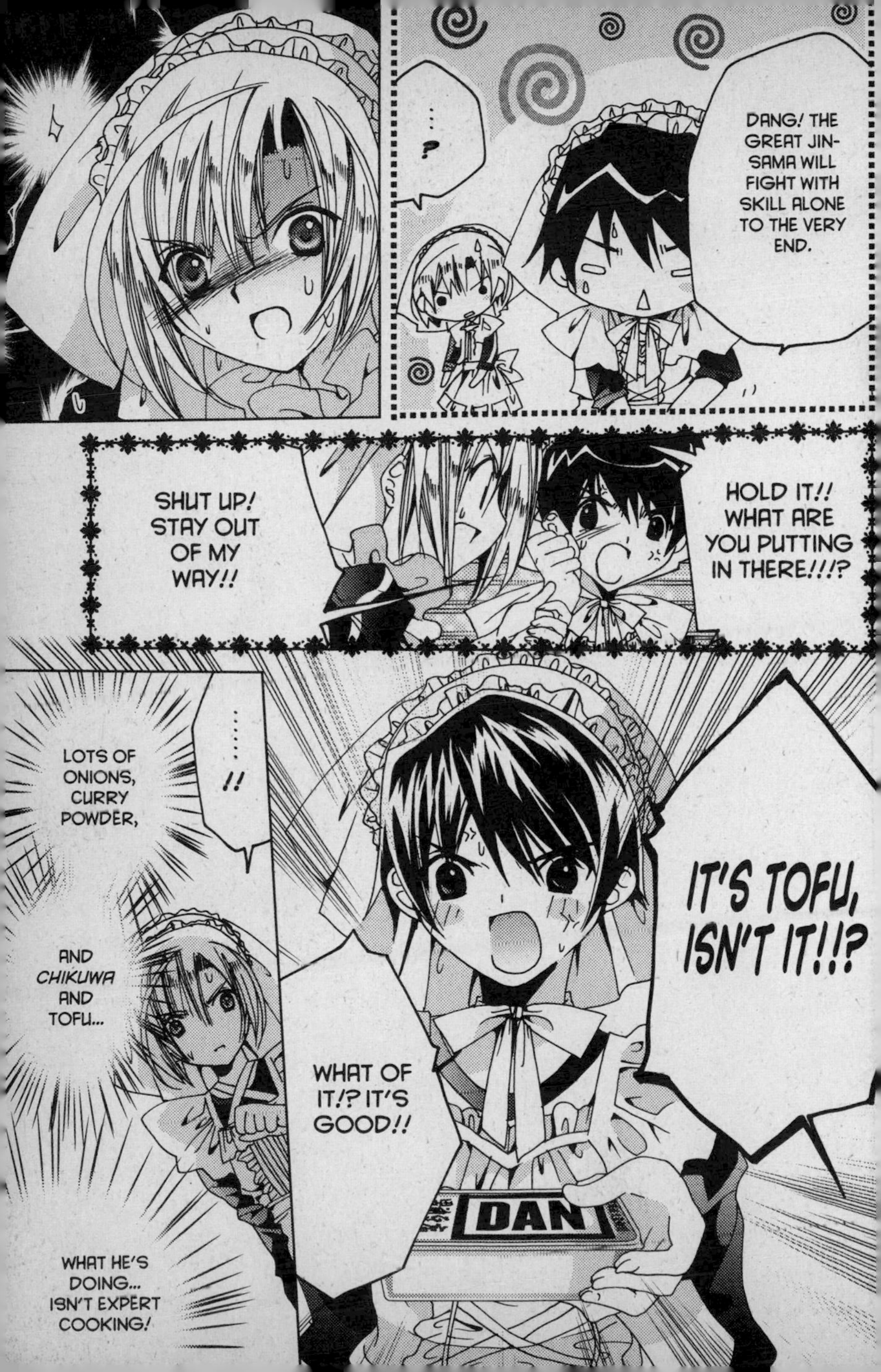
DANG! THE GREAT JIN-SAMA WILL FIGHT WITH SKILL ALONE TO THE VERY END.
...?
HOLD IT!! WHAT ARE YOU PUTTING IN THERE!!!?
SHUT UP! STAY OUT OF MY WAY!!
IT'S TOFU, ISN'T IT!!?
WHAT OF IT!? IT'S GOOD!!
......!!
LOTS OF ONIONS, CURRY POWDER,
AND *CHIKUWA* AND TOFU...
WHAT HE'S DOING... ISN'T EXPERT COOKING!
DAN

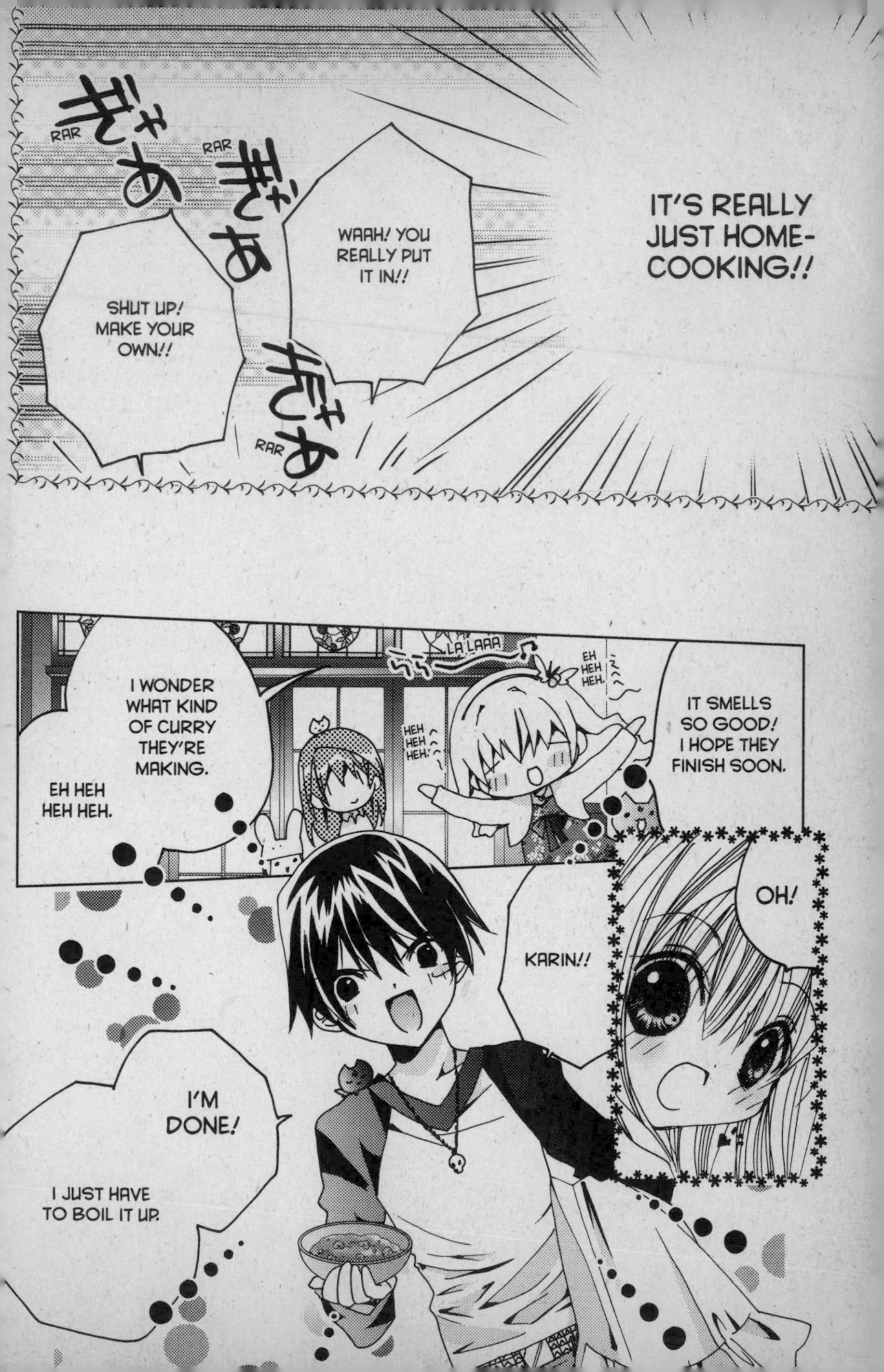
IT'S REALLY JUST HOME-COOKING!!
WAAH! YOU REALLY PUT IT IN!!
ぎゃあ RAR
ぎゃあ RAR
ぎゃあ RAR
SHUT UP! MAKE YOUR OWN!!
IT SMELLS SO GOOD! I HOPE THEY FINISH SOON.
EH HEH HEH.
ららー LA LAAA
HEH HEH HEH.
I WONDER WHAT KIND OF CURRY THEY'RE MAKING.
EH HEH HEH HEH.
OH!
KARIN!!
I'M DONE!
I JUST HAVE TO BOIL IT UP.

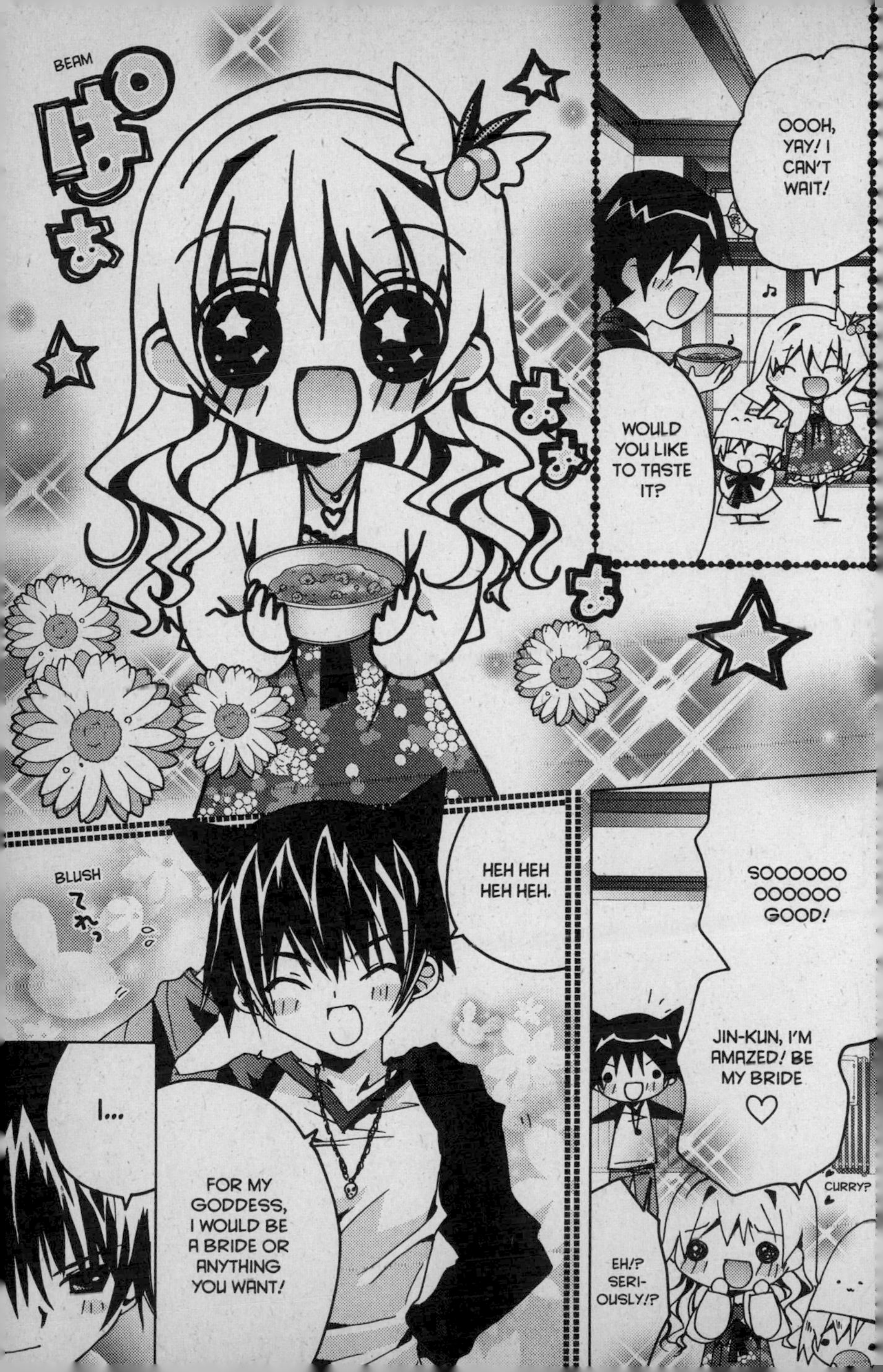
OOOH, YAY! I CAN'T WAIT!
WOULD YOU LIKE TO TASTE IT?
BEAM
SOOOOOO OOOOOO GOOD!
JIN-KUN, I'M AMAZED! BE MY BRIDE ♡
CURRY?
EH!? SERI-OUSLY!?
HEH HEH HEH HEH.
BLUSH
てれっ
FOR MY GODDESS, I WOULD BE A BRIDE OR ANYTHING YOU WANT!
I...

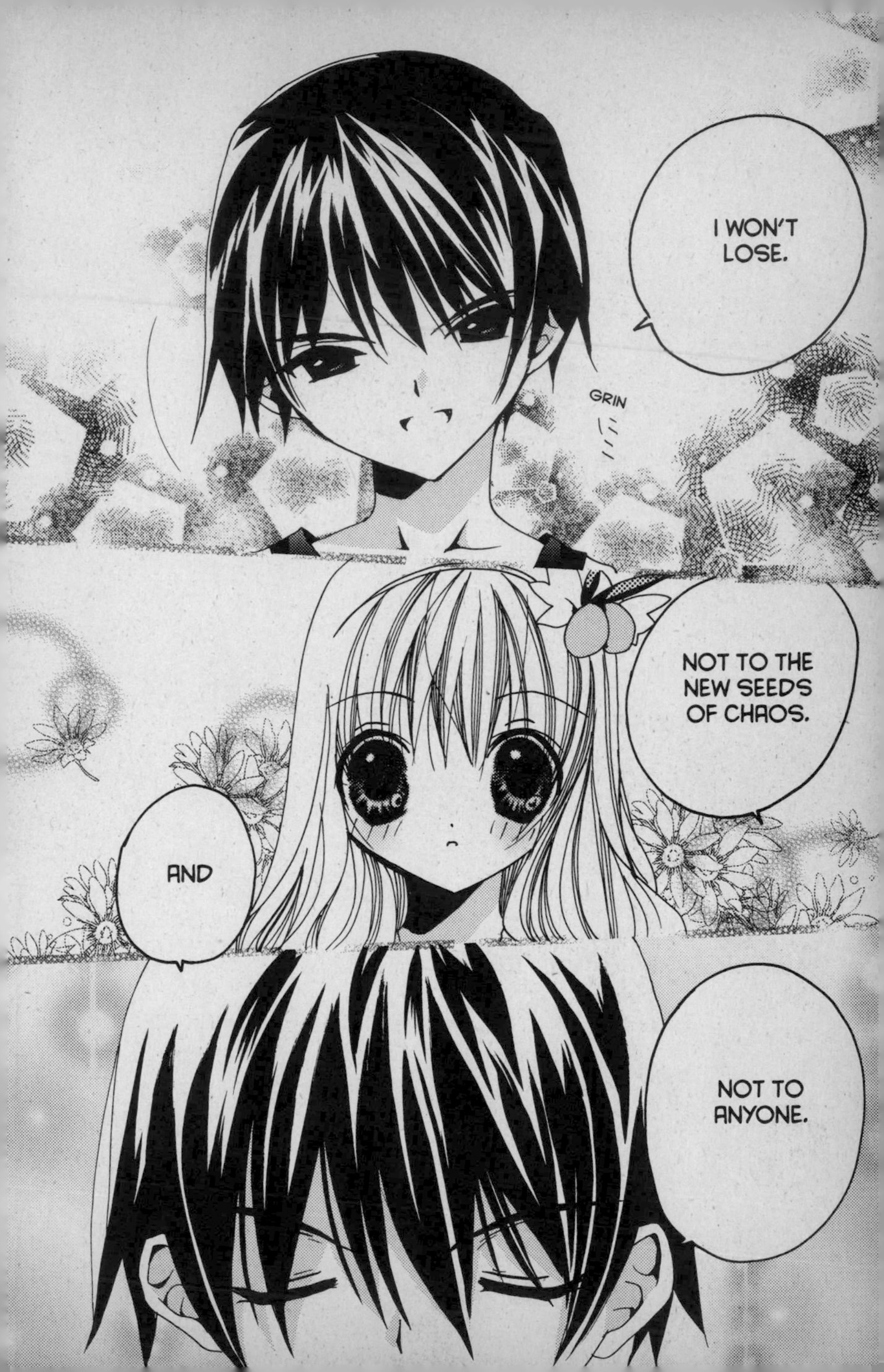
I WON'T LOSE.
GRIN
NOT TO THE NEW SEEDS OF CHAOS.
AND
NOT TO ANYONE.

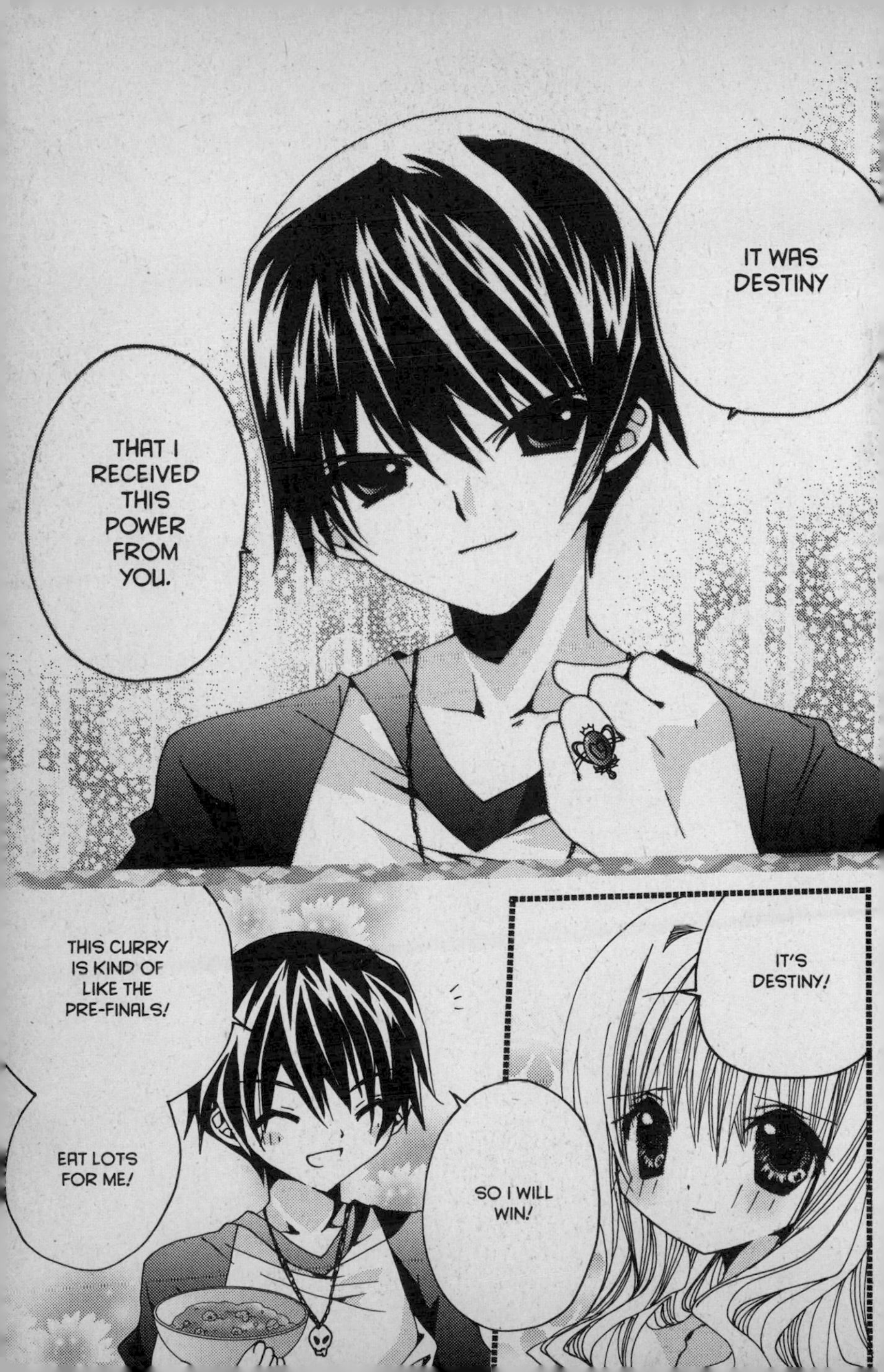
IT WAS DESTINY
THAT I RECEIVED THIS POWER FROM YOU.
IT'S DESTINY!
THIS CURRY IS KIND OF LIKE THE PRE-FINALS!
EAT LOTS FOR ME!
SO I WILL WIN!

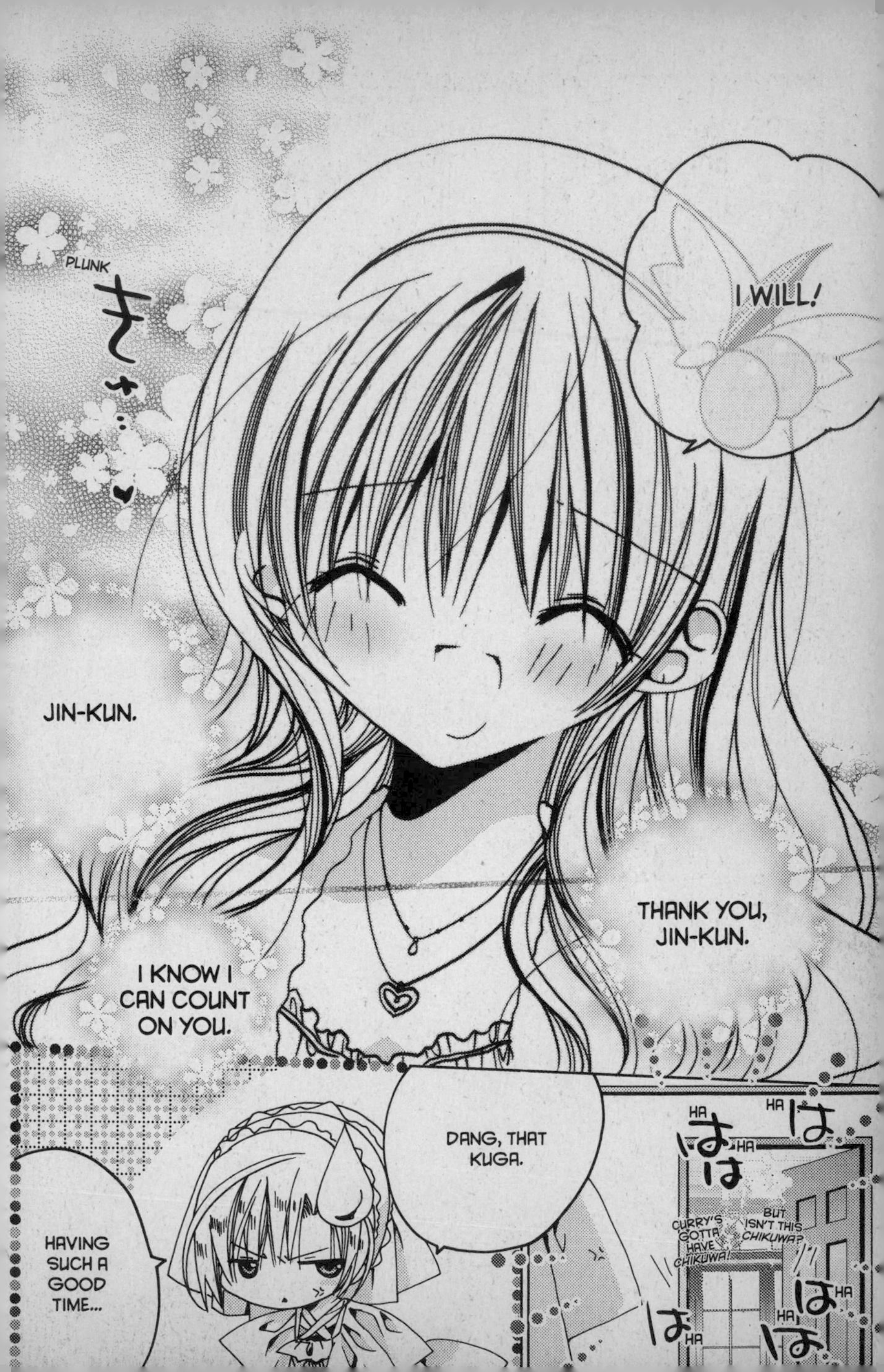
I WILL!
PLUNK
JIN-KUN.
THANK YOU, JIN-KUN.
I KNOW I CAN COUNT ON YOU.
HA HA HA
BUT ISN'T THIS CHIKUWA?
CURRY'S GOTTA HAVE CHIKUWA!
HA HA HA
DANG, THAT KUGA.
HAVING SUCH A GOOD TIME...

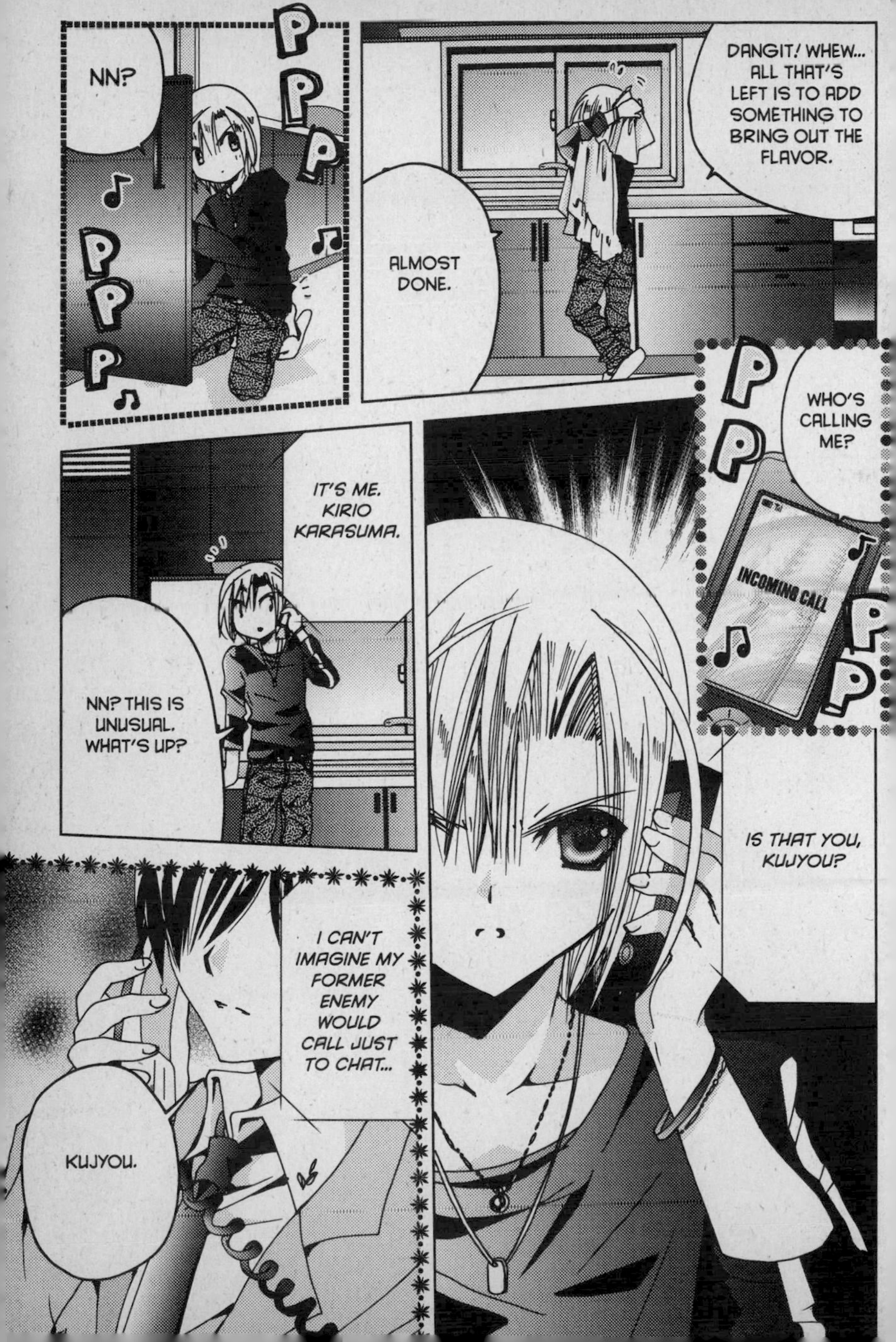
DANGIT! WHEW... ALL THAT'S LEFT IS TO ADD SOMETHING TO BRING OUT THE FLAVOR.
ALMOST DONE.
P P P
NN?
P P P
P P
WHO'S CALLING ME?
INCOMING CALL
P P
IS THAT YOU, KUJYOU?
IT'S ME. KIRIO KARASUMA.
NN? THIS IS UNUSUAL. WHAT'S UP?
I CAN'T IMAGINE MY FORMER ENEMY WOULD CALL JUST TO CHAT...
KUJYOU.

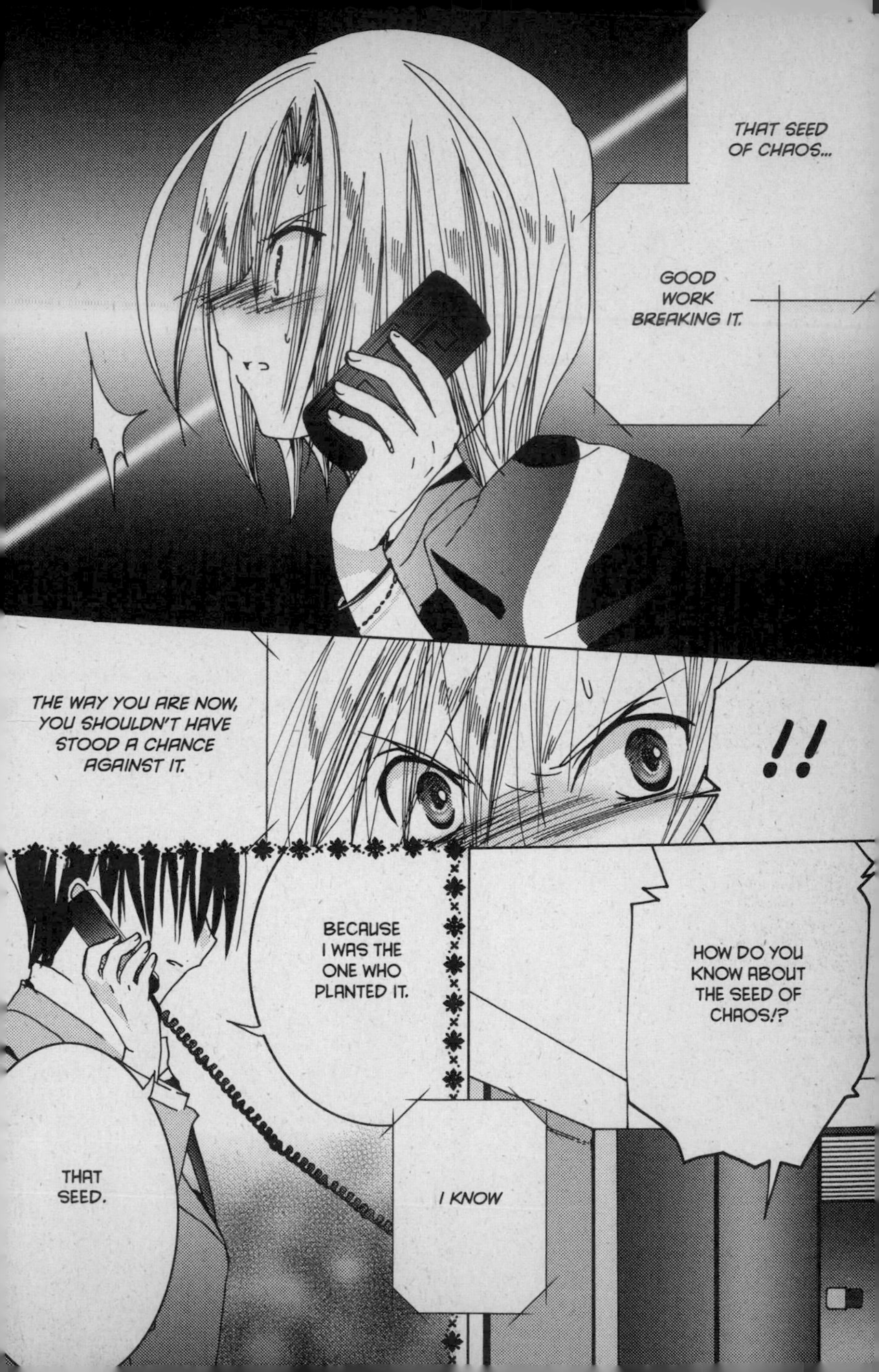
THAT SEED OF CHAOS...
GOOD WORK BREAKING IT.
!!
THE WAY YOU ARE NOW, YOU SHOULDN'T HAVE STOOD A CHANCE AGAINST IT.
HOW DO YOU KNOW ABOUT THE SEED OF CHAOS!?
BECAUSE I WAS THE ONE WHO PLANTED IT.
I KNOW
THAT SEED.

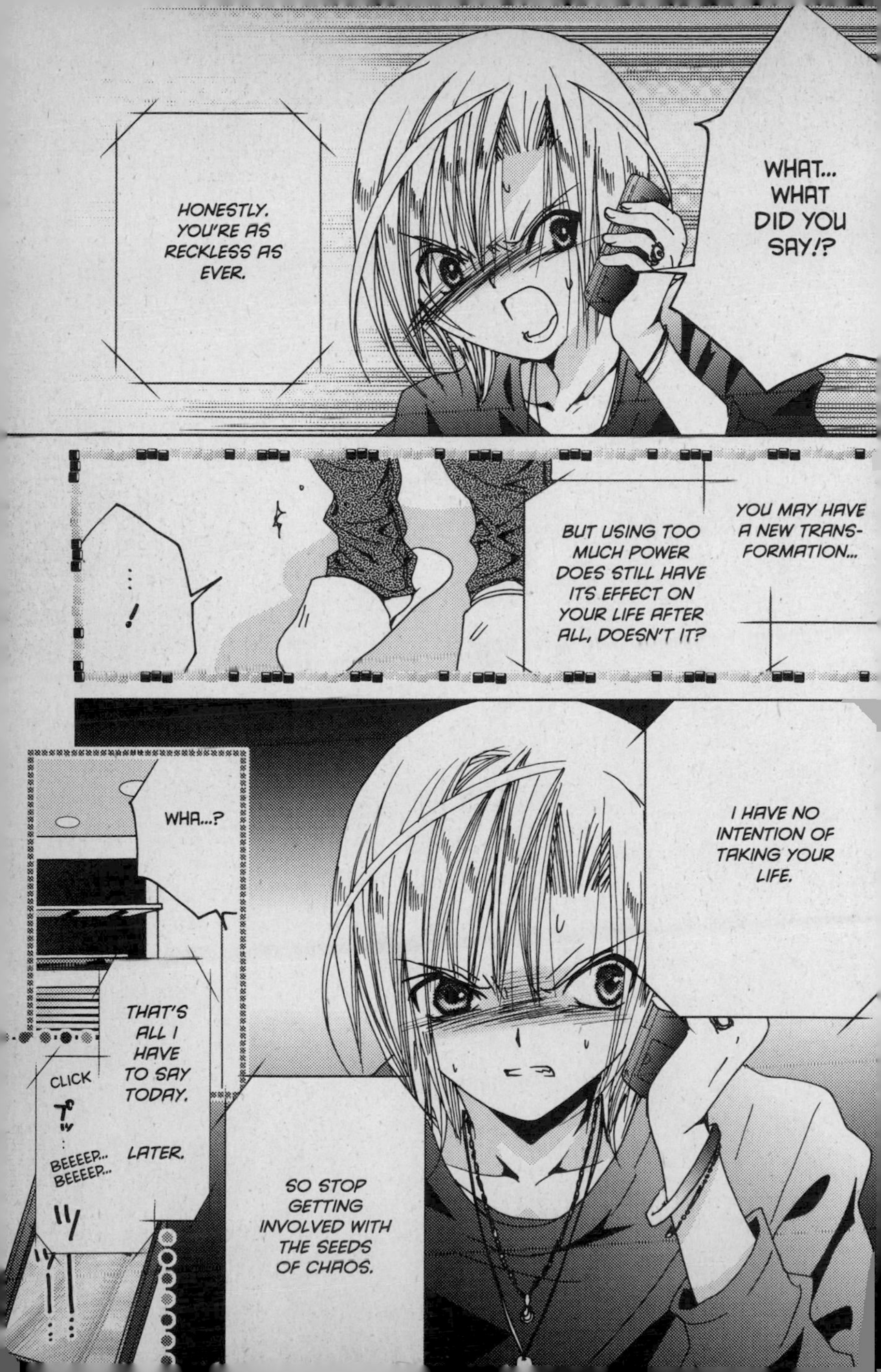
WHAT... WHAT DID YOU SAY!?
HONESTLY. YOU'RE AS RECKLESS AS EVER.
YOU MAY HAVE A NEW TRANS-FORMATION...
BUT USING TOO MUCH POWER DOES STILL HAVE ITS EFFECT ON YOUR LIFE AFTER ALL, DOESN'T IT?
...!
I HAVE NO INTENTION OF TAKING YOUR LIFE.
SO STOP GETTING INVOLVED WITH THE SEEDS OF CHAOS.
WHA...?
THAT'S ALL I HAVE TO SAY TODAY.
LATER.
CLICK
BEEEEP... BEEEEP...

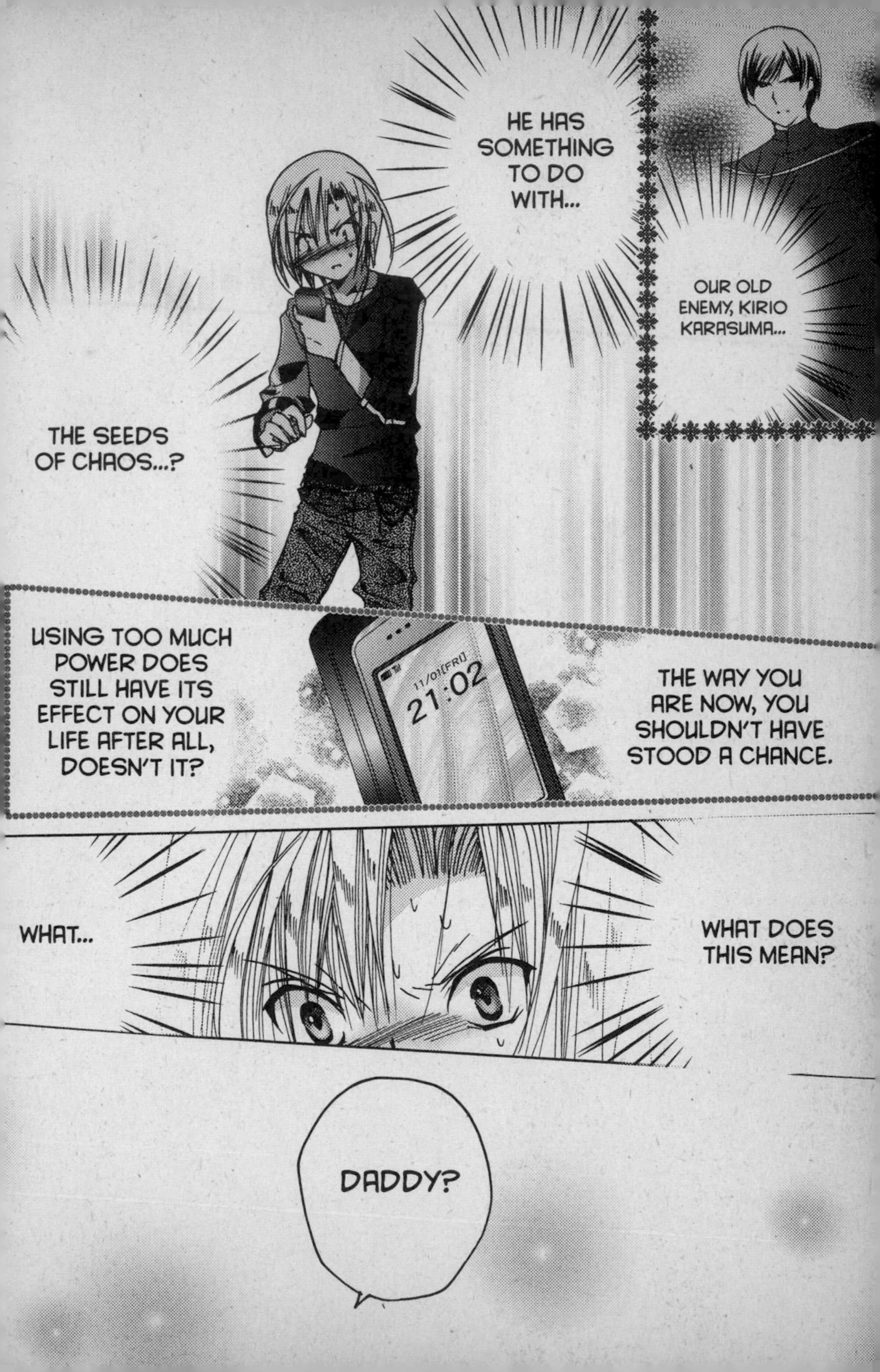
HE HAS SOMETHING TO DO WITH...
OUR OLD ENEMY, KIRIO KARASUMA...
THE SEEDS OF CHAOS...?
THE WAY YOU ARE NOW, YOU SHOULDN'T HAVE STOOD A CHANCE.
11/01[FRI]
21:02
USING TOO MUCH POWER DOES STILL HAVE ITS EFFECT ON YOUR LIFE AFTER ALL, DOESN'T IT?
WHAT DOES THIS MEAN?
WHAT...
DADDY?

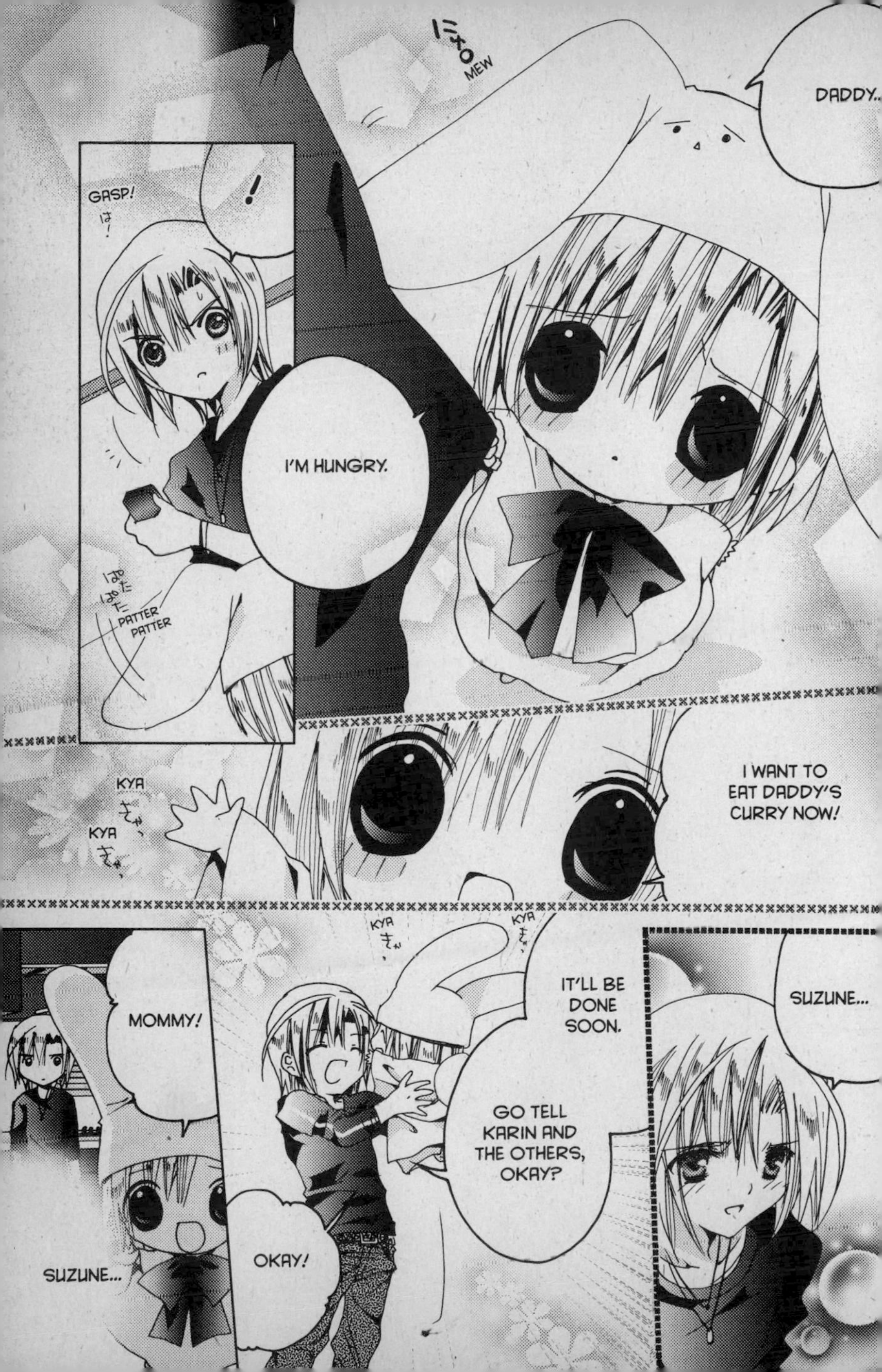
にゃ
MEW
DADDY..
I'M HUNGRY.
!
GASP!
は!
ぱたぱた
PATTER PATTER
I WANT TO EAT DADDY'S CURRY NOW!
KYA
きゃ
KYA
きゃ
SUZUNE...
IT'LL BE DONE SOON.
GO TELL KARIN AND THE OTHERS, OKAY?
KYA
きゃ
KYA
きゃ
OKAY!
MOMMY!
SUZUNE...

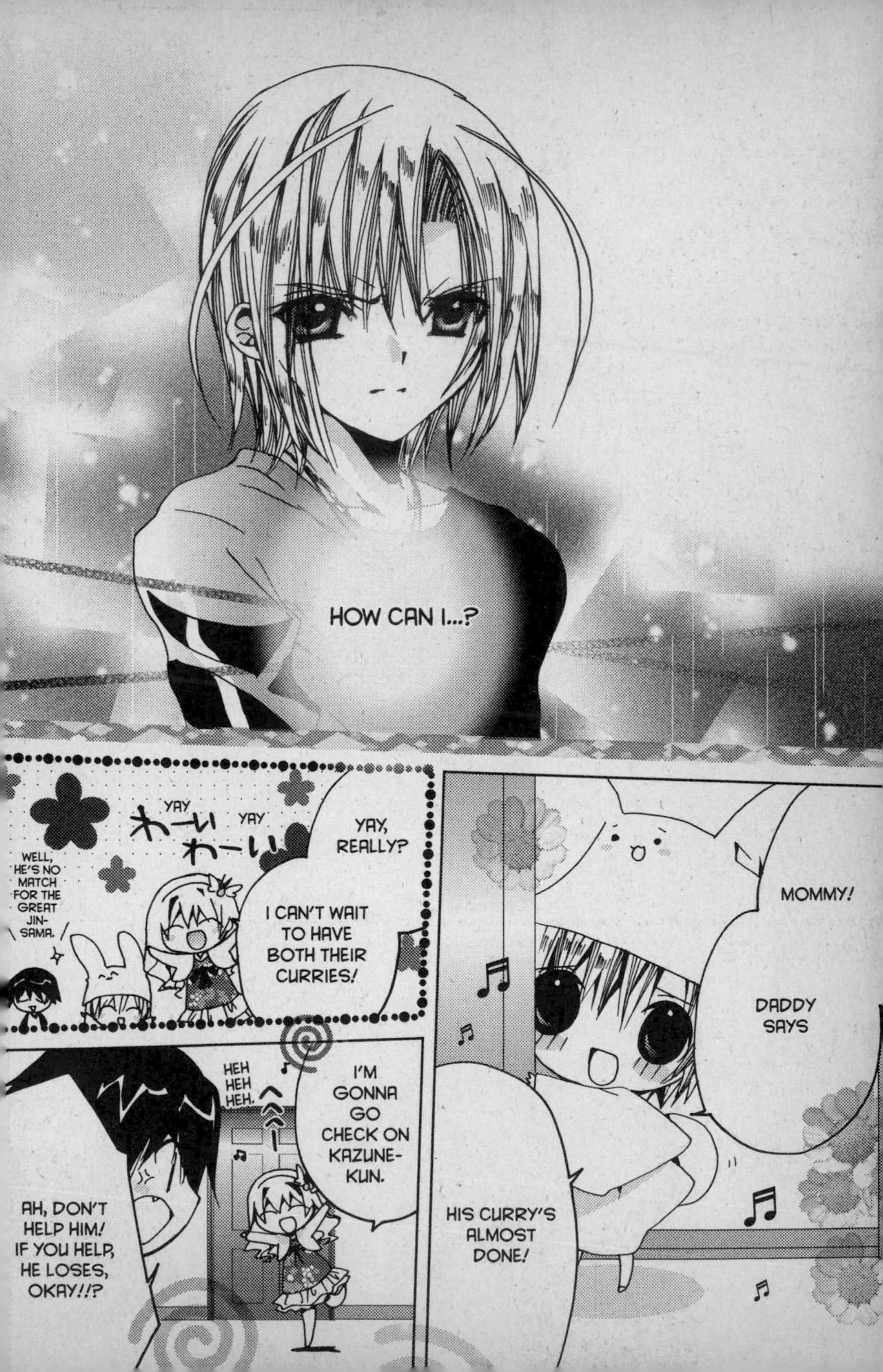
HOW CAN I...?
MOMMY! DADDY SAYS
HIS CURRY'S ALMOST DONE!
わーい わーい
YAY YAY
YAY, REALLY?
I CAN'T WAIT TO HAVE BOTH THEIR CURRIES!
WELL, HE'S NO MATCH FOR THE GREAT JIN-SAMA.
I'M GONNA GO CHECK ON KAZUNE-KUN.
HEH HEH HEH.
AH, DON'T HELP HIM! IF YOU HELP, HE LOSES, OKAY!!?

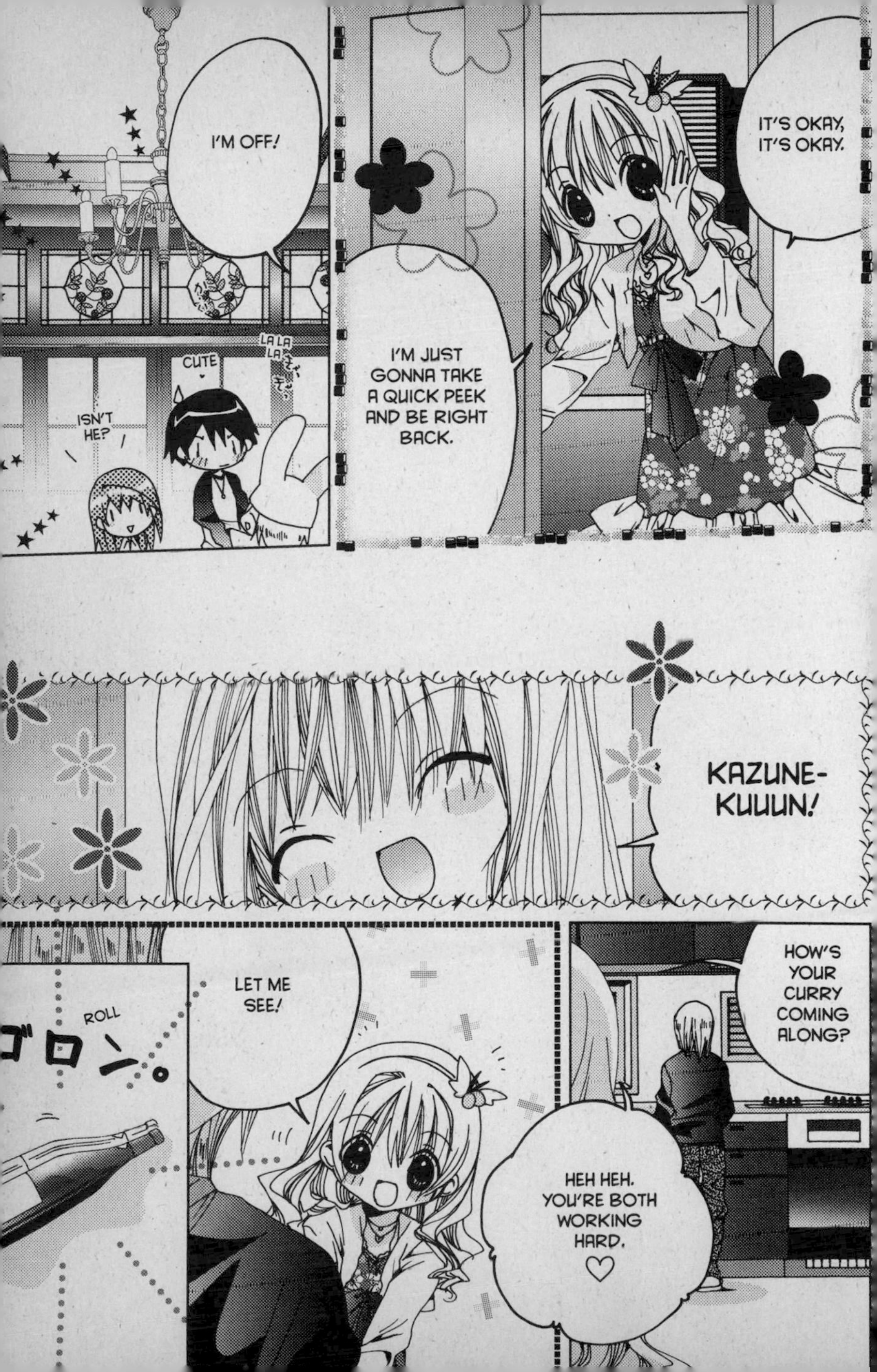
IT'S OKAY, IT'S OKAY.
I'M JUST GONNA TAKE A QUICK PEEK AND BE RIGHT BACK.
I'M OFF!
LA LA LA
CUTE
ISN'T HE?
KAZUNE-KUUUN!
HOW'S YOUR CURRY COMING ALONG?
HEH HEH. YOU'RE BOTH WORKING HARD. ♡
LET ME SEE!
ROLL
ゴロン

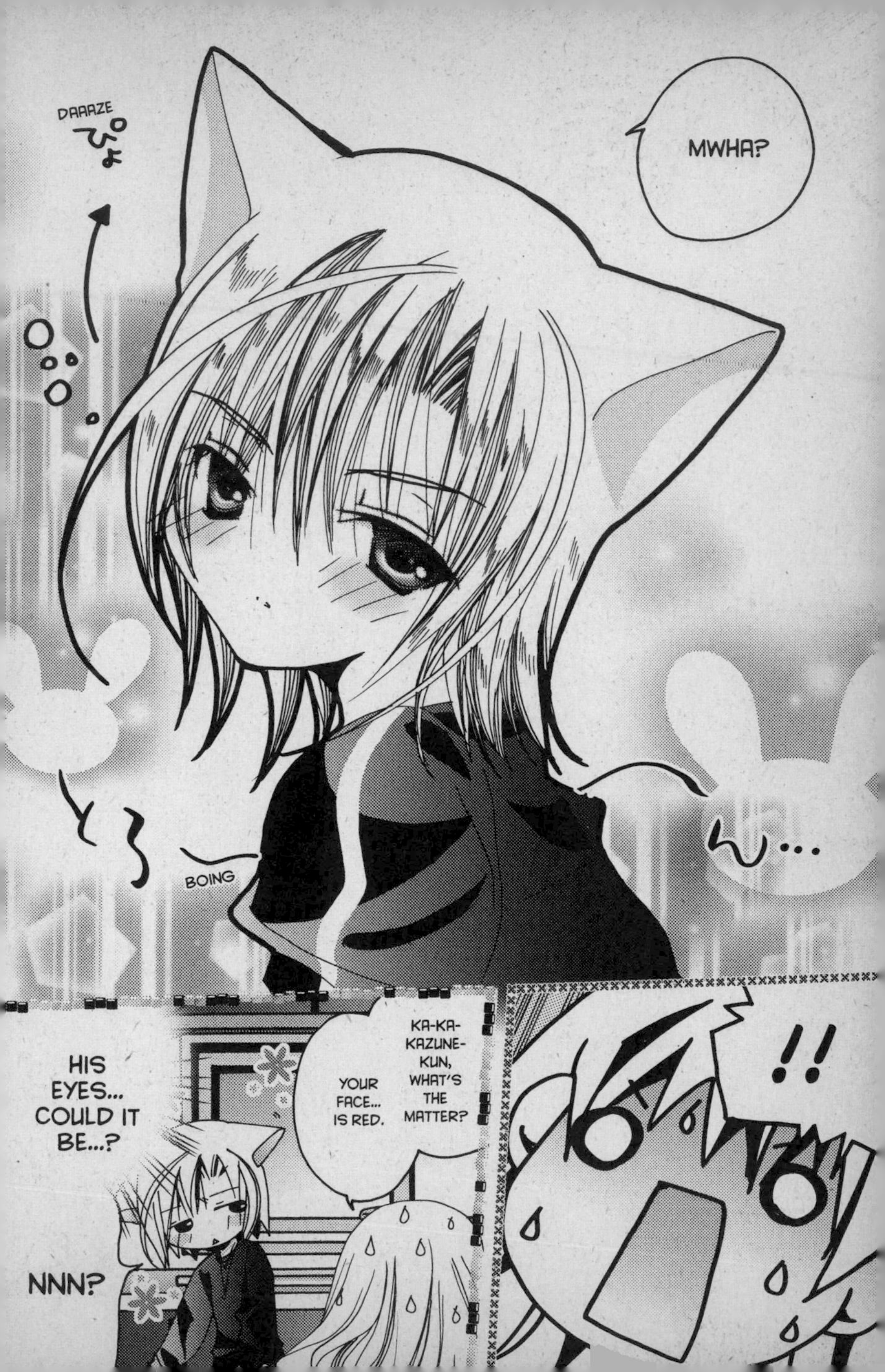
MWHA?
DAAAZE
ぴょ
ん...
とろ
BOING
!!
KA-KA-KAZUNE-KUN, WHAT'S THE MATTER?
YOUR FACE... IS RED.
HIS EYES... COULD IT BE...?
NNN?

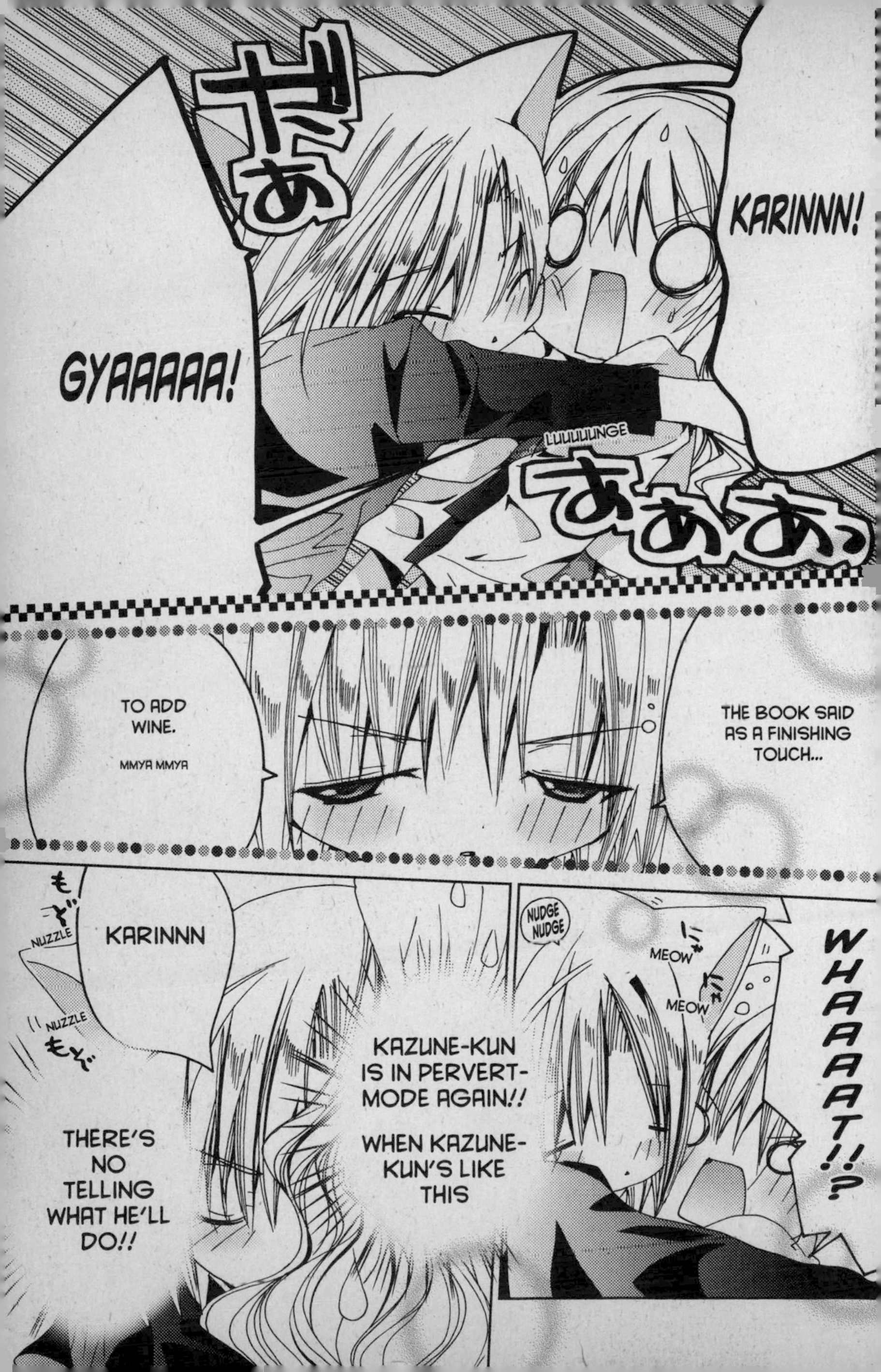
KARINNN!
LUUUUUNGE
GYAAAAAA!
THE BOOK SAID AS A FINISHING TOUCH...
TO ADD WINE.
MMYA MMYA
WHAAAAAT!!?
NUDGE NUDGE
MEOW
MEOW
KARINNN
NUZZLE
NUZZLE
KAZUNE-KUN IS IN PERVERT-MODE AGAIN!!
WHEN KAZUNE-KUN'S LIKE THIS
THERE'S NO TELLING WHAT HE'LL DO!!

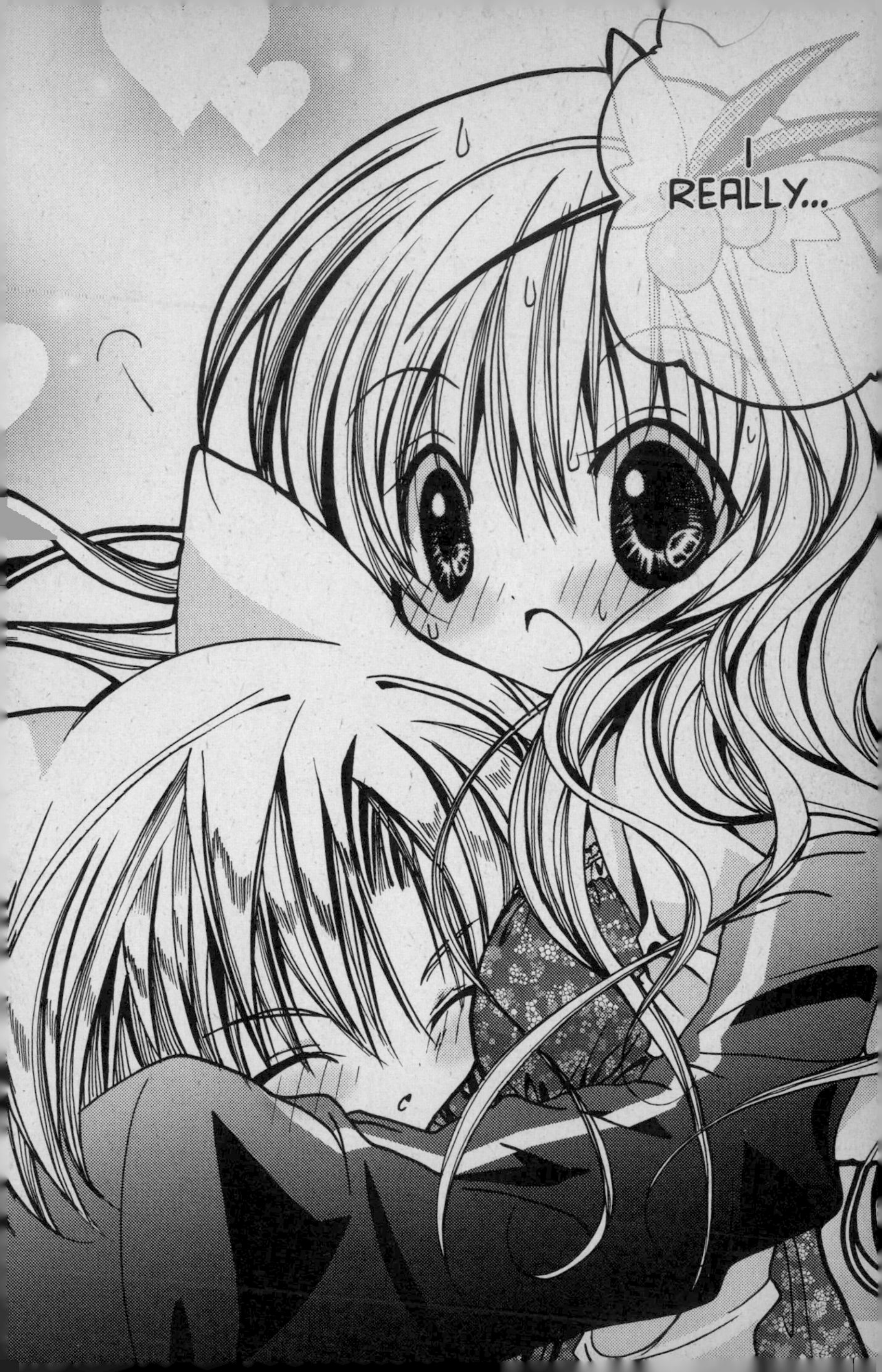
I REALLY...

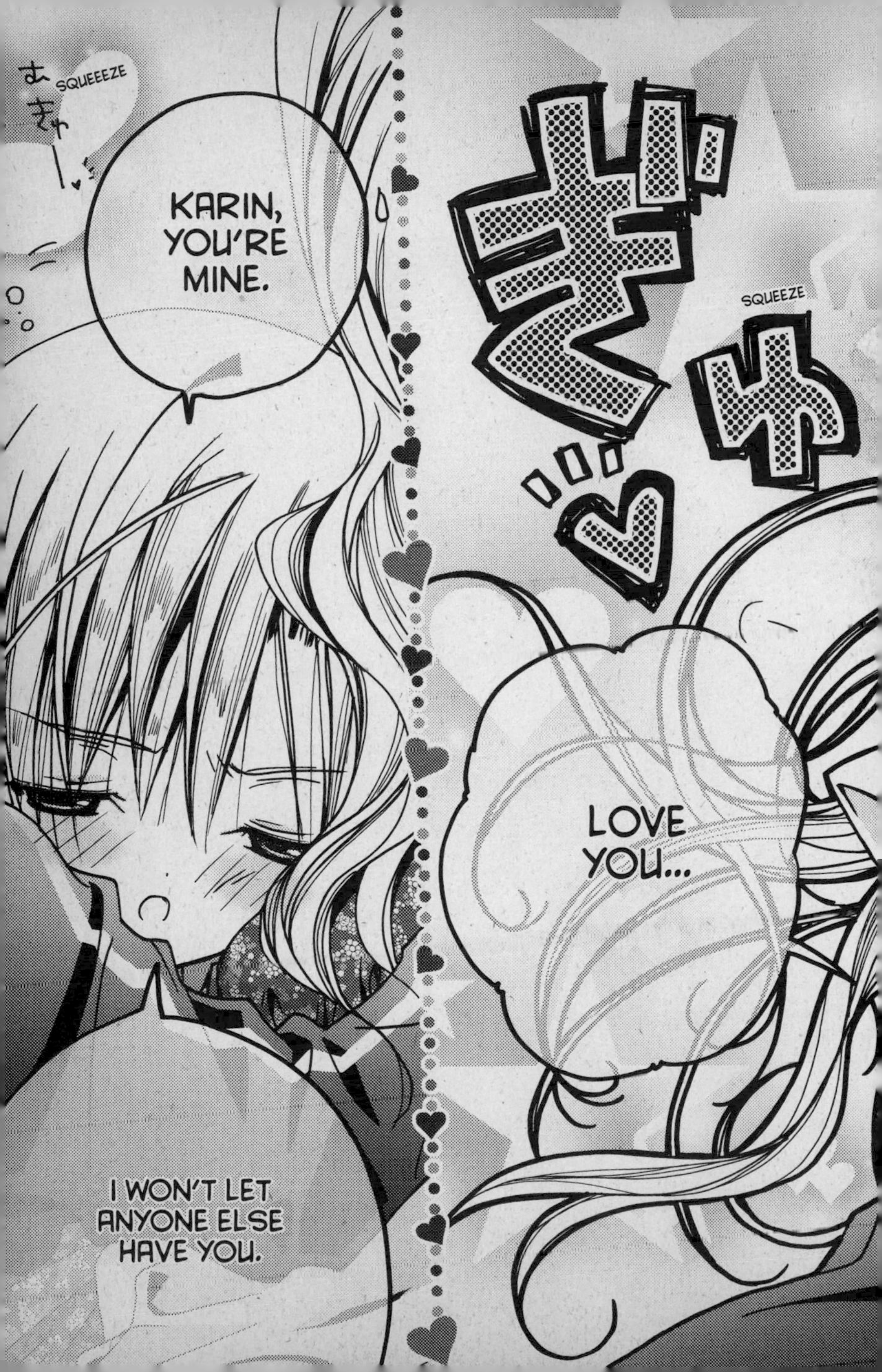
SQUEEZE
LOVE YOU...
KARIN, YOU'RE MINE.
SQUEEEZE
I WON'T LET ANYONE ELSE HAVE YOU.

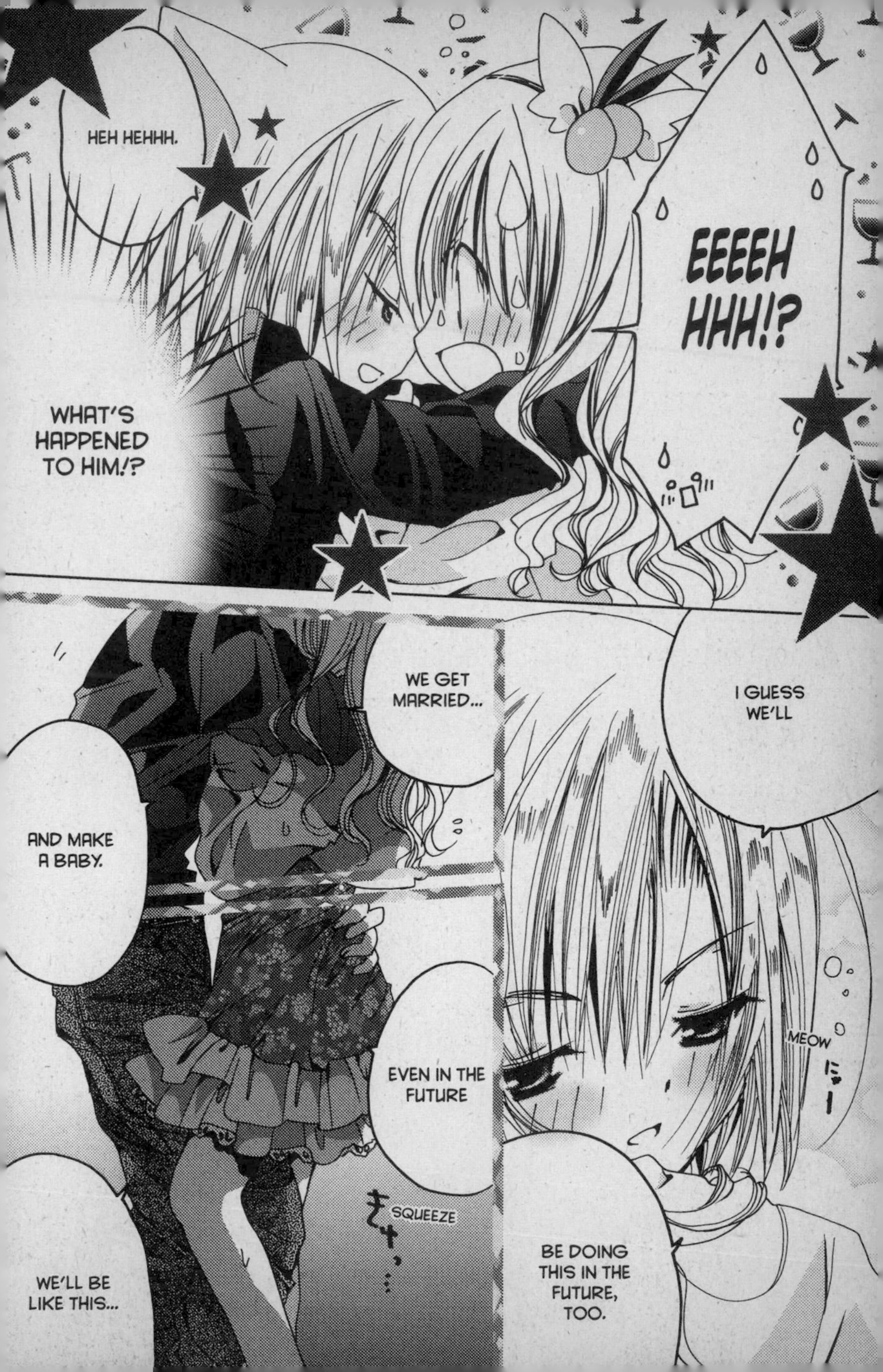
EEEEH HHH!?
HEH HEHHH.
WHAT'S HAPPENED TO HIM!?
I GUESS WE'LL
MEOW
BE DOING THIS IN THE FUTURE, TOO.
WE GET MARRIED...
AND MAKE A BABY.
EVEN IN THE FUTURE
SQUEEZE
WE'LL BE LIKE THIS...

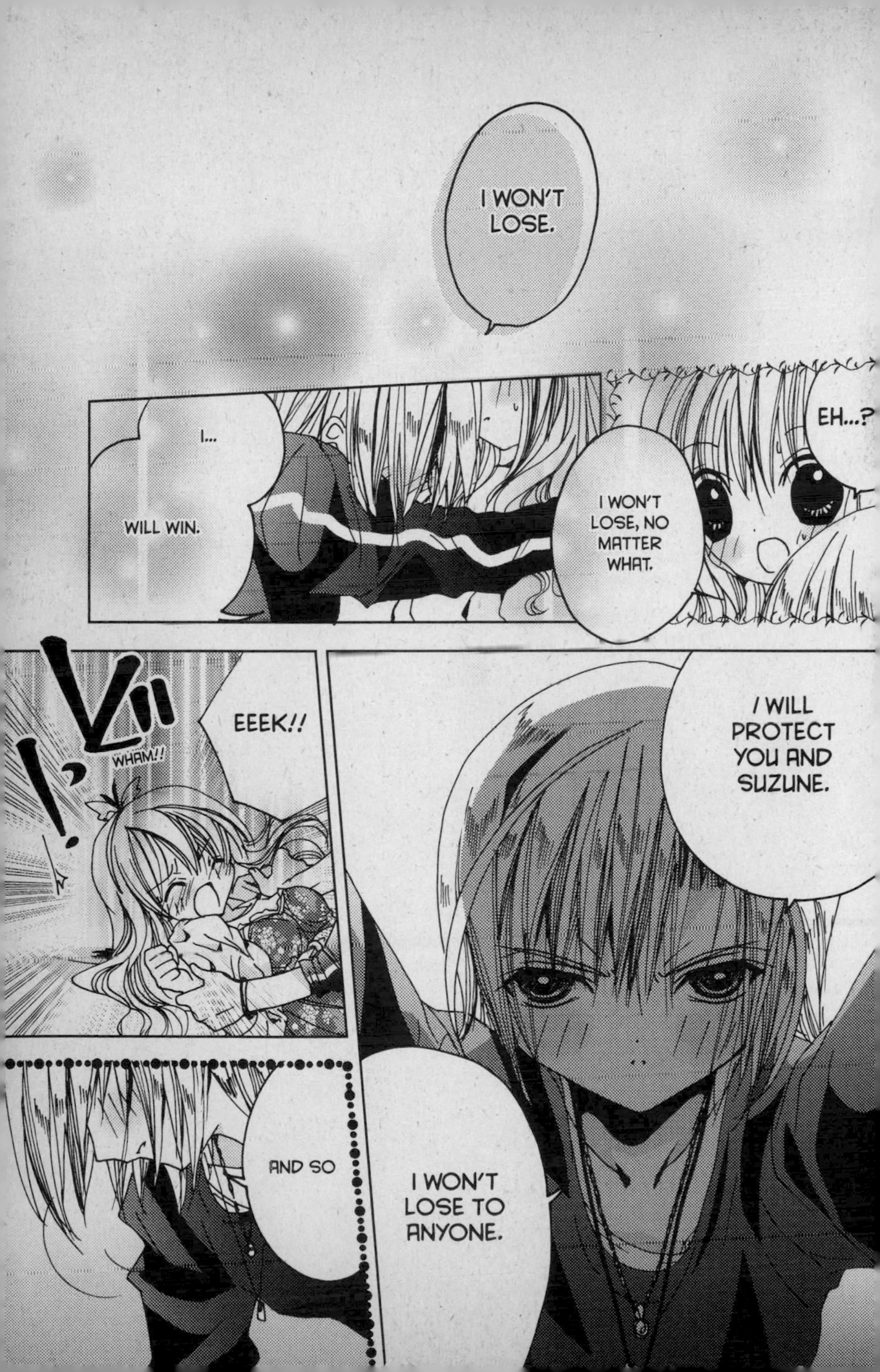
I WON'T LOSE.
EH...?
I WON'T LOSE, NO MATTER WHAT.
I...
WILL WIN.
I WILL PROTECT YOU AND SUZUNE.
EEEK!!
WHAM!!
AND SO
I WON'T LOSE TO ANYONE.

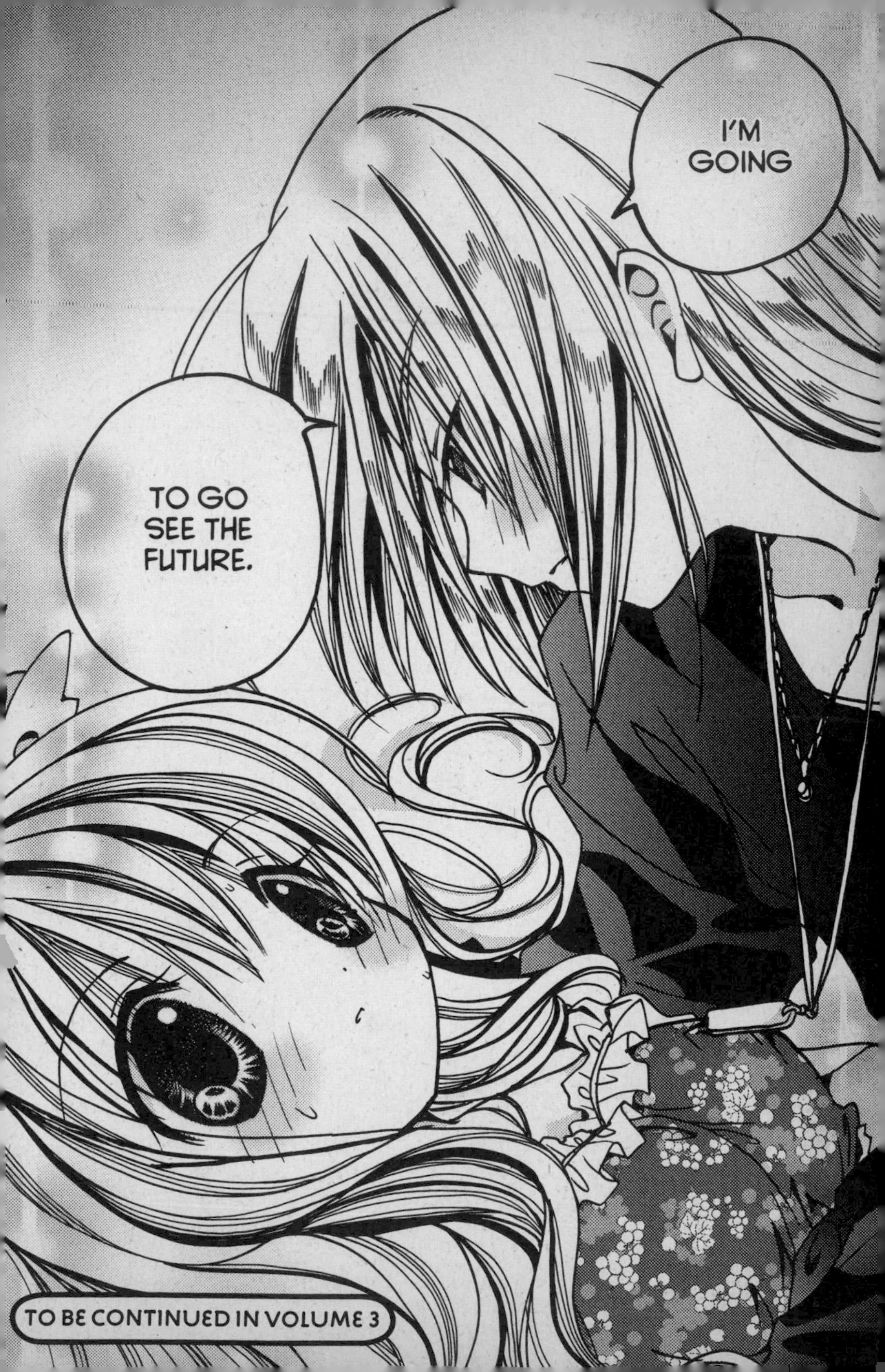
I'M GOING
TO GO SEE THE FUTURE.
TO BE CONTINUED IN VOLUME 3

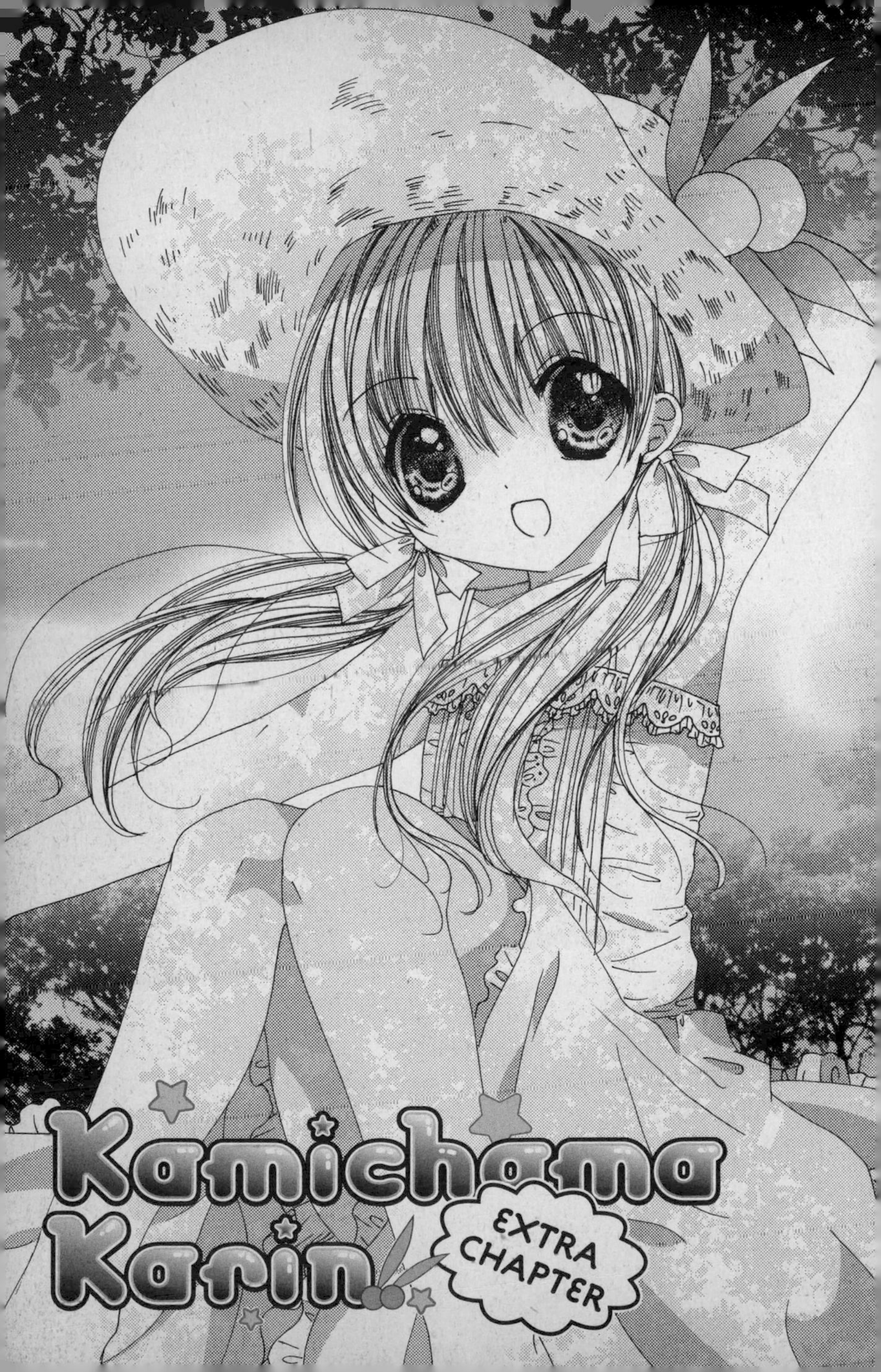
Kamichama Karin
EXTRA CHAPTER

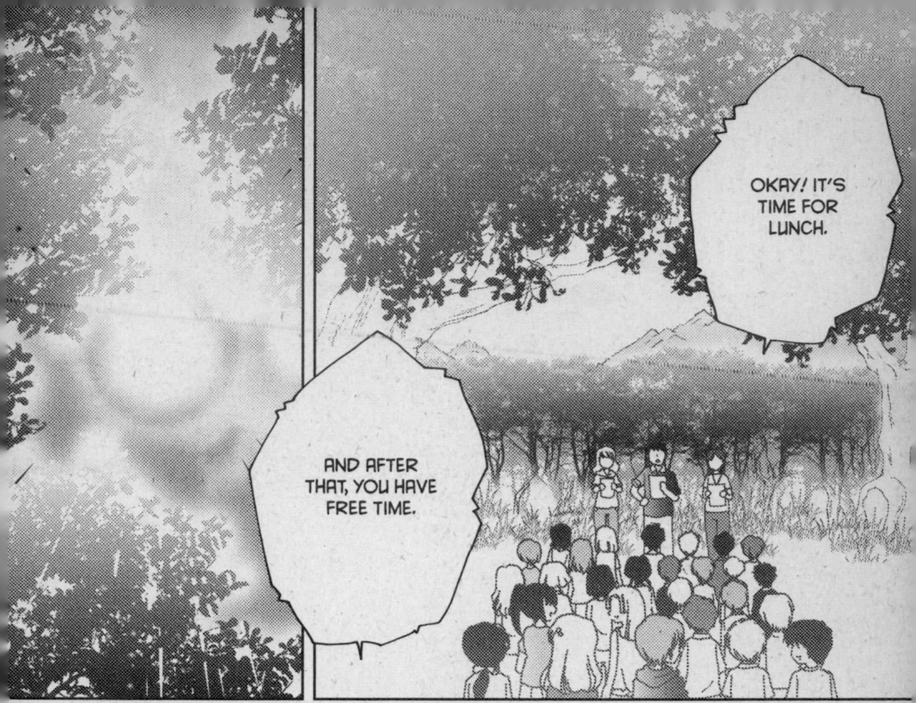
OKAY! IT'S TIME FOR LUNCH.
AND AFTER THAT, YOU HAVE FREE TIME.

KAMICHAMA KARIN WORLD

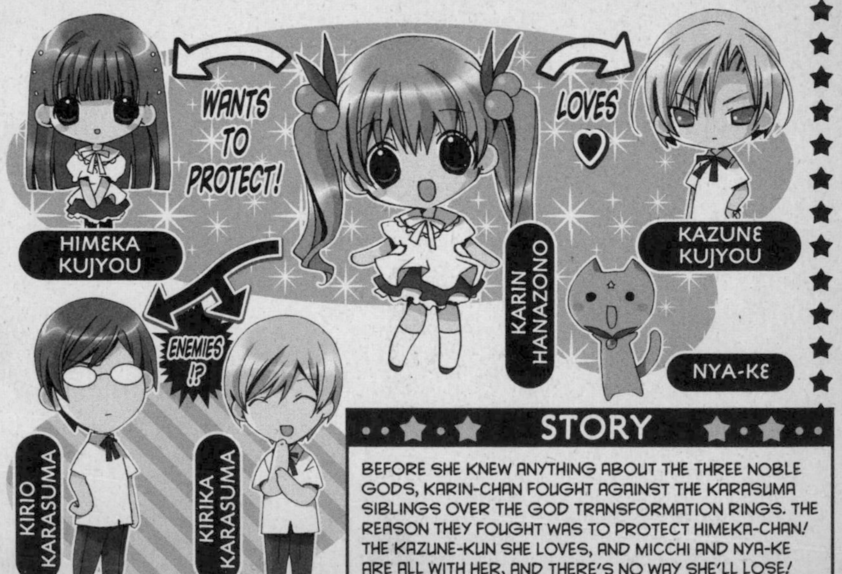
WANTS TO PROTECT!
LOVES
HIMEKA KUJYOU
KARIN HANAZONO
KAZUNE KUJYOU
ENEMIES !?
NYA-KE
KIRIO KARASUMA
KIRIKA KARASUMA

STORY

BEFORE SHE KNEW ANYTHING ABOUT THE THREE NOBLE GODS, KARIN-CHAN FOUGHT AGAINST THE KARASUMA SIBLINGS OVER THE GOD TRANSFORMATION RINGS. THE REASON THEY FOUGHT WAS TO PROTECT HIMEKA-CHAN! THE KAZUNE-KUN SHE LOVES, AND MICCHI AND NYA-KE ARE ALL WITH HER, AND THERE'S NO WAY SHE'LL LOSE! THESE ARE THE CIRCUMSTANCES IN WHICH WE FIND KARIN-CHAN IN THIS SUMMER STORY.

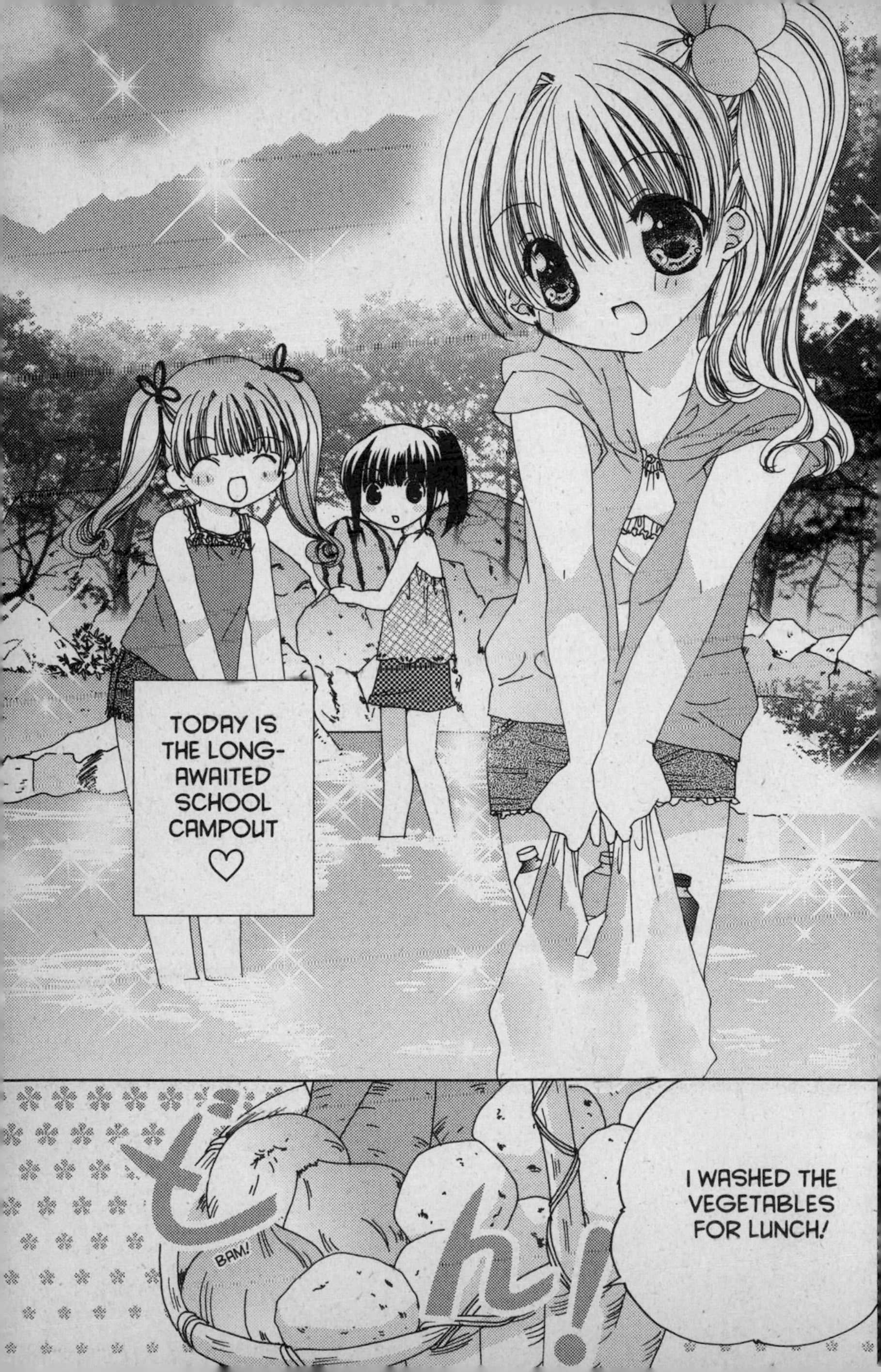
TODAY IS THE LONG-AWAITED SCHOOL CAMPOUT ♡
I WASHED THE VEGETABLES FOR LUNCH!
BAM!

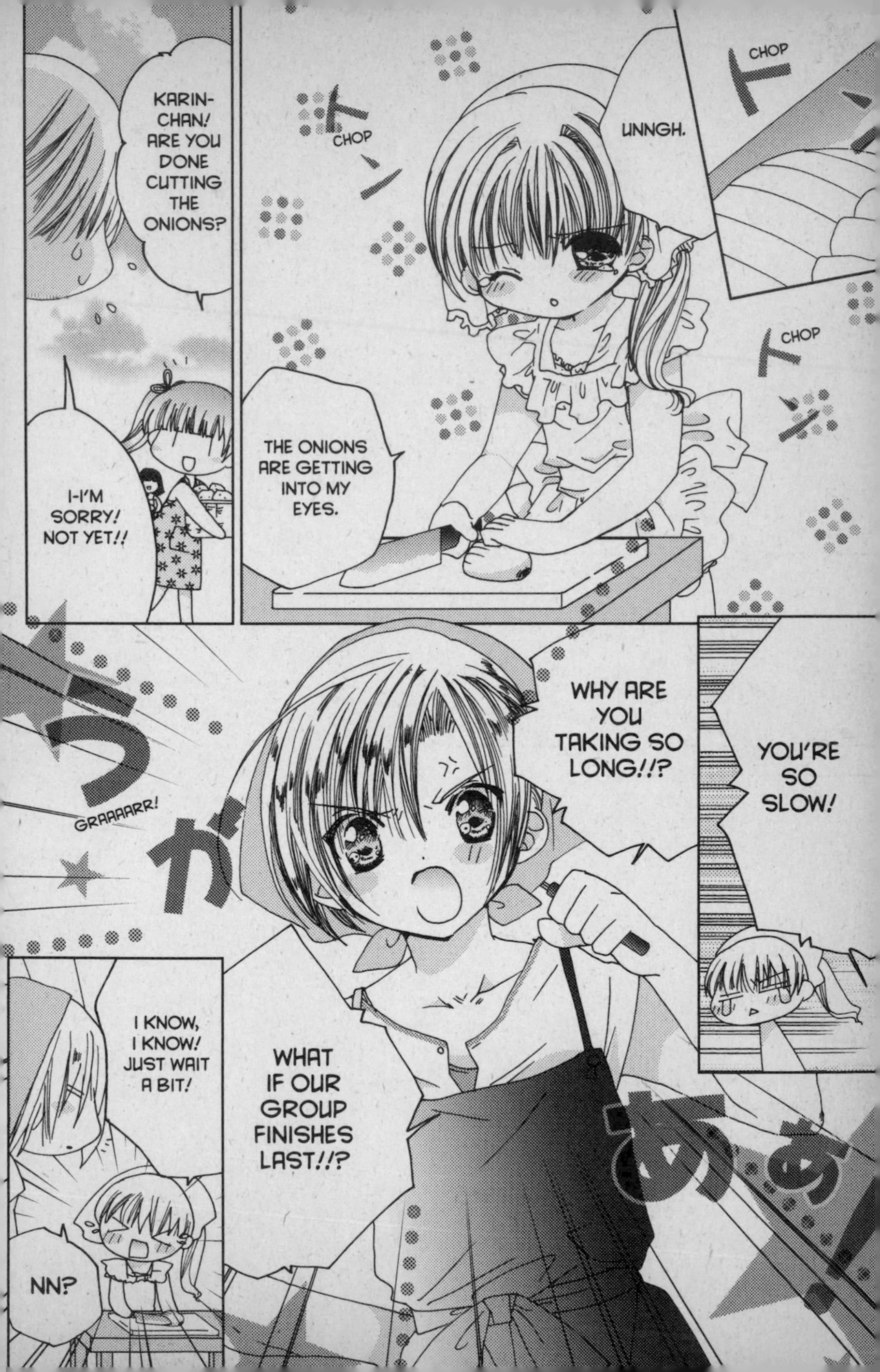

CHOP
UNNGH.
CHOP
CHOP
THE ONIONS ARE GETTING INTO MY EYES.
KARIN-CHAN! ARE YOU DONE CUTTING THE ONIONS?
I-I'M SORRY! NOT YET!!
YOU'RE SO SLOW!
WHY ARE YOU TAKING SO LONG!!?
GRAAAARR!
WHAT IF OUR GROUP FINISHES LAST!!?
I KNOW, I KNOW! JUST WAIT A BIT!
NN?

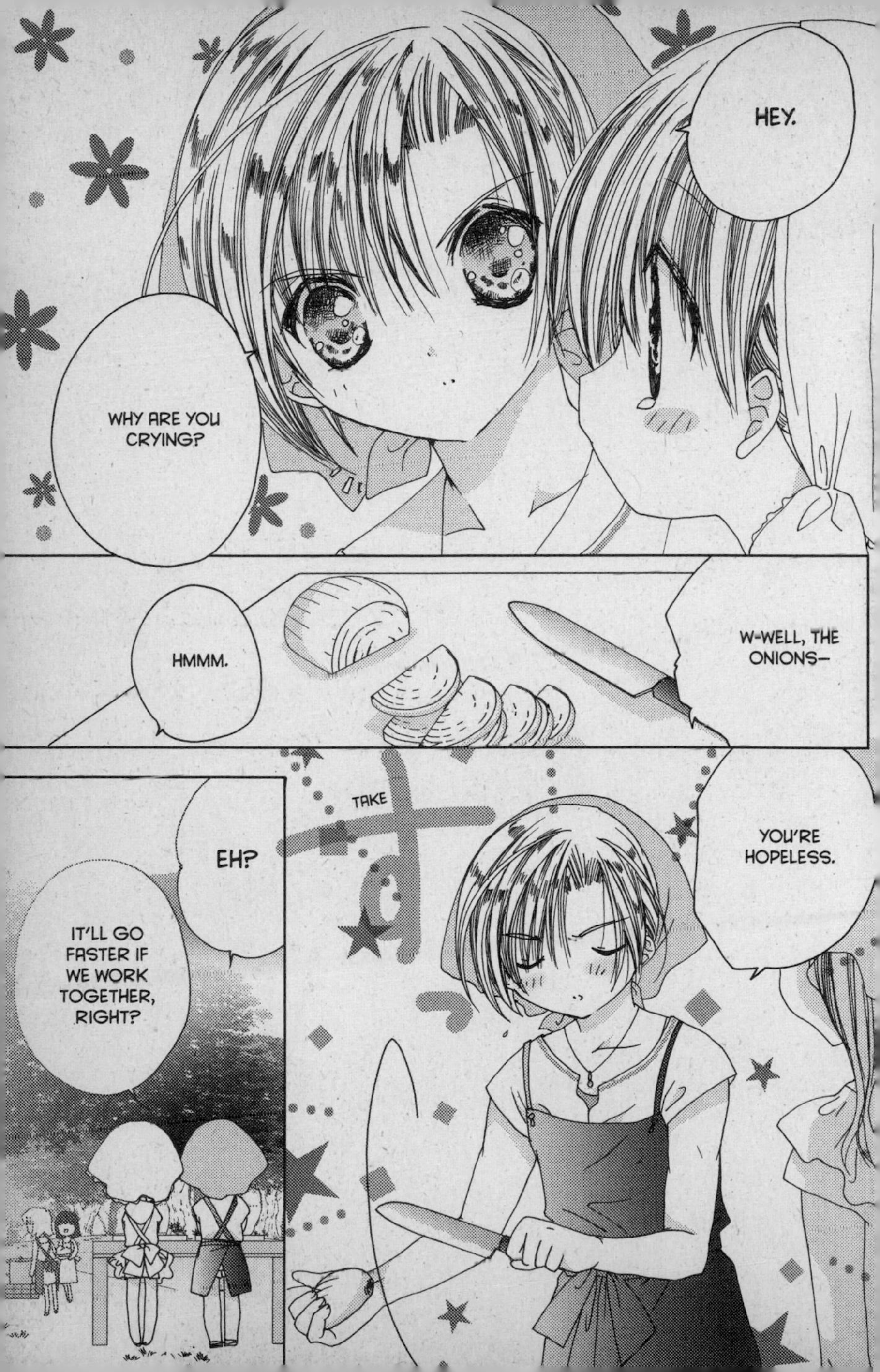
HEY.
WHY ARE YOU CRYING?
W-WELL, THE ONIONS—
HMMM.
YOU'RE HOPELESS.
TAKE
EH?
IT'LL GO FASTER IF WE WORK TOGETHER, RIGHT?

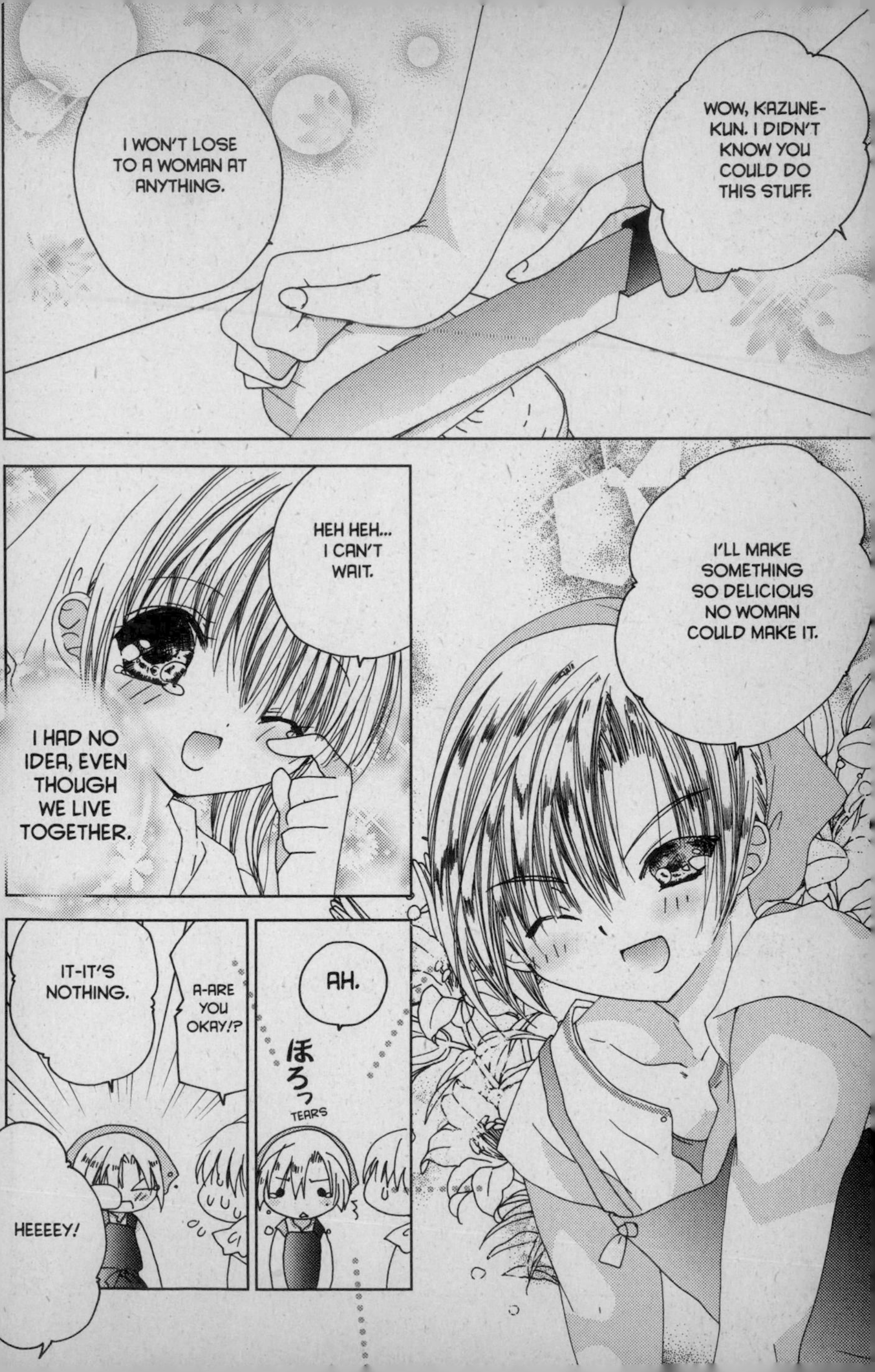

WOW, KAZUNE-KUN. I DIDN'T KNOW YOU COULD DO THIS STUFF.
I WON'T LOSE TO A WOMAN AT ANYTHING.
I'LL MAKE SOMETHING SO DELICIOUS NO WOMAN COULD MAKE IT.
HEH HEH... I CAN'T WAIT.
I HAD NO IDEA, EVEN THOUGH WE LIVE TOGETHER.
AH.
ほろっ
TEARS
A-ARE YOU OKAY!?
IT-IT'S NOTHING.
HEEEEY!

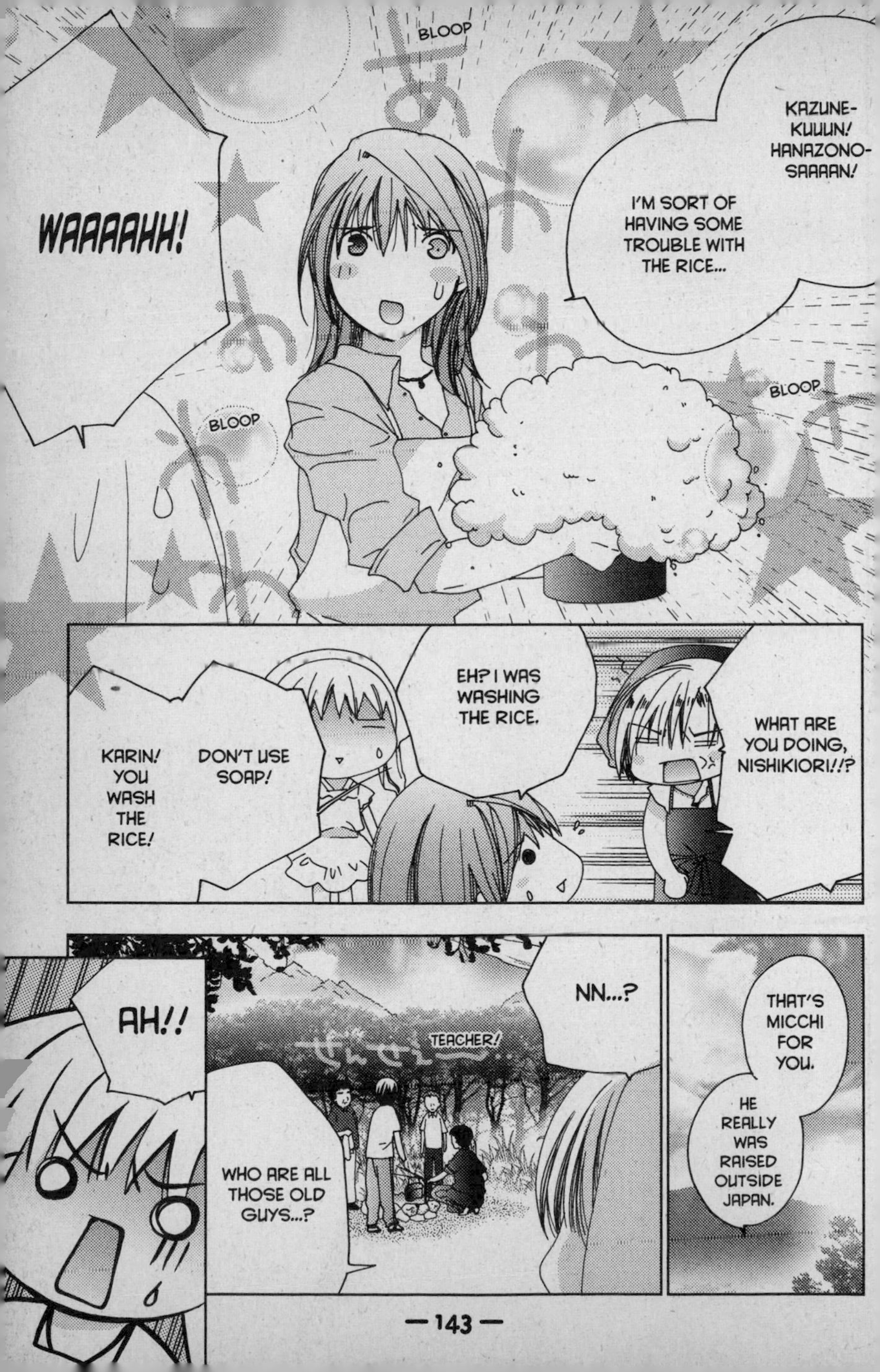
BLOOP
KAZUNE-KUUUN! HANAZONO-SAAAAN!
I'M SORT OF HAVING SOME TROUBLE WITH THE RICE...
BLOOP
BLOOP
WAAAAHH!
WHAT ARE YOU DOING, NISHIKIORI!!?
EH? I WAS WASHING THE RICE.
DON'T USE SOAP!
KARIN! YOU WASH THE RICE!
THAT'S MICCHI FOR YOU.
HE REALLY WAS RAISED OUTSIDE JAPAN.
NN...?
TEACHER!
WHO ARE ALL THOSE OLD GUYS...?
AH!!

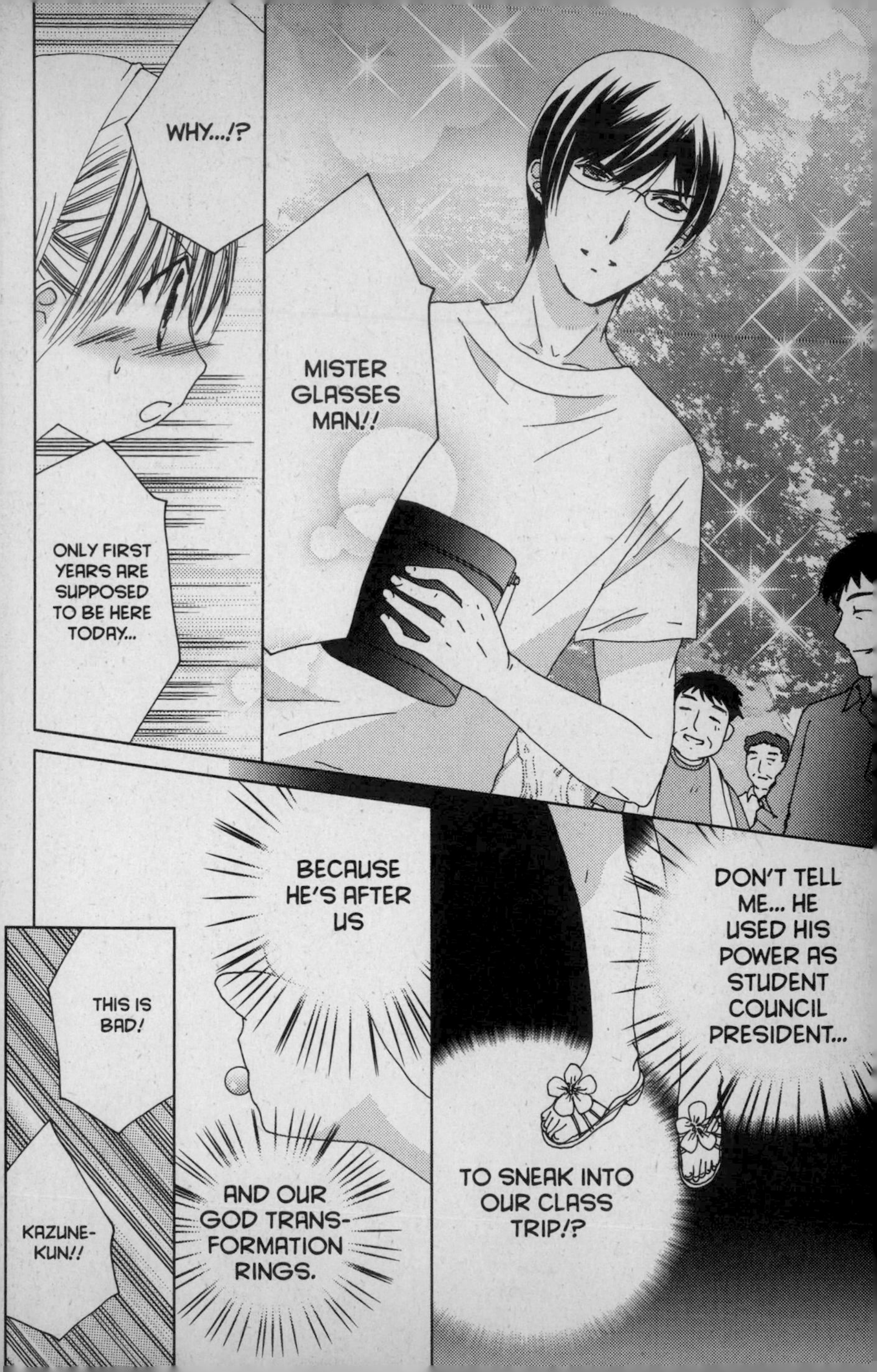
MISTER GLASSES MAN!!
WHY...!?
ONLY FIRST YEARS ARE SUPPOSED TO BE HERE TODAY...
DON'T TELL ME... HE USED HIS POWER AS STUDENT COUNCIL PRESIDENT...
TO SNEAK INTO OUR CLASS TRIP!?
BECAUSE HE'S AFTER US
AND OUR GOD TRANS-FORMATION RINGS.
THIS IS BAD!
KAZUNE-KUN!!

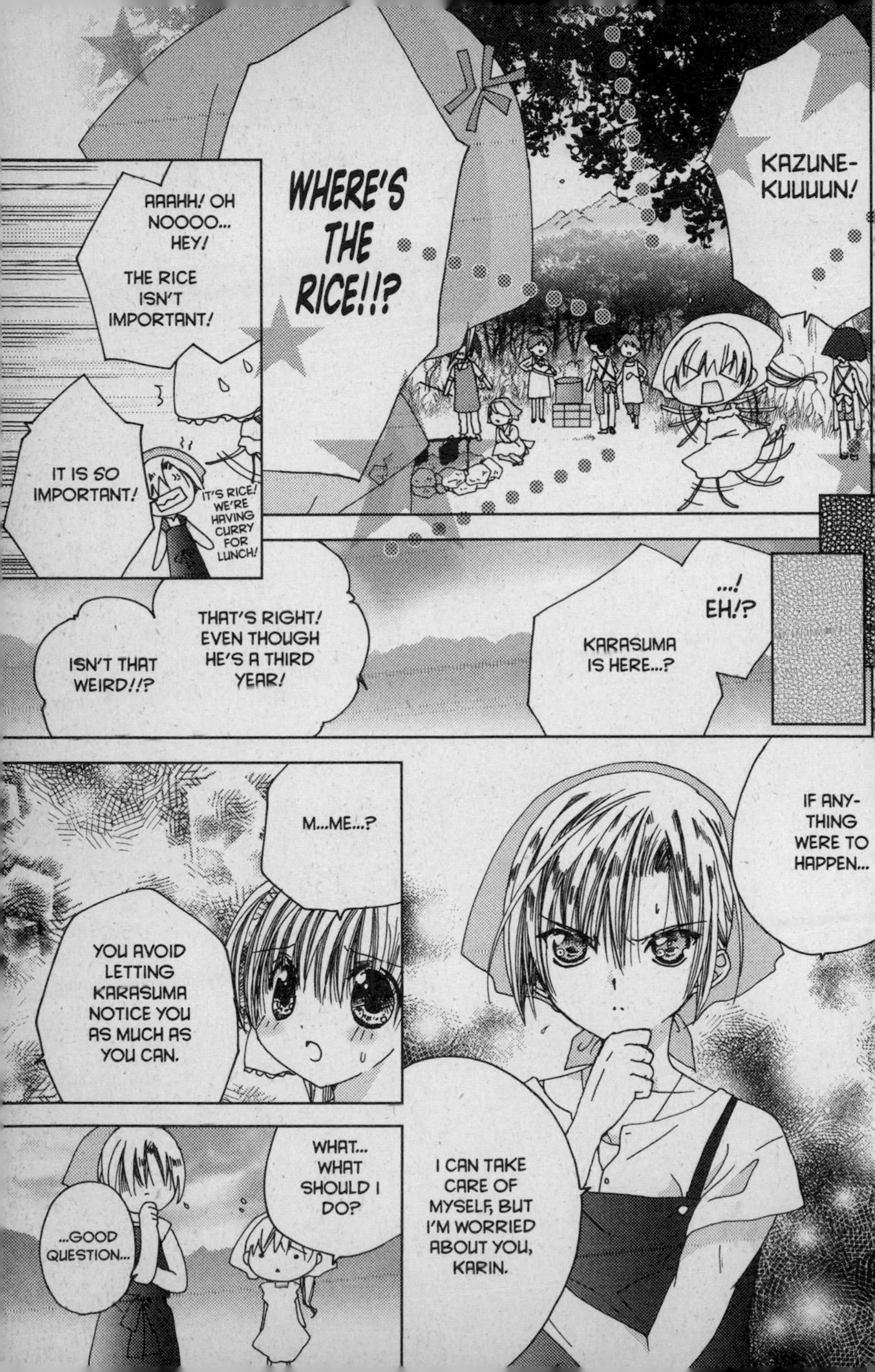
KAZUNE-KUUUUN!
WHERE'S THE RICE!!?
AAAHH! OH NOOOO... HEY!
THE RICE ISN'T IMPORTANT!
IT IS SO IMPORTANT!
IT'S RICE! WE'RE HAVING CURRY FOR LUNCH!
...! EH!?
KARASUMA IS HERE...?
THAT'S RIGHT! EVEN THOUGH HE'S A THIRD YEAR!
ISN'T THAT WEIRD!!?
IF ANYTHING WERE TO HAPPEN...
I CAN TAKE CARE OF MYSELF, BUT I'M WORRIED ABOUT YOU, KARIN.
M...ME...?
YOU AVOID LETTING KARASUMA NOTICE YOU AS MUCH AS YOU CAN.
WHAT... WHAT SHOULD I DO?
...GOOD QUESTION...

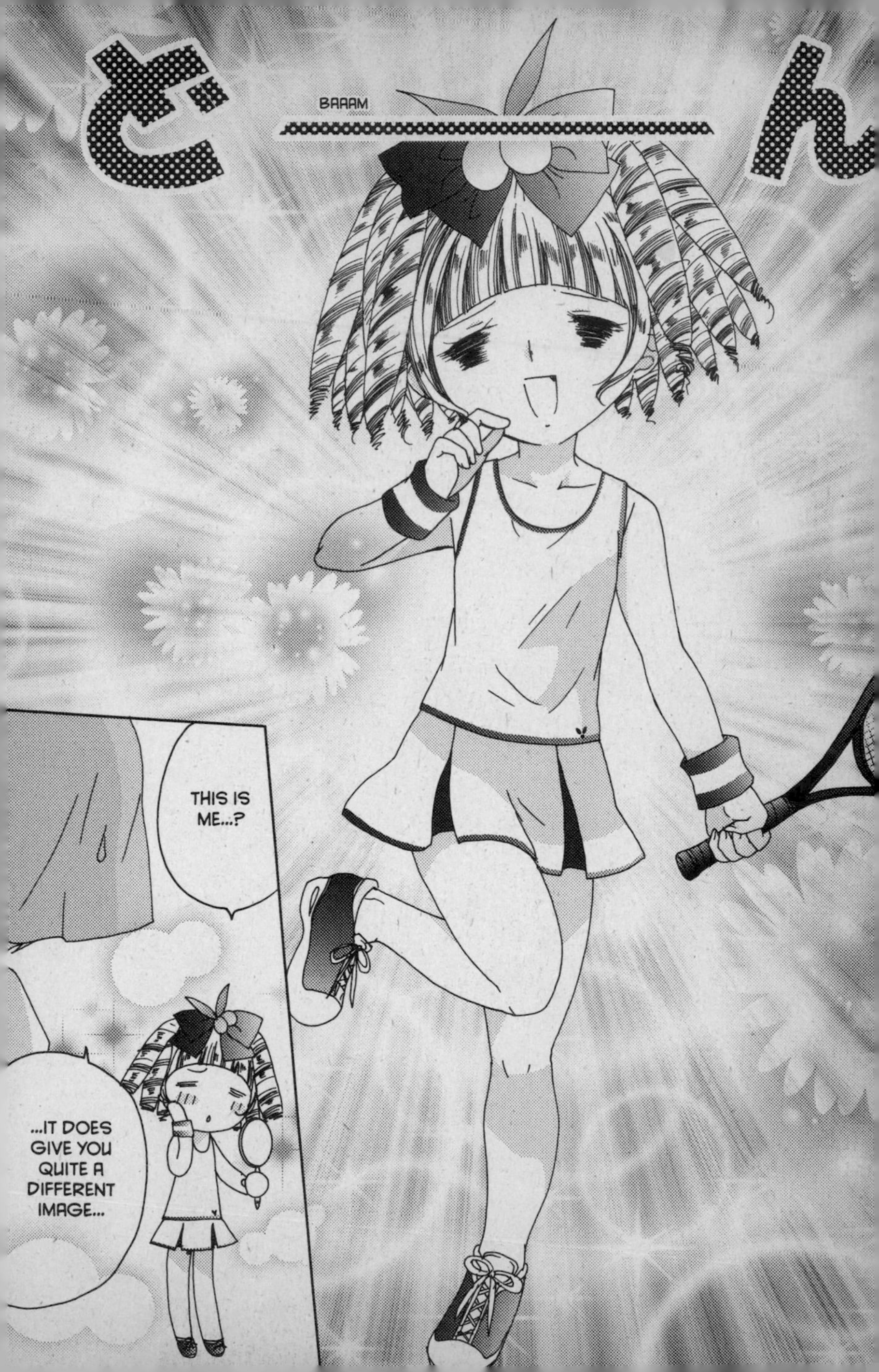
どーん
BAAAM
THIS IS ME...?
...IT DOES GIVE YOU QUITE A DIFFERENT IMAGE...

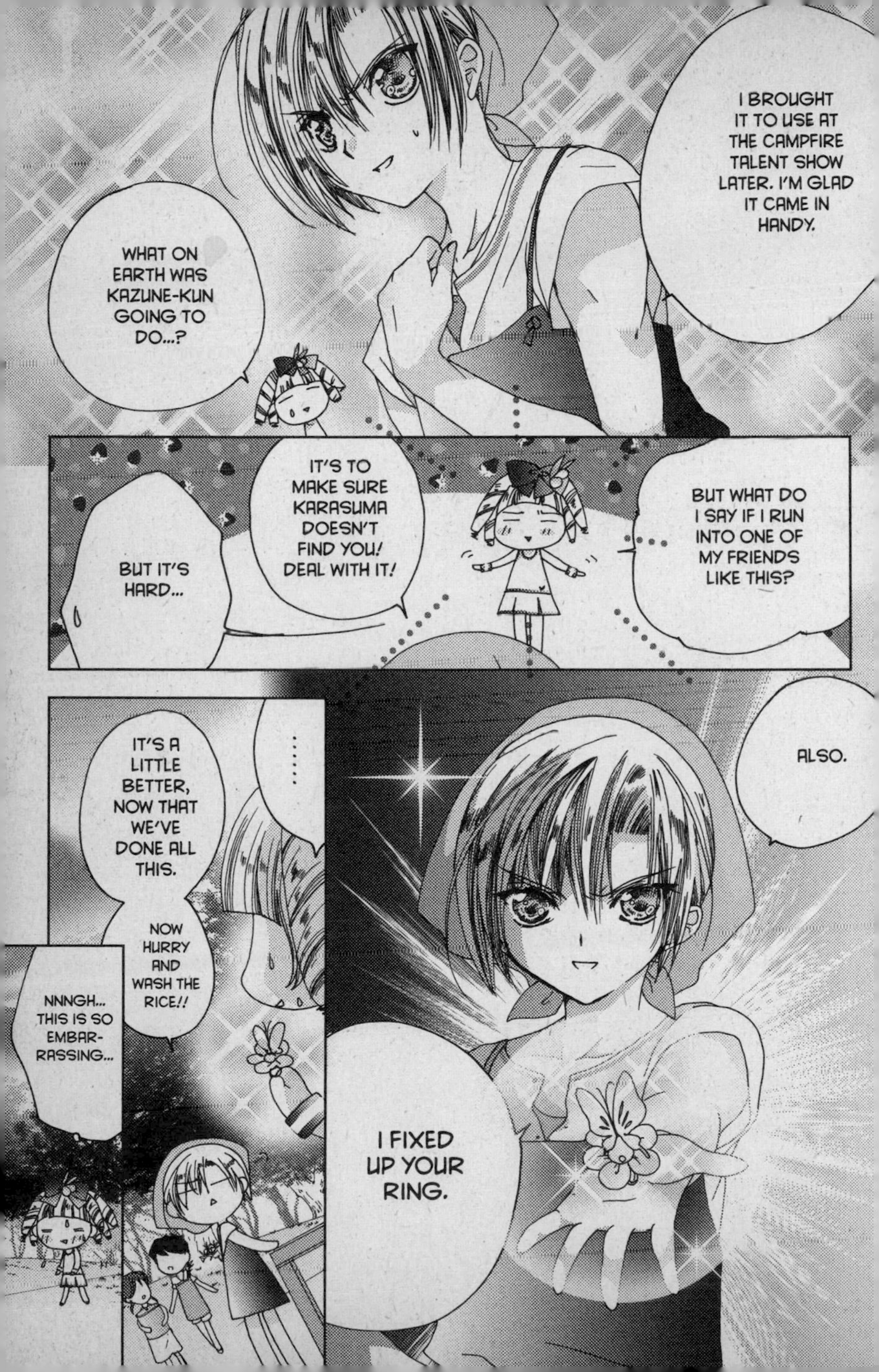
I BROUGHT IT TO USE AT THE CAMPFIRE TALENT SHOW LATER. I'M GLAD IT CAME IN HANDY.
WHAT ON EARTH WAS KAZUNE-KUN GOING TO DO...?
BUT WHAT DO I SAY IF I RUN INTO ONE OF MY FRIENDS LIKE THIS?
IT'S TO MAKE SURE KARASUMA DOESN'T FIND YOU! DEAL WITH IT!
BUT IT'S HARD...
ALSO.
I FIXED UP YOUR RING.
......
IT'S A LITTLE BETTER, NOW THAT WE'VE DONE ALL THIS.
NOW HURRY AND WASH THE RICE!!
NNNGH... THIS IS SO EMBARRASSING...

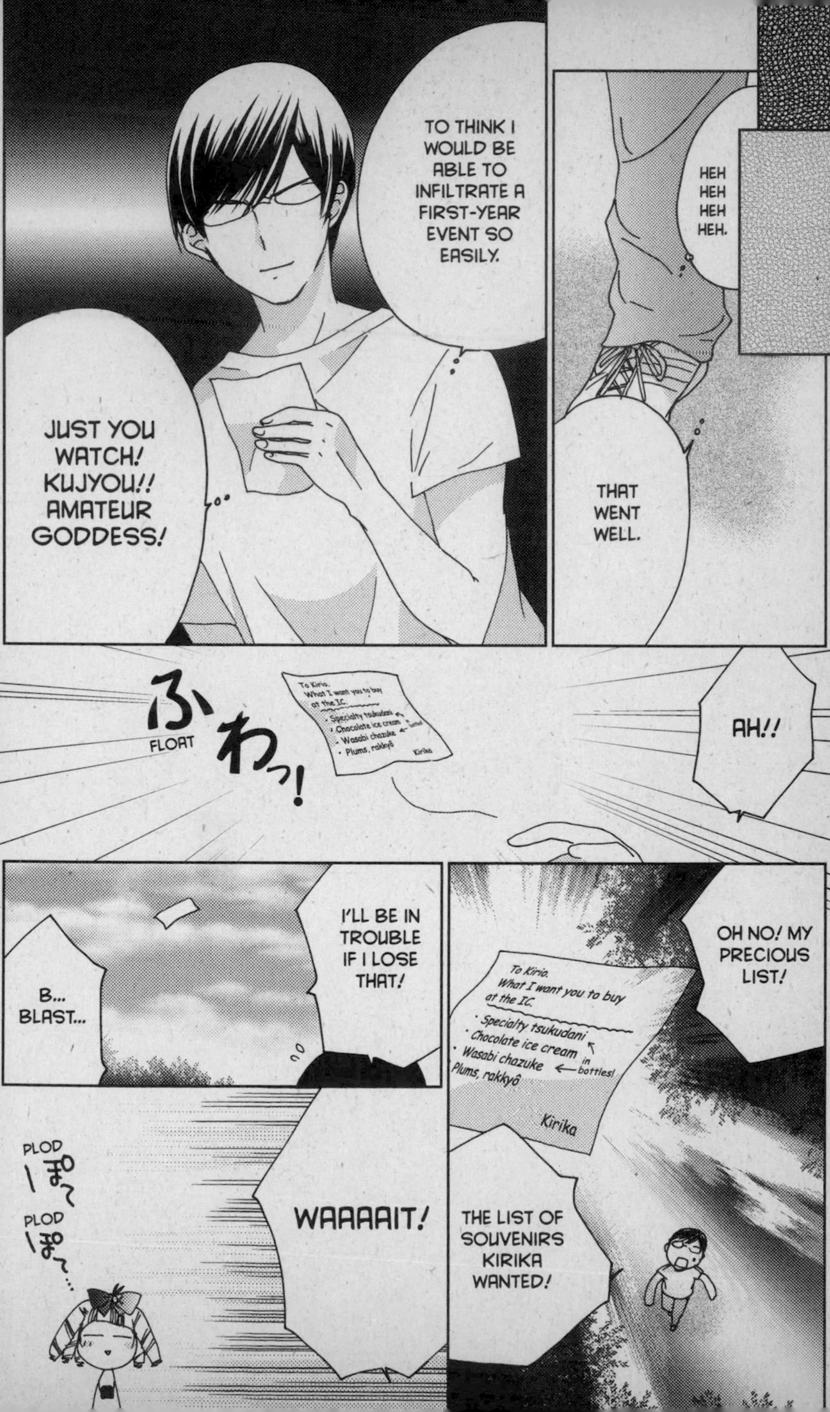
HEH HEH HEH HEH.
THAT WENT WELL.
TO THINK I WOULD BE ABLE TO INFILTRATE A FIRST-YEAR EVENT SO EASILY.
JUST YOU WATCH! KUJYOU!! AMATEUR GODDESS!
AH!!
To Kirio, What I want you to buy at the IC.
· Specialty tsukudani
· Chocolate ice cream
· Wasabi chazuke
· Plums, rakkyô
Kirika
ふわっ!
FLOAT
OH NO! MY PRECIOUS LIST!
To Kirio. What I want you to buy at the IC.
· Specialty tsukudani
· Chocolate ice cream
· Wasabi chazuke
Plums, rakkyô
in bottles!
Kirika
THE LIST OF SOUVENIRS KIRIKA WANTED!
WAAAAIT!
I'LL BE IN TROUBLE IF I LOSE THAT!
B... BLAST...
PLOD
ぽて
PLOD
ぽて~...

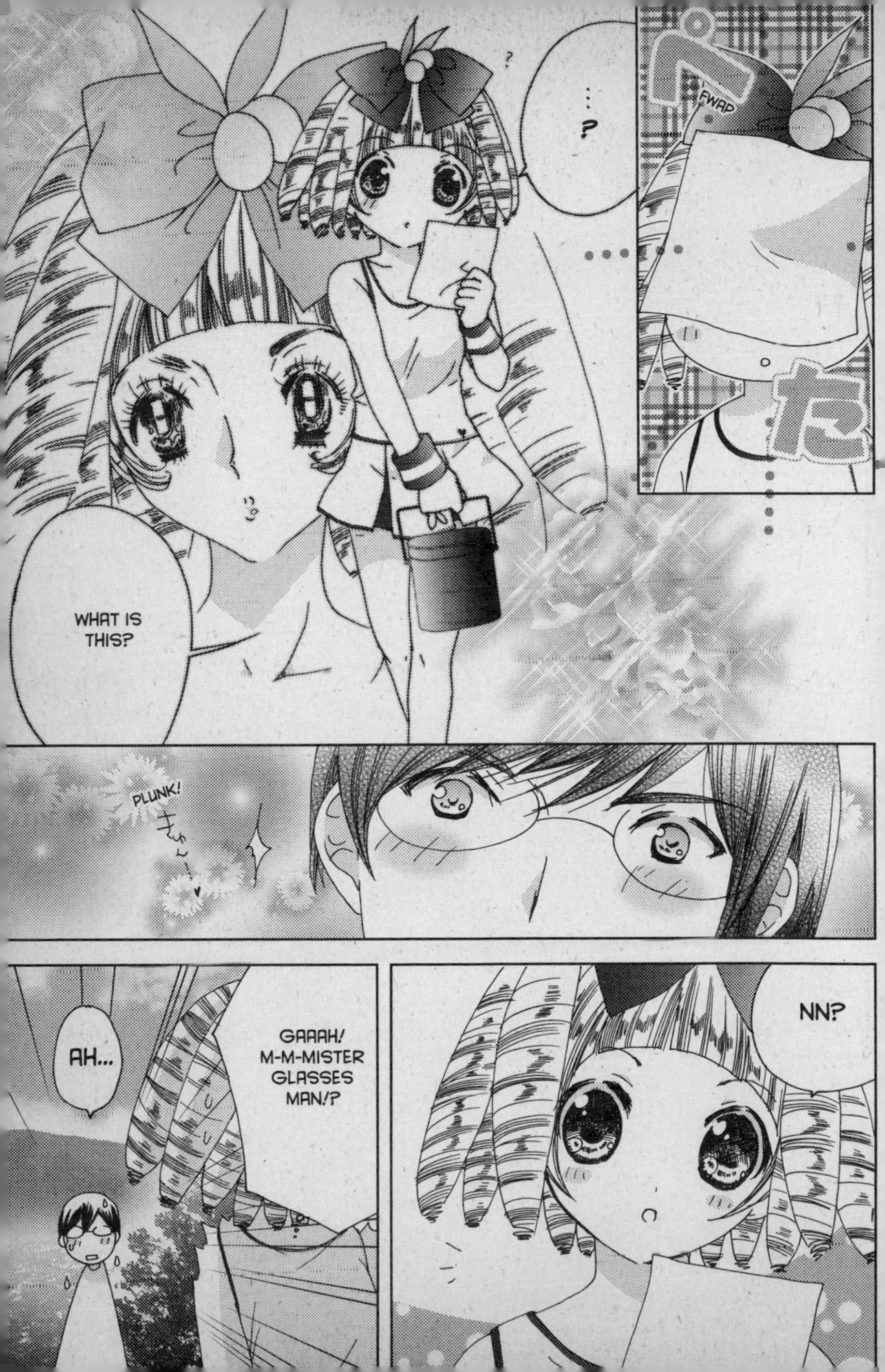
FWAP
ぱた
...?
WHAT IS THIS?
PLUNK!
NN?
GAAAH! M-M-MISTER GLASSES MAN!?
AH...

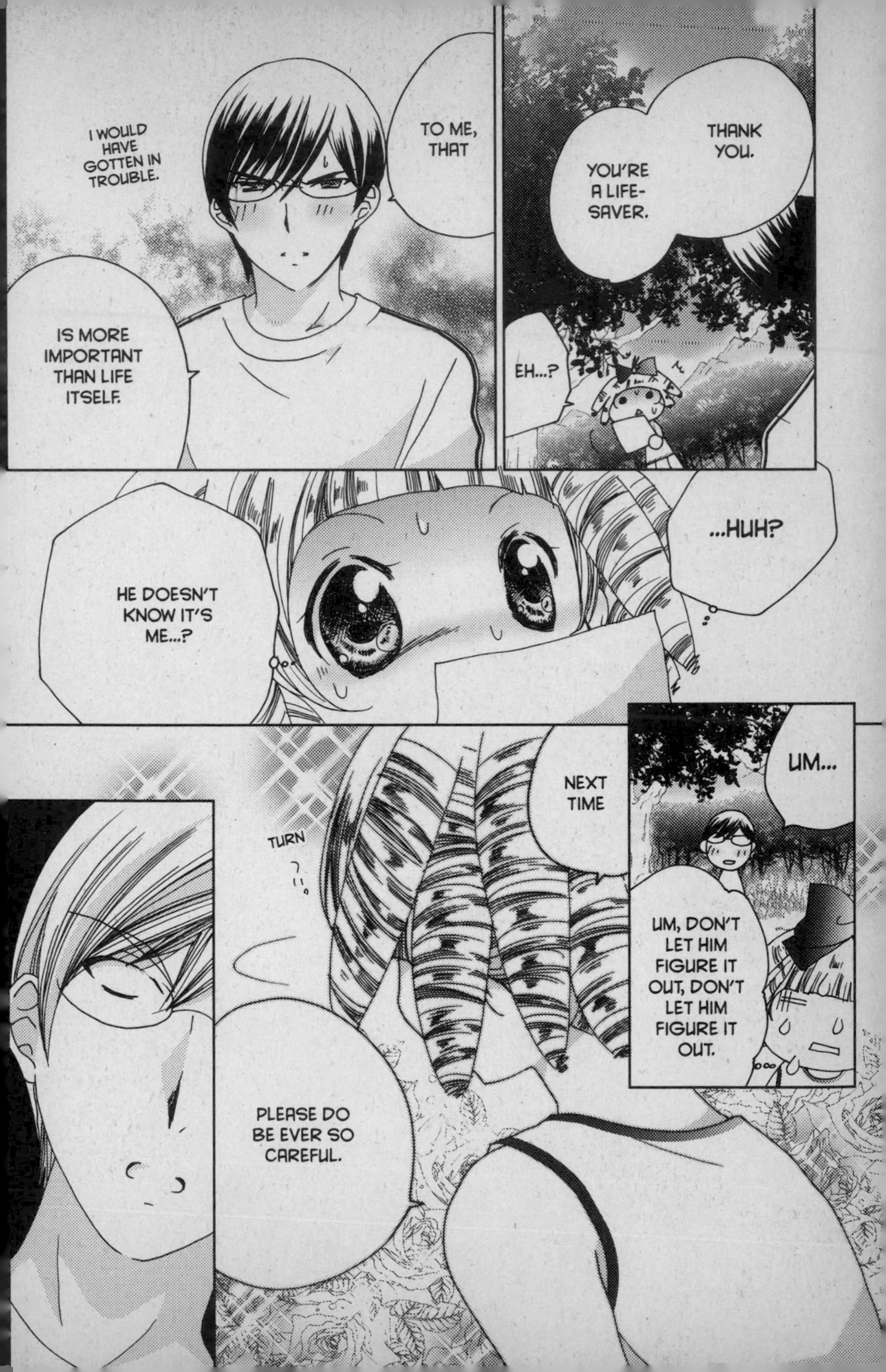
THANK YOU.
YOU'RE A LIFE-SAVER.
EH...?
TO ME, THAT
I WOULD HAVE GOTTEN IN TROUBLE.
IS MORE IMPORTANT THAN LIFE ITSELF.
...HUH?
HE DOESN'T KNOW IT'S ME...?
UM...
UM, DON'T LET HIM FIGURE IT OUT, DON'T LET HIM FIGURE IT OUT.
NEXT TIME
TURN
PLEASE DO BE EVER SO CAREFUL.

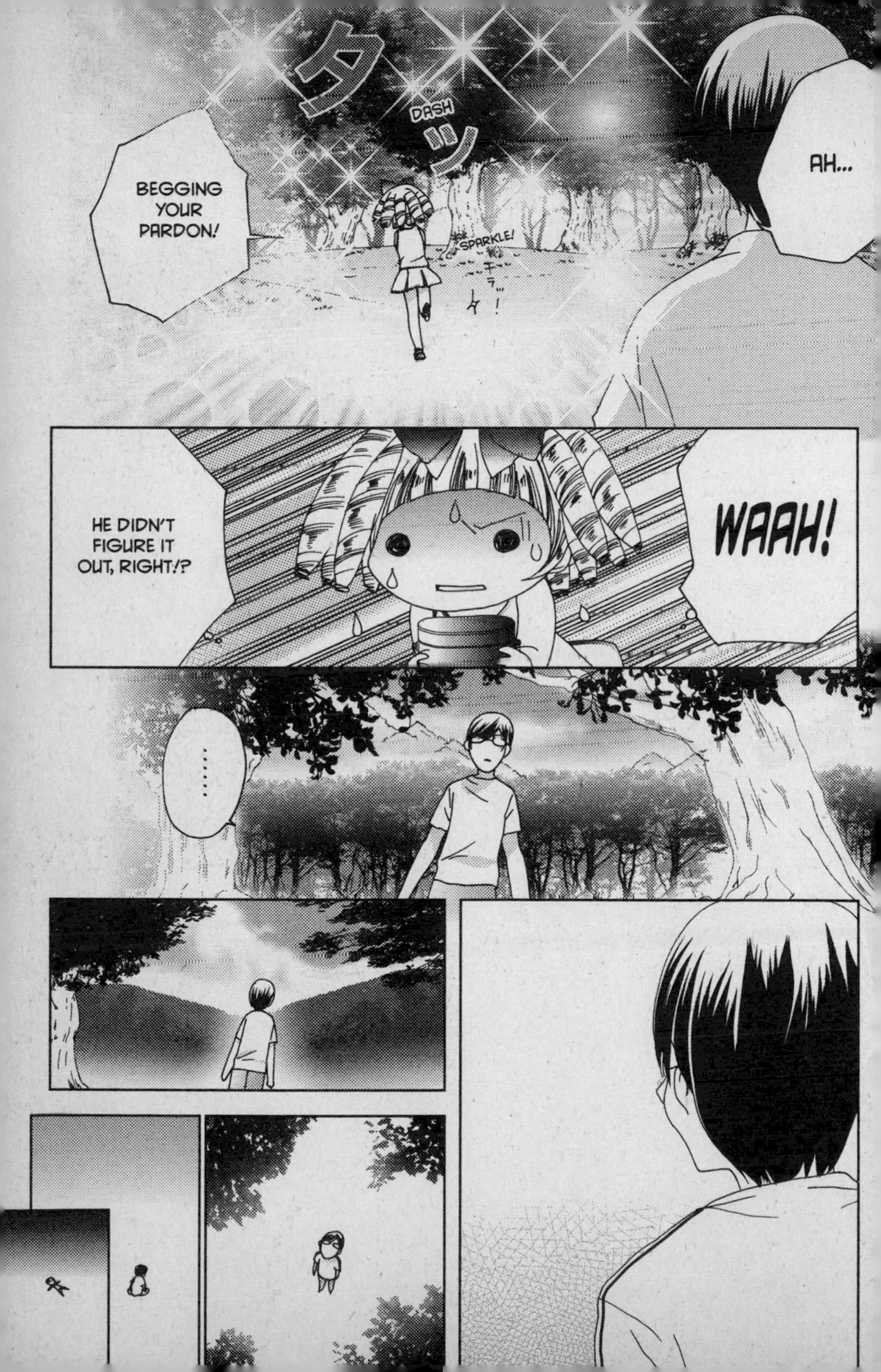
AH...
DASH
BEGGING YOUR PARDON!
SPARKLE!
WAAH!
HE DIDN'T FIGURE IT OUT, RIGHT!?
......

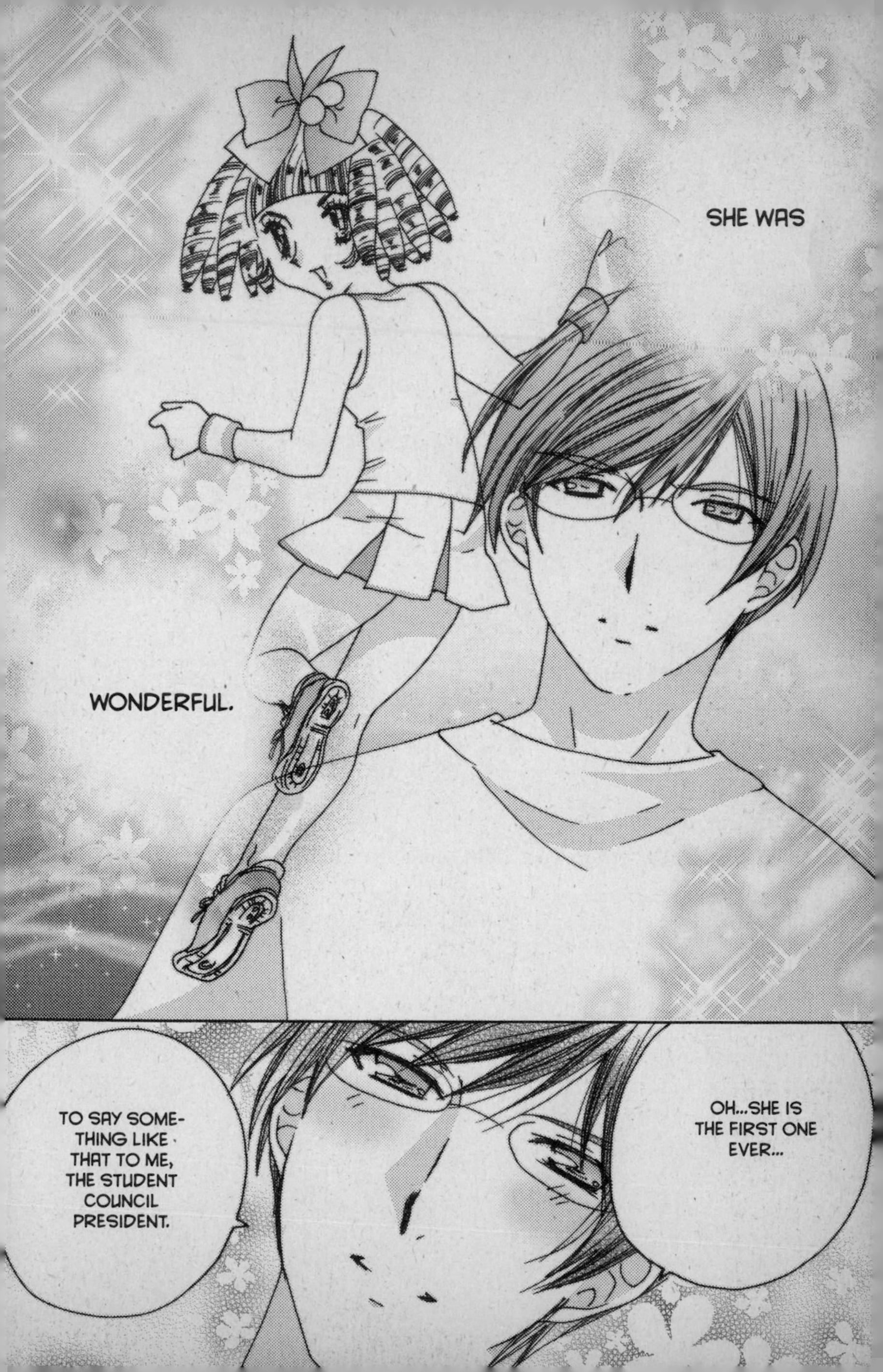
SHE WAS
WONDERFUL.
OH...SHE IS THE FIRST ONE EVER...
TO SAY SOME-THING LIKE THAT TO ME, THE STUDENT COUNCIL PRESIDENT.

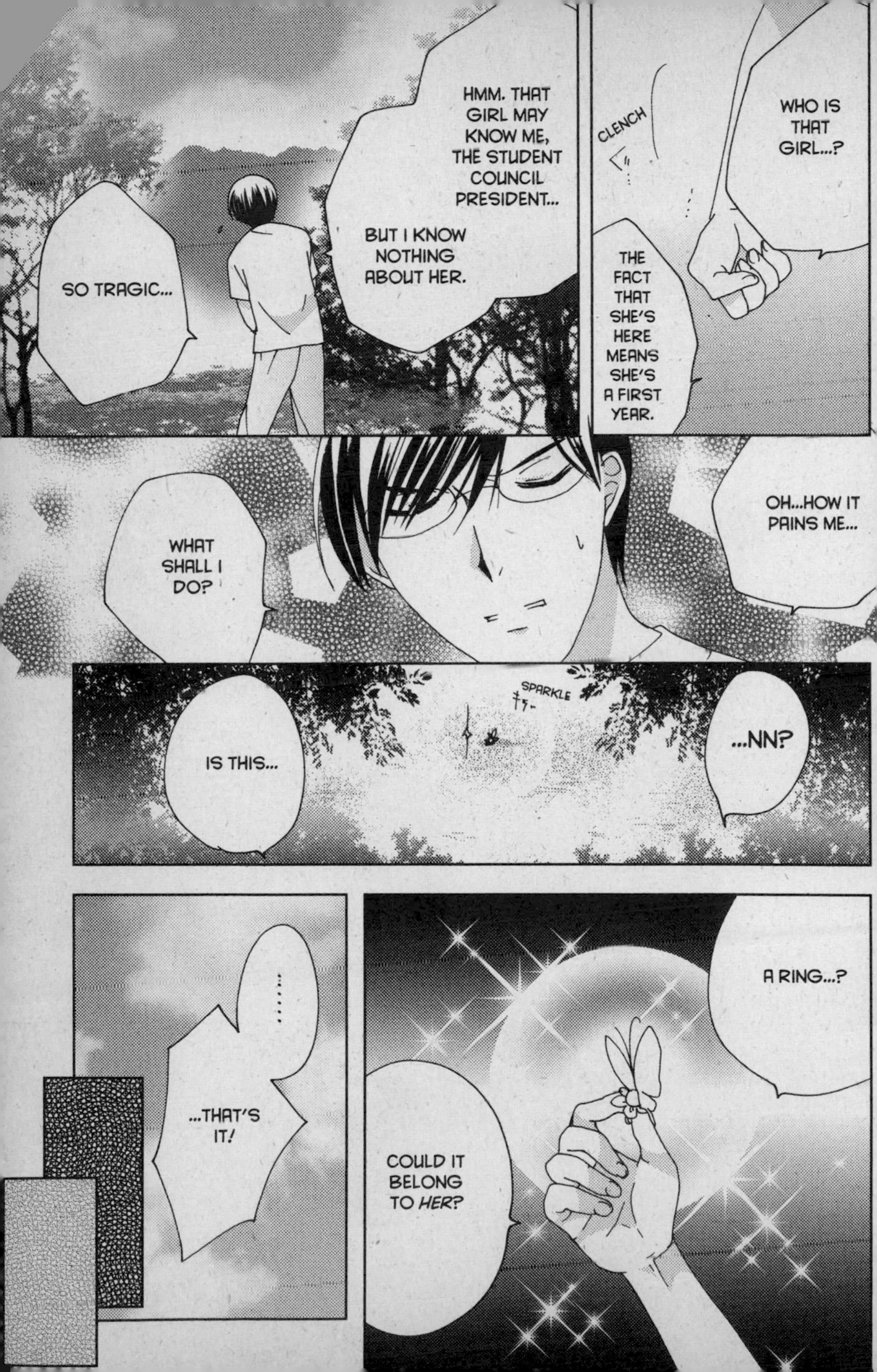
WHO IS THAT GIRL...?
CLENCH
THE FACT THAT SHE'S HERE MEANS SHE'S A FIRST YEAR.
HMM. THAT GIRL MAY KNOW ME, THE STUDENT COUNCIL PRESIDENT...
BUT I KNOW NOTHING ABOUT HER.
SO TRAGIC...
OH...HOW IT PAINS ME...
WHAT SHALL I DO?
...NN?
SPARKLE
IS THIS...
A RING...?
COULD IT BELONG TO *HER*?
......
...THAT'S IT!

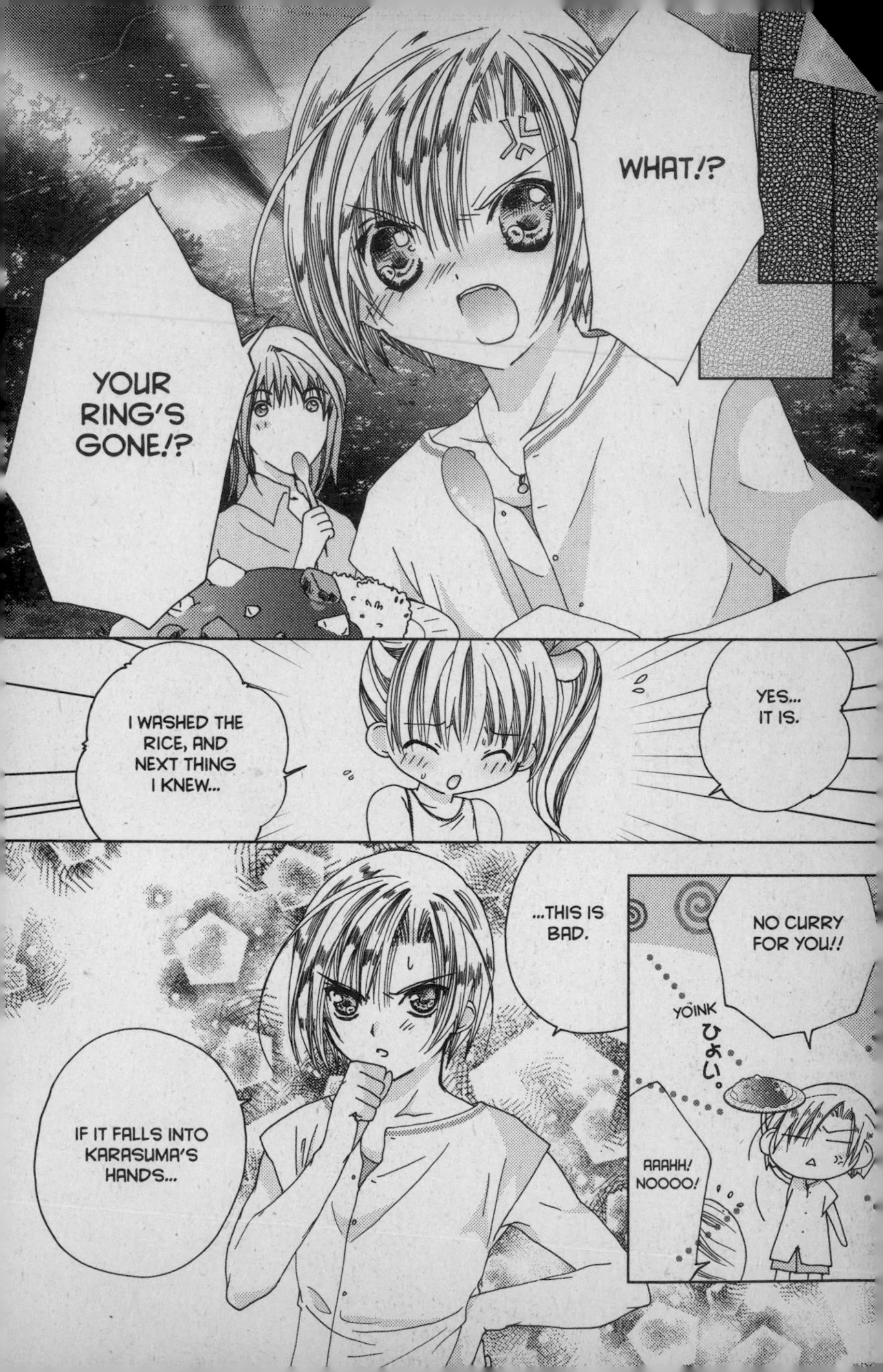
WHAT!?
YOUR RING'S GONE!?
YES... IT IS.
I WASHED THE RICE, AND NEXT THING I KNEW...
NO CURRY FOR YOU!!
YOINK ひょい。
AAAHH! NOOOO!
...THIS IS BAD.
IF IT FALLS INTO KARASUMA'S HANDS...

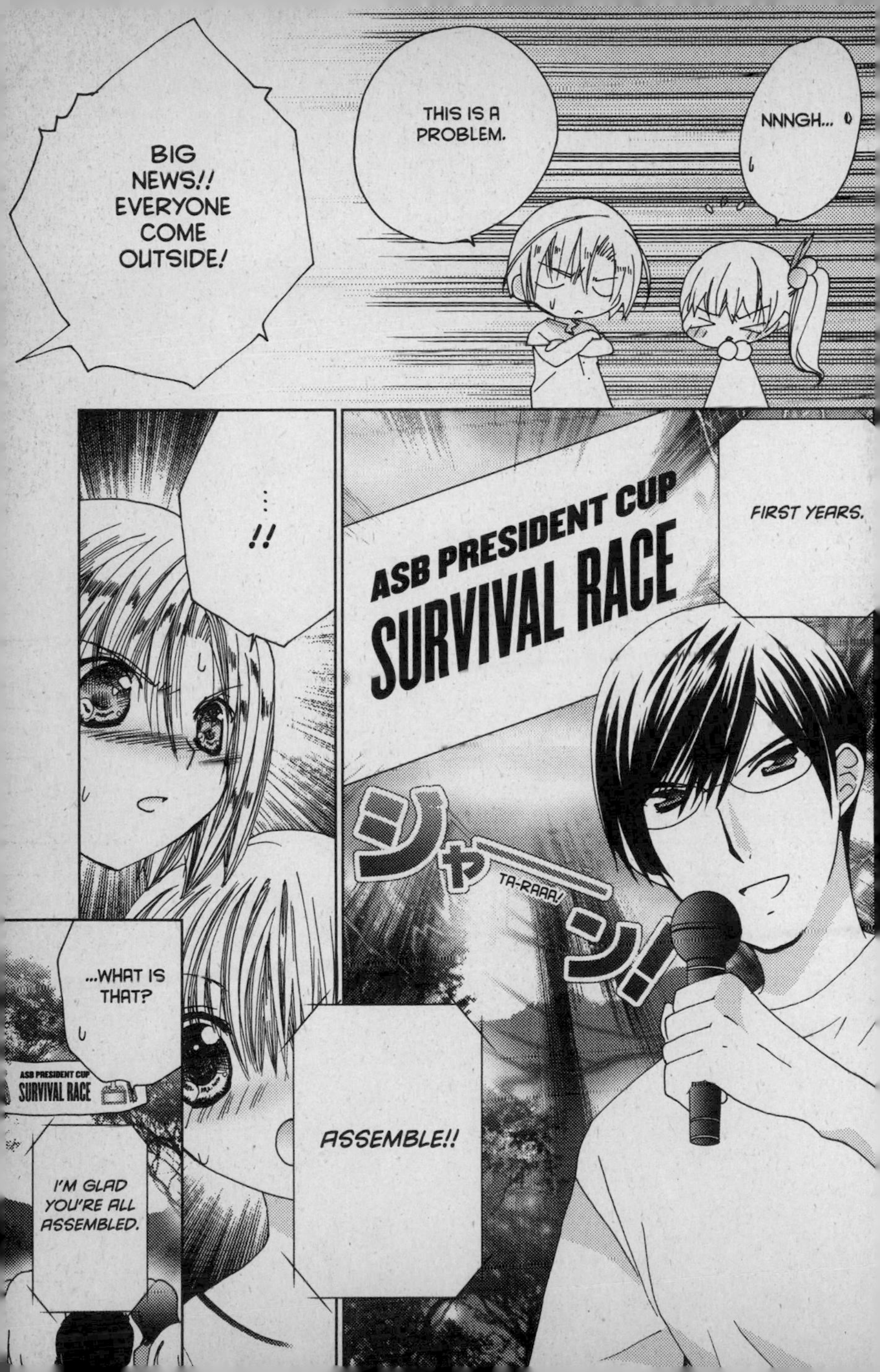
NNNGH...
THIS IS A PROBLEM.
BIG NEWS!! EVERYONE COME OUTSIDE!
FIRST YEARS.
ASSEMBLE!!
I'M GLAD YOU'RE ALL ASSEMBLED.
ASB PRESIDENT CUP SURVIVAL RACE
TA-RAAA!
...!!
...WHAT IS THAT?
ASB PRESIDENT CUP SURVIVAL RACE

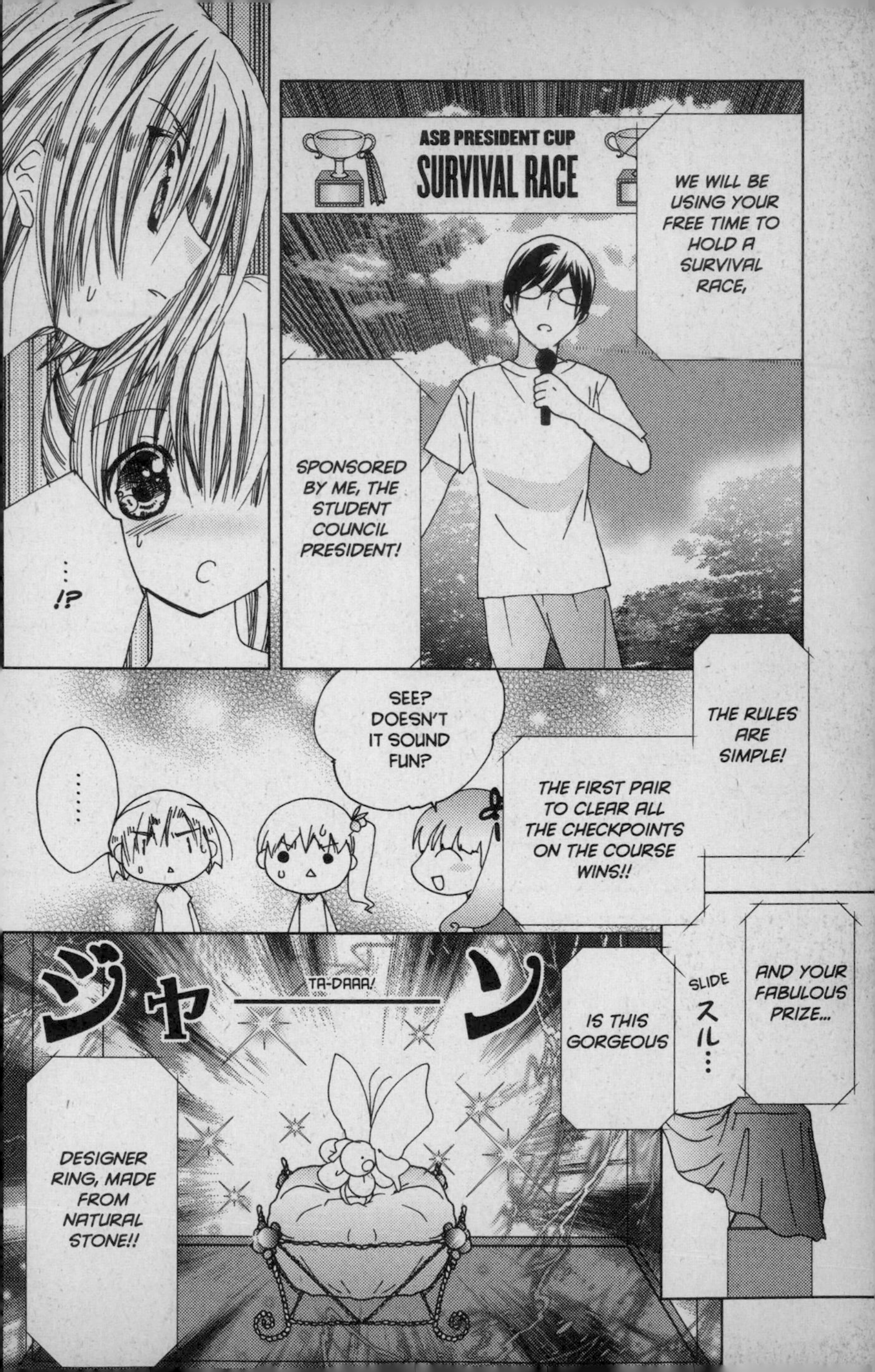
ASB PRESIDENT CUP
SURVIVAL RACE
WE WILL BE USING YOUR FREE TIME TO HOLD A SURVIVAL RACE,
SPONSORED BY ME, THE STUDENT COUNCIL PRESIDENT!
...!?
THE RULES ARE SIMPLE!
THE FIRST PAIR TO CLEAR ALL THE CHECKPOINTS ON THE COURSE WINS!!
SEE? DOESN'T IT SOUND FUN?
......
AND YOUR FABULOUS PRIZE...
SLIDE
スル…
IS THIS GORGEOUS
ジャーン
TA-DAAA!
DESIGNER RING, MADE FROM NATURAL STONE!!

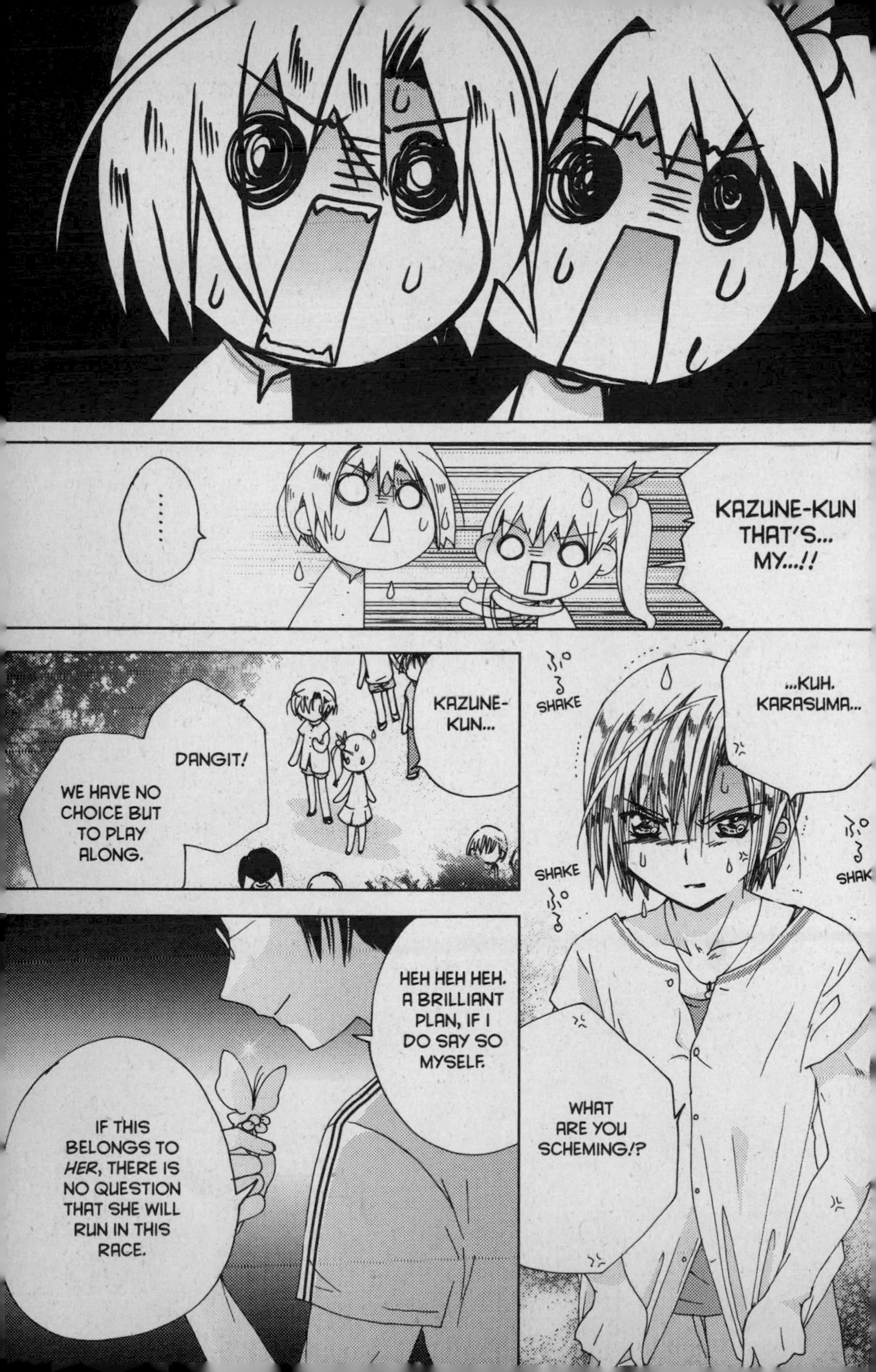
KAZUNE-KUN THAT'S... MY...!!
......
...KUH. KARASUMA...
SHAKE
SHAKE
SHAK
WHAT ARE YOU SCHEMING!?
KAZUNE-KUN...
DANGIT!
WE HAVE NO CHOICE BUT TO PLAY ALONG.
HEH HEH HEH. A BRILLIANT PLAN, IF I DO SAY SO MYSELF.
IF THIS BELONGS TO *HER*, THERE IS NO QUESTION THAT SHE WILL RUN IN THIS RACE.

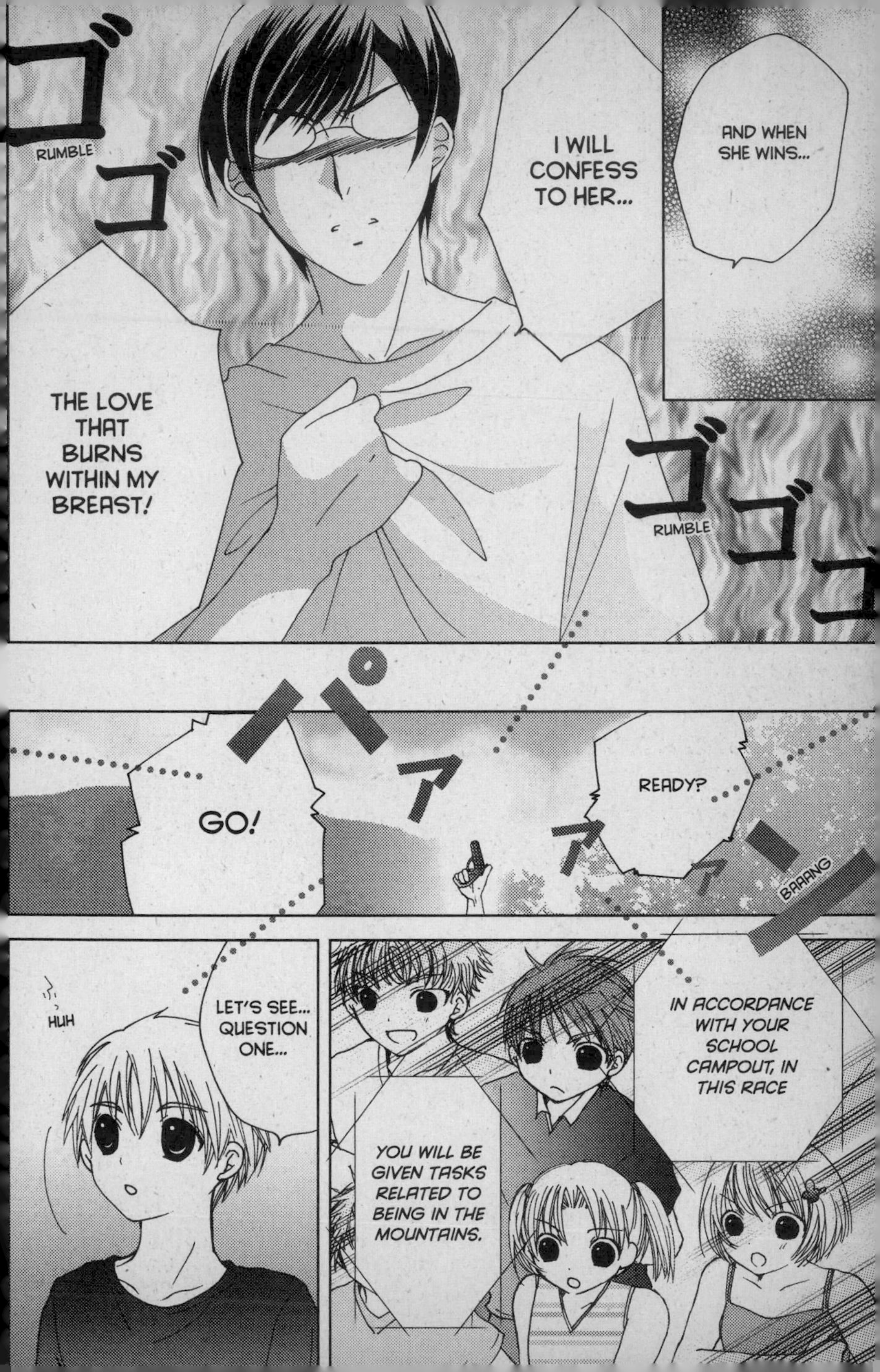
AND WHEN SHE WINS...
I WILL CONFESS TO HER...
RUMBLE
RUMBLE
THE LOVE THAT BURNS WITHIN MY BREAST!
READY?
BAAANG
GO!
IN ACCORDANCE WITH YOUR SCHOOL CAMPOUT, IN THIS RACE
YOU WILL BE GIVEN TASKS RELATED TO BEING IN THE MOUNTAINS.
LET'S SEE... QUESTION ONE...
HUH

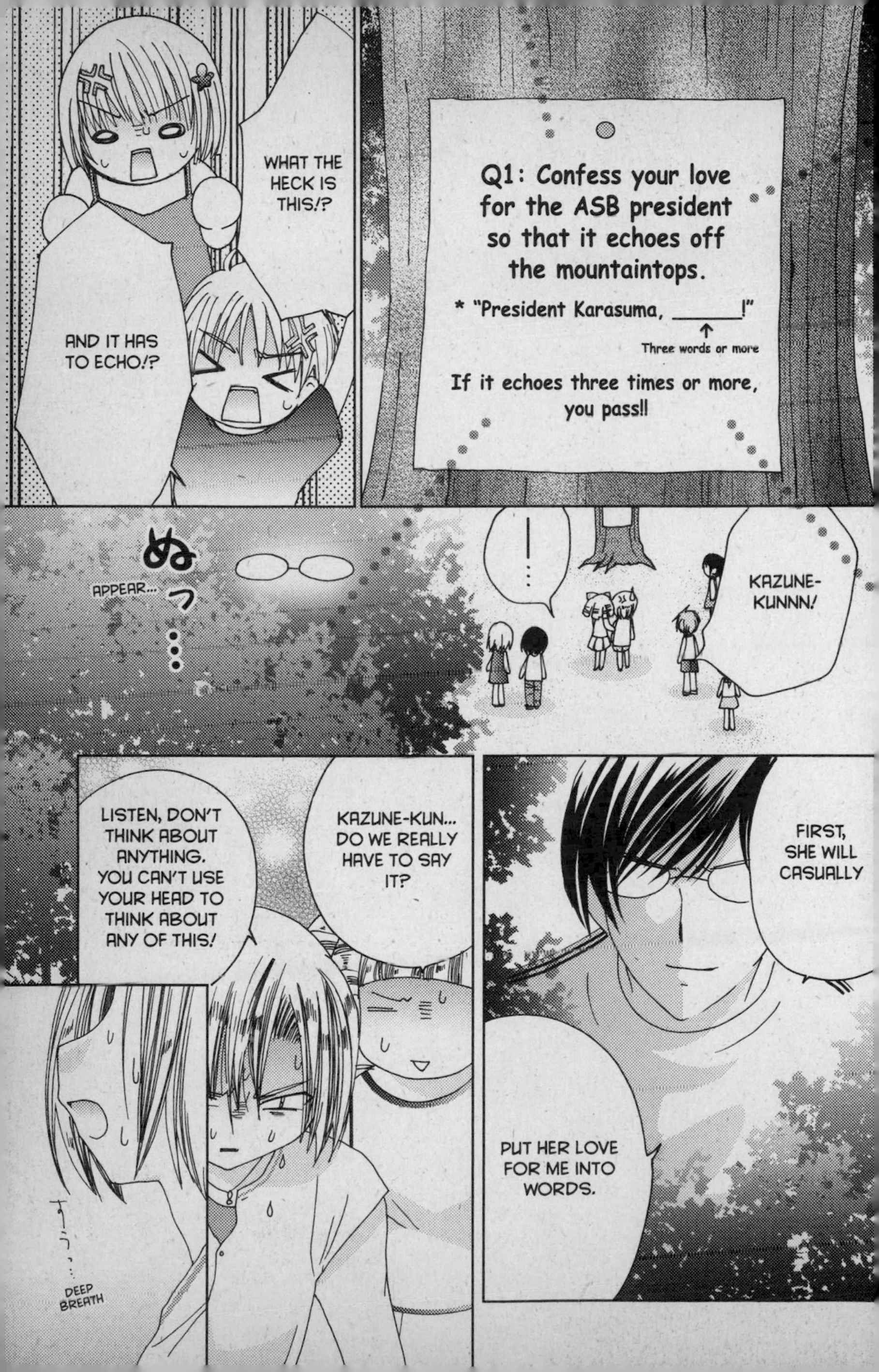
Q1: Confess your love for the ASB president so that it echoes off the mountaintops.
* "President Karasuma, ______!"
Three words or more
If it echoes three times or more, you pass!!
WHAT THE HECK IS THIS!?
AND IT HAS TO ECHO!?
KAZUNE-KUNNN!
!...
ぬっ…
APPEAR...
FIRST, SHE WILL CASUALLY
PUT HER LOVE FOR ME INTO WORDS.
KAZUNE-KUN... DO WE REALLY HAVE TO SAY IT?
LISTEN, DON'T THINK ABOUT ANYTHING. YOU CAN'T USE YOUR HEAD TO THINK ABOUT ANY OF THIS!
DEEP BREATH

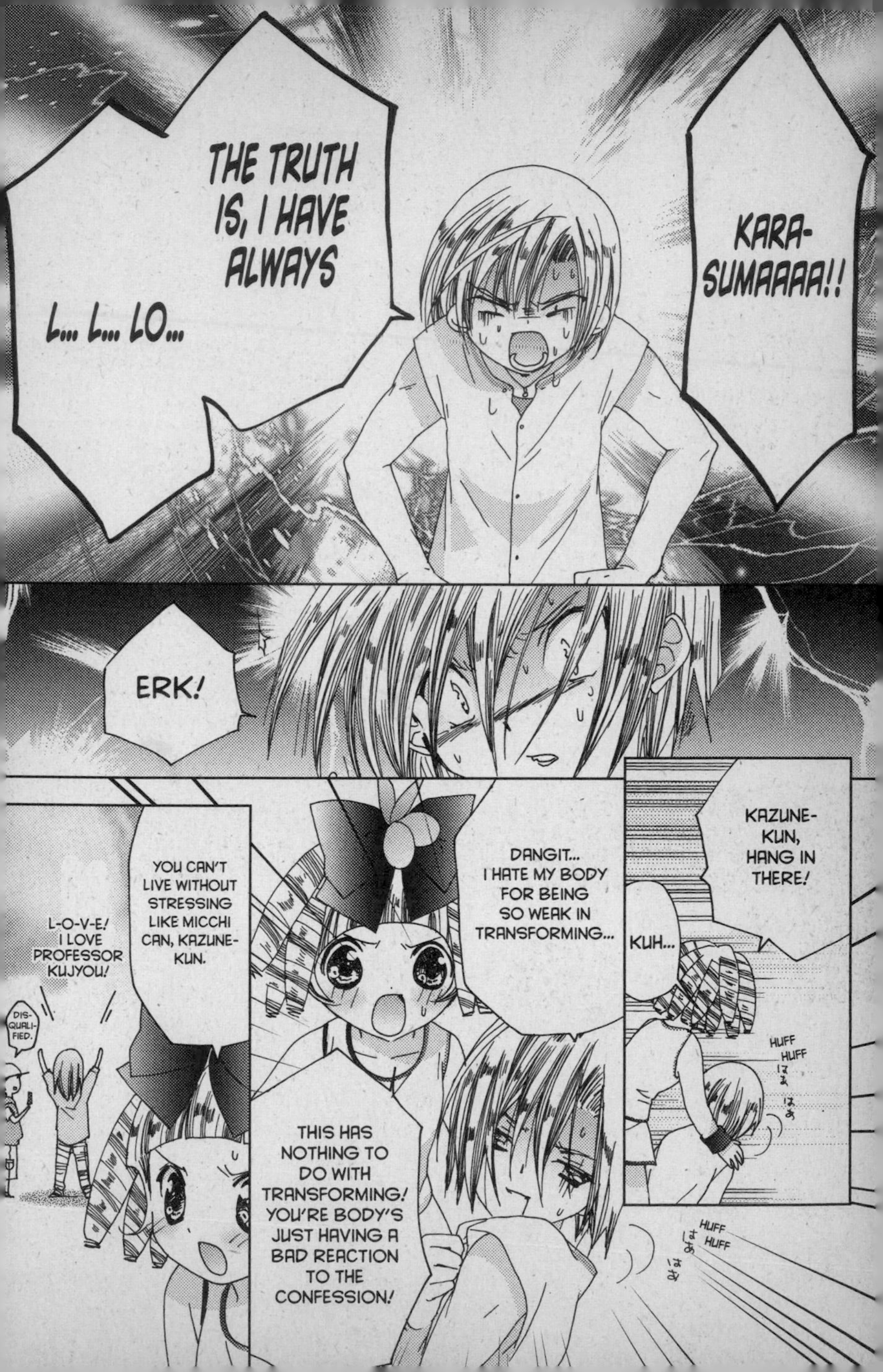
KARA-SUMAAAA!!
THE TRUTH IS, I HAVE ALWAYS
L... L... LO...
ERK!
KAZUNE-KUN, HANG IN THERE!
KUH...
HUFF HUFF
DANGIT... I HATE MY BODY FOR BEING SO WEAK IN TRANSFORMING...
THIS HAS NOTHING TO DO WITH TRANSFORMING! YOU'RE BODY'S JUST HAVING A BAD REACTION TO THE CONFESSION!
HUFF HUFF
YOU CAN'T LIVE WITHOUT STRESSING LIKE MICCHI CAN, KAZUNE-KUN.
L-O-V-E! I LOVE PROFESSOR KUJYOU!
DIS-QUALI-FIED.

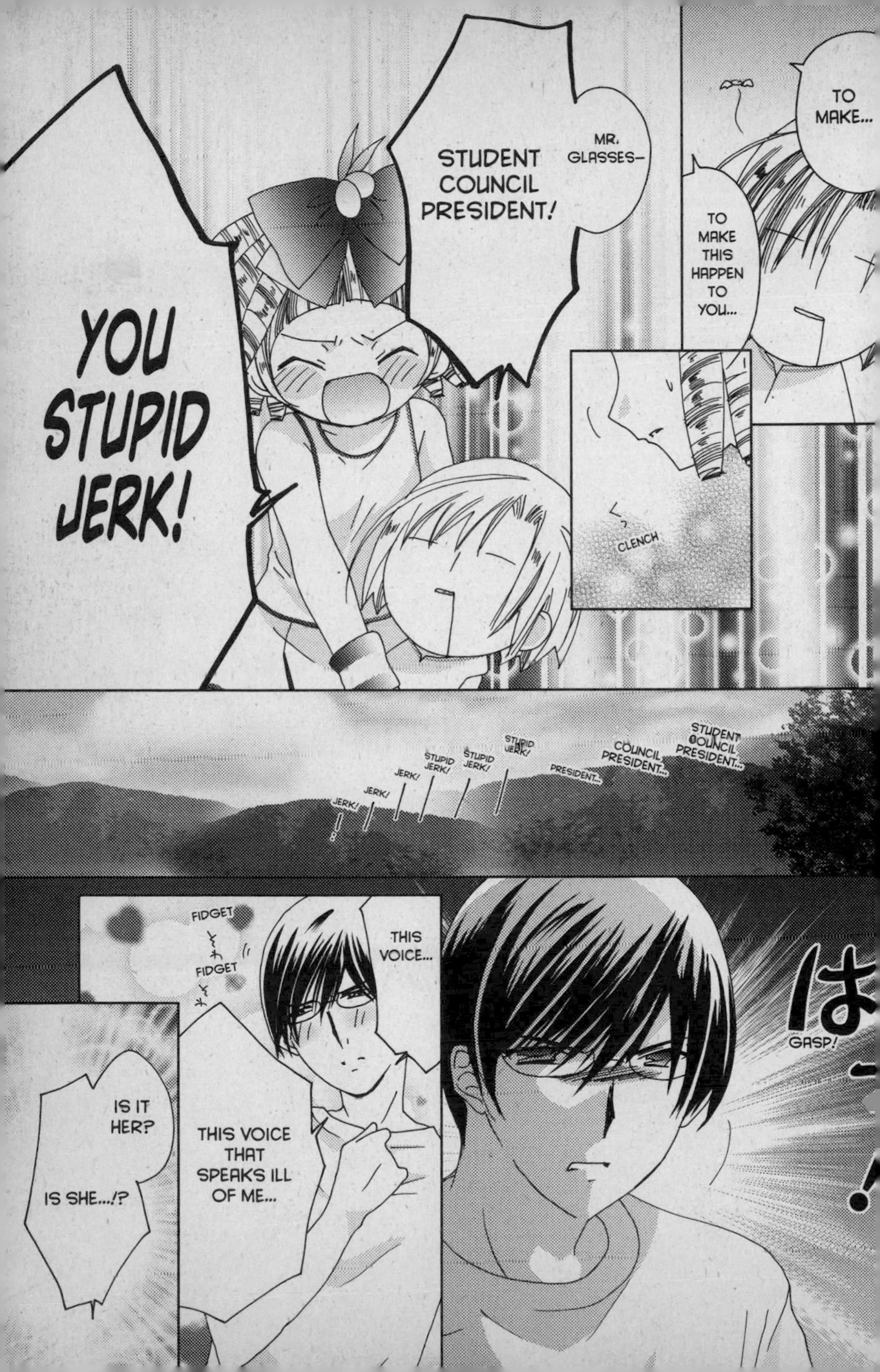
TO MAKE...
TO MAKE THIS HAPPEN TO YOU...
CLENCH
MR. GLASSES—
STUDENT COUNCIL PRESIDENT!
YOU STUPID JERK!
STUDENT COUNCIL PRESIDENT...
COUNCIL PRESIDENT...
PRESIDENT...
STUPID JERK!
STUPID JERK!
STUPID JERK!
JERK!
JERK!
JERK!
は
GASP!
THIS VOICE...
FIDGET
FIDGET
THIS VOICE THAT SPEAKS ILL OF ME...
IS IT HER?
IS SHE...!?

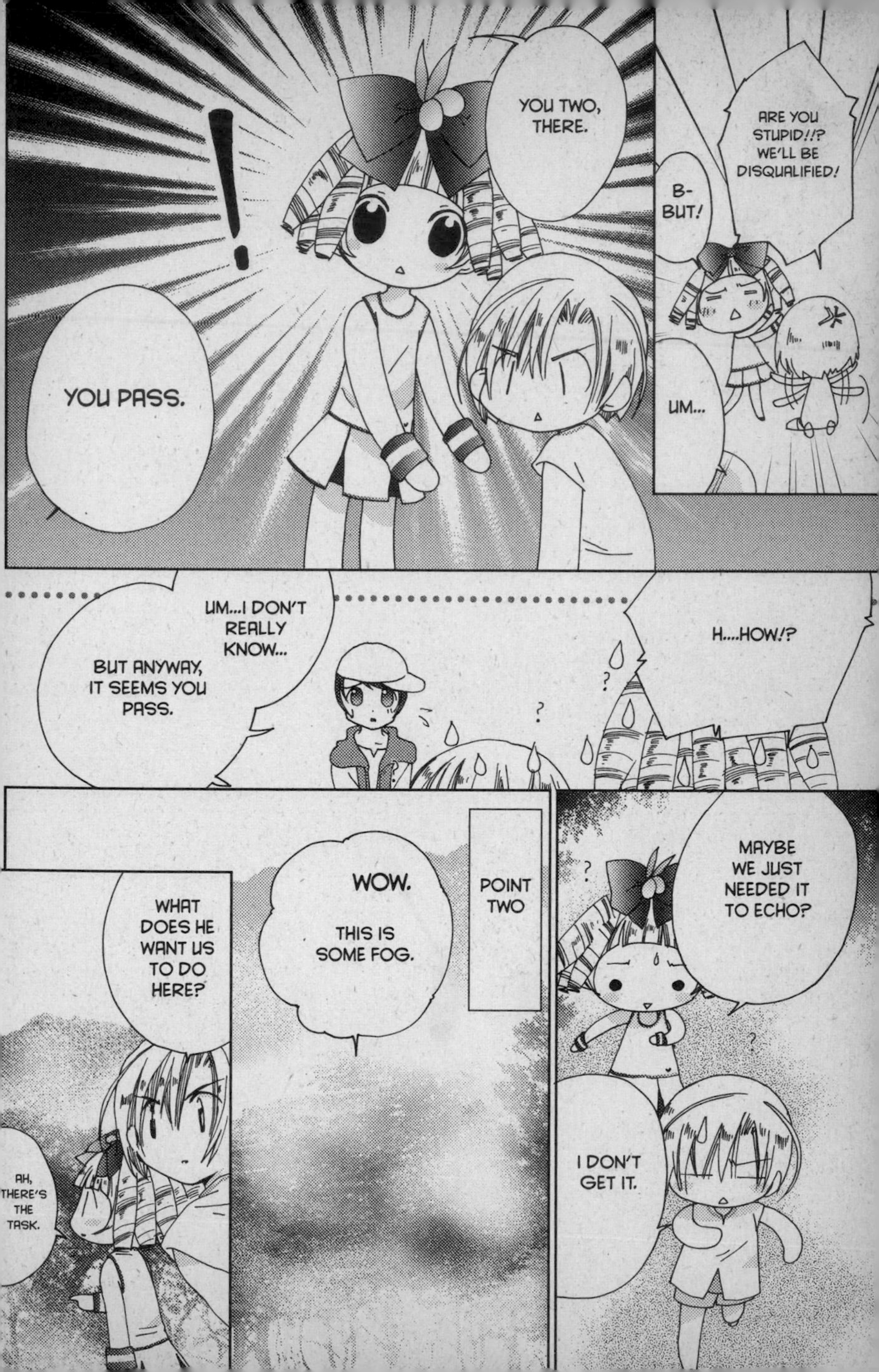
ARE YOU STUPID!!? WE'LL BE DISQUALIFIED!
B-BUT!
UM...
YOU TWO, THERE.
YOU PASS.
H....HOW!?
UM...I DON'T REALLY KNOW...
BUT ANYWAY, IT SEEMS YOU PASS.
MAYBE WE JUST NEEDED IT TO ECHO?
I DON'T GET IT.
POINT TWO
WOW.
THIS IS SOME FOG.
WHAT DOES HE WANT US TO DO HERE?
AH, THERE'S THE TASK.

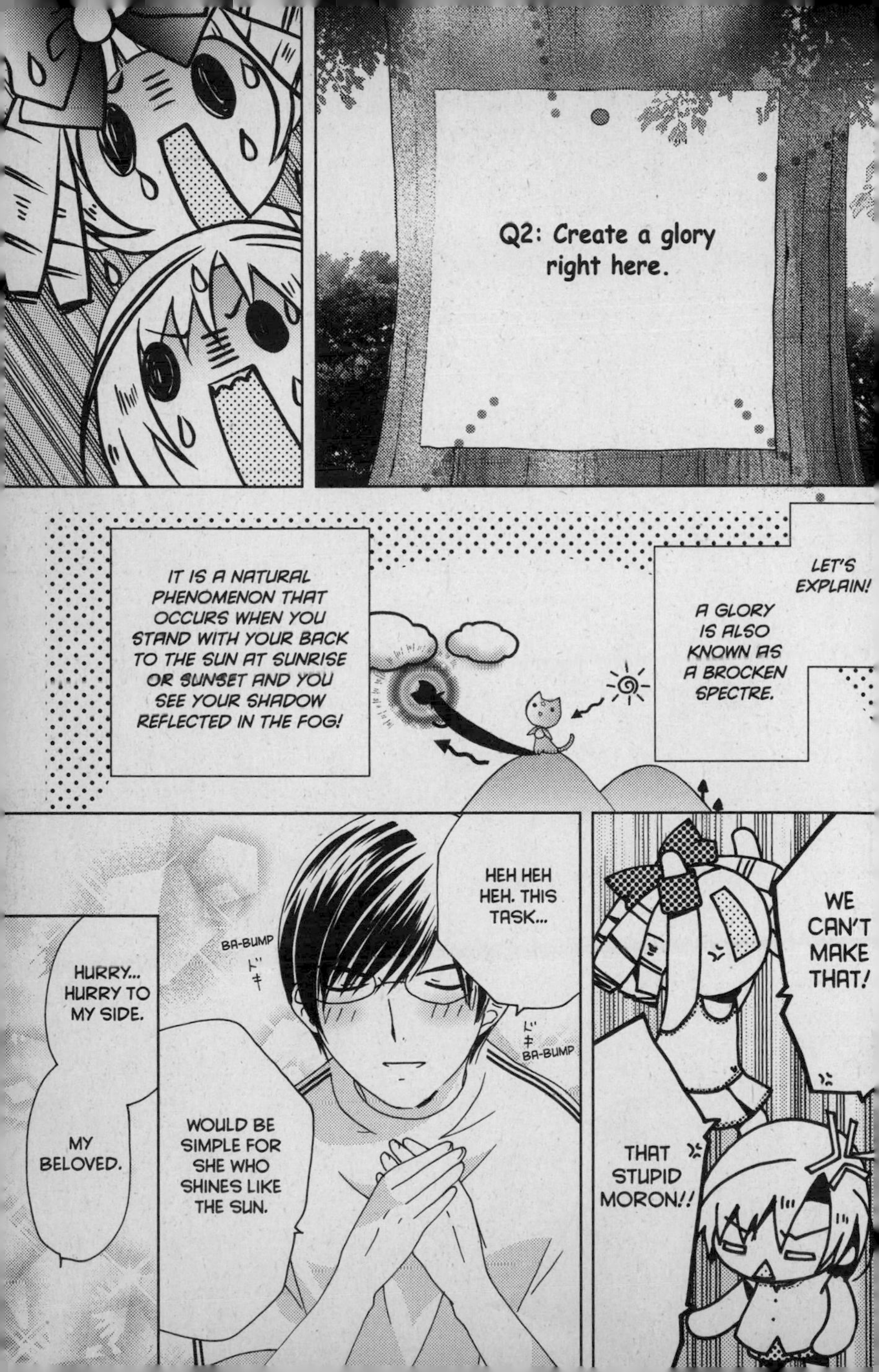
Q2: Create a glory right here.
LET'S EXPLAIN!
A GLORY IS ALSO KNOWN AS A BROCKEN SPECTRE.
IT IS A NATURAL PHENOMENON THAT OCCURS WHEN YOU STAND WITH YOUR BACK TO THE SUN AT SUNRISE OR SUNSET AND YOU SEE YOUR SHADOW REFLECTED IN THE FOG!
WE CAN'T MAKE THAT!
THAT STUPID MORON!!
HEH HEH HEH. THIS TASK...
ドキ
BA-BUMP
ドキ
BA-BUMP
WOULD BE SIMPLE FOR SHE WHO SHINES LIKE THE SUN.
HURRY... HURRY TO MY SIDE.
MY BELOVED.

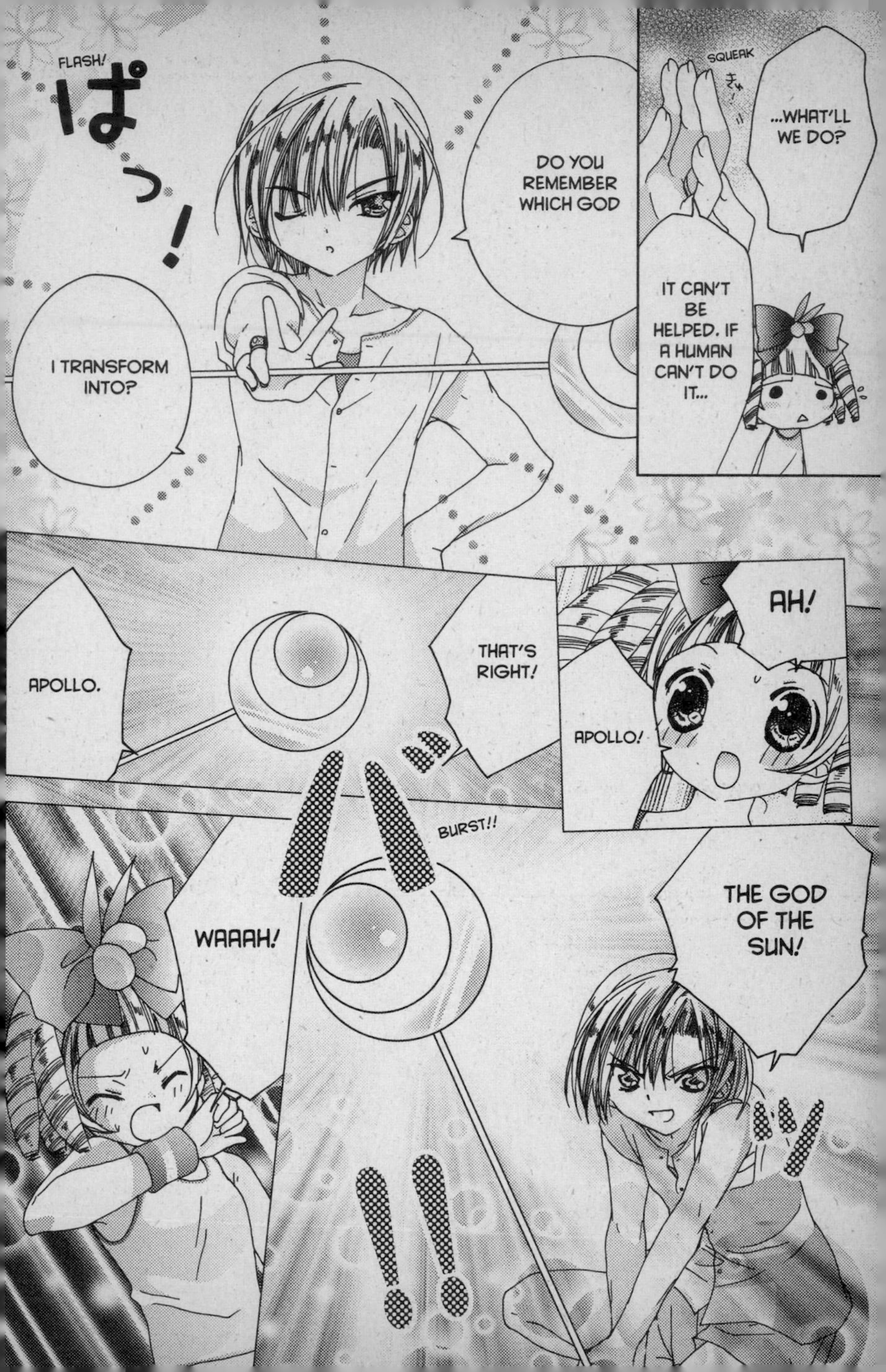
SQUEAK
...WHAT'LL WE DO?
IT CAN'T BE HELPED. IF A HUMAN CAN'T DO IT...
FLASH!
ぱっ!
DO YOU REMEMBER WHICH GOD
I TRANSFORM INTO?
AH!
APOLLO!
THAT'S RIGHT!
APOLLO.
THE GOD OF THE SUN!
BURST!!
WAAAH!

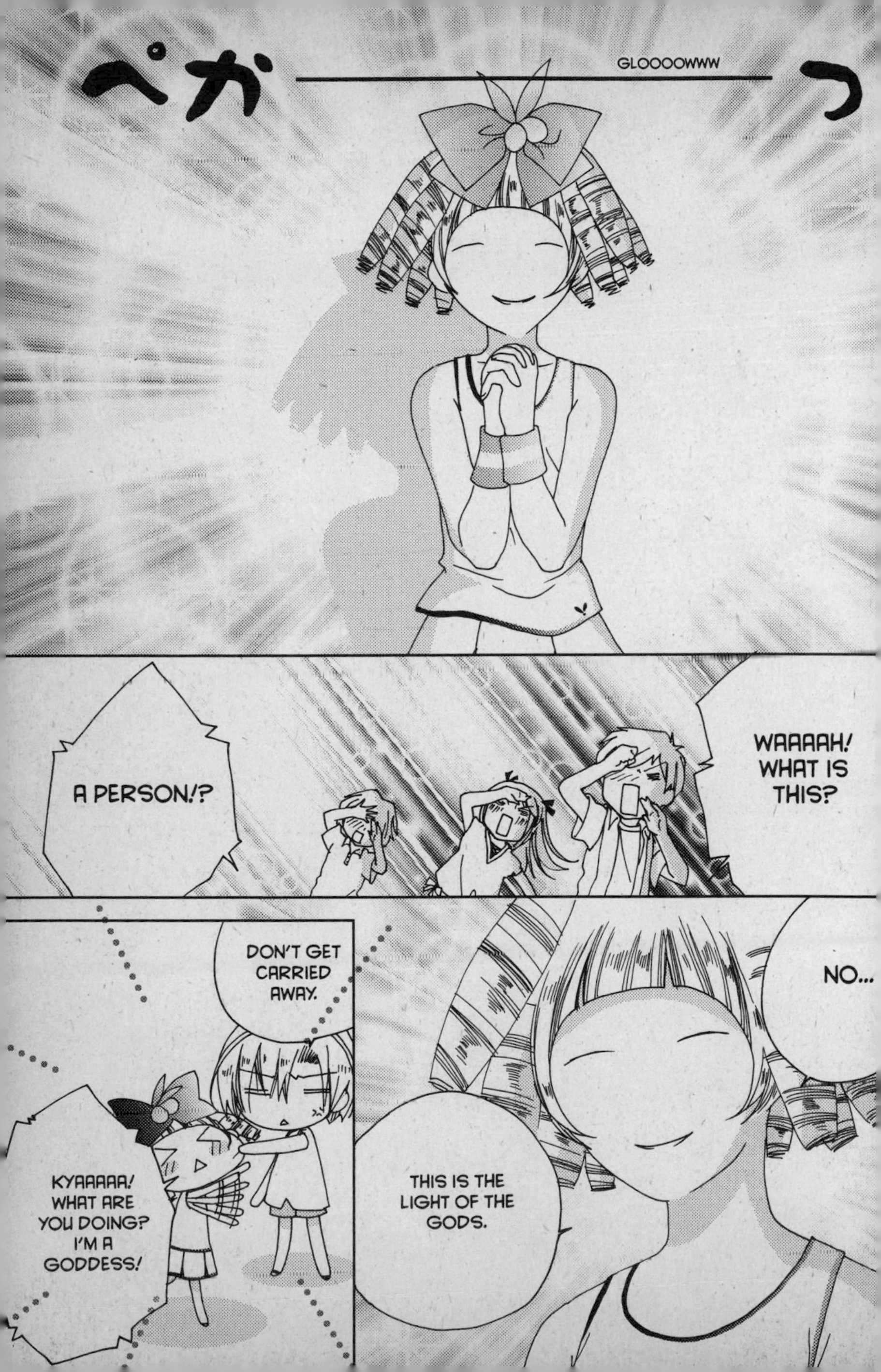
ペカーっ
GLOOOOWWW
WAAAAH! WHAT IS THIS?
A PERSON!?
NO...
THIS IS THE LIGHT OF THE GODS.
DON'T GET CARRIED AWAY.
KYAAAAA! WHAT ARE YOU DOING? I'M A GODDESS!

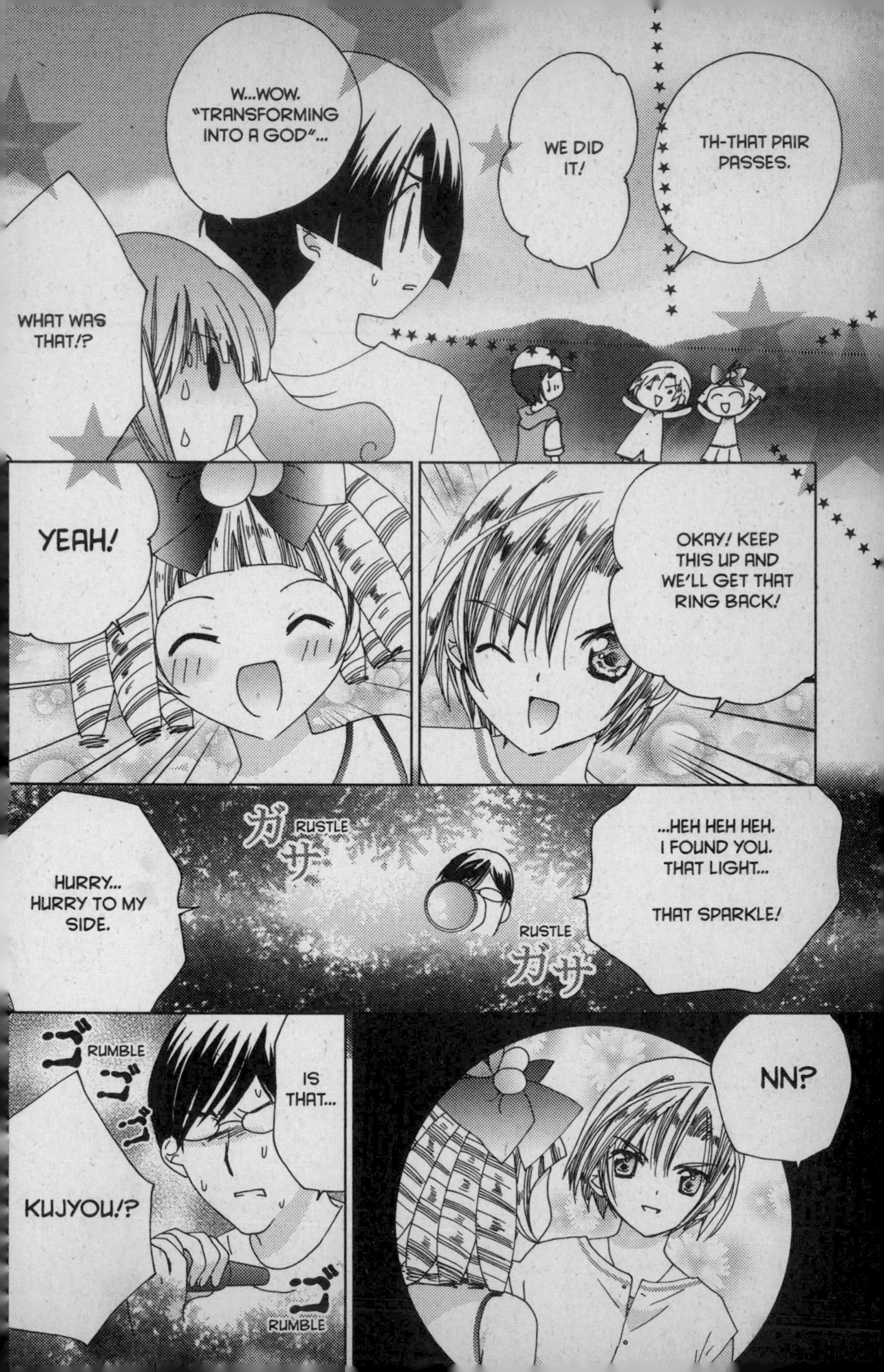
TH-THAT PAIR PASSES.
WE DID IT!
W...WOW. "TRANSFORMING INTO A GOD"...
WHAT WAS THAT!?
OKAY! KEEP THIS UP AND WE'LL GET THAT RING BACK!
YEAH!
...HEH HEH HEH. I FOUND YOU. THAT LIGHT...
THAT SPARKLE!
ガサ RUSTLE
ガサ RUSTLE
HURRY... HURRY TO MY SIDE.
NN?
ゴゴゴ RUMBLE
IS THAT...
KUJYOU!?
ゴ RUMBLE

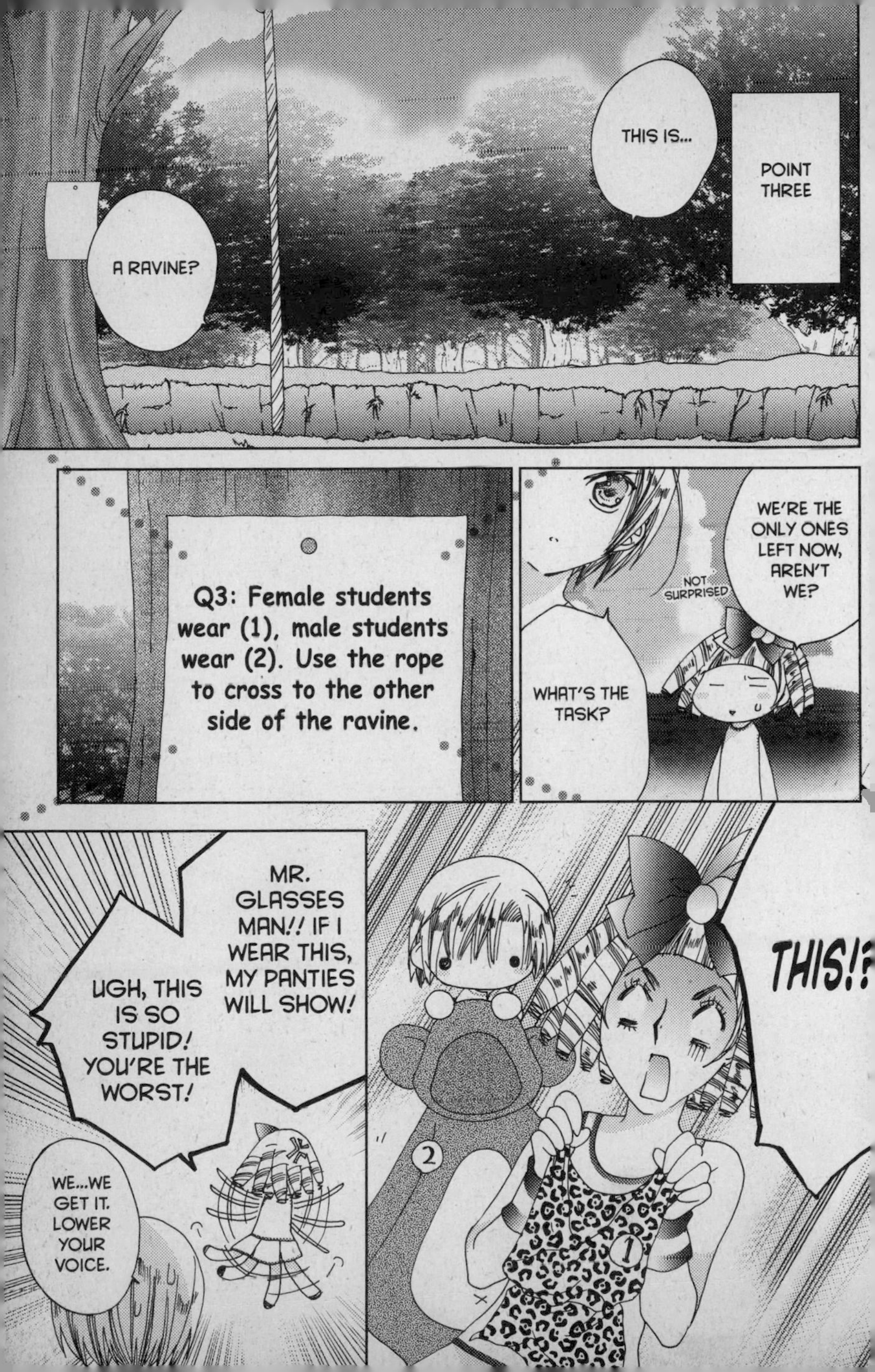
POINT THREE
THIS IS...
A RAVINE?
WE'RE THE ONLY ONES LEFT NOW, AREN'T WE?
NOT SURPRISED
WHAT'S THE TASK?
Q3: Female students wear (1), male students wear (2). Use the rope to cross to the other side of the ravine.
THIS!?
MR. GLASSES MAN!! IF I WEAR THIS, MY PANTIES WILL SHOW!
UGH, THIS IS SO STUPID! YOU'RE THE WORST!
WE...WE GET IT. LOWER YOUR VOICE.

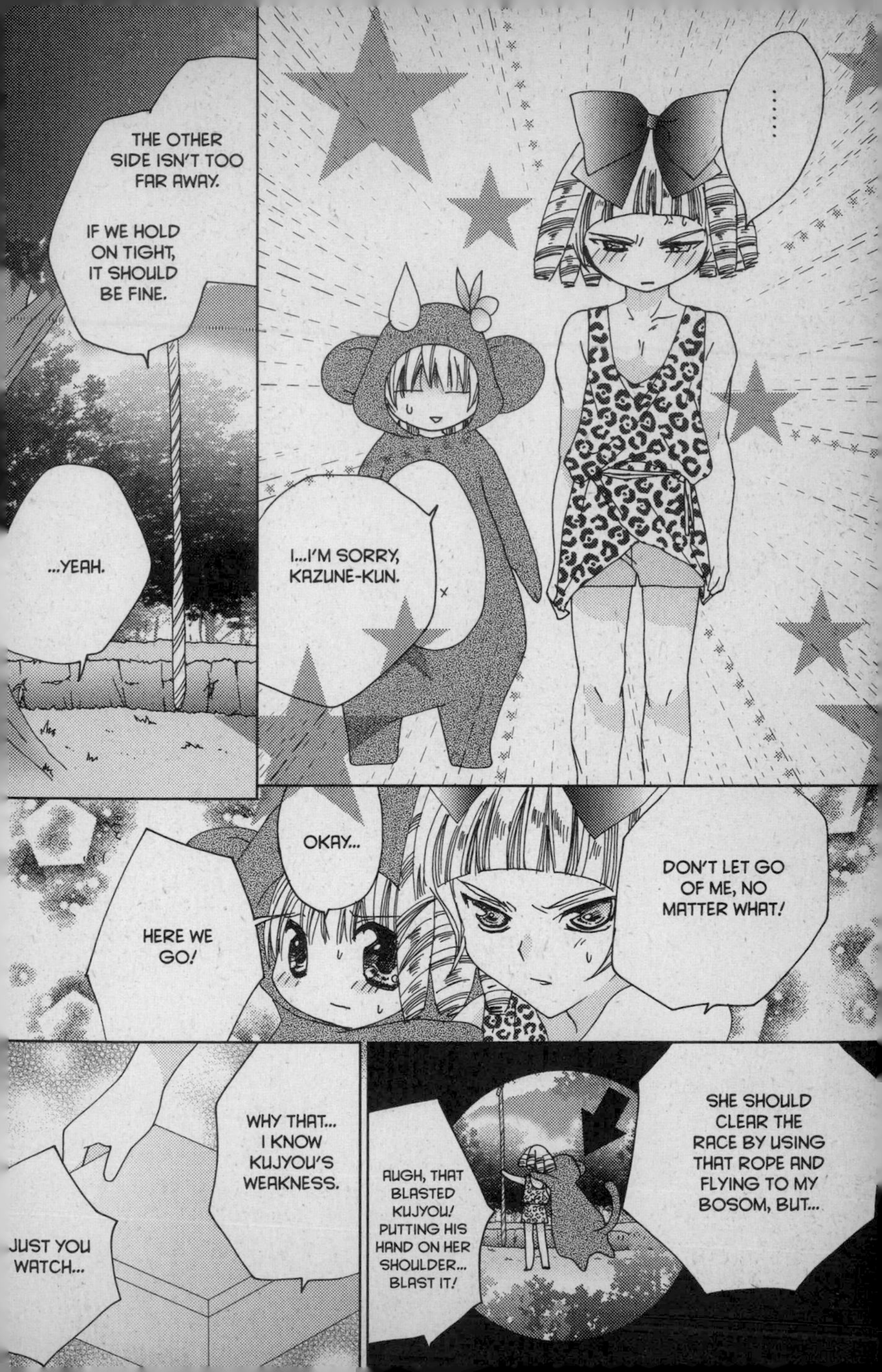
......
I...I'M SORRY, KAZUNE-KUN.
THE OTHER SIDE ISN'T TOO FAR AWAY.
IF WE HOLD ON TIGHT, IT SHOULD BE FINE.
...YEAH.
DON'T LET GO OF ME, NO MATTER WHAT!
OKAY...
HERE WE GO!
SHE SHOULD CLEAR THE RACE BY USING THAT ROPE AND FLYING TO MY BOSOM, BUT...
AUGH, THAT BLASTED KUJYOU! PUTTING HIS HAND ON HER SHOULDER... BLAST IT!
WHY THAT... I KNOW KUJYOU'S WEAKNESS.
JUST YOU WATCH...

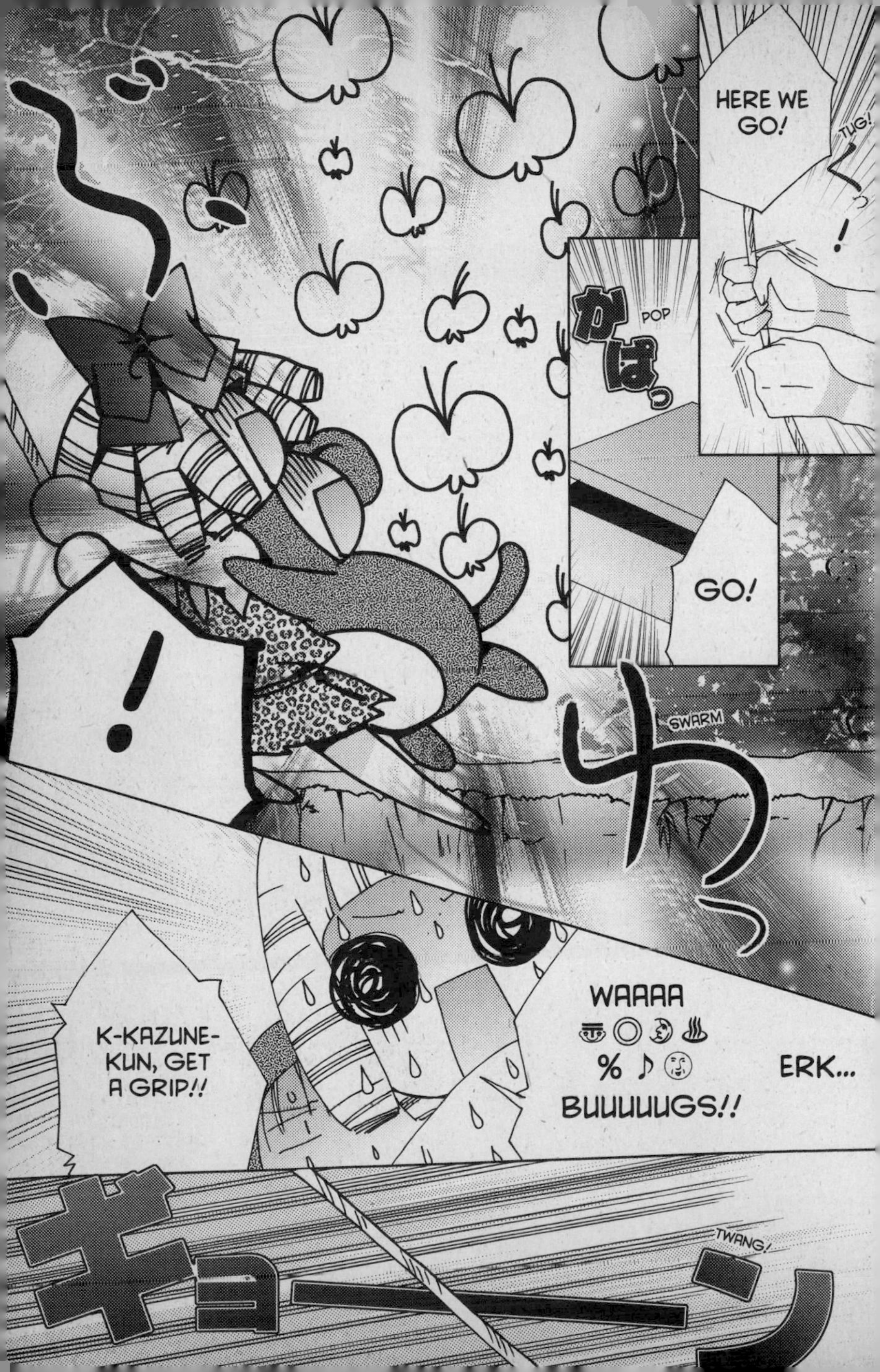
HERE WE GO!
TUG!
く!
POP
かぱっ
GO!
!
SWARM
わっ
ERK...
WAAAA
BUUUUUGS!!
K-KAZUNE-KUN, GET A GRIP!!
TWANG!
キョーン

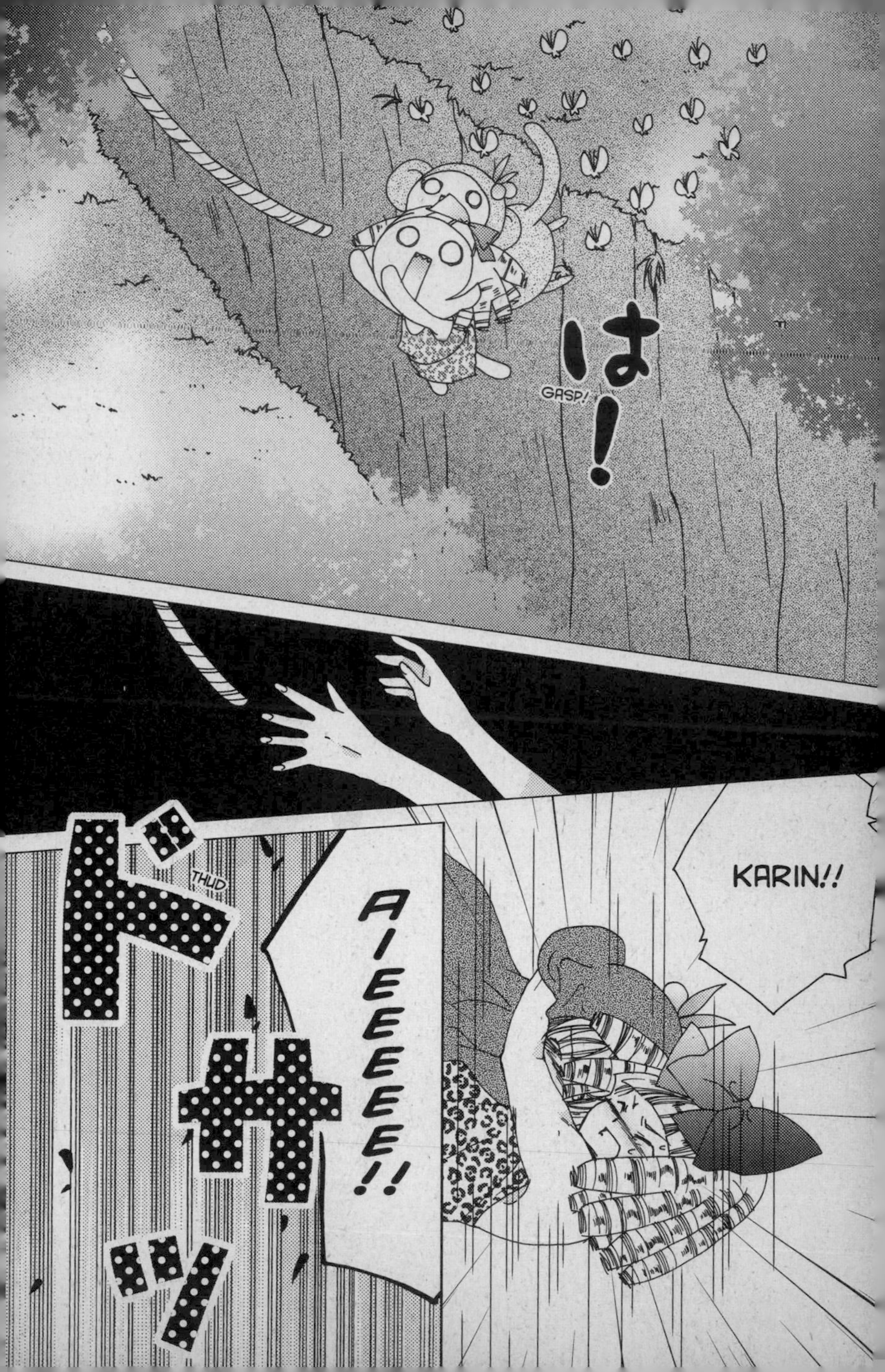
は!
GASP!
KARIN!!
AIEEEEEE!!
ドサッ
THUD

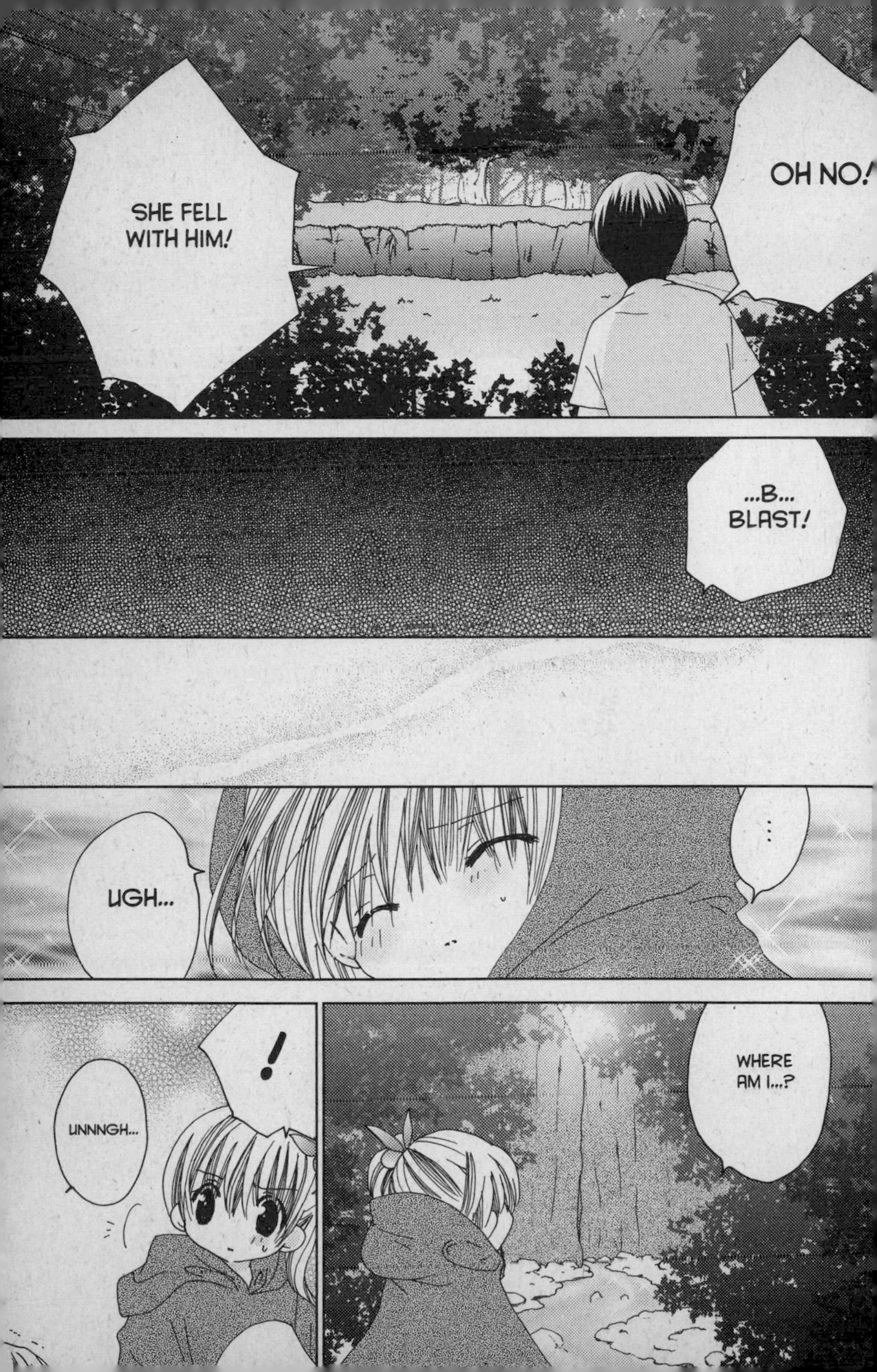
OH NO!
SHE FELL WITH HIM!
...B... BLAST!
...
UGH...
WHERE AM I...?
!
UNNNGH...

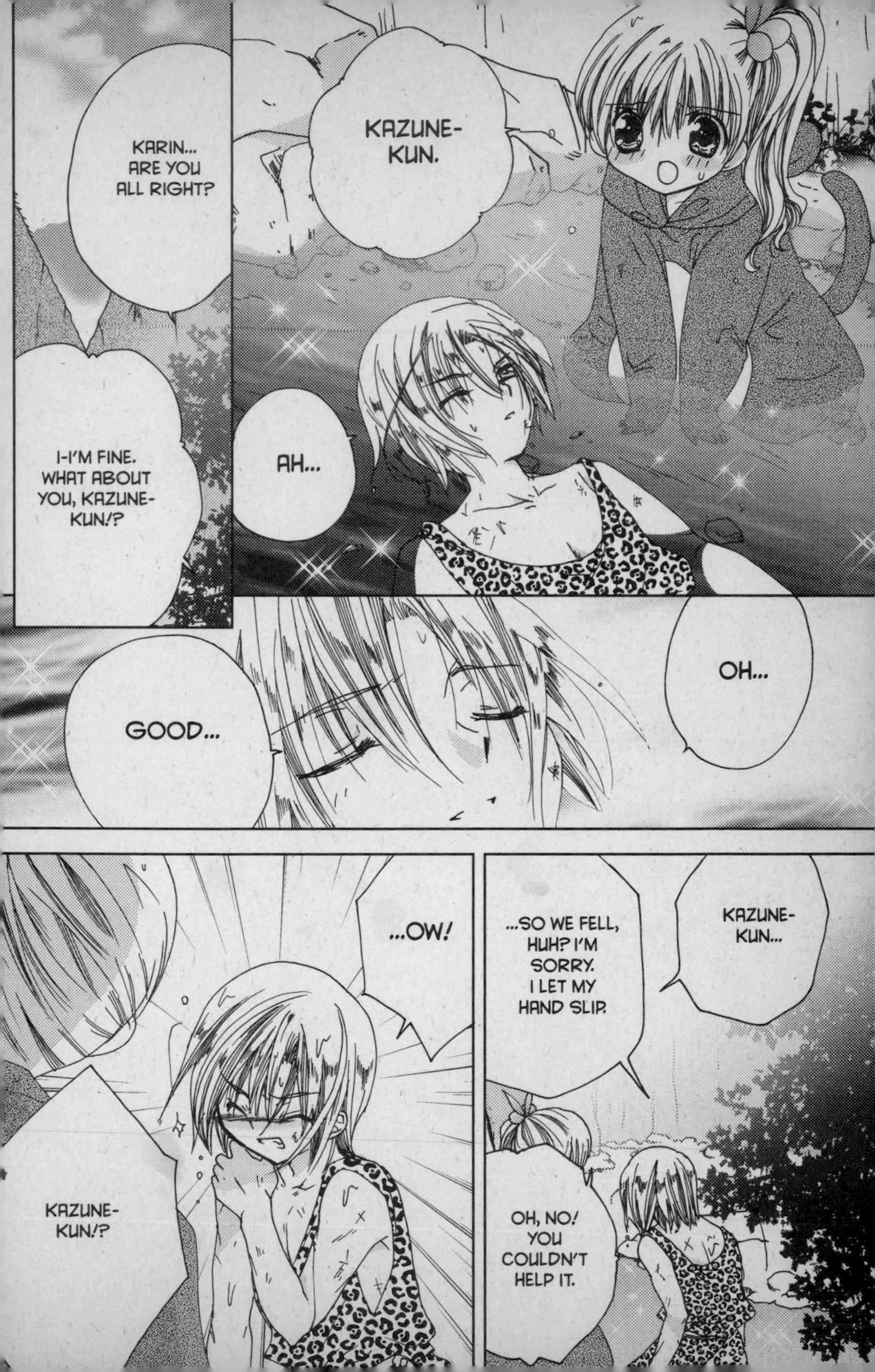
KAZUNE-KUN.
AH...
KARIN... ARE YOU ALL RIGHT?
I-I'M FINE. WHAT ABOUT YOU, KAZUNE-KUN!?
OH...
GOOD...
KAZUNE-KUN...
...SO WE FELL, HUH? I'M SORRY. I LET MY HAND SLIP.
OH, NO! YOU COULDN'T HELP IT.
...OW!
KAZUNE-KUN!?

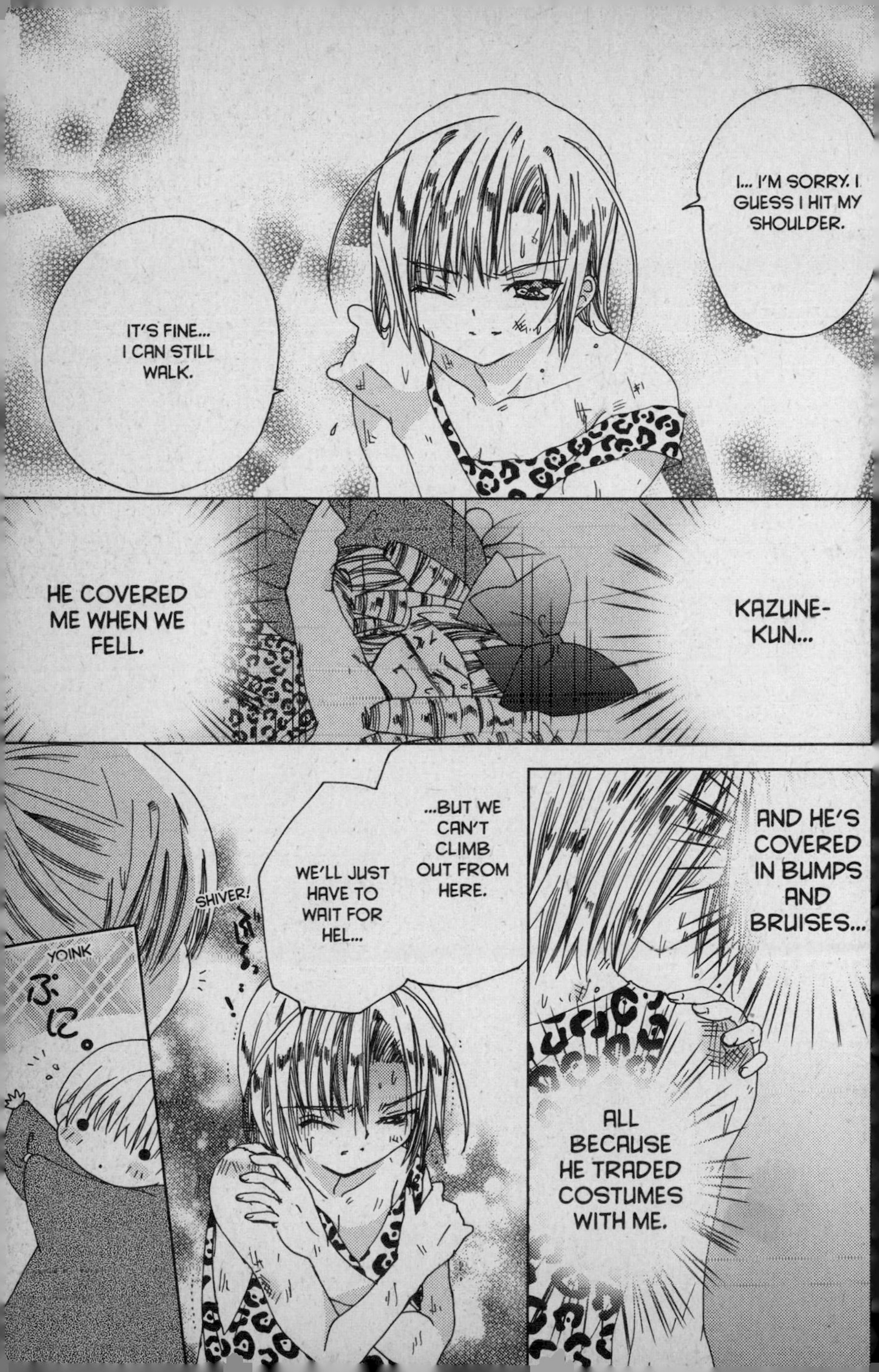

I... I'M SORRY. I GUESS I HIT MY SHOULDER.
IT'S FINE... I CAN STILL WALK.
KAZUNE-KUN...
HE COVERED ME WHEN WE FELL.
AND HE'S COVERED IN BUMPS AND BRUISES...
ALL BECAUSE HE TRADED COSTUMES WITH ME.
...BUT WE CAN'T CLIMB OUT FROM HERE.
WE'LL JUST HAVE TO WAIT FOR HEL...
SHIVER!
YOINK
ふに。

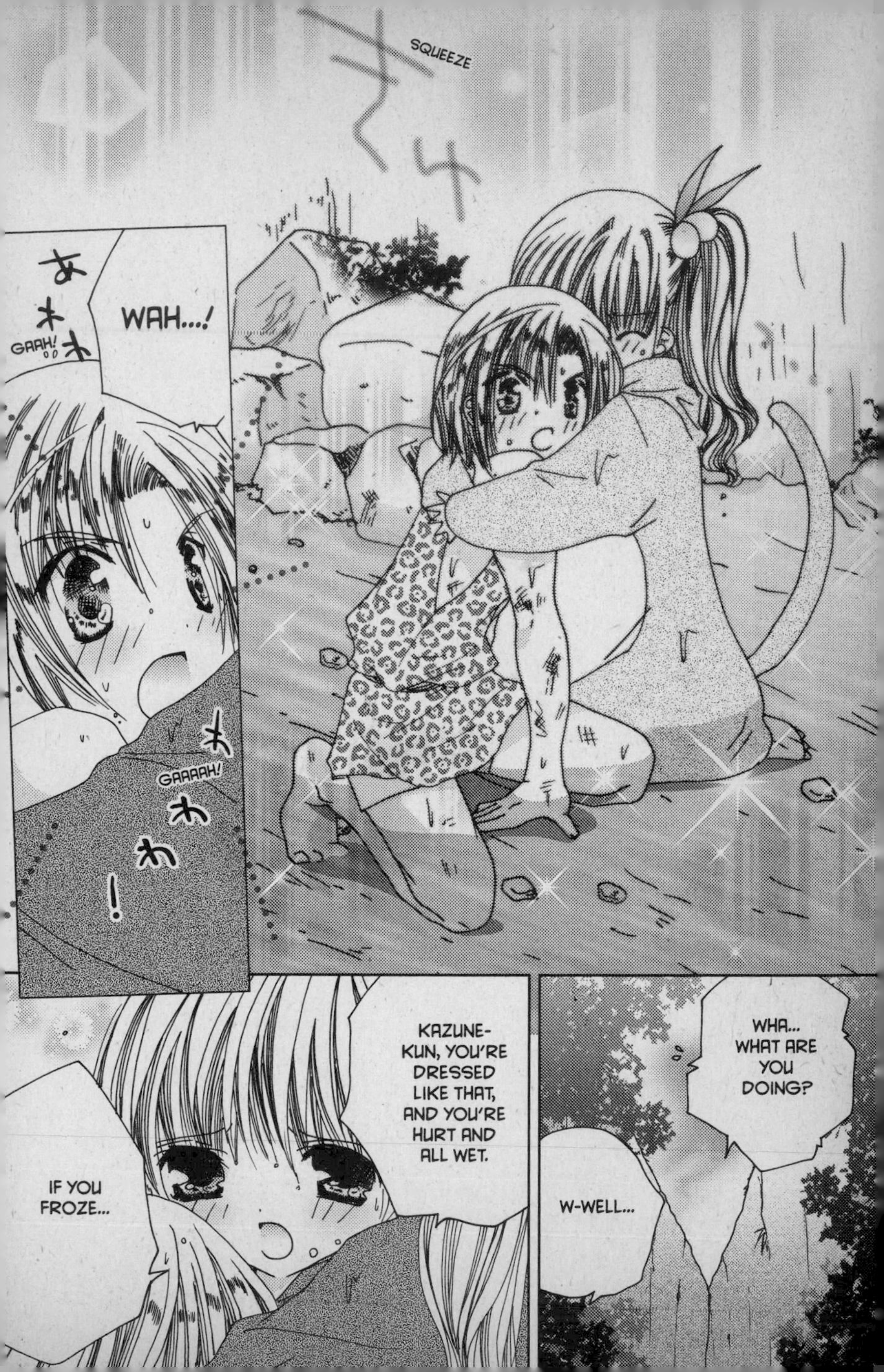
SQUEEZE
WAH...!
GAAH!
GAAAAH!
WHA... WHAT ARE YOU DOING?
W-WELL...
KAZUNE-KUN, YOU'RE DRESSED LIKE THAT, AND YOU'RE HURT AND ALL WET.
IF YOU FROZE...

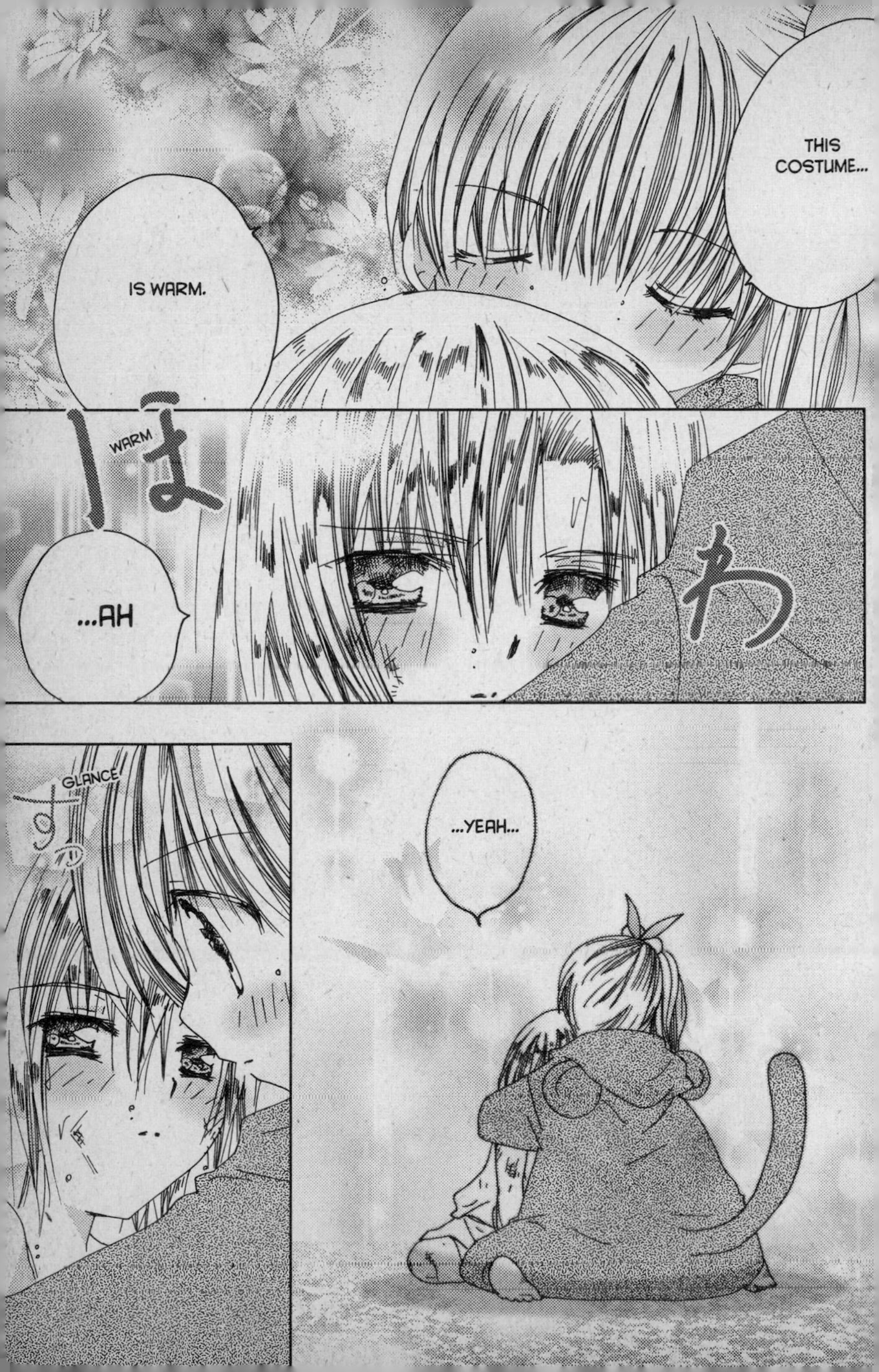
THIS COSTUME...
IS WARM.
ほわ
WARM
...AH
...YEAH...
GLANCE

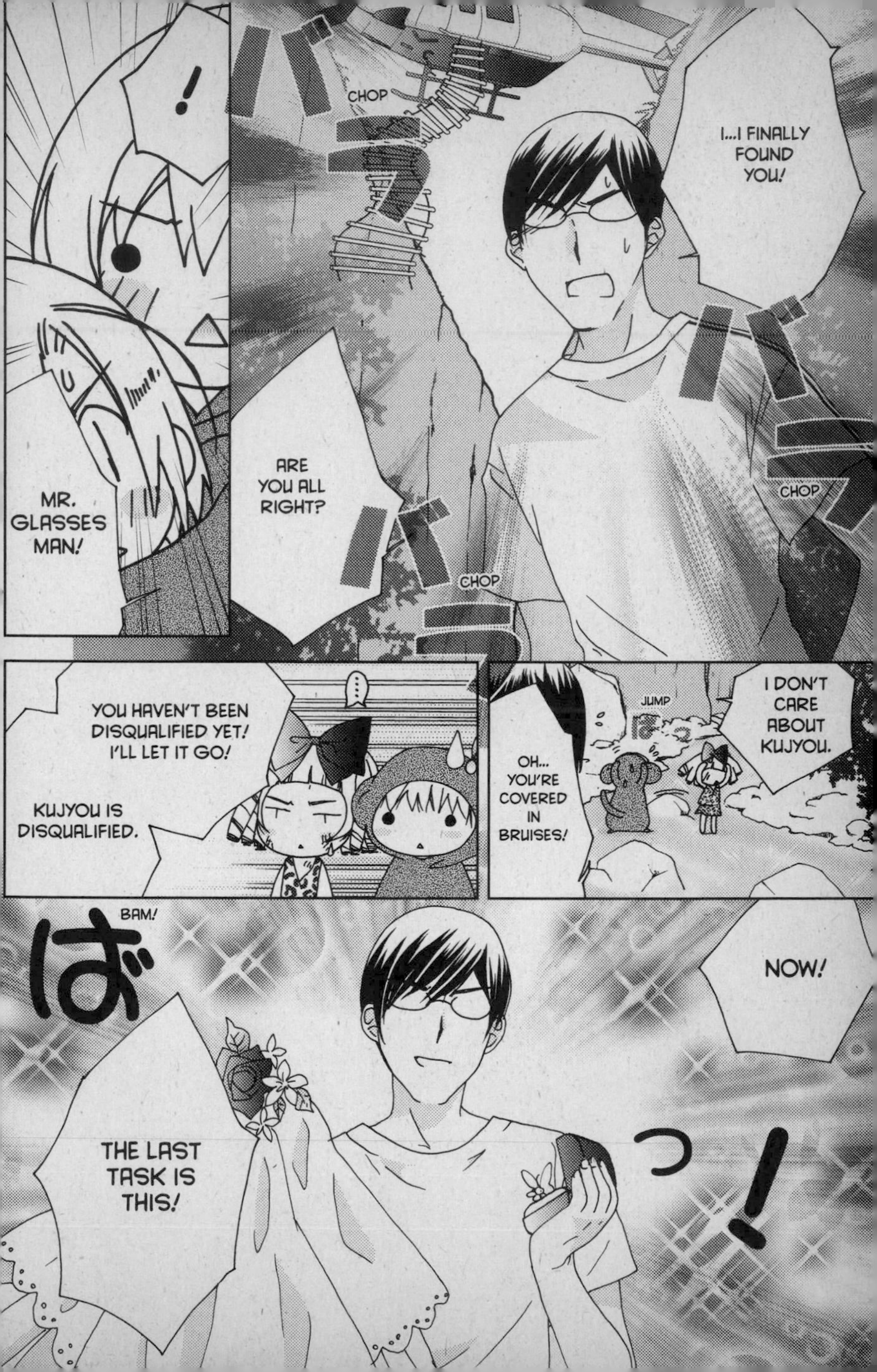
I...I FINALLY FOUND YOU!
CHOP
CHOP
ARE YOU ALL RIGHT?
CHOP
!
MR. GLASSES MAN!
I DON'T CARE ABOUT KUJYOU.
JUMP
OH... YOU'RE COVERED IN BRUISES!
...
YOU HAVEN'T BEEN DISQUALIFIED YET! I'LL LET IT GO!
KUJYOU IS DISQUALIFIED.
NOW!
BAM!
THE LAST TASK IS THIS!

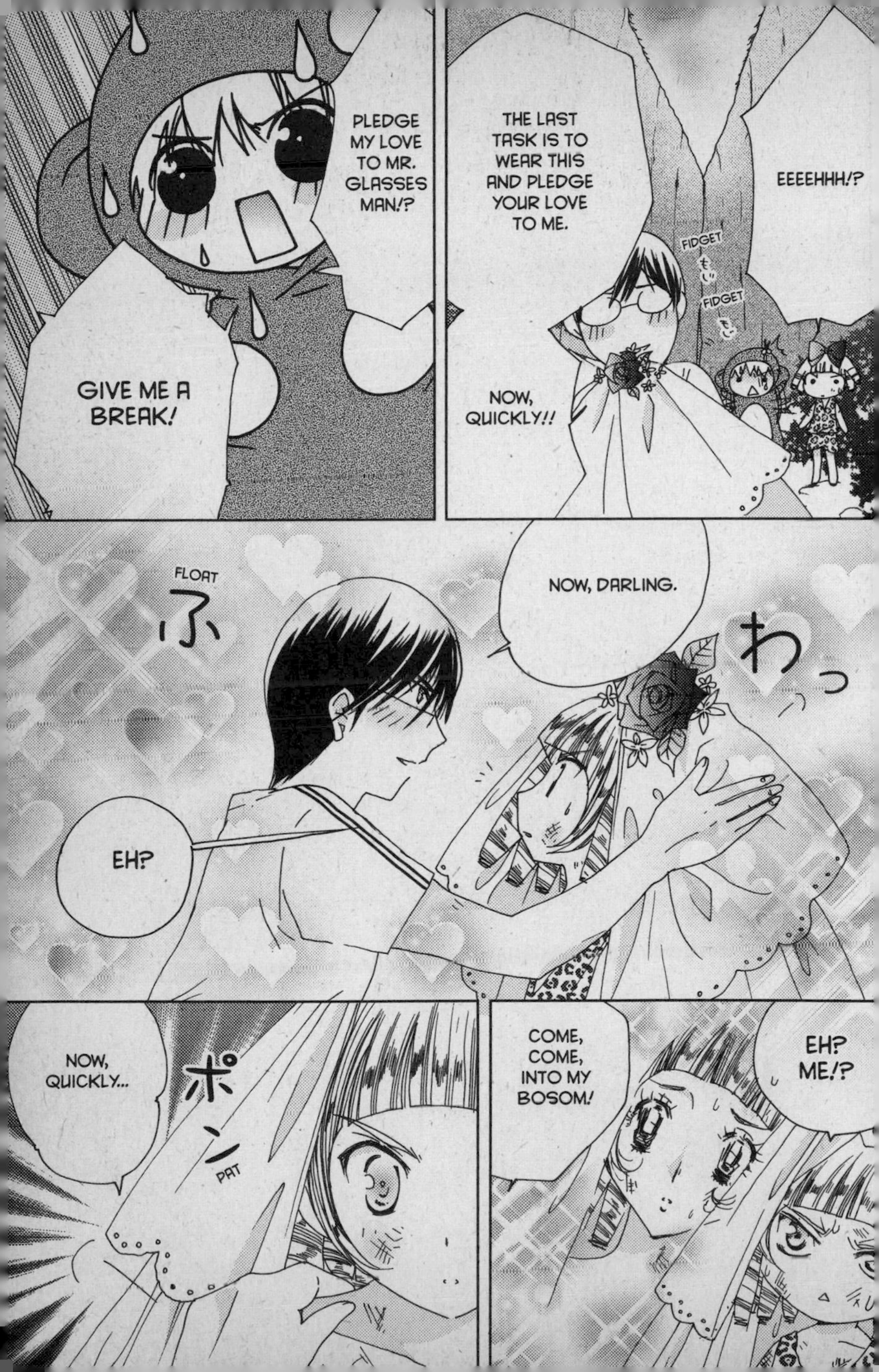
THE LAST TASK IS TO WEAR THIS AND PLEDGE YOUR LOVE TO ME.
EEEEHHH!?
FIDGET
もじ
FIDGET
もじ
NOW, QUICKLY!!
PLEDGE MY LOVE TO MR. GLASSES MAN!?
GIVE ME A BREAK!
わっ
NOW, DARLING.
FLOAT
ふ
EH?
EH? ME!?
COME, COME, INTO MY BOSOM!
NOW, QUICKLY...
ポン
PAT

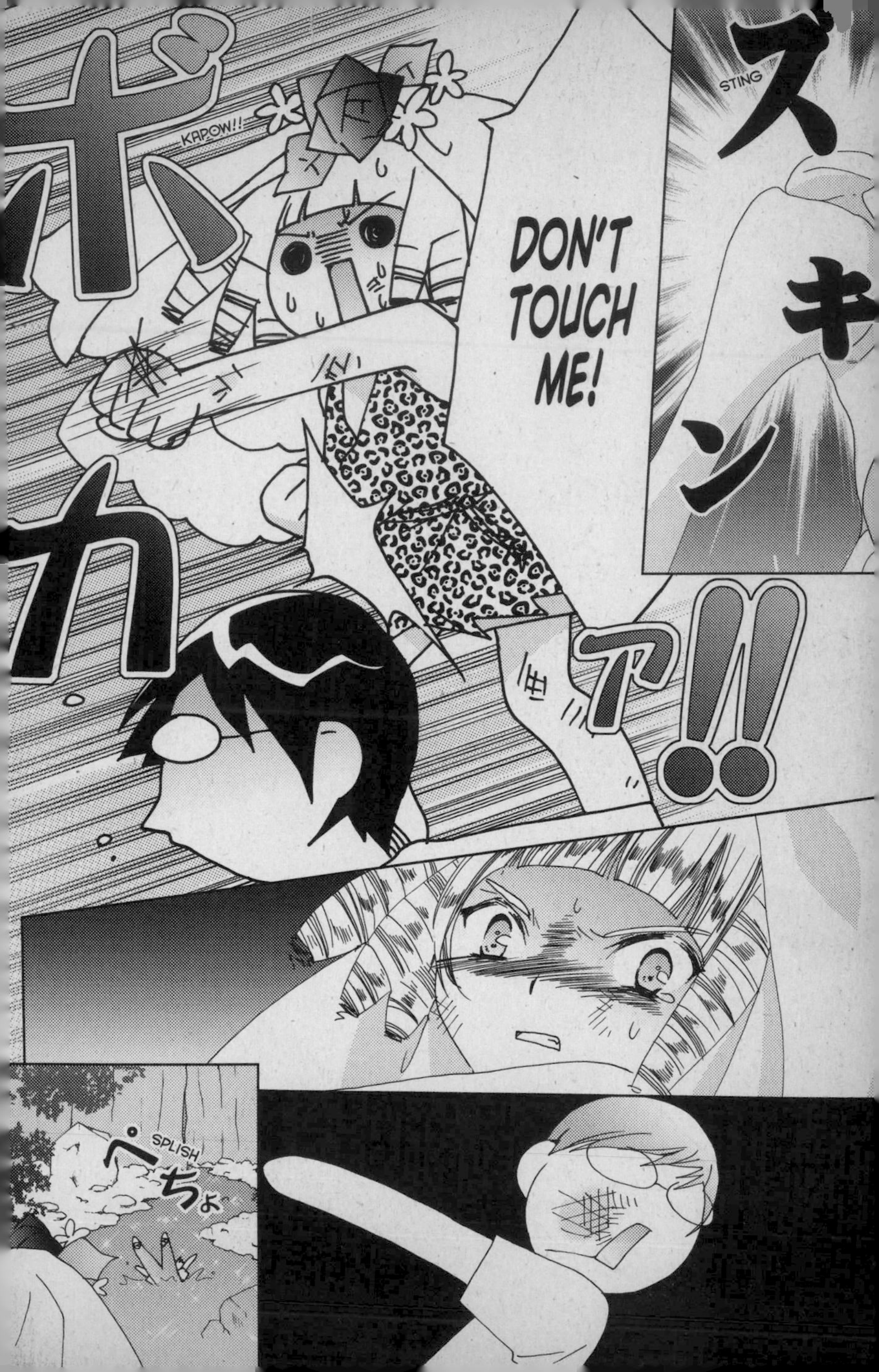

STING
スキン
KAPOW!!
ポカァ!!
DON'T TOUCH ME!
SPLISH
ぺちょ

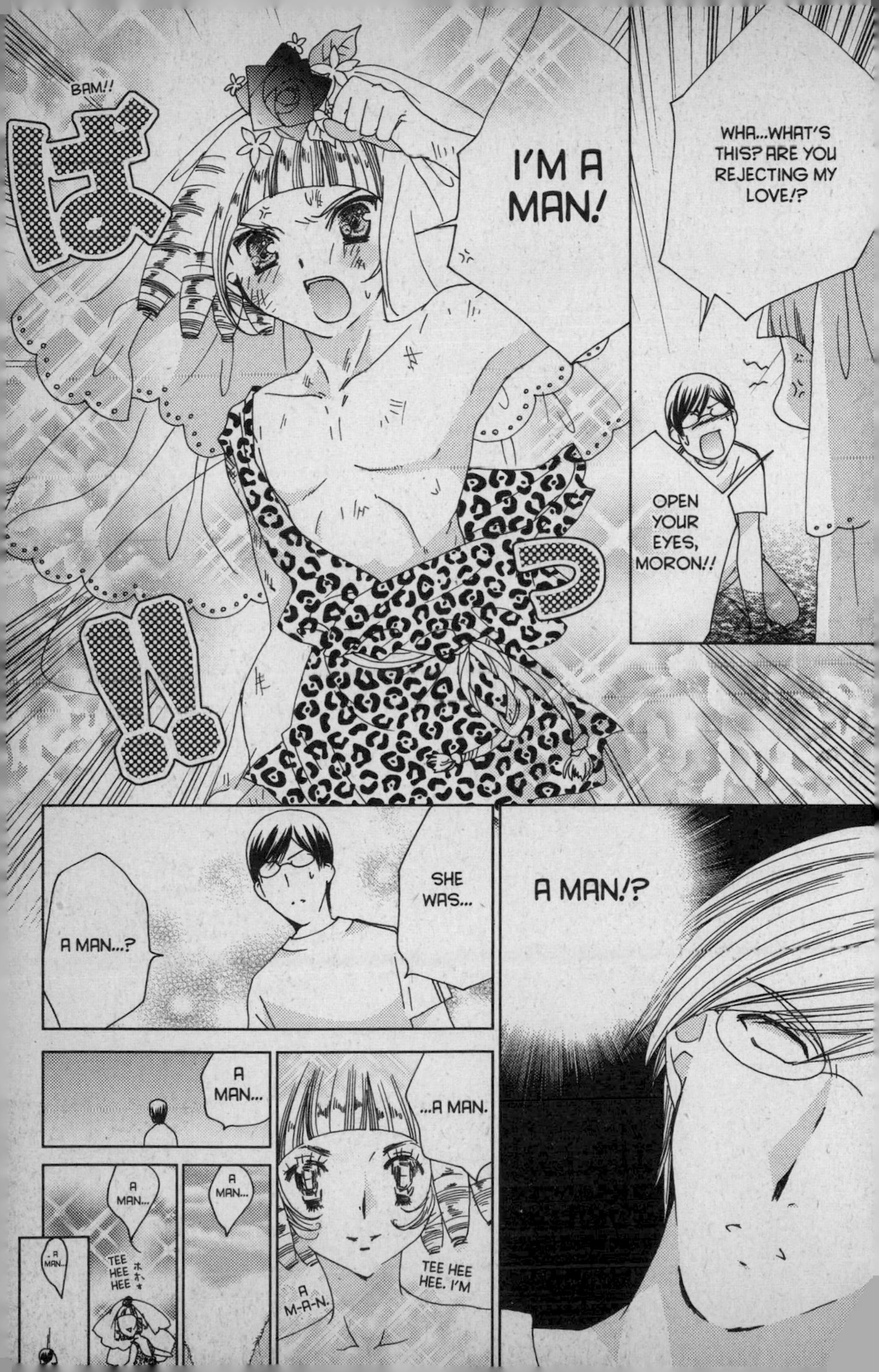
WHA...WHAT'S THIS? ARE YOU REJECTING MY LOVE!?
OPEN YOUR EYES, MORON!!
I'M A MAN!
BAM!!
A MAN!?
SHE WAS...
A MAN...?
...A MAN.
TEE HEE HEE. I'M
A M-A-N.
A MAN...
A MAN...
A MAN...
TEE HEE HEE
A MAN...

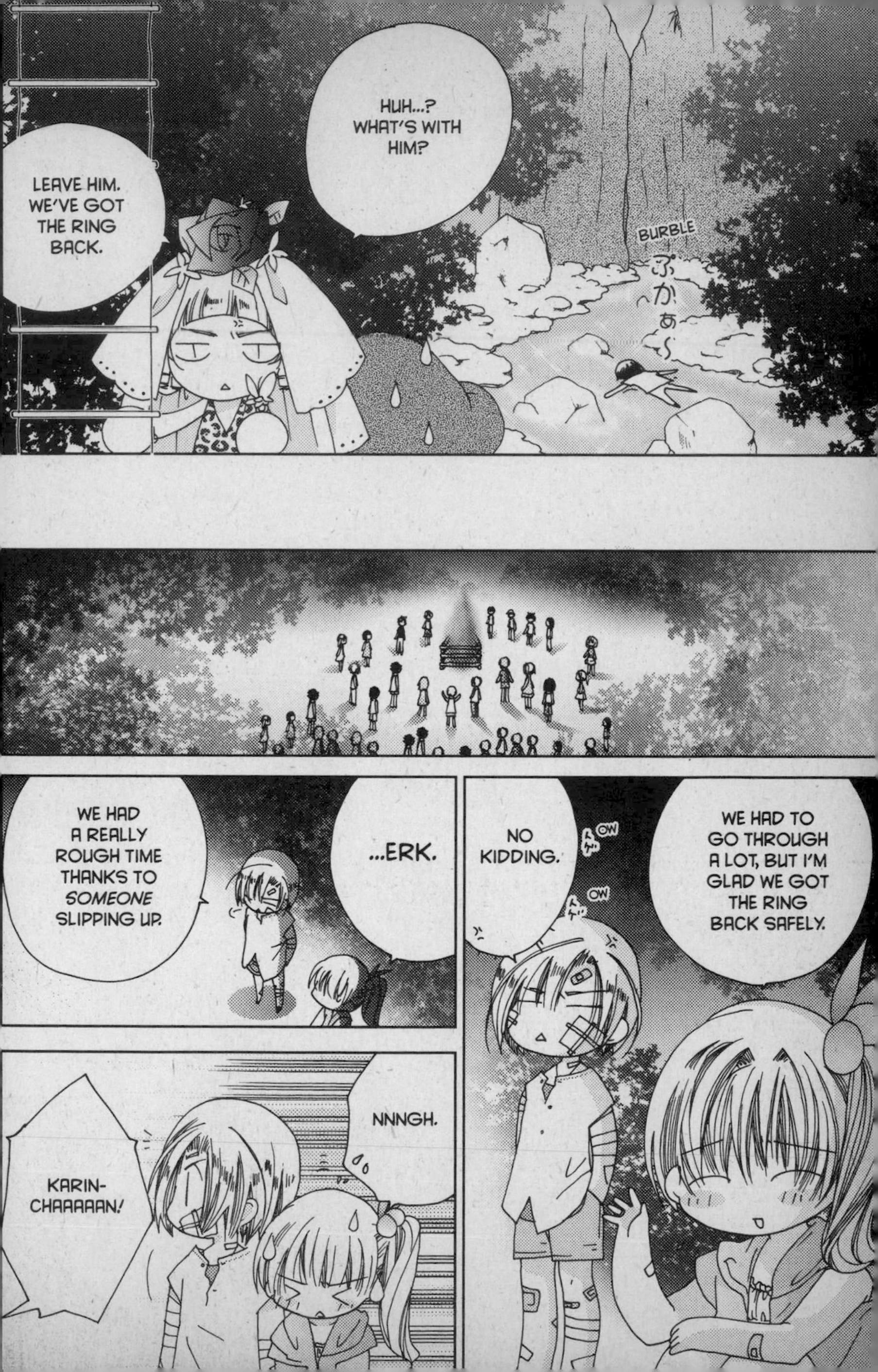
BURBLE
ぷかぁ〜
HUH...? WHAT'S WITH HIM?
LEAVE HIM. WE'VE GOT THE RING BACK.
WE HAD TO GO THROUGH A LOT, BUT I'M GLAD WE GOT THE RING BACK SAFELY.
NO KIDDING.
OW
OW
WE HAD A REALLY ROUGH TIME THANKS TO *SOMEONE* SLIPPING UP.
...ERK.
NNNGH.
KARIN-CHAAAAAN!

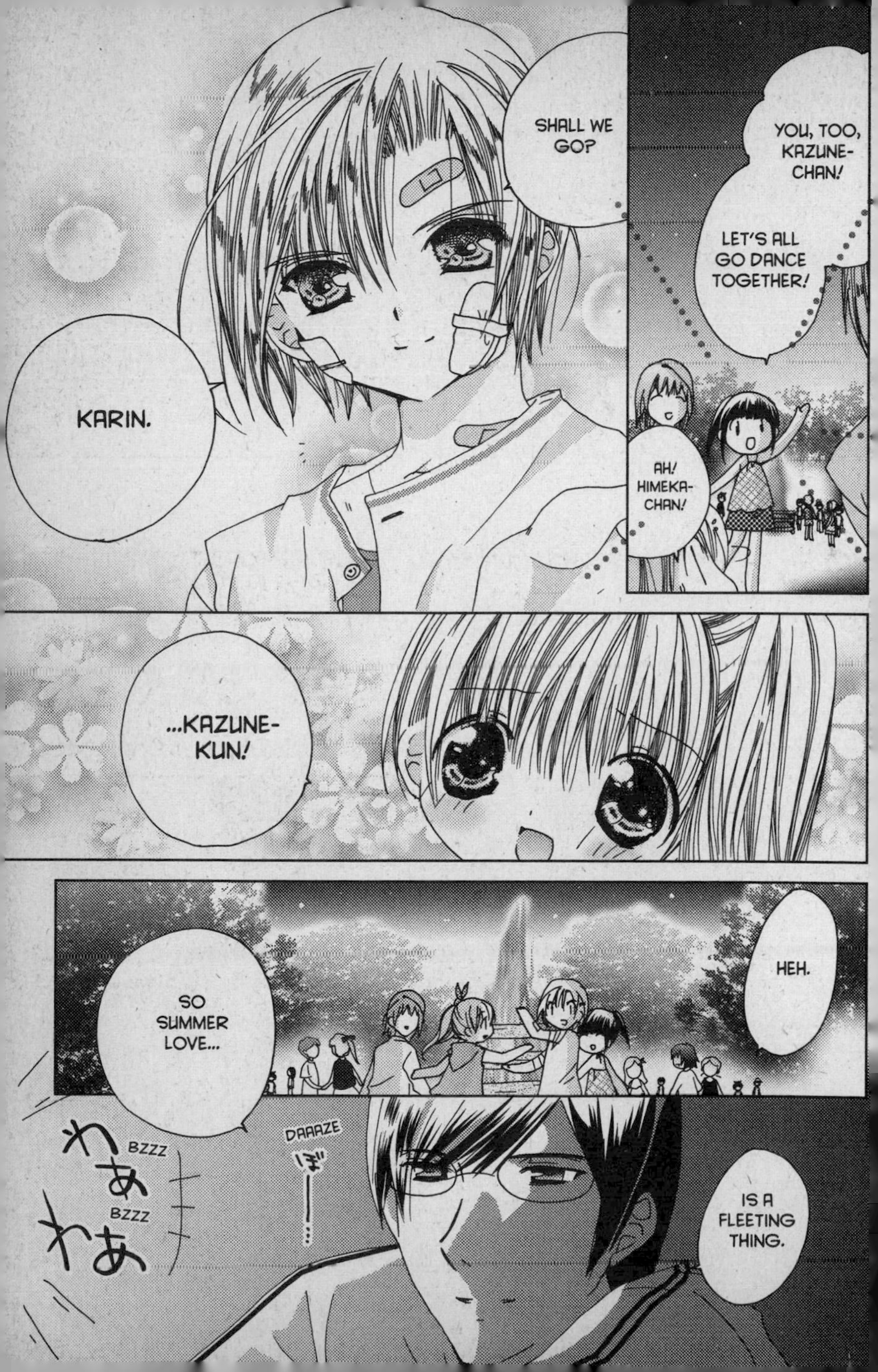
YOU, TOO, KAZUNE-CHAN!
LET'S ALL GO DANCE TOGETHER!
AH! HIMEKA-CHAN!
SHALL WE GO?
KARIN.
...KAZUNE-KUN!
HEH.
SO SUMMER LOVE...
IS A FLEETING THING.
ぼー…
DAAAZE
わあ BZZZ
わあ BZZZ

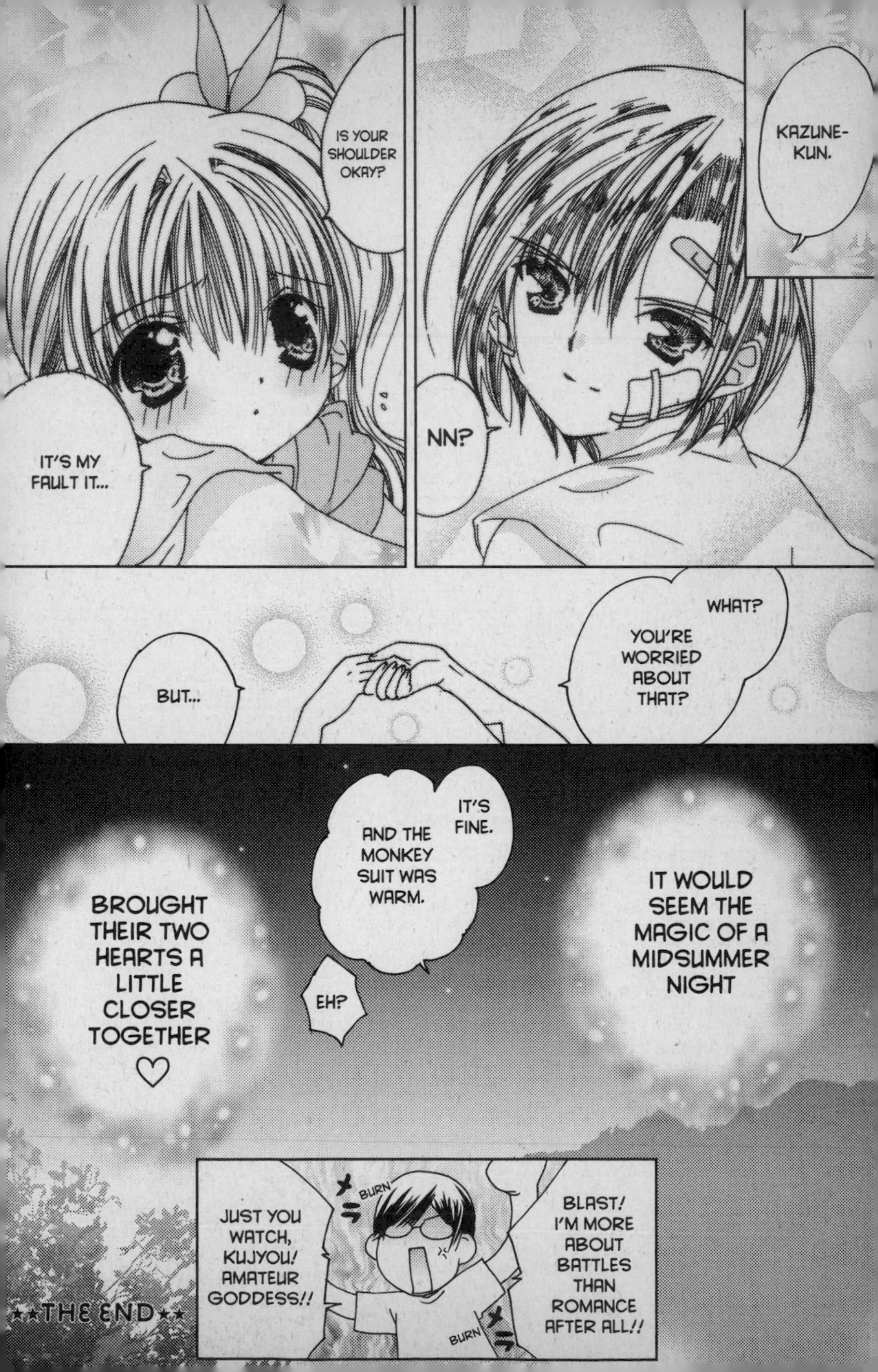
KAZUNE-KUN.
NN?
IS YOUR SHOULDER OKAY?
IT'S MY FAULT IT...
WHAT?
YOU'RE WORRIED ABOUT THAT?
BUT...
IT WOULD SEEM THE MAGIC OF A MIDSUMMER NIGHT
IT'S FINE.
AND THE MONKEY SUIT WAS WARM.
EH?
BROUGHT THEIR TWO HEARTS A LITTLE CLOSER TOGETHER ♡
BLAST! I'M MORE ABOUT BATTLES THAN ROMANCE AFTER ALL!!
BURN
BURN
JUST YOU WATCH, KUJYOU! AMATEUR GODDESS!!
THE END

Pardon our intrusion! & ASSISTANTS

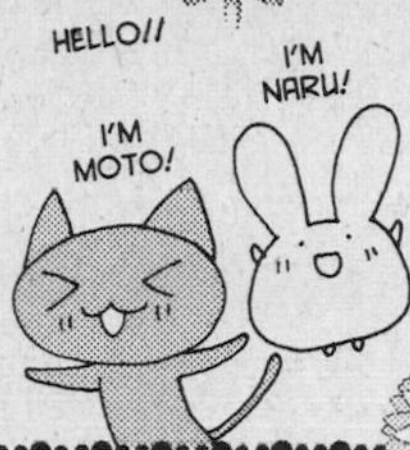
HELLO!!
I'M MOTO!
I'M NARU!

PRESENTING: OUR WORKROOM!

SENSEI AND HER ASSISTANTS ALL WORK HERE.

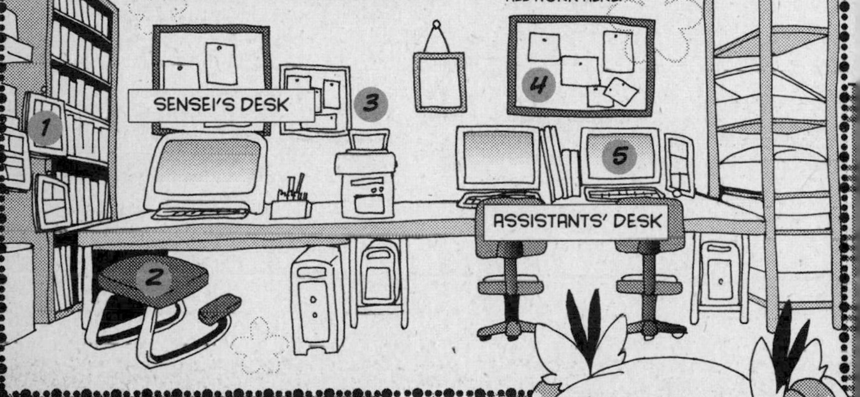
1
SENSEI'S DESK
3
4
5
ASSISTANTS' DESK
2

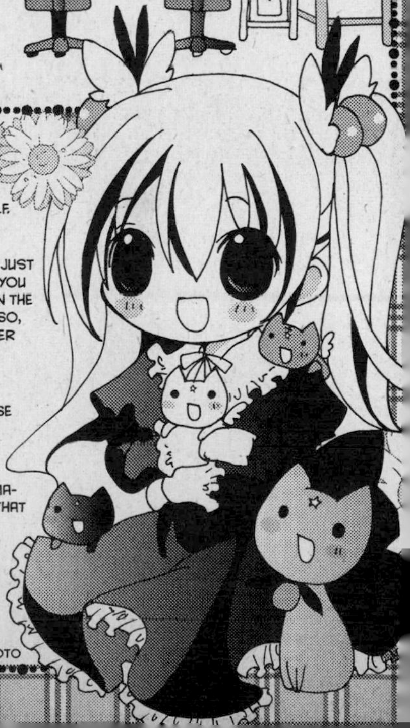

1. A LOT OF ROUGH DRAFTS AND MANUSCRIPTS FOR *KAMICHAMA KARIN CHU* ARE HUNG UP NEAR THE BOOKSHELF.

2. THIS IS THE CHAIR SENSEI SITS IN.
BECAUSE SHE SITS FOR A LONG TIME, SHE HAS A HARD TIME JUST MAINTAINING CORRECT POSTURE. OR SO SHE SAYS. AND IF YOU HAVE BAD POSTURE, YOU GET STIFF SHOULDERS AND PAIN IN THE HIPS, AND IT PUTS PRESSURE ON YOUR INTERNAL ORGANS, SO, THINKING OF HER HEALTH, SHE SITS IN A CHAIR THAT HELPS HER SIT WITH CORRECT POSTURE WITHOUT TOO MUCH EFFORT.

3. DVD, VIDEO, RADIO-CASETTE PLAYER.
SOMETIMES WE BRING ANIME AND HAVE A SCREENING. WE USE THE RADIO-CASETTE PLAYER WHEN WE'RE EXERCISING.

4. CORKBOARD.
IT HAS IMPORTANT MEMOS AND STORY AND DESIGN INFORMATION POSTED ON IT. THERE'S A WHITEBOARD, TOO. IT'S SO THAT WE CAN ALL UNDERSTAND WHAT'S GOING ON IN THE STORY.

5. COMPUTER.
WE TOUCH UP THE LINES SENSEI DRAWS ON THE COMPUTER. WE WORK RIGHT NEXT TO EACH OTHER, SO THAT WE CAN ALWAYS CHECK ON WHAT OUR NEIGHBOR IS DOING.

DRAWING BY MOTO

DRAWING BY NARU

Our comments.

PLEASED TO MEET YOU. I AM MOTO, ONE OF THE ASSISTANTS. CONGRATULATIONS ON THE RELEASE OF *KAMICHAMA KARIN CHU* VOLUME TWO AND GETTING IT ANIMATED*!!* MOTO'S FAVORITE EPISODE IS THE COOKING SHOWDOWN. JIN-KUN LEFT A BIG IMPRESSION BY PUTTING TOFU AND *CHIKUWA* IN HIS CURRY, SO ALL ANY OF US COULD TALK ABOUT WAS JIN-KUN'S TOFU. I WANT TO EAT CURRY EVERY TIME I SEE THAT CHAPTER. IT WOULD SEEM THAT SENSEI WAS THE SAME WAY BECAUSE SHE WENT TO EAT CURRY A LOT AFTER LOOKING AT THIS CHAPTER. BUT REALLY, THERE WAS A MORE IMPORTANT INCIDENT IN THAT CHAPTER, WASN'T THERE...? I REALLY CAN'T WAIT TO SEE MORE OF THE EXCITING, ADORABLE KARIN-CHAN! YOU CAN'T MISS IT.

NARU BUNNY!

NICE TO MEET YOU, EVERYONE! I AM NARU. THIS TIME, KOGE-SENSEI TOLD US, "YOU ASSISTANTS CAN WRITE WHATEVER YOU WANT!" AND GAVE US A COUPLE OF PAGES, SO I WILL SHAMELESSLY TAKE UP SOME SPACE. TH-THIS DOES MAKE ME NERVOUS... BADUMP, BUMP. WELL THEN, ABOUT *KAMICHAMA KARIN CHU* VOLUME TWO. HMM. ACTUALLY, I SECRETLY LOVE JIN-KUN'S MANAGER AND SHINGEN-KUN, SO THE HIGHLIGHTS I RECOMMEND ARE THE FRAMES THEY SHOW UP IN AND KIRIO-SAN'S HIGH SCHOOL UNIFORM, WHICH LOOKS JUST TOO PERFECT ON HIM ★ PLEASE MAKE SURE TO CHECK THEM OUT! OKAY, PARDON MY INTRUSION!

DAAAZE

OOF

OOF

Please continue to think kindly of us!!

YAAY!

ASSISTANT BLOG
[HTTP://KOGE2.BLOG68.FC2.COM/]
*THE ASSISTANTS TAKE TURNS UPDATING THEIR JOURNAL WITH INFORMATION ON OUR ART CIRCLE AND THINGS THAT HAPPEN WHILE DRAWING THE MANUSCRIPTS.

MOTO'S HOMEPAGE
[HTTP://MISHIBA.GOOGLEPAGES.COM/]

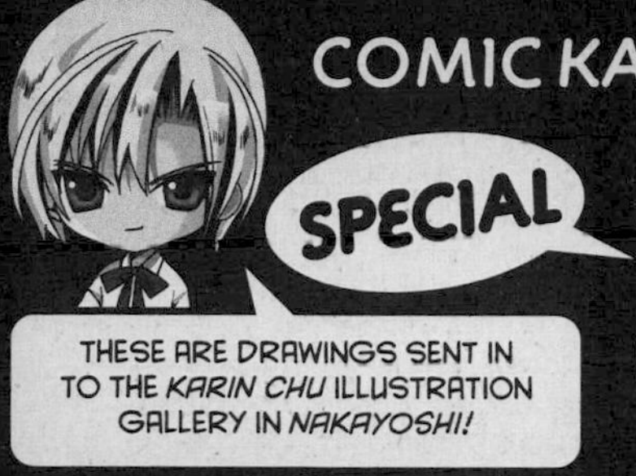
SPECIAL
THESE ARE DRAWINGS SENT IN TO THE *KARIN CHU* ILLUSTRATION GALLERY IN *NAKAYOSHI!*

COMIC KAMICHAMA KARIN CHU
ILLUSTRATION GALLERY

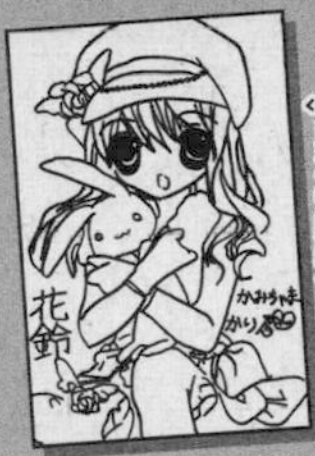
かみちゃま
かりん
花鈴
KAEDE KATÔ, IWATE PREFECTURE

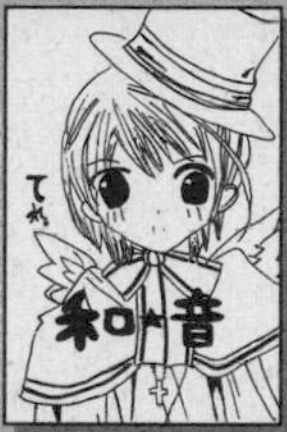
和音
HIROMI UDA, SAITAMA PREFECTURE

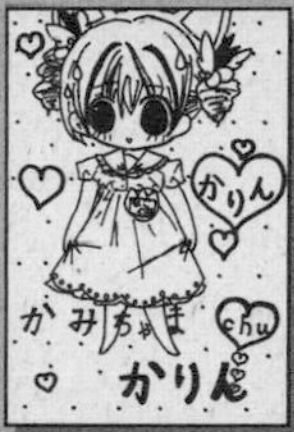
かりん
かみちゃま
chu
かりん
SHIORI TANAKA, NAGANO PREFECTURE

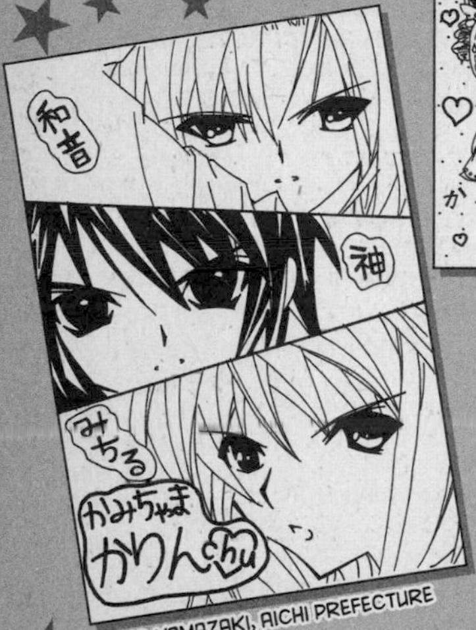
和音
神
みちる
かみちゃま
かりんchu
RIKO YAMAZAKI, AICHI PREFECTURE

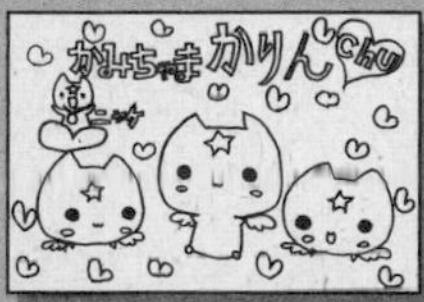
かみちゃまかりんchu
NAGISA SEYA, IBARAKI PREFECTURE

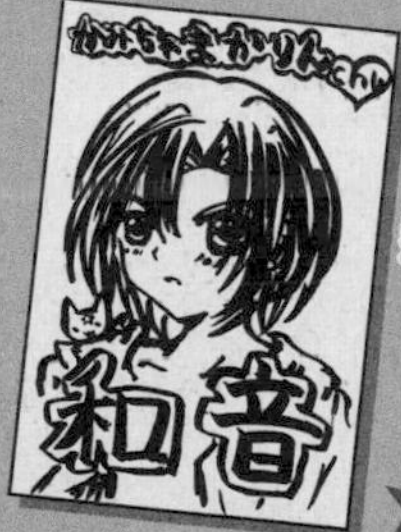
かみちゃまかりんchu
和音
KANE TOSHIMA, FUKUOKA PREFECTURE

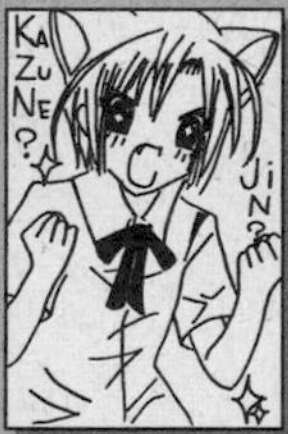
KAZUNE?
JIN?
YURIKA KIKUCHI, SHIZUOKA PREFECTURE

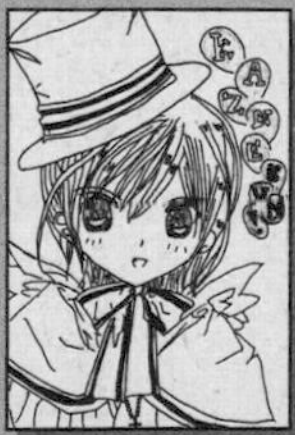
KUMI MAEDA, HOKKAIDO

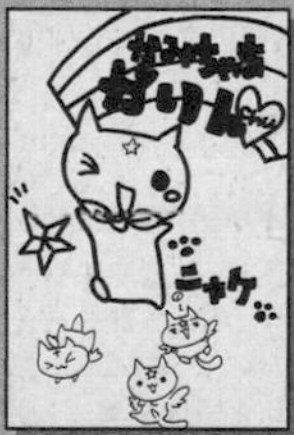
かみちゃま
かりん
ニャケ
TOMOE YOKOZAWA, IWATE PREFECTURE

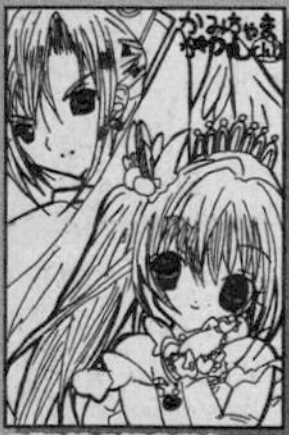
REINA INAGAKI, GUNMA PREFECTURE

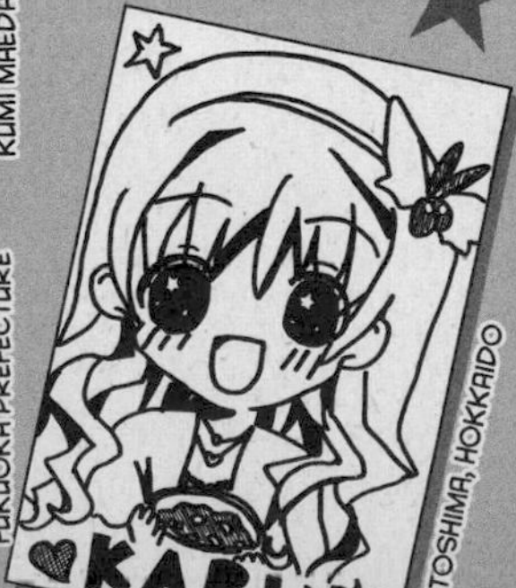
KARIN
SAHO TOSHIMA, HOKKAIDO

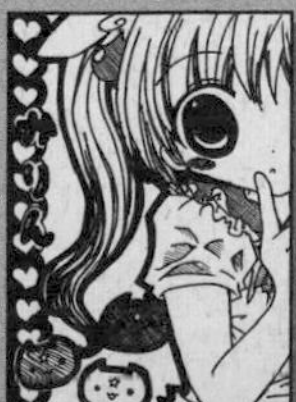
かりん
YUKINA MATSUMURA, FUKUOKA PREFECTURE

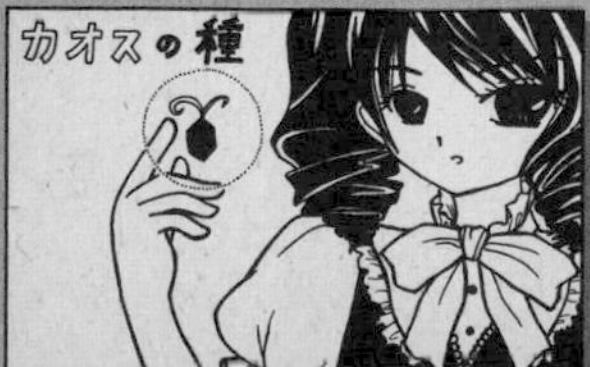
カオスの種
YÛKO YANASE, AICHI PREFECTURE

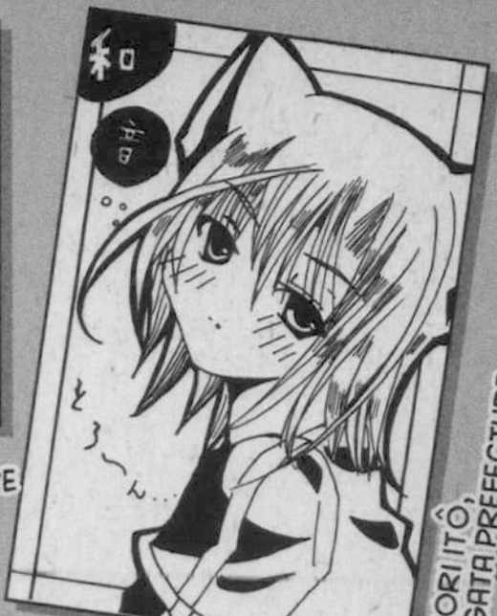
和音
とろ～ん…

SHIORI ITÔ, NIIGATA PREFECTURE

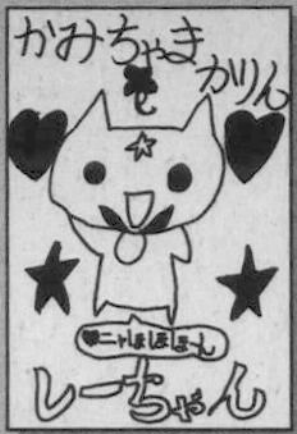
かみちゃまかりん
レーちゃん

RINA MIZUHASHI, NIIGATA PREFECTURE

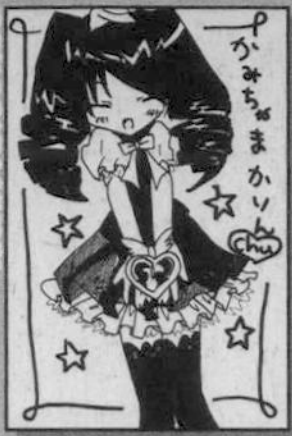
chu

MISATO IMAI, AICHI PREFECTURE

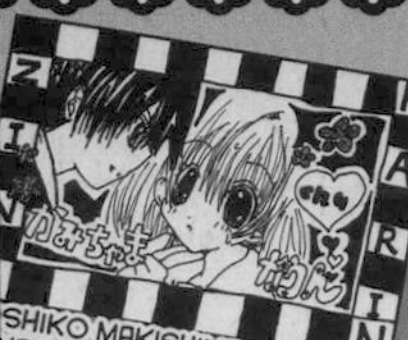
KARIN
かみちゃま

SHIKO MAKISHIMA, NAGAWA PREFECTURE

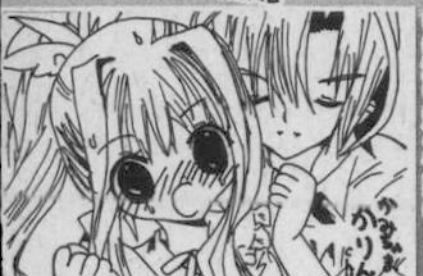

SAKI YOSHIDA, MIYAGI PREFECTURE

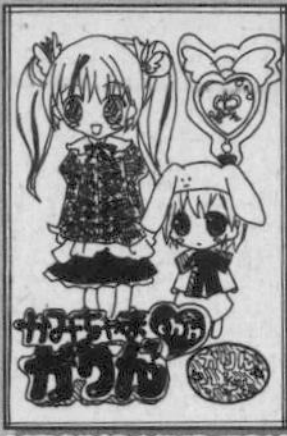

MAYUKO MITA, TOKYO

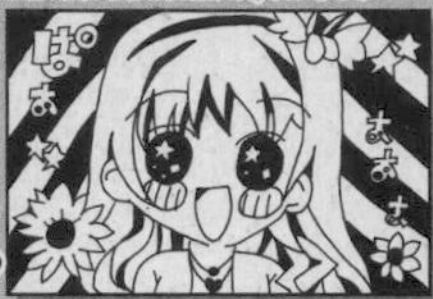

YÛNA NAKAMURA, KYOTO

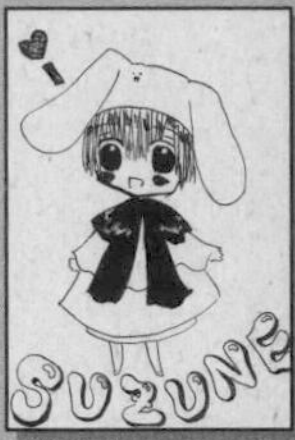
SUZUNE

AYAMI ONAKA, KANAGAWA PREFECTURE

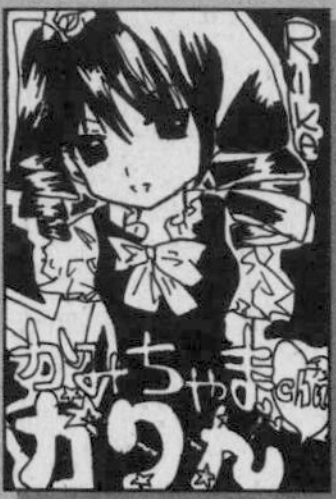
かみちゃま
かりん

MARI NASA, CHIBA PREFECTURE

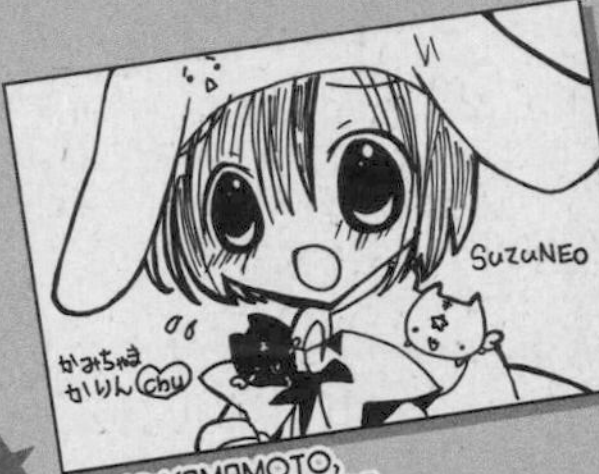
SUZUNEO
かみちゃま
かりん chu

NAHO YAMAMOTO, KOUCHI PREFECTURE

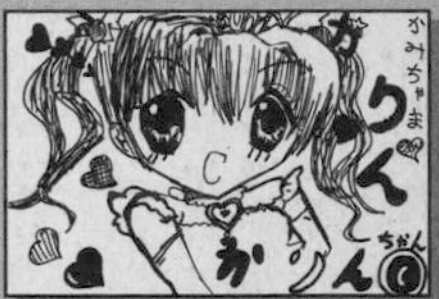

NATSUMI TSUJINO, YAMAGUCHI PREFECTURE

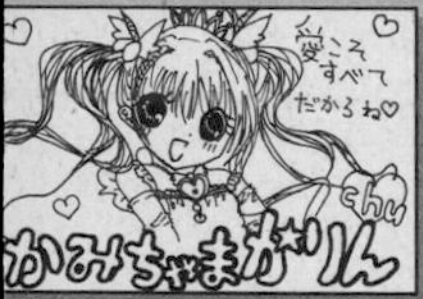
愛こそすべてだからね♡
かみちゃまかりん

MOMIJI OCHI, HOKKAIDO

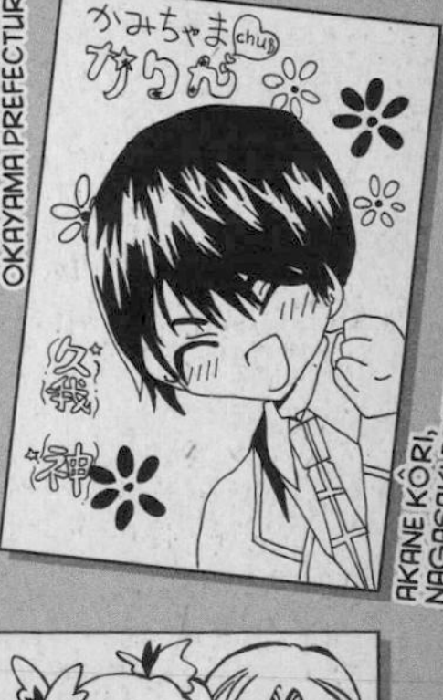
かみちゃま chu
かりん

AKANE KÔRI, NAGASAKI PREFECTURE

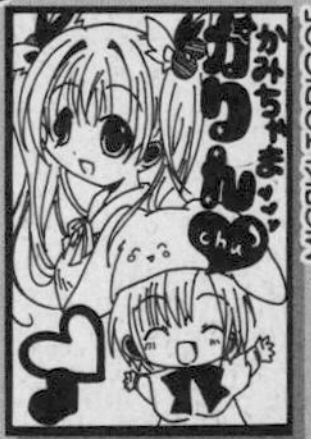
かみちゃま
かりん
chu

MISAKI TORIGOE, OKAYAMA PREFECTURE

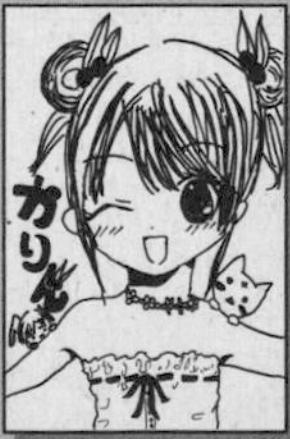

AOI AKIMARU, FUKUOKA PREFECTURE

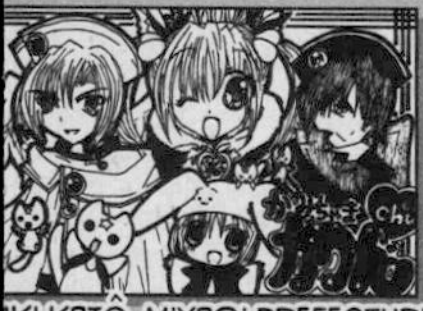
chu

AKI KATÔ, MIYAGI PREFECTURE

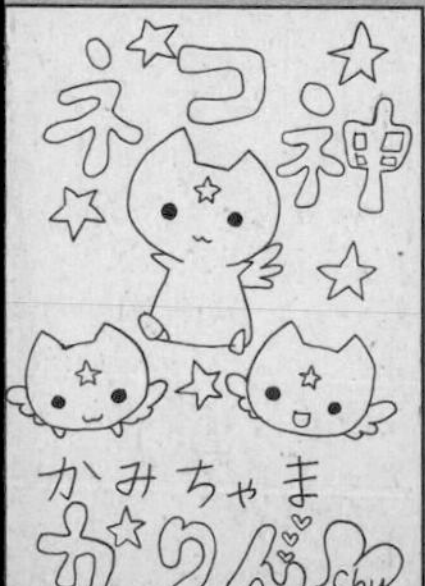
ネコ神
かみちゃま
かりん
chu

HIKARI SHIBUYA, FUKUOKA PREFECTURE

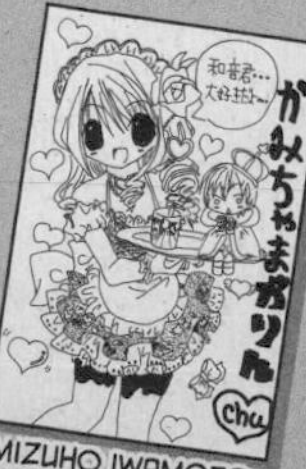
かみちゃまかりん
chu

MIZUHO IWAMOTO, IBARAKI PREFECTURE

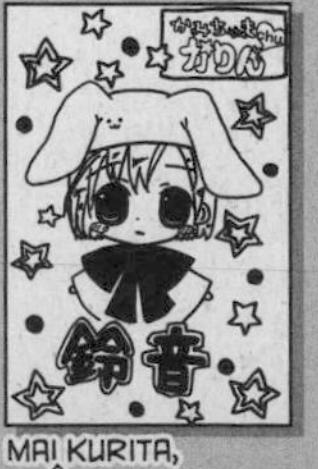
鈴音

MAI KURITA, HYÔGO PREFECTURE

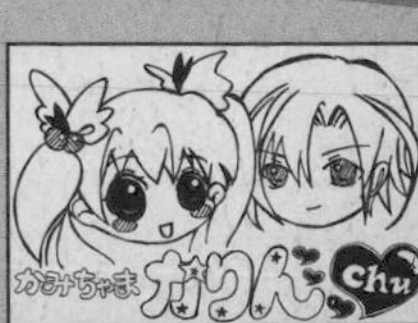
かみちゃま
chu

SAKI KAWAHARA, TOYAMA PREFECTURE

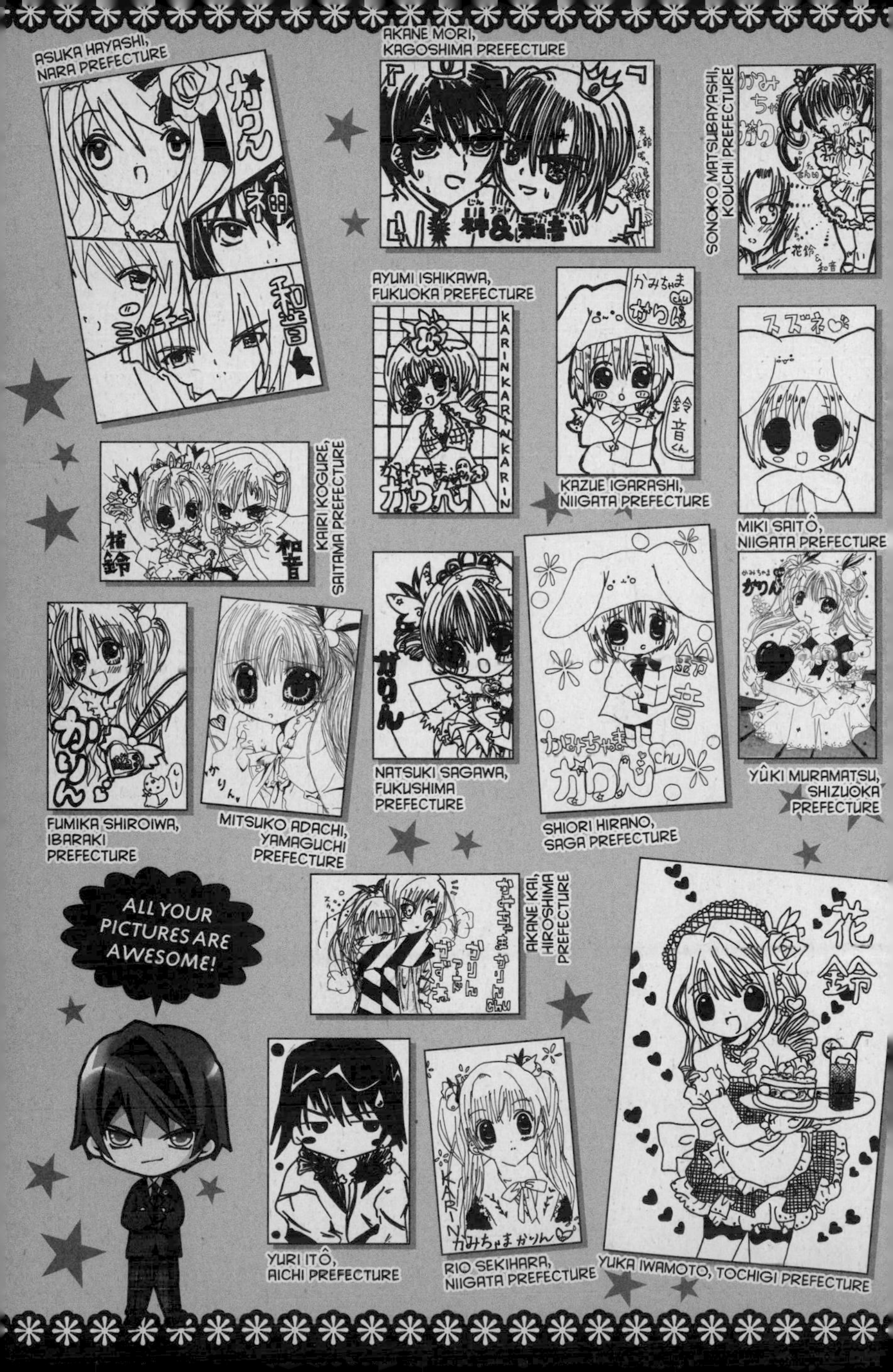
ASUKA HAYASHI, NARA PREFECTURE
AKANE MORI, KAGOSHIMA PREFECTURE
SONOKO MATSUBAYASHI, KOUCHI PREFECTURE
AYUMI ISHIKAWA, FUKUOKA PREFECTURE
KAZUE IGARASHI, NIIGATA PREFECTURE
MIKI SAITÔ, NIIGATA PREFECTURE
KAIRI KOGURE, SAITAMA PREFECTURE
NATSUKI SAGAWA, FUKUSHIMA PREFECTURE
SHIORI HIRANO, SAGA PREFECTURE
YÛKI MURAMATSU, SHIZUOKA PREFECTURE
FUMIKA SHIROIWA, IBARAKI PREFECTURE
MITSUKO ADACHI, YAMAGUCHI PREFECTURE
ALL YOUR PICTURES ARE AWESOME!
AKANE KAI, HIROSHIMA PREFECTURE
YURI ITÔ, AICHI PREFECTURE
RIO SEKIHARA, NIIGATA PREFECTURE
YUKA IWAMOTO, TOCHIGI PREFECTURE

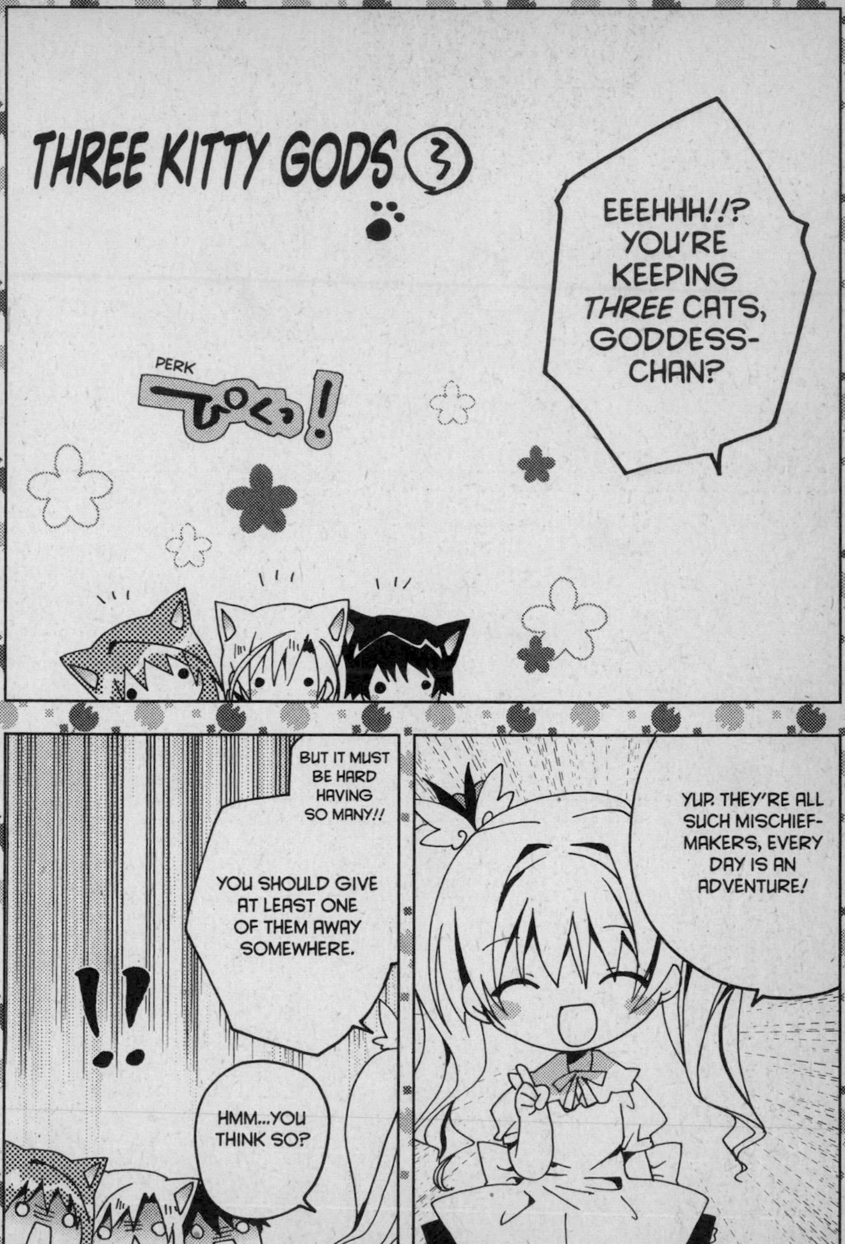
EEEHHH!!? YOU'RE KEEPING *THREE* CATS, GODDESS-CHAN?
THREE KITTY GODS ③
PERK
YUP. THEY'RE ALL SUCH MISCHIEF-MAKERS, EVERY DAY IS AN ADVENTURE!
BUT IT MUST BE HARD HAVING SO MANY!!
YOU SHOULD GIVE AT LEAST ONE OF THEM AWAY SOMEWHERE.
!!
HMM...YOU THINK SO?

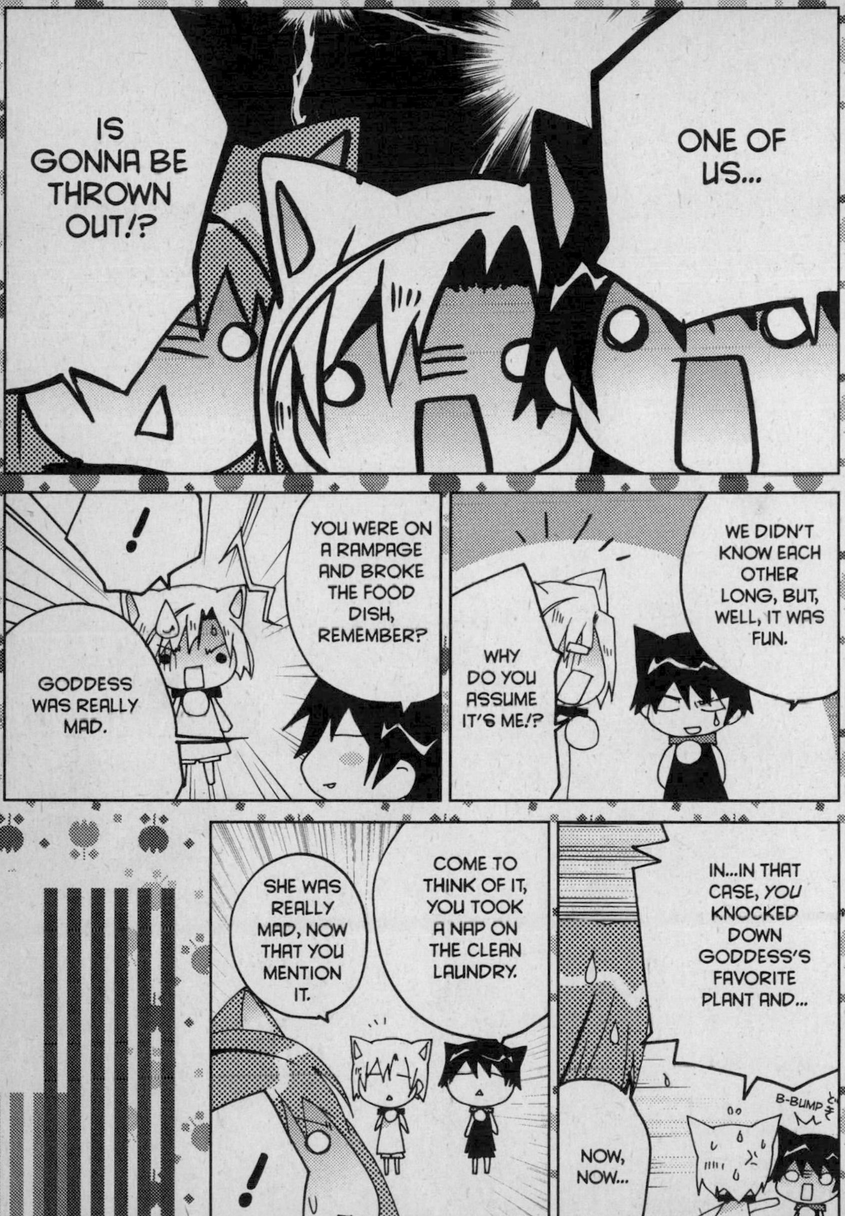
ONE OF US...
IS GONNA BE THROWN OUT!?
WE DIDN'T KNOW EACH OTHER LONG, BUT, WELL, IT WAS FUN.
WHY DO YOU ASSUME IT'S ME!?
!
YOU WERE ON A RAMPAGE AND BROKE THE FOOD DISH, REMEMBER?
GODDESS WAS REALLY MAD.
IN...IN THAT CASE, *YOU* KNOCKED DOWN GODDESS'S FAVORITE PLANT AND...
B-BUMP
NOW, NOW...
COME TO THINK OF IT, YOU TOOK A NAP ON THE CLEAN LAUNDRY.
SHE WAS REALLY MAD, NOW THAT YOU MENTION IT.
!

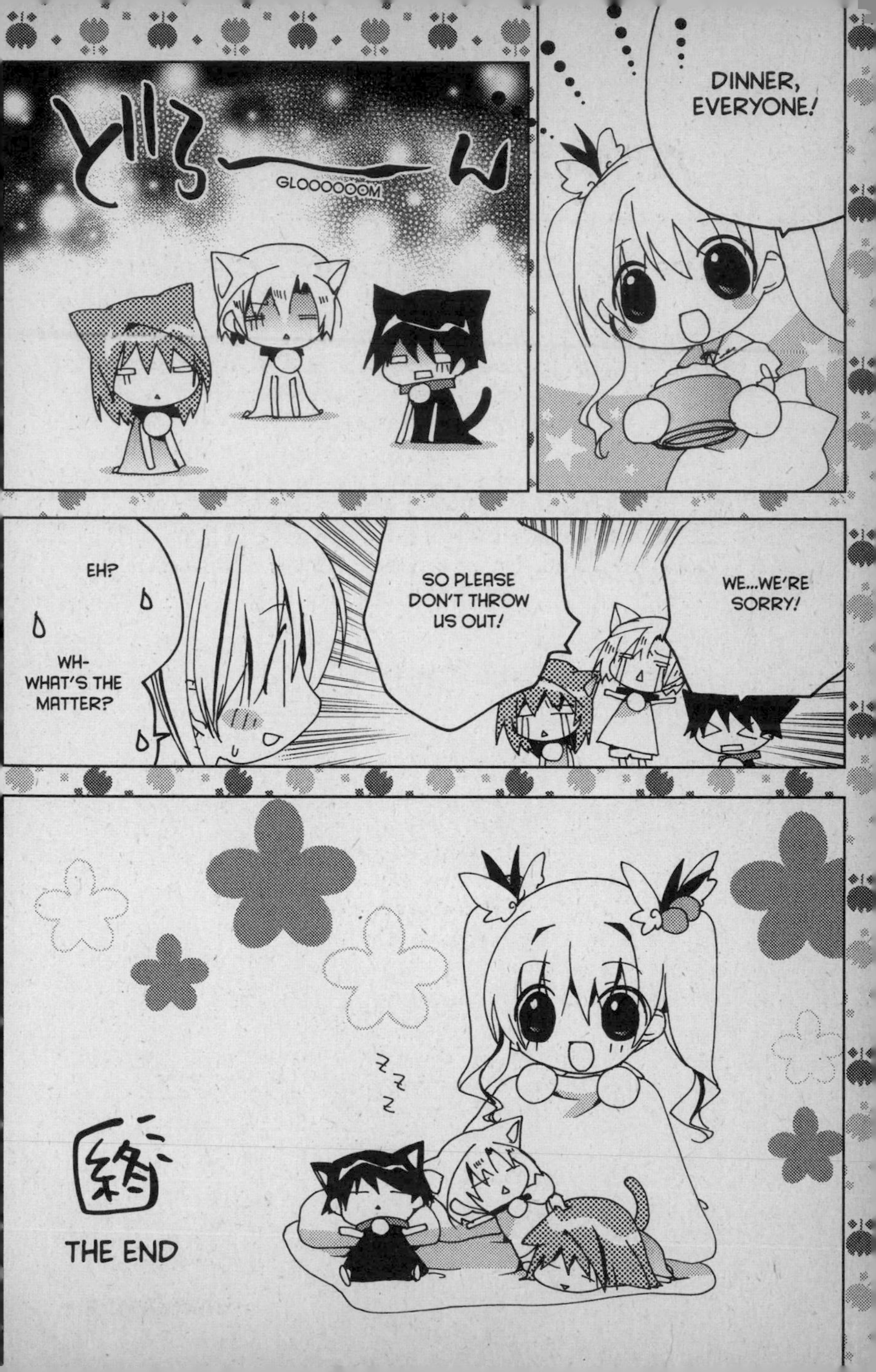
DINNER, EVERYONE!
とろーーん
GLOOOOOOM
WE...WE'RE SORRY!
SO PLEASE DON'T THROW US OUT!
EH?
WH- WHAT'S THE MATTER?
Z Z Z
終
THE END

About the Creator

Koge-Donbo, *Kamichama Karin Chu*

Koge-Donbo, who also creates under the pen name Kokoro Koharuno, chose this unusual pseudonym in honor of Akira Toriyama's cat! This popular and prolific creator is currently working on several manga series including *Di Gi Charat* and *Kamichama Karin Chu*.

Born on February 27, Koge-Donbo is a Pisces with blood type A. She loves traditional Japanese culture: She was a member of her college's aikido club and is now studying the art of Noh drama. Koge-Donbo is also fond of traveling and eating curry, ramen, and *okonomiyaki*.

Works

Current

Di Gi Charat
Kon Kon Kokon
Kamichama Karin Chu
Sumo Ou
Princess Concerto
Aquarian Age

Completed

Pita-Ten
Tiny Snow Fairy Sugar
Kamichama Karin
Koihime Soshi
Yoki Koto Kiku

I'M SO HAPPY ♪

Translation Notes

Japanese is a tricky language for most Westerners, and translation is often more an art than a science. For your edification and reading pleasure, here are notes on some of the places where we could have gone in a different direction, or where a Japanese cultural reference is used.

Kamichama Karin chu, title page

Kami is the Japanese word for a god. When talking about a great, powerful god, normally it would be referred to as *kami-sama*, because *-sama* is used to confer great respect. In Kazune's opinion, however, Karin is not great enough to be called *kami-sama*, at least at first. So he says she's more like a *kami-chama*, because *-chama* is like a baby-talk version of *-sama*, and conveys her cute childishness as a goddess. *Chu* is a Japanese pronunciation of the English "two," and it's also the sound a kiss makes, very fitting of this sequel to *Kami-chama Karin* ❤

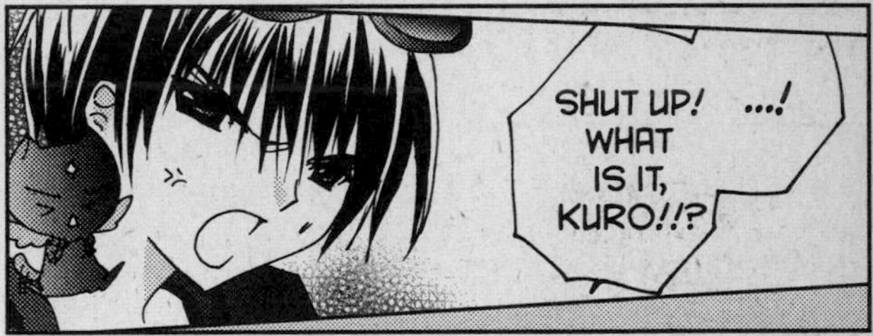
...!
SHUT UP! WHAT IS IT, KURO!!?

Cat god Kuro, page 20

Meaning black in Japanese, *Kuro* is an excellent, but not very original, name for Hades's black cat.

Just got into Narita, page 80

Narita Airport is Japan's number one international airport. Since Jin was in Hawaii, Narita would be an important stop on his way back to his home in Japan.

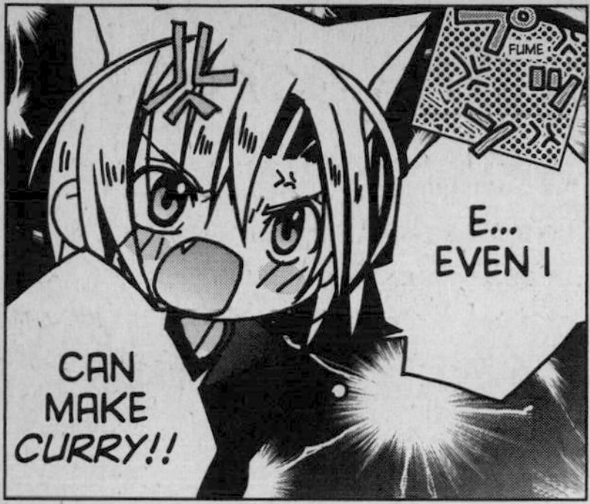
FUME
E...
EVEN I
CAN
MAKE
CURRY!!

Even I can make curry, page 108

Like macaroni and cheese in America, curry is one of the easiest things to cook in Japan and is often made on school campouts. Usually a mix is used to make a sauce, and vegetables and meat are included to suit the cook's taste. It is then served on rice.

"Sunday Night Chubaw?," page 110

A show much like the Japanese cooking show "Saturday Night Chubaw!" Guests come on and cook in the master chef's kitchen, or *chubaw*. At the end of the show, the guests' dishes are judged and given stars. The maximum amount of stars is three, so to get four stars, you have to be a pretty amazing cook.

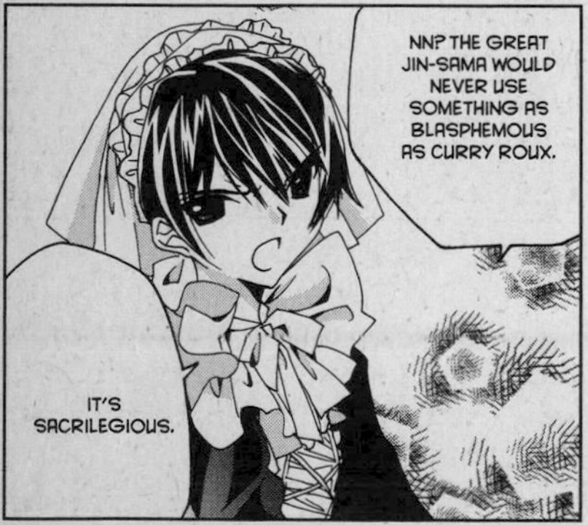
NN? THE GREAT JIN-SAMA WOULD NEVER USE SOMETHING AS BLASPHEMOUS AS CURRY ROUX.
IT'S SACRILEGIOUS.

Curry roux, page 112

Curry roux is the sauce mix normally used to make curry. Because of the added convenience, it would cost more than making curry completely from scratch.

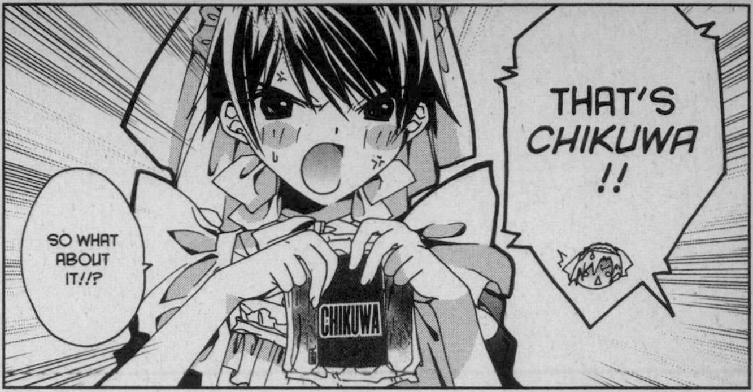
THAT'S CHIKUWA !!
SO WHAT ABOUT IT!!?
CHIKUWA

Chikuwa, page 116

Chikuwa is a kind of fish sausage. Meat is fairly expensive in Japan, so things like *chikuwa* and tofu are used as substitutes, in order to save money.

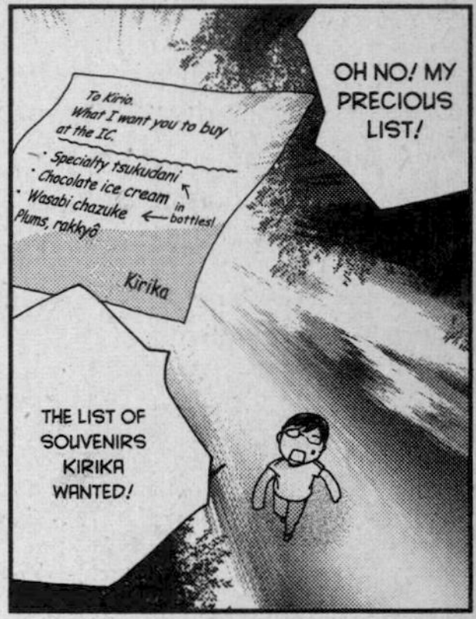
OH NO! MY PRECIOUS LIST!
To Kirio.
What I want you to buy at the IC.
· Specialty tsukudani
· Chocolate ice cream
· Wasabi chazuke
Plums, rakkyô
in bottles!
Kirika
THE LIST OF SOUVENIRS KIRIKA WANTED!

Kirika's souvenir list, page 148

Because Kirio has left Kirika behind, it's only natural that he buy some souvenirs as a gift. Kirika wants *tsukudani* (fish boiled in soy), chocolate ice cream, wasabi-flavored *chazuke* (rice with Japanese tea poured on it), plums, and *rakkyô* (a kind of Japanese onion).

Okonomiyaki, page 191

Loosely translated as "fried to your liking," an *okonomiyaki* is a pizzalike pancake fried with various ingredients—whatever you like.

Preview of
Kamichama Karin Chu, Volume 3

We're pleased to present you with a preview from volume 3.
Please check our website (www.delreymanga.com) to see when
this volume will be available in English. For now, you'll have to
make do with the Japanese!

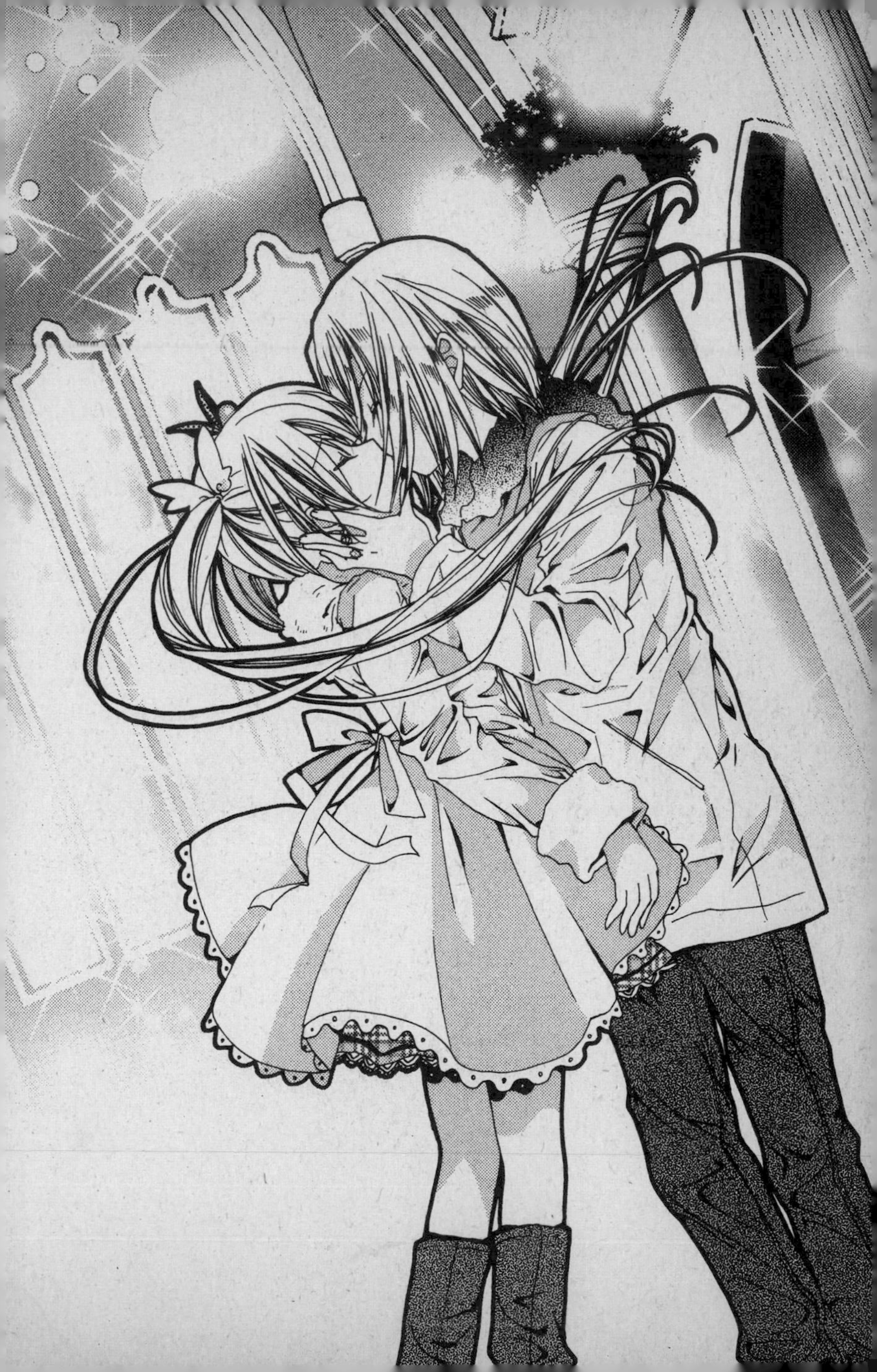

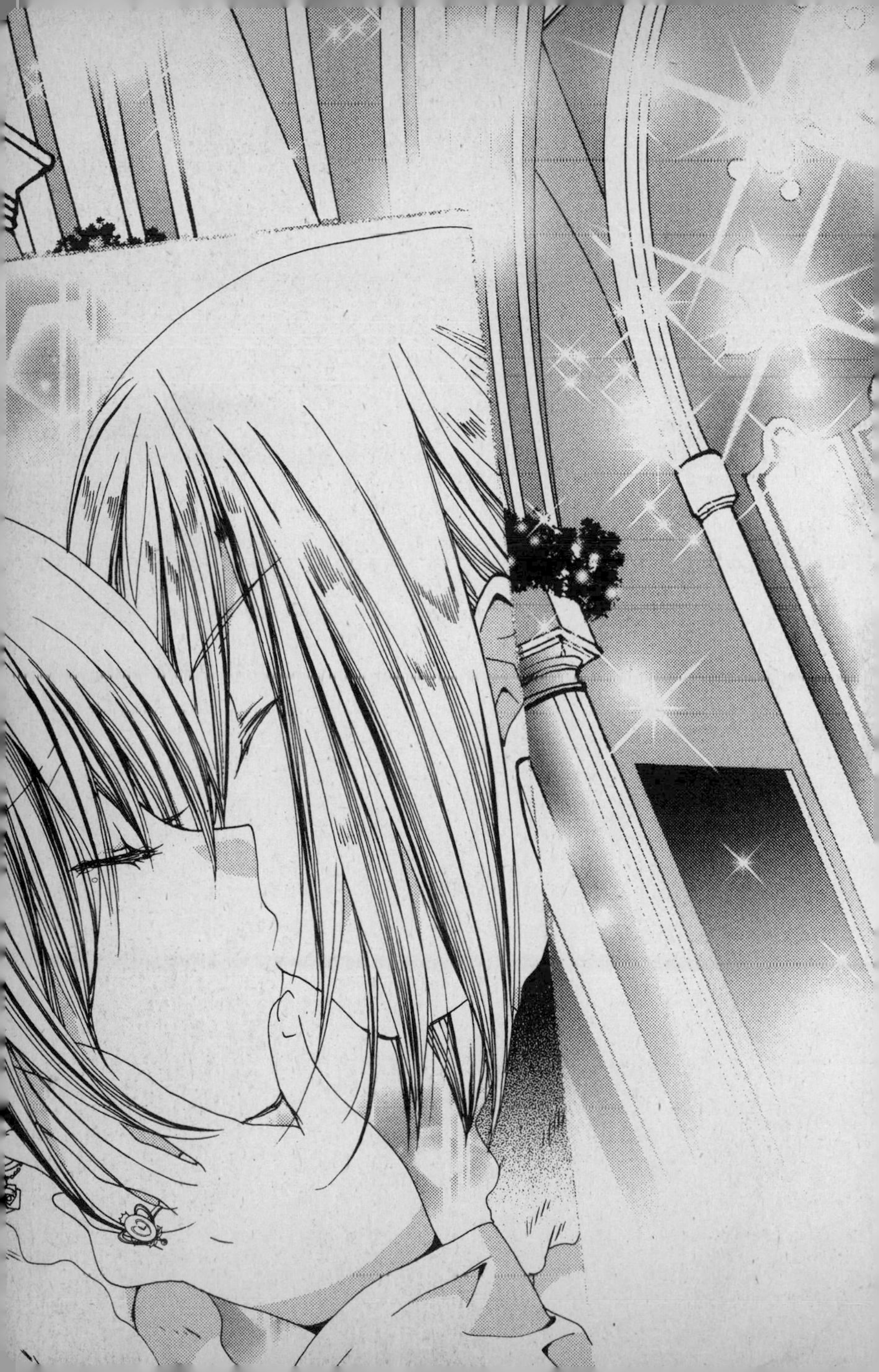

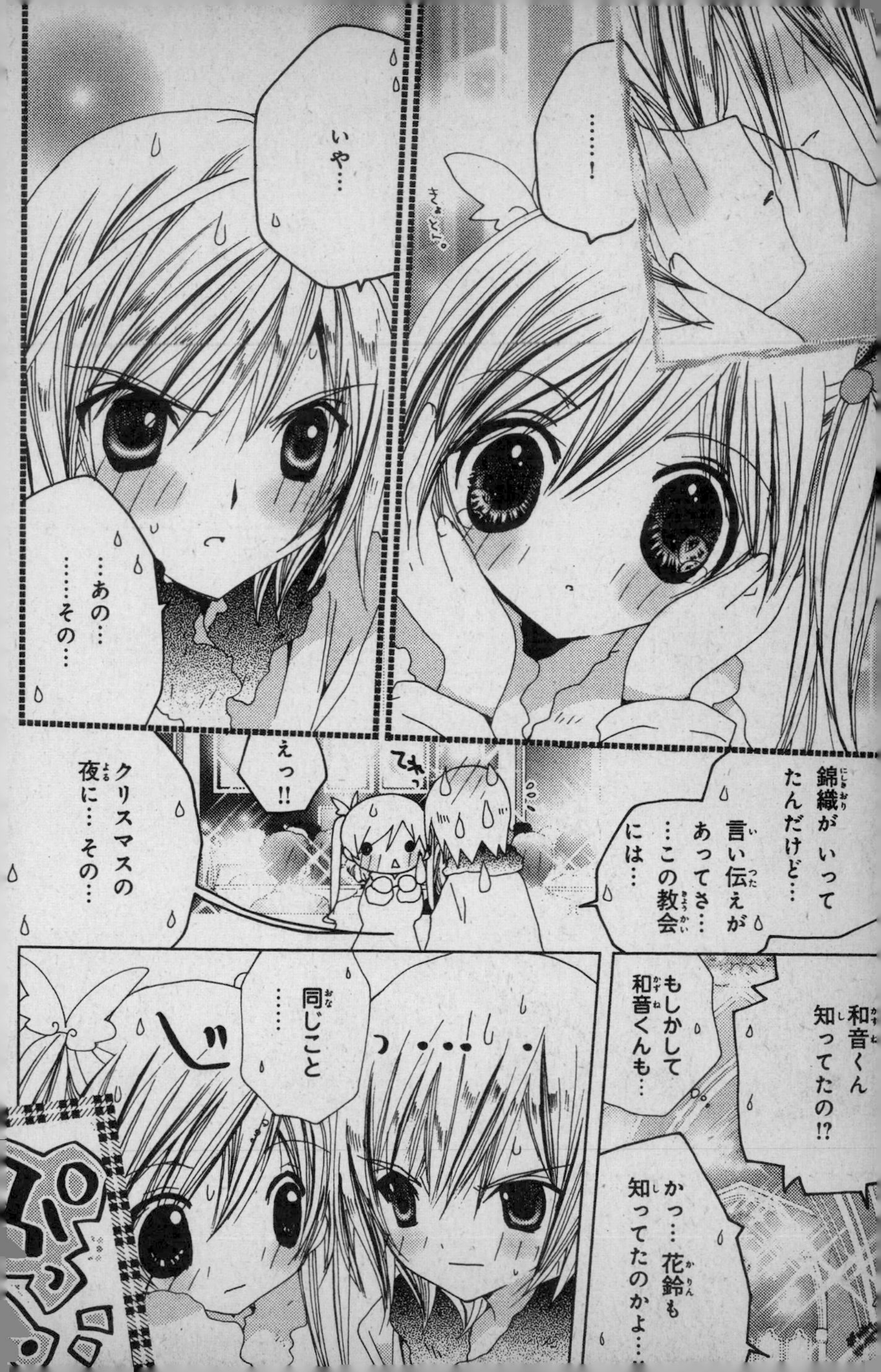
……!
きょとん。
いや…
…あの…
……その…
錦織がいってたんだけど…
言い伝えがあってさ…
…この教会には…
えっ!!
てれっ
クリスマスの夜に… その…
和音くん知ってたの!?
もしかして和音くんも…
かっ…花鈴も知ってたのかよ…
同じこと……
じっ……
ぱっ

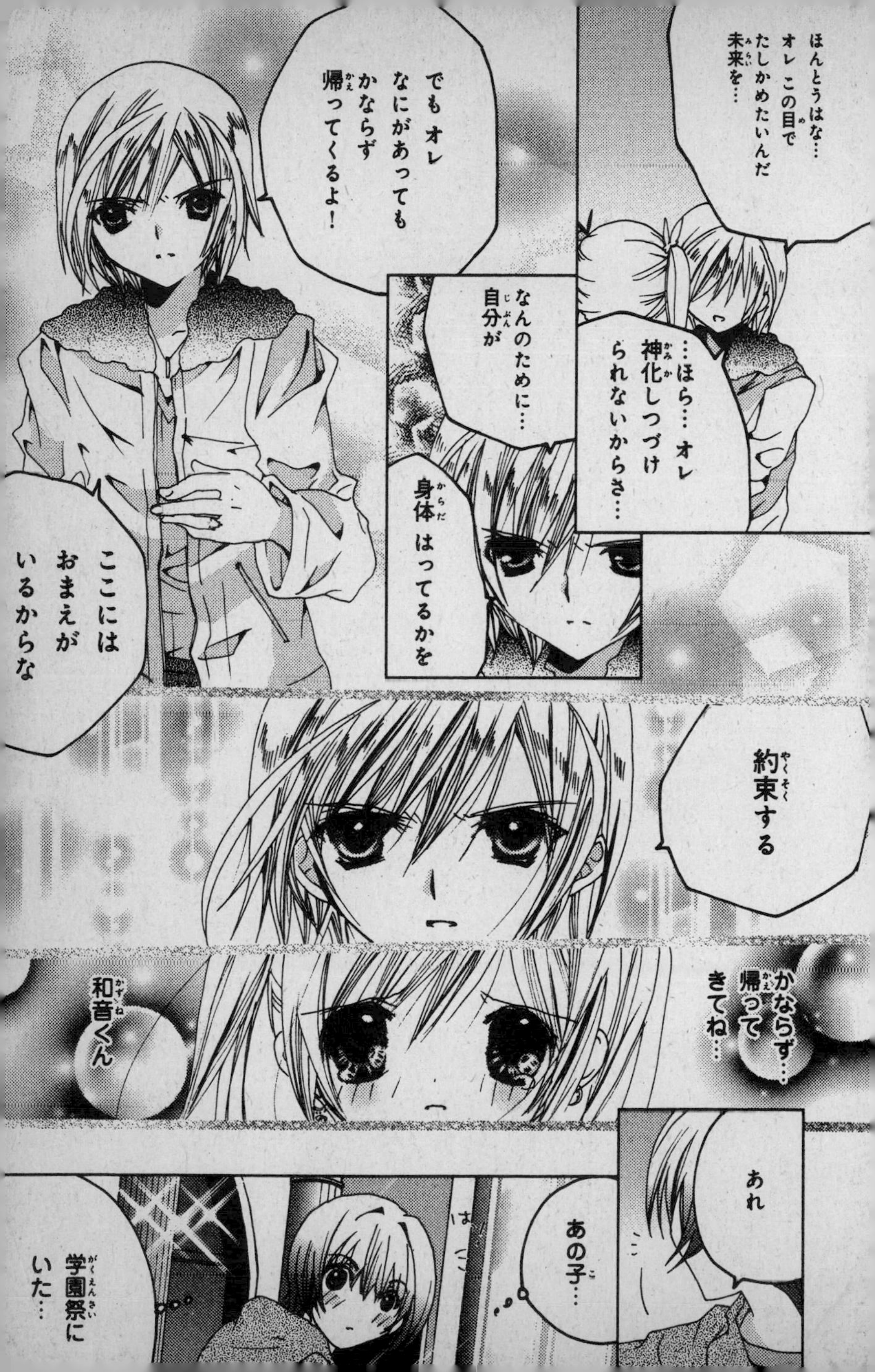
ほんとうはな…
オレ この目で
たしかめたいんだ
未来を…
…ほら… オレ
神化しつづけ
られないからさ…
なんのために…
自分が
身体 はってるかを
でも オレ
なにがあっても
かならず
帰ってくるよ!
ここには
おまえが
いるからな
約束する
かならず…
帰って
きてね…
和音くん
あれ
あの子…
はっ
学園祭に
いた…

KITCHEN PRINCESS

STORY BY MIYUKI KOBAYASHI
MANGA BY NATSUMI ANDO
CREATOR OF ZODIAC P.I.

HUNGRY HEART

Najika is a great cook and likes to make meals for the people she loves. But something is missing from her life. When she was a child, she met a boy who touched her heart—and now Najika is determined to find him. The only clue she has is a silver spoon that leads her to the prestigious Seika Academy.

Attending Seika will be a challenge. Every kid at the school has a special talent, and the girls in Najika's class think she doesn't deserve to be there. But Sora and Daichi, two popular brothers who barely speak to each other, recognize Najika's cooking for what it is—magical. Could one of the boys be Najika's mysterious prince?

Special extras in each volume! Read them all!

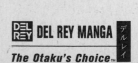

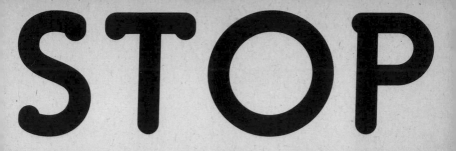

STOP

TOMARE!

You're going the wrong way!

MANGA IS A COMPLETELY DIFFERENT TYPE OF READING EXPERIENCE.

TO START AT THE BEGINNING, GO TO THE END!

THAT'S RIGHT!

Authentic manga is read the traditional Japanese way— from right to left, exactly the *opposite* of how American books are read. It's easy to follow: Just go to the other end of the book, and read each page—and each panel—from right side to left side, starting at the top right. Now you're experiencing manga as it was meant to be!